Praise for The Food Explorer

"Original, colorful, and irresistibly charming."
—Candice Millard,
author of *Hero of the Empire*

"A delightful tale of science and wanderlust."
—Hampton Sides,
author of *In the Kingdom of Ice*

"Fascinating."
—*The New York Times Book Review*

"Stone is an amiable narrator who balances
botany, culinary history, and travelogue with
fast-paced adventure writing and a well-drawn
cast of characters."
—*The Wall Street Journal*

More Praise for THE FOOD EXPLORER

"Daniel Stone draws the reader into an intriguing, seductive world, rich with stories and surprises. *The Food Explorer* shows you the history and drama hidden in your fruit bowl. It's a delicious piece of writing."

—Susan Orlean, *New York Times* bestselling author of *The Orchid Thief*

"Daniel Stone has written an elegant food history, a thrilling tour of a lost world—sometimes glamorous, sometimes dangerous, and always highly entertaining." —Luke Barr, *New York Times* bestselling author of *Provence, 1970*

"Daniel Stone spins a fascinating tale of a most unusual explorer. Any American who has ever savored a cashew or a nectarine has David Fairchild to thank. With a sharp eye and a deft touch, Stone has brought to life an intriguing new hero and his Gilded Age adventures around the globe."

—Evan Thomas, *New York Times* bestselling author of *Being Nixon*

"I think I had almost as much fun reading about Fairchild's adventures as he had living them."

—Candice Millard, *New York Times* bestselling author of *Hero of the Empire*

"Daniel Stone brings a forgotten era of American food back to the table. . . . [he] brings drama, humor, and perspective." —Associated Press

"Narrated in vividly realized, richly descriptive text with accompanying photographs, Stone's biography reanimates the legacy of an important contributor to the botanical diversity of America. . . . An erudite and entertaining historical biography of a food pioneer." —*Kirkus Reviews*

"Foodies and scientists alike will appreciate Stone's informative and entertaining book." —*Publishers Weekly*

"*The Food Explorer* does a wonderful job bringing Fairchild's story to life and giving this American original some overdue recognition." —*BookPage*

"[Stone] captures the flavor of an adventurous age, using Fairchild's voluminous writings to launch vivid descriptions of his travels." —*Booklist*

"This fascinating read will appeal to those interested in American history and food culture, travel narratives, and agriculture."

—*Library Journal* (starred review)

"A must-read for foodies." —*HelloGiggles*

David Fairchild

THE
FOOD
EXPLORER

The True Adventures of the Globe-Trotting Botanist
Who Transformed What America Eats

Daniel Stone

DUTTON

DUTTON

An imprint of Penguin Random House LLC
penguinrandomhouse.com

Previously published as a Dutton hardcover, 2018
First trade paperback printing, February 2019

Copyright © 2018 by Daniel Stone

Maps and illustrations by Matthew Twombly

The Library of Congress has catalogued the hardcover edition as follows:

Names: Stone, Daniel (Daniel Evan), 1985– author.
Title: The food explorer : the true adventures of the globe-trotting botanist
who transformed what America eats / Daniel Stone.
Description: New York, New York : Dutton, an imprint of Penguin Random House,
[2018] | Includes bibliographical references and index.
Identifiers: LCCN 2017030324 | ISBN 9781101990582 (hardcover) | ISBN 9781101990605 (epub)
Subjects: LCSH: Fairchild, David, 1869–1954—Biography. |
Botanists—United States—Biography.
Classification: LCC QK31.F2 .S76 2018 | DDC 580.92—dc23
LC record available at https://lccn.loc.gov/2017030324

Printed in the United States of America
1 3 5 7 9 10 8 6 4 2

Dutton trade paperback ISBN: 9781101990599

Book Design by Cassandra Garruzzo

For Walter Steinberg, my life's Lathrop

Never to have seen anything but the temperate zone is to have lived on the fringe of the world. Between the Tropic of Capricorn and the Tropic of Cancer live the majority of all the plant species, the vast majority of the insects, most of the strange and dangerous and exciting quadrupeds, all of the great and most of the poisonous snakes and large lizards, most of the brilliantly colored sea fishes, and the strangest and most gorgeously plumaged of the birds. Not to struggle and economize and somehow see the tropics puts you, in my opinion, in the class with the boys who could never scrape together enough pennies to go to the circus. They never wanted to badly enough, that's all.

—David Fairchild

The greatest service which can be rendered any country is to add [a] useful plant to [its] culture.

—Thomas Jefferson

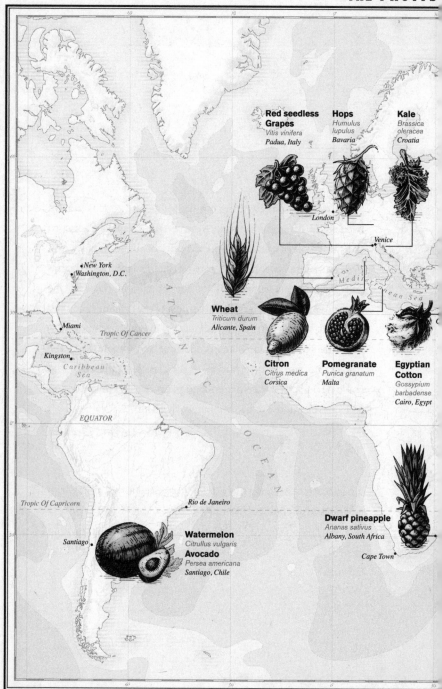

Red seedless Grapes
Vitis vinifera
Padua, Italy

Hops
Humulus lupulus
Bavaria

Kale
Brassica oleracea
Croatia

London

Venice

New York

Washington, D.C.

Mediterranean Sea

Wheat
Triticum durum
Alicante, Spain

Miami

Tropic Of Cancer

Kingston

Caribbean Sea

Citron
Citrus medica
Corsica

Pomegranate
Punica granatum
Malta

Egyptian Cotton
Gossypium barbadense
Cairo, Egypt

EQUATOR

ATLANTIC OCEAN

Tropic Of Capricorn

Rio de Janeiro

Dwarf pineapple
Ananas sativus
Albany, South Africa

Santiago

Watermelon
Citrullus vulgaris
Avocado
Persea americana
Santiago, Chile

Cape Town

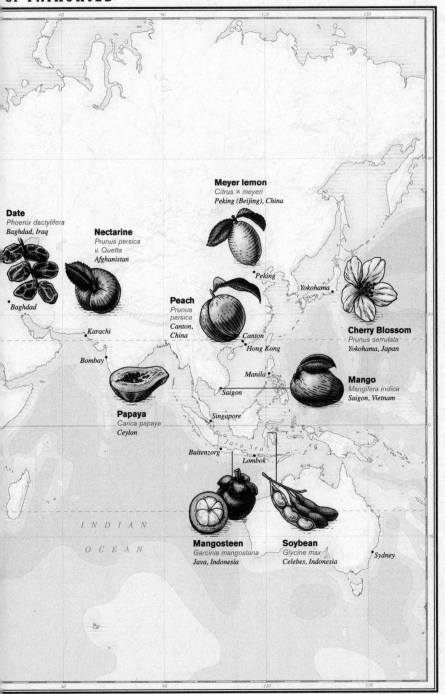

Date
Phoenix dactylifera
Baghdad, Iraq

• *Baghdad*

Nectarine
Prunus persica
v. Quetta
Afghanistan

Meyer lemon
Citrus × meyeri
Peking (Beijing), China

• *Peking*

Yokohama

Cherry Blossom
Prunus serrulata
Yokohama, Japan

Peach
Prunus persica
Canton, China

Karachi

• *Canton*
Hong Kong

Bombay

Manila

Saigon

Mango
Mangifera indica
Saigon, Vietnam

Papaya
Carica papaya
Ceylon

Singapore

Java Sea

Buitenzorg
Lombok

INDIAN

OCEAN

Mangosteen
Garcinia mangostana
Java, Indonesia

Soybean
Glycine max
Celebes, Indonesia

• *Sydney*

CONTENTS

AUTHOR'S NOTE

One of the humbling parts of being an American is the regular reminder that no matter how swollen America's pride or power, nothing has been American for very long. A few years ago, it occurred to me that the same way immigrants came to our soil, so did our food.

I was at my desk one morning researching a story for *National Geographic* when I came across a map showing where popular crops were first domesticated. Florida's famous oranges grew first in China. The bananas in every American supermarket originated in Papua New Guinea. Apples that Washington claims as its heritage came from Kazakhstan, and Napa's grapes saw their first light in the Caucasus. To ask when these became American crops seemed a little like asking how people from England became Americans. It was, in a word, complicated.

But as I continued to dig, deeper and deeper, there appeared to be a moment of clarity, a moment in history when new foods arrived on America's shores with the suddenness of a steamship entering a harbor. The late nineteenth century—a time known as the Gilded Age, the rise of industrial America, the golden age of travel— was a formative era in the United States. The opening of oceans and countries allowed a young scientist named David Fairchild to scour the planet for new foods and plants and bring them back to enliven his country. Fairchild saw world-changing innovation, and in a time that glorified men of science and class, he found his way into parlors of distinction not by pedigree but through relentless curiosity.

The way I became obsessed with this story seems, in retrospect, predictable. All my life I've been fascinated by fruit, the more tropical the better. When I was a kid, my parents took my sister and me to Hawaii because my dad thought we needed to "see things." I ate two whole pineapples, followed by a stomachache that burned hotter than Mauna Loa. Sometimes at home my mom would cut me a mango by shaving down the sides, and while I ate the pieces, she'd keep whittling away at the stone. It was mangoes, not my dentist, that taught me the value of floss.

In college, I worked on a farm, walking the hot rows of an orchard grading peaches. The goal was to find the superior varieties to prioritize for the following season, like performing eugenics on fruit. But distraction came easy. I'd finish shifts with the juice of dozens of peaches soaking my shirt, and, again, usually a stomachache. Before I moved to Washington, D.C., to write about politics, a friend offered me a job on his farm, picking fruit and selling it at the kind of Northern California farmers' markets where people use words like "varietals" and "terroir." I declined so I could follow a dream, although I spent years sitting in congressional hearings imagining my alter ego, windows down in a pickup truck, on empty farm back roads.

Several years later, when I heard about Fairchild, what struck me first was that this was a man who had made fruit his job—and not just familiar crops, but things no one had ever tasted. When I told friends how Fairchild had given the United States its first official avocados, people wanted to nominate him for sainthood. I started to enjoy reciting his greatest hits—dates, mangoes, pistachios, Egyptian cotton, wasabi, cherry blossoms—and watching people's eyebrows go up. Almost every time they would say something like,

"Gosh, it never dawned on me someone *brought* those things here." We tend to think of food from the ground as a type of environmental entitlement that predates humans, a connection with the raw planet itself. But what we eat is no less curated than a museum exhibit. Fairchild saw the opportunity in a bare canvas to add new color and texture.

Fairchild's life is the story of America's blooming relationship with the world at the turn of the twentieth century. He visited more than fifty countries, almost all by boat, before airplanes and automobiles shrank the planet. His passions and interests preceded our modern-day fixation on food and what the economic, biological, and ecological effects are of a meal's cultivation, transport, and consumption. Fairchild was the embodiment of boundless hunger and insatiable wanderlust, and his life's work was a quest to answer, *What else is out there?*

And yet his story is also one of frustration and drama, of being on a deadline as America's excitement for the world turned to a xenophobic fear of the unknown. Fairchild's star was attached to America's, and as its attention scattered in the onset of world war, Fairchild's ingenuity faced the angry criticism of a nation crouched in fear.

He was a man with a lot to say, and he wrote everything down. I read his love letters, his rough drafts, his ponderings on the backs of envelopes and napkins. I read as he recalled his encounters with Alexander Graham Bell, Teddy Roosevelt, and George Washington Carver. I could sense how much he'd hate to see a book written about him, to receive credit even though, as in so many stories, his life's path was made possible by other people's work, money, and sign-off.

There's a wistfulness in Fairchild's story, of seeing a man and a moment no longer possible. A world interconnected by culture, science, and communication, a world where people can travel thousands of miles in a day, can make someone reasonably ask, *Is there anything on Earth left unexplored?* I've spent many hours wondering what Fairchild would say to this, whether he'd see the aftermath of his life as a terminal end to the grand quests of earlier eras.

Then one day a few summers ago, I found myself in Florida in the living room of Helene Pancoast, Fairchild's eighty-one-year-old granddaughter. She used to take long drives with her granddad from Miami to Nova Scotia, during which he'd pepper her with questions and encourage her curiosities. She now lived just a few blocks from where she grew up, and her backyard had the palms Fairchild had fallen in love with in Indonesia. I asked her about what I'd been wondering so long: whether Fairchild would still find new questions in a world full of answers. She grabbed my arm and looked me square in the eye. "He used to say, 'Never be satisfied with what you know, only with what more you can find out.'"

THE
FOOD
EXPLORER

PART I

CHAPTER ONE

Chance Encounters

The trip had been punishing, a rocky overnight voyage over rough seas. Humid air, the kind that clings to one's face, stifled romantic visions of the Mediterranean. Even David Fairchild, a twenty-five-year-old from the prairielands of Kansas, was surprised by the small town of Bastia, Corsica's eastern outpost where the boat docked. "I had been accustomed to a certain degree of dirt but the town of Bastia appeared unbelievably filthy," he wrote of his first impression. Shabby dogs circled him on the dusty street as he stumbled around, disoriented, in the early light of day.

Had he been closer to home, he'd have found the scene easier to stomach. But here, on the French island, Fairchild was as far as anyone in his family had ever ventured. His journey had taken him from Kansas to Washington, across the Atlantic to Italy, north to Germany, and then south again across the Alps to the port where he met the boat. Such distance might have filled him with pride or pleasure if the last leg hadn't stirred a deep ailing in his stomach.

Sometime during the night, it had become December 17, 1894. Fairchild had spent his youth dreaming of traveling overseas, and now, finally, he was on his first assignment. He waited for the post office to open, and when it did, a man handed him an envelope crowded with forwarding addresses, and inside, a short message.

Secretary refuses authorization.

As an agent for the United States government, Fairchild had

been cautioned to keep secret his mission in Corsica. This sort of undertaking had rarely been tried, and without a treaty or informal diplomatic agreement, or even the definitive knowledge that such a visit was legal, the best Washington could hope for was that its man could get in and out without causing a scene.

Fairchild had little direction and, as had now become clear, even less money. The order from the secretary of agriculture to go to Corsica had been nullified by the same man, who refused to cable money for his agent to complete the job. Fairchild liked the idea of espionage, but he was as skilled at covert action as he was at ball-room dancing, having done neither. He was a botanist, an agent of plants, and not a good one.

Without money, Fairchild couldn't afford to stay long. But already on the island, he figured he might as well try to complete the objective. He flagged a cab drawn by a single horse that trotted south along the coast. To think clearly, he needed to eat. He also needed a lead. Corsica was hilly, hot, and too big to wander blindly.

He stopped at a roadside restaurant, where he was the only customer. While he waited to eat, he mentioned casually to the restaurant's owner that he was interested in plants. Where, he asked in a mix of English, broken Italian, and arm gestures, could he see some of the island's trees? Perhaps its famous citron?

The man lit with purpose. He took Fairchild behind the restaurant to sample figs he had grown, each one a mouthful of syrup. He suggested that Fairchild see the mayor of Borgo, a town at the top of a nearby mountain in the center of the citron region, and gave Fairchild a note of introduction. "There I was, with an adventure on my hands, and I enjoyed it," Fairchild wrote. He walked outside and hired a donkey to carry him up, observing the view at every switchback up the mountain, oblivious to the fact that Corsicans could be wary of outsiders.

The mayor of Borgo was a red-faced man, skin baggy and

sagging, "a bandit of a fellow," Fairchild jotted in his red pocket notebook. The mayor's house sat on wooden stilts atop a pigsty caked in mud. Fairchild had to navigate the snorting beasts to deliver the note from the man who had served him lunch.

As he might have expected, the mayor spoke no English and Fairchild knew almost no French, but the mayor made it understood that he had to leave for a funeral. He poured Fairchild a glass of wine and told his guest to wait. When the mayor left, Fairchild noticed a gray patch of mold floating on the wine and emptied it through a crack in the floorboards onto the pigs. Then he moved to the window, where he looked for a long moment at the deep valleys and orchards filled with fruit. It occurred to him: So long as he was waiting, what difference would it make to wait outside?

Efforts to be inconspicuous were betrayed by his large camera, an Eastman Kodet that folded like an accordion and had a cloth curtain. On the street, a small crowd gathered around him murmuring about the peculiar contraption and the man holding it. He stopped to photograph a group of women in long black skirts. A man urged Fairchild to photograph the view off the side of the mountain. Another woman asked him to take an image of her daughter. He obliged the woman's request but ignored the man, who turned and marched away.

While his head was concealed by the curtain, he felt someone grab his arm.

"*Vos papiers, s'il vous plaît.*"

It was a policeman. Or perhaps a soldier.

Fairchild had no papers to show, nor could he respond in a way the man understood. The minimal French learned in school left his head at the precise moment it might have been useful.

In just a few hours on the island, two hours into his first assignment working in a foreign land on behalf of the American government, Fairchild found himself arrested. If he knew anything about

*1894. A large camera identified Fairchild as an outsider, as did the way
he pointed it at women on the street. Moments after he took this image
in Borgo, Corsica, he was arrested.*

this type of work, he demonstrated the opposite. He had made his mission known to a government official. He had drawn attention to himself in the streets. And worst of all, he would now be interrogated. If he couldn't hold his resolve, the man would compel him to divulge what he had come for, and who had sent him.

The gendarme escorted Fairchild to a small house that doubled as the town's jail. He gestured for Fairchild to empty his pockets. The man picked up Fairchild's red pocket notebook and began to thumb through its pages. He asked in staccato what each word meant. Some of the scratches were in English, others in German and Italian, his attempt to practice languages he didn't know. Fairchild was filled half with fear, half with indignation, neither of which compelled him to cooperate.

In the corner of the room sat a woman in a black robe with a baby perched at her breast. As she rocked, she barked orders in Corsican French to the man. He paid her no attention, his gaze affixed on the notebook.

It struck Fairchild that the man mistook him for a spy, which he technically was, but the kind seeking more serious secrets. How else to explain the notebook with suspicious writings? Why the camera? Owing to the heat, his growing annoyance, and the creeping fear that he could spend his life in a Corsican prison, blood began to rush from Fairchild's face. "On an errand that was not likely to be pleasing if explained to the guard, with no papers in my pocket, with a captor whose very look was enough to terrify anyone, and in a jail that would rival in filthiness any that the Inquisition ever had, I think there are few men who would not have paled," he later wrote.

The policeman was familiar with the game of espionage, with foreigners arriving innocently but looking for political or economic secrets—or worse, to survey the land's value. The island had been war-torn for centuries, a plaything of European empires that fought for the rights to a Mediterranean oasis rich in crops, water, and fertile soil. America wasn't a threat, but the superpower Spain was, as was Italy, France's neighbor, which saw rich promise in a nearby island. A European spy hoping to steal strategic secrets from Corsica would be wise to impersonate a bumbling American who could barely speak French.

If the money had arrived from Washington, Fairchild would have had papers to prove his identity, his employer, and his mission, which, at the very least, was less threatening than looking for military secrets. Instead, all he had remaining in the bottom of his pockets was an old reimbursement check for fifteen dollars for work as a government contractor.

With nothing left to offer, Fairchild tossed the crumpled envelope containing the check onto the desk. But something caught both men's eyes. There on the envelope was the muscular visage of Ulysses S. Grant.

"Oo-lissies Grant," Fairchild said, pointing at the imprint. *"Americano!"*

The woman with the baby stared.

The man held the envelope up to study it. He seemed more taken by Grant's brawny gaze than by Fairchild's flailing insistence.

Then slowly, he pushed the red notebook back at Fairchild and uttered a string of words that sounded like a warning never to come back.

Fairchild stumbled out of the house, sweating lightly and breathing hard. With his head down he walked past the group of Corsicans watching him, then hoisted himself onto the donkey he had hired and kicked its side. As the animal trotted away, Fairchild peered over his shoulder every few paces, wary of being pursued.

Halfway down the mountain, when he felt confident he wasn't being followed, he dismounted. An orchard of yellow fruit had caught his eye, and he dashed into the grove of citron trees. He checked over both shoulders as he crouched in the dirt. Then he broke off four small bud sticks, the part of the tree where two thin branches merge into one. He tucked them into his breast pocket. These cuttings could later be grown into new trees, the Corsican citron mimicked in American soil. Then he plucked three small fruit from the tree's branches. If the buds didn't survive, the seeds inside these citrons might.

Back on the trail, Fairchild slowed the donkey. Success was in reach, but only if he could safely leave the island. The smartest thing he could do was to depart Corsica from a different city, where port agents wouldn't recognize him or have reason to inspect his camera and search his pockets.

In Bastia, he hailed another horse-drawn cab to drive him to the west-side city of Ajaccio. There, he asked an old man in an orchard for one of the few French terms he did remember, *pommes de terre*, potatoes. Fairchild paid for the stolen citron buds with agricultural knowledge: he demonstrated for the man a method he had once read about in a book—he stuck the sticks into the starchy centers of potatoes so that the cuttings would survive the lengthy trip to Washington. The freight bill would be a few cents. And after that, the remaining coins dangling in Fairchild's pocket were just enough to get him back to Naples.

The United States, barely a century old, was still young. The continent may have been green and vibrant, but as a culinary canvas, it was still fresh and white in 1869, the year David Fairchild was born one April day on the thawing plains of Lansing, Michigan.

America at one hundred hadn't developed a culinary identity of its own; there wasn't anything that could reasonably be called "American food." The choice of what to eat was most often confined to the items English colonists had brought over from their native land: meats and cheeses. Only the southern states could farm year-round, and when they did, root vegetables sprouted easiest, cabbage and green beans with a bit of extra work. "The fare of the Puritan farmers was as frugal as it was wholesome," Ben Perley Poore, a newspaper columnist, wrote in 1856 about the food of America's early days. "Porridge for breakfast; bread, cheese, and beer or cider for luncheon; a 'boiled dish,' or 'black broth,' or salt fish, or broiled pork, or baked beans, for dinner; hasty pudding and milk for supper." Slaves tended to get leftovers, and if there were none, they'd subsist on a combination of rice, beans, and potatoes.

Luck was the most critical factor in cultivating wheat. Bread was the product of corn, wheat, or rye, and in the harshest winters, most households could usually rely on bread, butter, and bacon. People preferred pigs to other proteins for the animal's indiscriminate diet, low water needs, and high calorie count. Flavor came in a distant fourth.

Fruits and vegetables were rare, and as a result, all things that sprouted from soil were dubious to medical authorities. "Woody tissue" was harder to process than animal muscle, which more closely resembled human flesh. Besides, the fruits of trees and shrubs were unpredictable, grown on such small scale and rejected by farmers who couldn't afford risks.

Food in every way was bland. Meals had bigger things to accomplish than merely to taste good. The food a person ate had a curious link to every aspect of his behavior, down even to his sexuality. The nineteenth century's avant-garde dieting theory came from Sylvester Graham, a Connecticut culinary reformer who developed a cracker—named after himself—to calm the body's "urges," sexual and otherwise. Women were said to faint at his speeches. Charles Elmé Francatelli, the closest thing the era had to a celebrity chef, warned in his popular 1846 cookbook, *The Modern Cook*, that "excess in the quantity and variety of spices and condiments . . . is especially to be guarded against. Nothing vitiates the palate more than a superabundant use of such stimulants." A generation later in

1875, George Napheys, a Philadelphia doctor, warned that highly seasoned food would stunt a person's development. Cravings of any kind were signs of weakness, he said, omens that a person wasn't properly "brought up."

There were right ways and wrong ways to eat food. Warnings percolated everywhere, in newspapers, in circulars, buzzed about in community centers. Sarah Tyson Rorer, the nineteenth century's Martha Stewart, issued a series of cookbooks that traded polite suggestion for blunt bossiness. In her most famous tome, *Good Cooking*, she advised:

> Eat only the proper amount for necessary nutrition; avoid excessive sweet mixtures, fried foods, complicated pastries, acids, such as pickles or foods covered with vinegar, excessively hot or very cold foods, or ice water, which is the most objectionable of liquids. A frequent cause of indigestion is the mingling of too great a variety of food in the mouth. Take one food, masticate and swallow it; then another. Do not take a mouthful of toast and then a swallow of tea, unless you wish to be a still further sufferer from indigestion.

Indigestion, otherwise known as dyspepsia, was the era's fashionable disease, which seemed to arrive in America so suddenly that no one could reasonably explain it. Some blamed it on eating hot foods with cold; others faulted the anxiety wives felt when their husbands left home for the workday. Indigestion provided an opening for some people to argue that stomach discomfort was a sure sign the country had degenerated from the greatness of the colonial period. The implied warning was that unless people changed their ways, starting with their diet, America's grand experiment in constitutional democracy would flame out.

When young Fairchild was learning to walk in the early 1870s, the purpose of food had begun to shift from survival and sufficiency to something resembling gastronomic pleasure. *The American Home Cook Book* proposed cooking eels with a little parsley. Another suggested terrapin turtles boiled with salt. The foot of a calf could be salvaged into a delicious jelly (the culinary ancestor of gelatin). Of thirteen million Americans in the labor force in those years, more than half were farmers, most of them small landholders simply trying to live off the land and, if they were lucky, make a little profit. Peaches could be boiled into preserves. A stew could last for many meals—more if one added flour biscuits. Before comfort food made people nostalgic for mom's home cooking, the same combination of meat, carbs, and dairy helped keep people full.

Around 1870 new advances started coming led by new companies with names like Pillsbury, Heinz, Quaker Mill, Lipton. A man named Ezra Warner invented a can opener with a handle and a rotating metal blade. Glass milk bottles appeared on doorsteps, along with orange crates. The crown jewel in home cookware was a tightly lidded pot that used pressure to expedite cooking, sometimes cutting the time in half. With new inventions food became less a chore and even, at times, an experiment.

David Fairchild's mother, Charlotte Pearl Halsted Fairchild, a petite woman just over five feet, was as much drawn to the fads as anyone. She traded tips with neighbors about the ways the kitchen was changing. She asked her husband, George, to fortify their kitchen with gadgets. She had been the first of eight children, and George the last of ten. Now she had five kids of her own, and cooking for an army was more methodical than inspired. Her dishes tended to include dry meats and boiled potatoes, and on special occasions a pie, named after America's first president, that called for sugar, butter, sweet milk, flour, egg, baking soda, and cream of tartar. "Spread with a nice sauce," the Washington pie recipe suggested. "It is nice without sauce but the sauce improves it."

Around the same time, "balanced" nutrition began to creep in as a reasonable factor in overall health. For those who could afford a visit to the sanitarium that John Harvey Kellogg was building in Battle Creek, Michigan, food innovation was under way, but primarily with existing ingredients, not new ones. In 1884, Kellogg, a doctor, was clumping together oats for something he'd later call granola. He pureed peanuts into butter, and soy into milk. Visitors to Kellogg's dining room found potatoes baked, mashed, or boiled. Eggs, for the most elite, came with the deluxe option of being poached, floated, runny, scrambled, made into cream, or drunk as nog. Food companies brought new products that demanded, for the first time, a type of culinary marketing. Chocolate milk and root beer excited young people in the summer of 1872, followed by margarine, its original name "butterine" (a name producers of *real* butter fought until it was changed). In 1876 at the World's Fair in Philadelphia, a delicacy called a banana, originally a crop of the Malay Islands, made its public debut in the United States, selling for a dime apiece and wrapped in tinfoil to prevent its phallic shape from offending the crowd's Victorian sensibilities. How else to eat one but with a fork and knife?

He didn't know it, but America had a need for David Fairchild. The bare agricultural landscape at the beginning of his life would transform by its end into a colorful portrait: yellows from tropical nectarines and Chinese lemons, reds of blood oranges from Mongolia, greens from Central American avocados and grapes from the Caucasus, even purple from dates, raisins, and eggplants that sprouted first in the Middle East.

Fairchild watched them all come to the United States, because many of them he carried himself or shipped from unexplored corners of the globe, mingling with indigenous people, outrunning police, and flirting with diseases that killed millions. By the time Harry Truman became president, the crops brought to North America to kick-start the United States' fledgling farms had helped create the most dominant system of agriculture the world had ever seen.

The insistence of his aunt Sue Halsted had pushed David Fairchild to Europe. But it was the influence of his father that had predetermined his life in agriculture. In 1878, the year before Fairchild turned ten, his father, George Fairchild, was named president of the State Agricultural College of Michigan, the recipient of the nation's first government land grant, provided the school teach the practical aspects of growing food. Nine million people were farmers, and more were needed. The land-grant system expanded, and a year later, when George was offered the presidency of Kansas State Agricultural College, the only sensible thing was to put his family on a train to Manhattan, Kansas.

The Fairchilds arrived in Kansas in 1879, a "grasshopper year." The groggy insects emerged from subterranean hibernations to mate with such volume, they darkened the sky. Fairchild was a slender blue-eyed boy, and having left Michigan's old-growth forests, he found new friendship in Kansas' limitless orchards and cornfields. He wandered through the neighbors' rows of apples, their names no more difficult to remember than his classmates'. He filled his hat with grapes as he walked, spitting the seeds in deference to the botanical cycle of rebirth.

A series of visiting professors and scientists who stopped in Manhattan to meet George Fairchild shaped his son's early years. The most important visit occurred by accident, in the sense that it almost didn't happen at all. One of Fairchild's friends, a boy named Charles Marlatt who was curiously obsessed with the grasshoppers and other insects, had heard that a white-bearded British naturalist with thin-rimmed glasses named Alfred Russel Wallace would be visiting Kansas. Marlatt told Fairchild, who then told his father. George Fairchild, the university's president, with a degree of influence, quickly offered to put up the famous scientist. Wallace accepted, and this chance encounter was enough to spark young Fairchild's ambition. "When

Wallace came he stayed at our house, and charmed us with his simplicity," Fairchild recalled. Wallace had once competed with another Brit, Charles Darwin, to be the first to publish on the theory of natural selection. Wallace researched how species changed over time in the Amazon River basin, and then later in the Malay Archipelago. Water provides isolation, so each of the archipelago's twenty-five thousand islands demonstrated how organisms diverged from their neighbors. Wallace completed his papers before Darwin did his, but Darwin's opus *On the Origin of Species* was more extensive and marketed better, thus solidifying his perch as the historical patriarch of evolution.

During that visit, Wallace gave a copy of his new book, bluntly titled *The Malay Archipelago*, to Fairchild, whose eyes widened at the imagery and wonder of such a faraway place. To an Englishman like Wallace, the islands between Asia and Australia were the least known parts of the world, and were more consistently wet than anyplace else on the planet. Wallace told Fairchild that they teemed with diverse animal species, rich plants, and wild fruits.

Most maps had neglected the region due to incomprehension, but Wallace explained that at least one island, Borneo, was bigger than France. And unlike anywhere in Europe, it was largely untouched by travelers, who considered the area too remote, too dangerous, and too prone to earthquakes. Fairchild found this fascinating, and later observed of his childhood, "When the formative years of one's life are spent among men such as these, it is little wonder if one becomes 'agricultural-minded.' Personally, I cannot imagine existence in a family where the parents are interested only in a social life, but I feel sure that it would be very boring."

Wallace's stories were magical. But to a young boy from Kansas, the Malay Islands may as well have been Jupiter. Fairchild was a boy who had never seen mountains, never heard a riverboat whistle, never listened to music beyond a church choir. He spent his days in a carpenter shop earning pennies and nickels laying shingles and cutting doorframes. Any Kansas boy could find work pulling weeds or raking hay, but never enough to fund a journey to the ocean, let alone across it.

So, out of practicality, the desire to see the Malay Islands would lie dormant in Fairchild's mind. His parents agreed that it was more sensible for him to spend his teenage years with his aunt and uncle in New Jersey. Uncle Byron had more connections to the grand thinkers along the corridor between New York and Washington, D.C. And Aunt Sue, who kept Beethoven, Chopin, and Dickens at her fingertips, would be his liaison to culture. New Brunswick, New Jersey, was a Dutch-influenced town with sloped roofs that poured sheets of rain onto the streets. Life there would be a useful shock to a boy from the plains, everything bigger, faster, and flush with high-minded attitude that demanded a certain way of doing things.

Fairchild would adapt, at least a little. But the indelibility of his childhood on the plains would steer his curiosities for a lifetime. At nineteen, pushed by his uncle and in letters from his father, Fairchild turned to courses in botany. He spent evenings studying agriculture journals so thoroughly he memorized the names of the researchers. Around the dinner table, he could recite who studied wheats, tubers, and fruits, and, perhaps more important, the elusive question that would vex farmers for a century to come: How could you inoculate an entire field from a pest without contaminating the crops with unhealthful sprays?

The decision to leave Kansas had turned out to be a smart one. A friend of Uncle Byron granted Fairchild the chance to move to Washington for a job as a junior scientist with the Department of Agriculture. The work wasn't glamorous, and neither was the building, four stories of old brick that reflected Washington's low regard for matters of food and farms. Agriculture was one of the country's biggest industries, along with steel and textiles, but the power lay with farmers, not the government.

For the majority of American history, affairs of agriculture had occupied a small office at the Department of State. Only on May 5, 1862, did President Abraham Lincoln create a Department of Agriculture all its own, which, despite its lack of cabinet-level status, he nicknamed "the people's department." Its first goal was to increase the number of calories Americans ate each day. And its first leader was a modest farmer coincidentally named Isaac Newton, a man said to have won the job because he delivered Lincoln's butter.

Eighty workers, all of them men, filled the headquarters of the Department of Agriculture at the corner of Fourteenth Street and Independence Avenue. The five men working on matters of plant pathology arrived to greet Fairchild on his first day, each presenting his name and the problem vexing farmers he was trying to solve. The reception was formal, particularly for a junior scientist, but the Division of Plant Pathology was small, and any newcomer notable. The men devoted most of their attention to viral diseases, such as one called peach yellows that made fruit ripen too fast while the flesh stayed bitter. One man, Theobald Smith, was investigating the cause of Texas cattle fever that inexplicably killed thousands of cows (it was a bacteria, he would discover, transmitted by a tick). Not long before, the Department had identified an infection responsible for destroying entire orchards of pears and fields of sweet potatoes.

Early agricultural work entailed this type of reactive problem solving, trying to curtail bad things rather than invent good ones. The work of a new scientist involved early-morning trips to places with more farmland than Washington. Fairchild spent two summers in Geneva, New York, trying to figure out why some young pear trees had prematurely stopped bearing fruit. He tied bags around tree branches to protect them from pollen in the air. It was Fairchild's discovery that blossoms on pear trees were sterile to their own pollen—a genetic revelation later applicable to other tree fruits.

Fairchild's flashiest assignment was to man a booth at the 1893 World's Fair. Chicago had won the honor to host the event, and,

1889. Fairchild's early days with the U.S. Department of Agriculture involved testing equipment, such as this knapsack sprayer, in search of new ways to help farmers keep their fields healthy and productive.

not to be outdone by Paris five years prior, opened the fair with a giant 264-foot wheel designed by George Washington Gale Ferris to rival Gustave Eiffel's sleek Paris tower on the banks of the Seine. Organizers expected more than fifteen million people to visit the fair. More than double actually came.

On a small stage in front of an even smaller crowd, Fairchild was to explain how plant diseases could decimate a crop.

"It's knowledge people can use!" his boss, Beverly Galloway, said when Fairchild complained that other presenters would have more exciting demonstrations. A giant wheel in the air was spectacular, Galloway conceded, but when people returned to their farms in Kansas, Iowa, and Illinois, Fairchild's lesson would prove most useful.

Each day as the cold wind blew off Lake Michigan, Fairchild, in a baggy shirt with no coat, showed how pear blight fungus killed one pear seedling after another. The fast-growing fungus would cover the seedlings and starve them of sunshine. Then the plants would lean to the side and droop dead. Hours earlier, he would have contaminated the plants with the fungus so that, at the precise moment the crowd gathered, the plants would begin to visibly die before everyone's eyes. If he timed it right, the onlookers would gasp. Farmers found it a useful lesson. Everyone else saw a magic trick.

As the wind battered his face and chapped his lips, Fairchild thought incessantly about two things.

One was the Malay Archipelago, and specifically the island of Java. His requests to be sent on assignment to study foreign plant diseases were met with the scoffs of men who saw no need for such irrelevant work and were unwilling to fund it. What insight could Javanese farmers possibly have into American problems? He daydreamed about going to Java on his own—a self-funded research expedition like those of the great explorers of Portugal and Spain who had once set off amid public doubt only to discover earth-changing things. But the daydreams were nothing more.

The other item occupying Fairchild's daily thoughts was

something Charles Wardell Stiles, a young zoologist, had told Fairchild before he left for Chicago. When Fairchild explained his longing
for overseas travel, Stiles suggested that he apply to the Smithsonian,
which had received a generous government grant to facilitate scientific exchange with several universities in Europe. One position
in Naples was still empty.

As Chicago's spring turned to summer, after another day of
shuttling pear seedlings and fungus to and from the demonstration
hall, Fairchild returned to his room to find a cablegram from Stiles.
He had secured the Smithsonian job for Fairchild—and with it, the
opportunity for him to leave his world and enter a new one. Fairchild spent the final days of the fair writing letters to his parents
and his aunt and uncle. He imagined them pleased to see him
granted the respect of a scientist.

What made Fairchild himself giddy was the idea of taking a
steamship across an ocean. In 1893, an age of glamorous travel reserved solely for the most moneyed, crossing the Atlantic even once
qualified as the rarest treat of a person's life. Fairchild would have
his own cabin, and his own seat in the dining room. There might
be people on board who had visited exotic locales, and would regale
him with illustrious stories of their adventures. He would buy a
stack of pocket notebooks and jot every detail.

The anticipation tantalized him during the last weeks of the fair.
Yet there was one pesky chore that remained. When he returned to
Washington, before he headed for the ocean-crossing steamship, before he peered over the railing into the blue Atlantic, before he got to
unpack his pocket microscope or try to decipher a menu in Italian,
Fairchild would have to go into the Department of Agriculture, the
agency that had given him the full sum of his opportunity, and quit.

Two months later, as fall's leaves disappeared under winter snow,
the most important conversation David Fairchild ever had occurred

on a seven-thousand-ton ocean liner named the SS *Fulda* that would cross the stormy Atlantic and leave Fairchild and his ambitions in Naples.

Sea travel at first proved more cumbersome than the notions of calm luxury he imagined. Relentless wind upturned deck tables. Dishes clattered.

It was a pair of pajamas that first caught Fairchild's eye. Only rich people wore pajamas—and so was the man wearing them. He stood in the doorway of the second officer's cabin, a space reserved for the star passenger. The man was tall and handsome, with a perfect mustache outlandish enough to make Fairchild stare in crude astonishment. For a brief moment, the man looked back at Fairchild, and then he was gone.

The next evening, Fairchild recalled the odd encounter to Raphael Pumpelly, a Harvard geologist on board with whom Fairchild dined. When he mentioned in a different breath his longing to go to the Malay Islands, Pumpelly's eyes lit up. The man in the pajamas was one Mr. Barbour Lathrop, esteemed world traveler. He had been to Java.

In fact, Barbour Lathrop had been around the world forty-three times. Perhaps more, perhaps less—the number changed each time someone asked, because Lathrop enjoyed demonstrating that he couldn't be bothered to keep track. On the long voyages when bored travelers would count days with scratch marks in journals, Lathrop would find any pair of ears with even the smallest interest in hearing stories of his globe-trotting and death-defying adventures. "That reminds me of a time in Japan . . ." he would occasionally say, before describing how, amid great danger, he crossed Japan's widest latitude on foot. Because of his status as a frequent traveler with deep pockets, Lathrop received the type of onboard treatment even the most regal dignitaries would envy.

In the smoking room aboard the *Fulda*, Fairchild met the man who would direct his destiny. Lathrop was wearing his formal tailcoat for an evening on board, and sat with a novel in one hand and a cigarette in the other. A forty-seven-year-old millionaire who financed his pleasure for travel on his father's real estate fortune, Lathrop was a man of intellect, some real, some imagined, whose ego fueled an impetuousness to speak his mind—and, just as often, to ignore the dull. He couldn't be moved to steal away from his book as Fairchild explained his yearning for Java. The older man nodded, half listening. Fairchild mentioned his meeting with Alfred Russel Wallace, and then his work studying plant fungus. Lacking prestigious credentials of his own, he described his father's agricultural pedigree.

Lathrop waved him quiet. He had already been to Java two times—or was it three?—and recalled between puffs of smoke the time he hunted rhinoceros on the western part of the island. As he talked, he would pause, empty his Turkish cigarette holder, and fill it with a new Egyptian cigarette.

"Why study microscopic stuff instead of plants that man can use?" Lathrop asked. His speech was impatient, as though his solution were obvious, and yet, only the revelation of a genius. "If you're a botanist, why don't you collect plant specimens for the Smithsonian Institution and pay for your trip that way?"

Fairchild stuttered. He wasn't that kind of botanist, he explained. He wanted to *study* plants and their diseases, not collect them. For him Java would be a laboratory, not a bazaar filled with goods to be chosen.

Lathrop was a man accustomed to holding court. His usual position was seated, leaning back, regaling curious commoners or anyone nearby with his stories of danger and drama, each one mounting to a punch line demonstrating that he had been omniscient all along. He wasn't interested in people who didn't share his brilliant view of himself. And so with a wave of his hand, he ended the encounter.

Lathrop's attention drifted back to his novel.

Fairchild showed himself out.

Behavior that anyone else would have thought rude made Fairchild feel something different entirely. He found Lathrop's disinterest to be the mark of a true cavalier, a man who had seen and experienced so much that he couldn't be distracted by minutiae. "I left quite awed, feeling that I had met one of the most widely traveled men in the world," he wrote.

An encounter so brief hardly qualified the men as acquaintances. Nor did their eyes meet again for the rest of the voyage. Fairchild saw him one more time, at the customary onboard banquet, as the *Fulda* passed the Azores. Lathrop played emcee to a room of tuxedos and high-necked gowns. Lacking formal clothes, Fairchild hid behind a pillar in the dining room long enough to hear Lathrop's witty introduction of every performer, writing down every uttered name in his notebook.

Before he even stepped onto foreign soil, ocean travel had become more exciting than Fairchild's greatest fantasy. The boy from the Midwest fancied the globe-trotting playboy Lathrop the "most fascinating man" he'd ever meet. Boys dreamed about travel, but gentlemen had the cunning to make such fantasies reality.

Lathrop, too, had been piqued by Fairchild. The young man was one of hundreds of cursory companions Lathrop encountered on the ocean. But there was something about his awkwardness, his inquisitiveness, the way he asked questions with naïve amazement. Lathrop had developed a penchant for people like Fairchild, young men who came to him with submissive awe.

When the ship docked at Gibraltar, the passengers learned that a group of mountain tribespeople in northern Morocco had staged a rebellion against their Spanish colonizers. The Foreign Legion had offered to help quell the violence. Lathrop rushed off to see the action, drawn to the dramatics and prestige of battle. But not before writing down the name of the young man from the steamer to remind himself, on another day, to find him again.

CHAPTER TWO

One Thousand Dollars

There was a time in North America before people ate fruits or vegetables, a time before people ate anything at all, because far enough back, there was no North America.

Earth has been around for 4.5 billion years, and life for at least 3.7 billion of them. The planet of that era would be unrecognizable to anyone alive today. Early life was almost entirely aquatic, and a few billion years passed before, about 450 million years ago, creatures started to creep onto land. Time has long ago swept away any record of what these early animals looked like, but they weren't much to look at, nor could they see very well, and, perhaps as a result, they lived short lives. A hundred million years after that, the planet for the first time had seeds—a part of an evolving form of reproduction in which female spores held their eggs in their outer tissue for the best odds of getting fertilized by male spores.

The planet circled the sun millions more times before two big things happened. One was the arrival of flowering plants, and the other was the arrival of dinosaurs. The asteroid that hit the Yucatán Peninsula sixty-six million years ago was brutal to the dinosaurs, and it was equally cruel to plants. The ash and smoke cloud cut off photosynthesis worldwide and effectively starved the majority of plant species into extinction.

Earth, as we know, is resilient, and once the cloud settled, mammals, birds, and plants began to evolve again, except this time, in a new way: in relation to one another. Plants developed showy flowers—the ones we're used to seeing—largely as a ploy to attract butterflies, moths, and bees. The success of plants led to more of them, and they spread everywhere that wasn't too cold.

Such botanical dexterity helped make human life possible. The earliest primates based part of their diets on plants. And plants, in turn, evolved to make themselves attractive (or repulsive), depending on how much they wanted to be eaten (or left alone). The truly wise ones—wise in the judgment of humans—are the plants that made themselves edible. Those include the plants that produce fruit, and often, their sweet flesh is a devious lure to attract something to hunt it, eat it, and spread it.

In a biological sense, a fruit is the developed ovary of a plant (the vessel that holds the plant's eggs), and examining a fruit gives clues about its past struggles. Before humans, the red flesh of strawberries was a decoy for flyby nibbles from birds. Avocados appealed to elephant-like creatures called gomphotheres, which had intestines wide enough for the animals to swallow the fruit and excrete its hefty seed somewhere else. The day gomphotheres went extinct, thankfully no one told avocados. Nine thousand years passed before the Aztecs invented guacamole.

As for what constitutes a fruit in 2018, sweetness has little to do with it. Tomatoes are fruits, but so are eggplants, peppers, and olives. Peanuts and almonds and walnuts are fruits. So are parts of the world's six top crops—wheat, corn, rice, barley, sorghum, and soy. Oftentimes, things that masquerade as vegetables, like pea pods, are technically fruits. Which is not to cast shade at vegetables; they are, by definition, *almost* fruits. To botanists, vegetables are any other edible part of the plant that doesn't contain seeds. Roots, such as carrots, potatoes, and parsnips, are vegetables. Lettuces are seedless, so they're vegetables, too, as is garlic.

Chefs and bakers have their own definitions for what separates a fruit (something sweet or sour) from a vegetable (everything else).

But there's no central authority to keep things consistent—no Supreme Court of Plants. Federal judges have tried to give vegetables their day in court. In 1893, the United States Supreme Court classified tomatoes as a vegetable so the government could collect higher tariffs than if they were fruit (which they are). If judges can change botanical laws, then anyone can. Spend an afternoon plucking every speck off a strawberry, and your fruit just became a vegetable.

Once North America became known as North America, the continent had rich botanical diversity. Yet such success was again interrupted. Glaciers of the last ice age, eighteen thousand years ago, pushed life south. When they retreated, the ice rivers left behind a chilled land mass slow to repopulate itself. Just as two people would take longer than one hundred to grow a civilization, North America took longer to botanically rebound than a bigger continent like Asia.

For a long time, wherever animals pooped out seeds, unique things grew. But that changed when modern humans arrived. Agriculture was the greatest advance in human history, but until it had a name, it was simply the process of domestication, of taming a wild species to help humans. Domestication let people produce food for unfavorable seasons and form a steady source of nutrition that allowed them to settle down and form villages. In places like North America with few humans, however, hunting and gathering was easier than organized domestication. The earliest North Americans rarely domesticated crops, leaving the continent a disorganized patchwork of loosely related plants.

In the thousands of years before European colonists landed in the West, the area that would come to be occupied by the United States and Canada produced only a handful of lasting foods—strawberries, pecans, blueberries, and some squashes—that had the durability to survive millennia. Mexico and South America had a respectable collection, including corn, peppers, beans, tomatoes, potatoes, pineapples, and peanuts. But the list is quaint when compared to what the other side of the world was up to. Early civilizations in Asia and Africa yielded an incalculable bounty: rice, sugar, apples, soy, onions, bananas, wheat, citrus, coconuts, mangoes, and thousands more that endure today.

If domesticating crops was an earth-changing advance, figuring out how to reproduce them came a close second. Edible plants tend to reproduce sexually. A seed produces a plant. The plant produces flowers. The flowers find some form of sperm (i.e., pollen) from other plants. This is nature beautifully at work. But it was inconvenient for long-ago humans who wanted to replicate a specific food they liked. The stroke of genius from early farmers was to realize they could bypass the sexual dance and produce plants *vegetatively* instead, which is to say, without seeds. Take a small cutting from a mature apple tree, graft it onto mature rootstock, and it'll produce perfectly identical apples. Millennia before humans learned how to clone a sheep, they discovered how to clone plants, and every Granny Smith apple, Bartlett pear, and Cavendish banana you've ever eaten leaves you further indebted to the people who figured that out.

Still, even on the same planet, there were two worlds for almost all of human time. People are believed to have dug the first roots of agriculture in the Middle East, in the so-called Fertile Crescent, which had all the qualities of a farmer's dream: warm climate; rich, airy soil; and two flowing rivers, the Tigris and Euphrates. Around ten thousand years before Jesus walked the earth, humans taught themselves how to grow grains like barley and wheat, and soon after, dates, figs, and pomegranates.

The next seismic era comes with Christopher Columbus. Credited and cursed for stumbling upon the Western Hemisphere, the Italian explorer had a little-known side gig as the father of globalized agriculture. Until the 1490s, the Western and Eastern hemispheres hadn't formally met. And Columbus' arrival on a Caribbean island in 1492 led to a frenzied exchange of crops. Potatoes, tomatoes, and corn from Central and South America became staples in Europe and

Asia. Crops from the Old World, like bananas, coffee, sugar, and citrus, found fertile growing conditions in the New World, so much so that within a few hundred years, the Americas became top producers of them all. Historians call that period the Columbian Exchange and mark it the official bridge to modern times, when two worlds fused into one.

Technically, Columbus never set foot in North America, nor did he do any agricultural swapping himself. And many of the people living there, the Native Americans that he believed were Indians, benefited little from the agricultural exchange. There were relatively few people on so much land—around fifty million on six billion acres. While Europeans were busy introducing to the New World foods that they thought would improve the native people's lives, they were also importing new diseases that ended them, such as smallpox, measles, cholera, and influenza. Smallpox alone is thought to have diminished Native American populations with horrific devastation rarely seen in history.

When English colonists landed, they found a heavily wooded continent, overgrown and underused, prime for them to create a portrait of their former lives. They brought carrots and, not long after, barley, wheat, and peaches. By the 1730s, the process of building a new colony meant building a sustainable system for growing food. James Oglethorpe, the British general keen to develop a colony called Georgia, split his time between governing and innovating food. He experimented with how weather affected crops, believing Georgia's winters were too cold for cotton. They could, however, support silk, hemp, and flax. The peach that made Georgia famous didn't arrive for another hundred years.

George Washington, too, realized he was best at waging revolt when he took breaks to hoe the soil. Before he was president, the general studied subtropical agriculture, pleading frequently to London for seeds. Tobacco did well under his watch, but there was more money in wheat. To Mrs. Washington's horror, he spent early mornings investigating the optimal fertilizer, mixing oddities like animal manure, mud, and black mold that grew on a hillside near his house. Count among Washington's gifts to his future nation his revelation that cows, rather than horses or sheep, provide the most potent dung.

Thomas Jefferson, president number three, spent America's early days in France. When he returned, he had the foresight to know that for a new nation to survive, it needed more food. "The greatest service which can be rendered any country is to add [a] useful plant to [its] culture," Jefferson wrote in 1800. He particularly liked grain, which was second in value only to oil, but he knew self-sufficiency required diversity. If the newly created foreign consuls were good for anything, they could send seeds—and consuls in France, England, Italy, and the Netherlands did. Thomas Jefferson loved fruits of the earth as much as he loved liberty. Which is why, for all his efforts, he sits beside Willie Nelson, crooner of the heartland, in the National Agricultural Hall of Fame.

In America's infancy, food wasn't a sector—it was almost the whole economy. Farmers accounted for 90 percent of the United States' labor force in 1790. Fifty years later, they were 60 percent. And a generation after that, they were just over half (today they're less than 2 percent). Accounting for America's swelling population during that time, from four million to thirty-one million, there were more individual farmers in the late nineteenth century than ever before (or again) in American history. Because of this, the government focused an extraordinary amount of attention and money on agrarian matters. In the years following Abraham Lincoln's presidency, courses on horticulture—the era's equivalent to modern biotechnology—were taught in nearly every university. Federal officials gave land to states to analyze crops, their diseases, and how to grow them at large scale.

Compared to today's political campaigns that rise and fall on money, media, and messaging, the first campaigns were a calculation of food. The earliest pork from Washington wasn't pork; it was

seeds for corn, wheat, and barley in small envelopes that congressmen would stuff in their pockets and, when home in their districts,
hand out with a wink. In 1881, William G. LeDuc, the agriculture
commissioner, wrote to his boss, Rutherford B. Hayes, that the
seed distribution program was a resounding success. "It is now generally conceded that the distribution of seeds from this department
is doing incalculable good." It was one way Washington worked
directly for the people, and for a congressman with deep pockets,
reason enough to vote for him again.

When Fairchild arrived in December of 1893, Naples greeted him
with an assault on the senses. Loud voices pierced the streets.
Horses trotted along, their ankles crusted in dung. To be a foreigner was distressing. When his steamship, the *Fulda*, docked, a
group of burly men, sweaty, with shimmering muscles, came to
unload the baggage, fighting with one another over every item,
and, with grand gestures, demanding tips for their service. "The
high-pitched, screaming voices, the continual gesticulations, and
the insistent demands for money, made it a nightmare to me," Fairchild recalled.

Outside the port, Naples was filled with an air of laziness that no
breeze could arouse. People walked during the day, sidestepping
piles of uncollected garbage, to sit on the grand seawall that protected the city from the dull waves of the Mediterranean. A traveling reporter for the *Chicago Sunday Tribune* found the city lethargic,
lacking drive and passion, as if hung over from the grand centuries
of artistic titans and extraordinary scholars of theology. "Sitting on
the sea-wall [in Naples] and dangling one's legs is not a very remu-
nerative employment, and yet crowds of able-bodied men spend
day after day in this easy occupation and in others that are like it,"
he reported to readers back home, many of whom had taken backbreaking roles in America's industrial revolution. Italy would soon

experience its own rapid economic growth as a result of advances in steelmaking and cotton milling, but that spurt hadn't arrived, and certainly not in Naples. There were hordes of *lazzaroni*, people who spent their days cooking atop stoves in the street, putting in enough work each week to afford only the macaroni they ate, the rest of the time filled with smoke, gossip, and catcalls.

Fairchild had gone to Naples without a place to live. Arranging a room in advance would have required a correspondent, and corresponding would have required a basic knowledge of Italian. An Italian painter on board the *Fulda* returning from America, where he'd exhibited paintings at the World's Fair in Chicago, sensed Fairchild's shock, took pity, and invited Fairchild to join him in a horse-drawn *carrozza* that clopped through the narrow streets, depositing him at the apartment of the artist's brother, who conveniently needed a boarder. The room had a view of Mount Vesuvius near a new funicular that carried a steam-powered railcar up a hill.

There was a fascination in the young man, the type one finds when landing in a foreign place, and he had to remind himself not to gawk at foreign peculiarities: the writing on signs; the sounds of an unfamiliar language; the people, how they dressed and looked, and how they seemed not to notice him. Fairchild filled his notebooks with fits and starts, giving the impression that he stopped every few feet to jot observations. The city was full of "pestiferous ragamuffins." His meals of hard bread were "disappointing" and his silverware "only sketchily washed." These small snubs were both memorable and insignificant. What truly delighted him was that, all around, he could hear nothing but Italian.

He spent the first few nights wandering the streets, first by himself and then with his landlord's son. They attempted to communicate in Italian until Fairchild's piecemeal vocabulary would sputter, and then they would slip into a theater for an inexpensive play, the kind where people stood and heckled the melodramatic actors. One play that particularly struck Fairchild had thirteen characters who were all killed scene by scene in increasingly gruesome ways, until only two were left, a pair of lovers who declared their devotion in a horrific double suicide.

The first day Fairchild reported for work, people were expecting someone older. The Smithsonian's Zoological Station was a place where men of science worked in secluded silence, unraveling the great mysteries of biological life. Fairchild, however, had come without a research goal. He had already achieved his principal objective, which was to travel somewhere outside the bounds of his country. All he had when he arrived in Italy was the eagerness of a twenty-four-year-old ready to stand over a microscope and help wherever needed.

When his adviser, Paul Mayer, a marine biologist, asked about his interests, Fairchild told him, "As a boy I watched termites build nests. But at the department we studied crop diseases." Mayer suggested that Fairchild study the cells of algae that grew in the Bay of Naples. Only recently had cells piqued the interest of scientists, particularly how cells divide, seemingly endlessly, suggesting they could perpetuate infinite life. Every morning, the station's head boatman dredged the bay and filled balloons with water that glowed green in the sunlight. Fairchild spent each afternoon and evening on the highest setting of his microscope, watching the process known as karyokinesis as the cells split.

Meanwhile, outside the lab were unlimited opportunities for distraction. He spent his evenings watching people in the city's Piazza del Plebiscito or wandering to the coast for a view across the water to the island of Capri. In Naples, where pizza was invented, Fairchild tasted his first cheesy flatbread, a punishing food for first-timers, whose mouths could be scorched with hot, lavalike cheese. He was enchanted by the various shapes of macaroni. And pastries were works of history. Naples' mixed heritage over several centuries from the French, Spanish, and Austrians resulted in flaky, sweet pastries, yeast cakes drowned in rum, and deep-fried doughballs known as zeppole, each one an ancestor of the modern doughnut.

Despite the contagion of indolence, there were few places more picturesque than Naples for one's first taste of foreign charm. Four thousand years of continuous history left deep footprints in art and culture. The bronze statues; the marble sculptures; the paintings that hadn't made it to New York City, let alone Manhattan, Kansas. In an old Bourbon palace known as the Capodimonte, the masterpieces of artists Fairchild had only read about—Michelangelo, Raphael, Botticelli—were on display in their original and full-color glory. Art was art, but no twenty-four-year-old could ignore that, often, the people in the paintings weren't wearing any clothes.

There was seaweed on his desk rotting and stinking the morning someone knocked on Fairchild's door. The person walked in with two thick pieces of paper—calling cards, each engraved with a name.

BARBOUR LATHROP

Chicago, Illinois

RAPHAEL PUMPELLY

Cambridge, Massachusetts

Fairchild first thought the men had left their cards, terrifying in itself. But there they were, climbing the stairs, at a moment when his room smelled of ocean bacteria and his shirt was stained green with chlorophyll. He hadn't remembered Lathrop's behavior:

blustery, unpredictable, and apathetic of his breach in etiquette at arriving unannounced. Lathrop answered only to Lathrop, and after his detour in Morocco, he'd asked Pumpelly, the professor from the boat, to help him find that young man who wanted to travel.

"The professor and I thought we'd come to see how you were getting along," Lathrop said as he mounted the last step and invited himself into the room.

With his military posture and gray mustache, Lathrop impressed Fairchild anew. Next to Lathrop, Pumpelly somehow looked more official, standing erect with piercing eyes—a jacket, a vest, a cane. Fairchild didn't speak. He had neither time nor anything to say, just the instinct that he had done something wrong, or was about to.

"I've been below here many times, but never knew there was anything like this in the upper story," Lathrop said, answering a question no one had asked.

He sat. Then took out his cigarette holder and lit a cigarette before asking, "One is allowed to smoke here?"

Lathrop asked him what he was working on.

"Karyokinesis," Fairchild said, pleased that his first word could be a large one.

"The what?" Lathrop cut in sharply.

"Karyokinesis. The way that a cell divides. I'm trying to observe the nuclei. I've been using the cells of green seaweed from—"

"You told me on the boat that you wanted to go to Java," Lathrop interrupted. "Have you given up that idea?"

"For now. The trip is beyond my means."

"Well, I've decided to give you a thousand dollars with which to go to Java," Lathrop said before inhaling deeply. "I want you to understand that I look upon this thousand dollars as an investment, nothing more. I have had you looked up, and you seem to be all right. You must understand that this is no personal matter. I want that clearly understood. It is merely my idea of making an investment in science."

Fairchild said nothing. Lathrop inhaled again, sat for another moment, and then he rose. Before he slipped through the doorway, he turned around again.

"Oh, and I'd like to have you lunch with me at the Tivoli Hotel at one o'clock."

Less than three minutes had passed and the men were descending the steps.

Fairchild's head was in a whirl. He tried to make sense of what had happened. He marveled first at the money, and then at the reality that he might actually see Java, and then back to the money. One thousand dollars, the modern equivalent of twenty thousand, was more than he had ever seen, twice the era's average salary for a full year. One Christmas, his aunt and uncle had given him fifty dollars, which to any young man would have felt like a fortune.

Lunch passed quickly, for much of it Lathrop recalling stories about his travels and triumphs, amusing himself more than anyone else, pausing characteristically for breaks from chewing to squint his eyes and nod slowly as though dusting off a distant memory. Fairchild understood his role was to listen, and for that Lathrop enjoyed his company.

After lunch, Lathrop suggested they see *Carmen*, a French opera about an undisciplined soldier lured away from his wife by a gypsy. The performance started at nine and lasted five hours, during which Fairchild was less entertained by the actors than by Lathrop's knowing sighs at turns in the plot.

It was three in the morning when they arrived at Fairchild's house. In the *carrozza*, Fairchild waited for Lathrop to finish his final story about the last time he had visited Naples. Lathrop seemed a peculiar man, talking in a flow of running consciousness, unconcerned about whether he retained his listener's attention.

Fairchild thanked Lathrop for the evening, then climbed down to the street.

"Well, don't you think you'd better have my address?" Lathrop called after him.

For the money. In Fairchild's attempt to remain polite, to come across as deferential and courteous, the money had slipped his mind. He took out his red notebook and, as Lathrop dictated, wrote the older man's address. *Barbour Lathrop Esquire. Bank of Scotland, 19 Bishopsgate Street Within, London. E, period, C, period.*

Although it had been longer, the second meeting of the two men confused Fairchild more than the first. It still wasn't clear whether Lathrop actually *liked* David Fairchild, or simply saw in him an opportunity to cure his glamorous boredom. And there was the matter of the money, which Lathrop emphasized was neither a gift nor a favor, but an investment that he expected to pay off.

How, he didn't say, because he didn't know. But as a millionaire, he could afford to find out later. The transaction would soon turn out to be wise, both for the men and for their country, but it would be some time before either man knew. As Fairchild turned toward the door to the house, Lathrop yelled, *"Avanti,"* and the coachman cracked his whip and whisked the carriage away.

CHAPTER THREE

East of Suez

The letters arrived with foreign postmarks. Cape Town, Singapore, Hong Kong, Oahu. In each one Lathrop was baffled by how long it was taking his young "investment" to get to Java. Over a year had passed since the meeting on the boat, and eleven months since Lathrop's surprise visit in Naples to discuss the particulars of the deal. To Lathrop, a man restless enough to circle the globe every year, Fairchild's foot-dragging was maddening at best, and at worst, just rude.

Fairchild had received Lathrop's letters, but despite the unsubtle push to get moving, he spent a year convincing himself that he wasn't ready for Java. An opportunity as big as what Lathrop offered shouldn't be squandered by insufficient preparation. "How foolish I would be to go to Java without a better training!" Fairchild wrote. The boyhood dream of seeing the Malay Islands at any cost had been replaced by the sensible reality that he had little to offer South Asia. Until he did, he'd keep the offer, and the money, on ice.

Fairchild was puzzled by Lathrop's demeanor. There was the older man's generosity, but Lathrop made it clear that his niceties were not nice. He called the money a business transaction but didn't specify what he expected from his investment. Lathrop seemed more personally interested in Fairchild, as if taking on a mentee, or a son, or something different entirely. Their age difference was curious, just twenty-two years—shorter, and they might be peers; longer, perhaps father-son. It surprised Fairchild, as it would most people, to receive such sudden and aggressive attention from an older man.

He wrote back to Lathrop telling him of his new work in Naples, and of the grand scientists he was meeting and valuable work they were doing, with each letter hoping to convince Lathrop that his grant was paying off even before a dime was exchanged. But Fairchild hesitated before sliding each note in the postbox, wary that the contents would aggravate Lathrop to the point that he'd revoke the offer altogether.

Fairchild's confidence grew after his heart-stopping trip to Corsica in pursuit of citron. While he was in Naples, a request had come from W. A. Taylor, assistant pomologist for the Department of Agriculture, who, with the endorsement of the secretary of agriculture, asked Fairchild to visit Corsica to acquire citron cuttings. The fruit itself was larger and more potent than most lemons, particularly because it existed first. Citrons were one of four major original citrus fruits, along with pomelos, mandarins, and papedas. The four mixed their genes together to make the modern orange, lemon, and grapefruit—each one eventually reproduced in the trillions. Future archaeologists would discover citrus to be among the most popular human foods, the rare mix of sweet, tart, and sumptuous, the centerpiece of American fruit salads, breakfast juice, and the all-American lemonade stand. All giving little credit to the fruits' hardy Asian ancestors.

Americans in the 1890s were familiar with citron. The country grew a little and imported two million pounds each year from abroad. The fruit had arrived not with explorers like Fairchild but with colonialism, traveling slowly over millennia from its birthplace in South Asia to Italy and Spain, and then brought by Spanish colonists, who planted the first citron groves in California. But by 1894, farmers in California had such antiquated fruit that they asked the federal government for better seeds. Taylor could think of only one man in Europe amenable to this kind of freelance work.

The trip was a success, even considering Fairchild's brief arrest. After the gendarme let him go, and after Fairchild escaped down the mountain on his mule, and after he acquired the citron cuttings and stuck them in potatoes, he managed to leave Corsica without any further incident. The cuttings arrived in Washington several weeks later, and several months after that, word returned to him that the cuttings had proved of "real value" to American citrus growers. The saplings would bolster California's citrus market for twenty years, from twenty thousand trees to more than a million. The fact that California's citron market later fell from dominance was bittersweet, for the fruit was replaced not by an aggressive fruit competitor, but by a fellow citrus, an orange from Brazil with a strange cavity on its underside that resembled a belly button.

Fairchild, meanwhile, was gaining an odd practicality for a man of twenty-five. Corsica had boosted his ego, but the run-in with the policeman had also awakened him to the dangers of plant espionage. Besides, in the laboratories of Germany were fascinating questions to research, and top scientists to shadow. One, Ted Nichols, was studying the pressure of light waves, supplying knowledge that would be crucial to the later invention of the radio. A man named Röntgen used electromagnetic radiation to produce a fuzzy photo of a key and purse, an early technology that the world would come to know as X-ray photography. Of sublime interest to Fairchild was the one-eyed mycologist Oskar Brefeld, whose servant one day arrived holding a heaping platter of horse excrement with the pride of a person carrying a cake.

For the next three weeks, Brefeld stood guard over the pile, his only good eye pressed to a microscope to inspect layer after layer of mold overtaking the dung. Fairchild needed breaks to calm his stomach, but he admitted that microscopic mold had an absorbing beauty. "Incredible as it may seem," he wrote, "after my first feeling of revulsion had passed, I spent three of the most entertaining and instructive weeks of my life studying the fascinating molds which appeared one by one."

Fairchild bided his time at night writing letters, first to his friends in Washington, and then, on a whim, an unsolicited missive to the botanical garden of Java. He wanted to inquire, sheepishly, if anyone needed help from an American fungus scientist-in-training.

When an envelope arrived several months later, the biggest surprise was that someone had bothered to write back at all. Correspondence soon blossomed between Fairchild and the garden's director, Melchior Treub, a Dutchman who had built Java's botanical garden into one of the most respected in the world.

It's possible that, at twenty-six, Fairchild might never have gone to the Malay Islands. Not because of self-doubt or laziness but for the relentless force of procrastination. In front of him were grand scientists with ambitious goals. Java could be a spectacular experience, but also a derailing distraction. The promise of one thousand dollars answered the question of how, but even one million couldn't unveil why. Imagining an exasperated Lathrop added urgency, yet the two had met once—twice, counting the cursory encounter on the boat—and despite Fairchild's urge to appease his impatient supporter, he wasn't about to alter his life's course to quell Lathrop's anxiety.

But in one letter, Fairchild had let slip to Treub that a rich man had promised a mound of silver for Fairchild to make the trip to the East Indies. In the early days of 1896, Treub responded to say he was soon coming to Europe, and that when he returned to Java, he wanted Fairchild to join him.

The Suez Canal was the great engineering marvel connecting the Mediterranean to the Red Sea. It was also the official maritime divider between West and East, and as such, there were strict codes aboard the Dutch steamer regarding what women could wear on either side of the world. The first morning east of the canal, Fairchild unknowingly wandered onto the deck and caught sight of barefoot women splayed under the sun in sarongs. Men weren't supposed to be on deck so early, he thought. But he was wrong. The women had changed to their native and more revealing Javanese garb as soon as the captain allowed. When he learned this, he returned with his camera.

Crossing Suez was a novel experience for anyone in the latter part of the nineteenth century, chiefly because the canal had only existed since 1869. The hundred-mile route through the narrowest part of Egypt was perfectly level, requiring no locks, and when the first ships passed through, the twenty-six-foot-deep canal cut the voyage, formerly around the Cape of Good Hope, by four thousand miles.

To mark its global centrality, the French sculptor Frédéric-Auguste Bartholdi asked the Egyptian government to let him build a ninety-foot statue of an Arab peasant woman wearing robes and holding a torch above her head to welcome Eastern travelers to the Mediterranean. When Egypt declined on account of the project's high cost, he took the idea to France, which financed the sculpture. Once the Muslim woman was refashioned into a Roman goddess, France gifted the statue to the United States, where the woman became a symbol of liberty for immigrants entering New York Harbor.

Over the next week, Fairchild reveled in his slow entrance to the tropics. The weather became warmer; the water bluer, and it teemed with birds and fish, including, occasionally, sharks. Then one day, from the ship's railing, Fairchild watched the islands of the Malay Archipelago approach. "You approach Java with a feeling of how beautiful and lovable everything seems," he wrote. He was taken first by the green richness. In an essay Fairchild wrote about his early impression of the tropics, he would five times use the word "verdure."

From his first night in Java, Fairchild was enchanted. Palms and bamboos covered every square inch of Batavia, the city on the west end of Java that would later be known as Jakarta. At night, loud buzzing insects filled the air with a soundtrack of "idyllic leisureliness" no

1895. Java had a feeling of "idyllic leisureliness," the warm sun, the buzzing insects, and the bare feet whose only sound when one walked was the soft crunch of grass.

one in Washington, D.C., had ever heard. From the patio of the tony
Hotel Bellevue, he could sit under tremendous banyan trees watching people shoulder bamboo sticks with buckets at both ends. No
shoes or pavement meant every step was placed in silence. The barefoot people ate rice and fish from wooden bowls, without the clang
of china. Even the soft and rhythmic language had the melody of a
quiet song.

For a first-time visitor to the tropics, the natural wonders were
like a dreamworld. Trees carried their roots above the soil, appear-
ing to walk across the ground. Fairchild saw a tiger orchid with a
thousand orange blooms, each so perfect and vibrant, as though
prepared for his arrival. His first experience breaking the purple
skin of a mangosteen was maddening, but far better than his first
whiff of a durian, the fruit whose sweetness was belied by its putrid
smell, which would linger on the lips for hours. He walked through
a jungle of rattan palms that attached themselves to his clothes, and
he marveled at the quick growth of bamboo, up to a foot a day.

The Dutch influence also saw that food was never in short supply for foreigners. At the Hotel Bellevue, meals were the highlight
of anyone's day, particularly Fairchild's, who wanted with every
bite to taste the simmering stew of the tropics. At lunch, he would
pile his plate high with rice, followed by bits of sardines, eggs, and
perhaps a banana dripping with hot oil. Down the buffet would be
tiny ears of corn and roasted coconut. India's mark in the region
meant that the chutneys and curries were, to Fairchild, "as hot as
liquid fire." A deep burning of the chest came next, but the pain
was a tolerable cost. The final course wasn't a food but a nap, keeping with the tropical custom delivered by the Spanish, rendering
the hotel silent between two and four o'clock.

Fairchild had never had a servant, but as a white man and a scientist
living the colonial life, he was granted one—and his name was

*1896. As a colonist in Java, Fairchild **(center)** donned the traditional white Dutch suit. He made friends with the European people living on the island and had his first encounters with coconuts and other curious fruits of the tropics.*

Mario. Fairchild had long been averse to slavery, and he also bristled at race-based servitude. Still, despite the barrier of language, the two chatted about girls in the area and the insufferable humidity. Fairchild told Mario about the marvels of the 1893 World's Fair, where there had been two replicas of the Liberty Bell, one made of rolled oats and the other of oranges.

In Java, the work that Fairchild decided was finally worth the lengthy trip was to study how termites built colonies. Termites struck Fairchild as ironic: blind and savage warriors that worked as elegant architects of the forest. But the question that had never been answered, at least as far as Fairchild knew, was how a colony functioned, an intricacy no other species copied. The termites would be born in an underground colony, grow wings, and then go from the dark burrows into the open air of the world. In broad daylight they coupled, two by two, and then, reveling in domestic bliss, would snap off their wings and burrow into the ground to start a new colony. Did they build the fungus gardens in their colonies, or simply eat mushrooms that were already there?

The termites weren't eager to reveal their secrets, especially not when exposed to paralyzing light. So finding out required killing thousands of them and opening their stomachs. One afternoon, Fairchild broke open a colony. The mud was dried solid; a hammer finally cracked it in half. Inside were no worker termites, just a king and queen termite, their plump bodies motionless as if flustered to be disturbed.

The queen, the larger of the two, was as big as Fairchild's thumb, and after he inspected her, he delayed dissecting her pudgy trunk to count the speed at which she excreted eggs. One per second, it turned out, an astounding eighty-five thousand in a day. Fairchild figured she'd give life to more than thirty million offspring, a calculation he completed twice to be sure. The work was solitary and more personally fulfilling than useful. But Fairchild believed he was discovering something new, and he imagined that studying termites could occupy him for decades.

It took two hours to get from Buitenzorg to the port in Tanjung-priok, on Java's north coast. On November 26, 1896, Fairchild would need every minute.

The series of events began when he received a letter from Chicago informing him that its sender, one Barbour Lathrop, would soon be arriving in Java with a small party consisting of his brother, his sister-in-law, and a woman about Fairchild's age by the name of Carrie McCormick. A trip from Chicago to Java may have taken a month, or longer, but since Lathrop had sent the letter only days before his party departed, the missive barely beat Lathrop to the island. Contained in his note was the unsubtle implication that Fairchild would be available to stand in as the group's tour guide.

This was the second time Lathrop called upon Fairchild, both times almost unannounced. Lathrop traveled constantly, but to journey straight from America to Java, an interminable ocean voyage few would envy and even fewer would take, makes one wonder at his motives to see, of all the people he had met in the world, this young man who had somehow captured his attention.

Fairchild rushed to the port. When he approached the group, out of breath, Lathrop was in the middle of a story.

He looked Fairchild up and down, his eyes lingering on his protégé's white Dutch suit that buttoned up to the chin. Months in the sweaty tropics had left Fairchild thin, almost emaciated. Lathrop said he was "shocked" at Fairchild's appearance. Never had so much money looked like so little.

Lathrop was not especially close with his brother, Bryan Lathrop, and he had agreed to the trip only after Bryan had begged. Traveling with people annoyed Barbour. Too many people brought too many opinions, which required compromise. Money was not the problem. The Lathrops were laden with means, owing to the lucrative banking career of their father, Jedediah Hyde Lathrop, who had made several wise investments, none wiser than a real estate play following the Great Chicago Fire of 1871. It was hardly a gamble: the fire created the biggest redevelopment opportunity in American history.

Barbour Lathrop was pleased with his lineage—he was the grandson of the respected Governor James Barbour of Virginia. But he never got along with his father. Jedediah had pushed his son to attend law school at Harvard, which Barbour did. But when he finished, Barbour decided he couldn't become a lawyer because, as he saw it, "a lawyer cannot tell the truth." His incensed father responded that young Barbour would not get another cent. In Barbour Lathrop's retelling of the story, he replied to the ultimatum with a shrug.

Poor in his early twenties, Lathrop committed his sharp wit and passion to the bombastic, first to New York, which didn't hold him, and then to California, an upstart state awash in ambition. In the 1870s the West was still a new frontier with a spirit unencumbered by the divisions over slavery that still hung in the East. Gold had attracted opportunists to California in the 1840s and '50s. By the seventies, the game was either mining silver or trying to predict its fluctuating price. In San Francisco, the rumor of someone discovering a new vein would cause a mining stock to rocket 1,000 percent, creating fortunes overnight. "The entire city buzzed with tales of chambermaids who bought the rooming houses they had worked in a few weeks earlier and of former ditchdiggers riding down newly fashionable Kearny Street in opulent carriages," one historian wrote of the era. Lathrop didn't care about wealth as much as he wanted to *be* somebody, so he took his first job as a reporter, or as he pretentiously put it, "a newspaperman," for the *San Francisco Morning Call*, where he'd have a front-row seat to important events. He dressed aspirationally, wearing fine suits and hats. He even bought a revolver from a gun salesman who fed Lathrop's ego by claiming—correctly—that a man of Lathrop's status would need to use it one day.

It turned out that his father's ultimatum had been good only in life, not in death. When Jedediah died in 1889, he made each of his three progeny instant millionaires. The money immediately changed Barbour Lathrop. He quit his job at the *Morning Call* and began smoking fatter cigarettes. He passed his days in the gentlemen-only Bohemian Club, a tall brick building near San Francisco's Union Square that attracted Lathrop's type: the wealthy, powerful, and artistically minded who sought out the company of men—and men only. Amid boisterous conversation with writers, musicians, and patrons of the arts, Lathrop emitted baritone guffaws and plotted pranks, such as the time he convinced a man with thinning hair to emulate the people in Timbuktu, who he claimed stimulated their scalps with raw onions steeped in gin. Lathrop became known as the "sire of high jinks."

At forty-three, Lathrop was uninterested in the path of most men his age, namely to invest in property, marry, and raise a large family. He rented a room on the top floor of the Bohemian Club. His only close friends were other men he met in the dining room and in the smoking parlor, or on the streets of San Francisco. Fraternal gossip seemed to delight him, but when boredom inevitably set in, the next itch to strike him was to travel.

By the fourth day of Fairchild's stint as a tour guide on Java, the group was reaching its limit. Bryan Lathrop, on his maiden voyage east, was unaccustomed to humidity, and he squabbled with his brother about the indignities of foreign travel, setting Barbour's nerves on edge. Meanwhile, Bryan's wife annoyed everyone with incessant questions fired in scattershot fashion.

Fairchild was unperturbed. He took the young woman, Carrie McCormick, on a boat ride near an island full of bats. Had he known she came from the venerable McCormick family—the great

Chicago dynasty of Robert McCormick, who invented the mechanized reaper, one of the greatest tools in agricultural history—he
might have thought twice about asking the man rowing the boat to
clap the oars together with such a loud thwack that bats blackened
the sky above them. A sight that delighted Fairchild left the young
woman rattled for days.

Lathrop, meanwhile, was anxious and lonely, and had exhausted
his patience. It didn't help that Fairchild's command of the Malay
language was poor, or that Lathrop banished him from the hotel
one afternoon after Fairchild ate a noxious-smelling durian.

"Fairchild, I don't like this traveling with a party," Lathrop said
one night in Bandung. "I'm not accustomed to it. They don't like
the same things that I do, and what's the use?" It was time, he felt,
to abandon the others and move on. He asked Fairchild to join him.
"There is nothing in those termites. Leave them alone and come
along with me and I will show you the world."

Fairchild replied sheepishly that he couldn't leave Java, that his
research had just begun, that he had only been on the island for
eight months. But Lathrop answered the excuses with his classic
dismissal.

"You're working too hard and you need a change," Lathrop said.

Fairchild felt guilty at the prospect of leaving the job Dr. Treub
had created for him. But Lathrop promised to cover every expense,
and to pay him the salary he would be forfeiting. Lathrop also enchanted him with a promise that, as soon as a boat could be arranged, they would head together up the west side of Sumatra, an
island rich in minerals, fruits, and tribes seen by few people with
white skin. Unable to say no, and convinced that Lathrop would
reject his refusal anyway, Fairchild accepted.

Lathrop arranged a steamer for his brother, sister-in-law, and
Carrie McCormick to return to the United States. As soon as they
departed, he made arrangements for himself and Fairchild.

Their boat left Batavia and traveled west, through the Sunda

Strait, where the passengers gathered on deck for a sight of the famous Krakatau volcano, which had erupted a decade earlier in an explosion so extraordinary that, three months afterward, officials in New York and Connecticut deployed fire engines when smoke in the distance erroneously indicated a massive blaze.

The boat turned north to Padang, the port on Sumatra's west coast. As the vessel approached land, Fairchild stood on the bow to watch the endless forests draw closer. The island appeared raw and green, a chain of protruding volcanoes stretching across the horizon like the backbone of a sleeping dinosaur.

As he awaited his ship's landing, Fairchild penned a letter to his mother in Kansas. A typical young man in the nineteenth century might live in his parents' home until he married. Yet Charlotte Fairchild's son had left not only his home, but his country, writing from as far from Kansas as one could possibly be. He told his mother of Barbour Lathrop, of his abundance of personality and money, and recounted his hasty departure from Java and the impending arrival in Sumatra. He assured her that, in all his time living abroad, he had yet to experience even one serious accident.

Fate can always be tempted. As he was sealing the letter, he heard a shriek.

A Malay man on board was tussling with a waiter in the passageway. One wielded a hatchet, the other a dirk, each flailing his appendages. They wrestled down the passageway attempting to stab each other, and then fell, their bodies interlocked, into Lathrop's cabin and doused his trunk with blood.

Lathrop yelled and shooed. He and the ship's captain tried to separate the pair. It took another minute to put them in restraints and for some soldiers to drag them away on their heels, their bodies dripping a crimson trail.

The glue on the envelope was still wet. Fairchild peeled it open and amended his letter with a postscript.

CHAPTER FOUR
Guest and Protégé

One of the biggest uncertainties for an American traveling in the East was what kind of people he'd meet, and whether they'd be friendly. The Malay tribes on Sumatra, in their colorful garments, looked more welcoming than the more serious people of Java. The most striking feature were women's earrings, which looked less like ornaments than ear buttons. After getting their ears pricked, toddlers wore rolled banana leaves to enlarge the holes. When the child reached fertility, the openings would be an inch in diameter. Only after she delivered her first child would she take them out, leaving her elongated lobes to flap against her cheeks.

Fairchild didn't know how long he and Lathrop would stay in Padang, so he wandered around to survey the area and maybe collect a few things. A yellow raspberry caught his eye, and he pulled it to taste—tart and mealy.

A moment later, he came across the tallest, thickest cane of bamboo he had ever seen, its shaft thirty feet tall and deep green. Bamboo isn't a tree, but an overgrown grass, and Fairchild shook it to test its strength. The hefty joints separated and the stalk cracked in half and tumbled down around him, the weight of two-by-fours barely missing his head. Fairchild would one day describe bamboo as "the most beautiful and useful of plants," but for the moment, he decided to leave it where it was.

As travel companions, the botanist and the playboy were a study in contrasts. Lathrop was always immaculately dressed and groomed, his collar left open, his mustache plumped. Fairchild, by comparison, wore baggy pants that didn't fit, and his necktie was never tied correctly. He couldn't dance or make small talk. At times, the two men rarely spoke.

The two-man odyssey was plagued by growing pains and, true to form, Lathrop quickly grew impatient with his companion. The tall, rich man was unable to slow down, and Fairchild, earnest and awkward, seemed incapable of moving faster. "Lathrop was a rapid traveler and I was a rather slow and deliberate collector," Fairchild later remembered. "He didn't propose to spend the rest of his life on that fever infested coast and I didn't see what was the use of just a glimpse of plants that there was no time to collect." If they had been closer to America, Lathrop at this point probably would have sent Fairchild home, conceding that the whole idea of traveling together had been foolish.

Lathrop believed an expedition could have only one leader—him. He made all the major decisions about where they'd go and where they'd stay. He sighed loudly in frustration. But once Fairchild had experienced the full range of Lathrop's moods, he realized that the older man's lectures were meant to be more therapeutic than instructional, and the harsh words lost their bite. Fairchild learned to listen without listening, if only in anticipation of the several quiet hours that would follow each outburst.

Lathrop came from Alexandria, Virginia, the kind of town that valued cultural refinement and a proper way of doing things, and where anything in violation could be decried as endangering "the public morality." The windswept plains of Kansas where Fairchild grew up had little to offer as high-minded culture or art. Other than the rotation of visiting professors who stopped by the Fairchild family's house, Fairchild's parents were hardly socialites. His sheltered upbringing may go some way toward explaining his gullibility and discomfort traveling with Lathrop, and in a group. When

Christmas 1896. Barbour Lathrop **(left)** *and David Fairchild aboard a steamer on the west coast of Sumatra.*

Lathrop told a story, Fairchild would stand nearby and laugh when others did. The rest of the time, he stayed quiet. A man on board with a camera asked to take their photo. Lathrop stared at the lens while Fairchild looked to the side, feeling as small and timid as he looked.

Most of the time, he simply didn't know what to say. One morning, after an entire breakfast filled with one-sided conversation, Lathrop stood up and threw his napkin down. "My god, man, can't you talk?" he yelled and stormed out.

And yet Fairchild looked at Lathrop with reverence so deep he might've drowned in it. "I was the guest and protégé of the greatest world traveler and one of the greatest interviewers America had produced," he would write of his deep fascination.

Fairchild's fawning obedience explains his eagerness to push on. But why would Lathrop, a man of such confidence and wealth, be drawn to compromise? Men who write little down cannot be easily analyzed. But Lathrop had developed a fondness for well-formed young men, those established in upbringing but still impressionable in character. Fairchild wasn't the first sidekick Lathrop had taken on. Two others had come prior but had left before long, one from impatience, and the other who annoyed Lathrop to the point of dismissal.

There's no evidence that Lathrop ever discussed his sexuality, but signs point to his discomfort in established society, not least his apathy toward marriage in an era when it was the norm, and his eagerness to remain in feverish motion, as if evading something he couldn't outrun. Lathrop identified himself as "bohemian," to describe both his lifestyle quirks and his unwillingness to conform.

It also explained where he lived. The Bohemian Club, the only place where Lathrop ever had a permanent address, was full of other men who styled themselves bohemian, a masking word for something that didn't quite have a name. The fashion of the so-called Gay Nineties in places like New York and San Francisco wasn't necessarily to *be* with other men, but simply to revel in the strangeness of it. Only a little before the 1890s was there a clinical term—homosexuality—to describe someone's sexual identity, and only *in* the 1890s did men begin to tiptoe more boldly toward the company of other men for reasons of inexplicable attraction in established smoking clubs on America's coasts.

If Lathrop was, in fact, drawn to men, he would have had good reason to be cagey. There was a stigma attached to being sexually different, and a deep risk of ostracism. Bans on gay bars and social clubs effectively regulated gender, outlining permissible speech patterns, attire, and demeanor in polite society. Policing gender came in the form of vigilante enforcement on the streets, where men thought to be queer were roughed up and jeered. Social punishment was worse: the loss of jobs, family, and social respect. Efforts to avoid this fate and still make oneself known to like-minded men caused distress, and from that anxiety came creative ways to both blend in and stand out. Gay men secretly announced themselves to each other with red ties and bleached hair. The best way to navigate was with multiple alibis, pushing most gay men to lead mirrored lives.

Lathrop lived in and seemed to pass with relative ease through a world where everything had double meanings, where people were mysterious because they had to be. One way to explain his constant travel may be that, in the distant places he visited, no one knew him well enough to judge.

"It's a collection expedition," Lathrop said matter-of-factly one morning, looking away from his newspaper. "We'll be collecting things."

Fairchild had built up the courage to ask Lathrop what, exactly, they were doing. He had been lured by the promise of luxury travel to untouched lands. But when he sat to write letters, he struggled to explain why he had left Java. He hardly knew where they were headed next.

After the novelty of travel began to fray, the wheels might have fallen off Fairchild and Lathrop's odyssey—if the odyssey had wheels to begin with. With more bluster than actual purpose, they were, in a real sense, floating. Lathrop's haughty aloofness masked the reality that he was flying blind.

Lathrop had seen more corners of the world than almost anyone alive, but his years of solo travel had lacked an objective, or even a general direction. At each port, he stumbled across things that, for a traveler, were simply there to observe and then leave behind. *Why not bring some of those oddities back?* was as much of a plan as Lathrop had considered. Something small here and there, altogether a few armloads to drop on the doorstep of the American people. What or for whom didn't matter so much as that Lathrop was repurposing personal enjoyment into a form of philanthropy.

He must have realized that to do it effectively meant doing it scientifically, and conducting science required a scientist. Lathrop had only the training of a nonpracticing lawyer and a short stint as a reporter. To bring his plan to life, he didn't want a botanist so much as need one.

The relationship between the two thinned further in Padang, the port city of Sumatra that was the terminus for the new West Sumatra Railway. In silence, Fairchild and Lathrop took the train, the world's first to work on a system of cogs with teeth carrying a locomotive up a steep mountain. Swampy jungle lined both sides of the track, punctuated with atap palms that rose from the jungle floor as small shrubs with large plumes of leaves. Jungle gave way to periodic waterfalls and beds of rising steam. The mud below them was tropical soup, home to snakes, leeches, and uncountable insects.

For hours, Fairchild, reluctant to talk and with little to say, stared out the windows, captivated by the foliage. Each plant had its own reason to be gawked at for a boy from the Midwest. If America's landscape was a black-and-white sketch on paper, Sumatra's was a nuanced portrait of watercolors.

At the hotel the next morning, Lathrop stood waiting beside his fully packed trunk. Without a word, Fairchild understood that he was ready to leave. Such an island offered thousands, even millions, of plants to collect. Fairchild could have spent a month there, three if he had his choice. But he also knew that Lathrop, when his mind was made up, couldn't be swayed. Fairchild's trunk joined Lathrop's on a horse carriage, which delivered them back to the train. Without one specimen collected, the two men returned down the mountain to Padang, where a steamer was waiting to continue up the coast.

As the steamer cut north, Fairchild and Lathrop kept to their separate quarters. One night when Lathrop and a group of Dutch officials were joking and gossiping in the smoking room, Lathrop slipped out to find Fairchild, who, with a lone candle, was hunched over a report. From the doorway, Lathrop delivered the closest thing yet to a compliment.

"You're a worker, Fairchild," he said, "whatever else you aren't."

When they arrived a day later in Fort de Kock, an area rich in waterfalls and sweeping gray cliffs, Fairchild left to collect. The ground was hard and the air dry, the perfect conditions for termites.

Yet this was a poor decision. When Lathrop discovered Fairchild hunched on all fours digging in the dirt, he let loose. One can assume that in Lathrop's entire life he had never had the occasion to position himself thus, in soil so dirty it had passed through the intestines of worms. Nor could a man of his stature understand why anyone would opt for behavior so undignified.

Fairchild stood up, circles of mud at his knees. For the first time, he spoke back. If he was to collect things, Fairchild said, he needed time to understand what he was collecting. Collecting useful things couldn't be done by grabbing indiscriminate handfuls of plants.

Lathrop let silence hang for a moment.

"If you're going to travel with me, I'll show you the world, but you can't stop every minute and collect specimens, or you won't get any general idea of the countries we travel through." Then he walked away.

1895. On Sumatra, simmering tension between Fairchild and Lathrop boiled over into full resentment. Their pact nearly unraveled completely. They stayed in a guesthouse with towering palms, but hardly talked.

Fairchild felt embarrassed by the exchange, but he was also emboldened by it. If he was going to be the scientific muscle behind the expedition, he might begin acting like it, starting with speaking to Lathrop as a peer.

The argument in the dirt gave Fairchild the confidence to seek out Lathrop that night as he read in his hotel room, novel in one hand, cherrywood cigarette holder in the other. Why, Fairchild wanted to know, had he left his unfinished studies in Germany, and his incomplete work in Java? Why had he agreed to travel to strange places and meet new people? Tourism was good enough for Lathrop, but not for Fairchild, who felt listless, anxious, and unfocused.

"Well," Lathrop began, a little impressed that Fairchild had grown a backbone, "what do you think we should collect?"

Fairchild answered that he had studied crop diseases for American farmers. But nothing on the other side of the world could solve the problem of a pear grower in Minnesota. While he enjoyed the exotic allure of the Indian Ocean, he didn't feel that he was helping farmers in need back home.

Lathrop sat and listened.

Fairchild continued by describing the World's Fair and the type of farmers who came to see his pear blight demonstrations. They were provincial and distressed, far too preoccupied with the problems in their fields to care about the novelties of a faraway land. Biologists could help them, perhaps by finding foreign predators of the pests on their farms, but that kind of work was targeted and deliberate, not accidental and haphazard.

At a pause in Fairchild's monologue, a Catholic priest appeared in the doorway. He'd heard there was a botanist on board. Fairchild, a little flummoxed, invited him to sit.

The priest, unaware of the tension in the room, described a vast collection of orchids he kept. He explained how he had built a garden of his own with new plants and rare flowers.

The minutes turned into several hours as the man described the wonders that plants held, and how people living in subtropical places like North America or Europe were oblivious to the wondrous diversity of the Earth. The priest bored Lathrop, but he also gave Lathrop an idea.

After the man left, Lathrop asked Fairchild if he remembered his first taste of a banana. What about a grapefruit, or even a durian? The answer was obviously yes. For a botanist, the first taste of a new plant was like meeting a new person, and recalling it flooded the mind with memories of where it had happened, what the tongue expected, and what it found instead. Lathrop explained that the sweet flavor and starchy texture of a banana was easy to remember because it had been *new*.

A man as traveled as Lathrop knew there were thousands of wild plants around the world, perhaps millions, that farmers had never seen. "If I was a botanist with the opportunity to travel, I'd collect native vegetables, and fruits. There are drug plants that can help cure ailments and all types of other useful plants still unknown in America."

Fairchild's citron adventure in Corsica was, at the moment, the best example. Lathrop seemed to be conjuring that episode to explain that it could be done repeatedly and for more crops—crops farmers had asked for and many more that they hadn't. Lathrop stood up and mounted to his grand proclamation. "As a botanist, you can help farmers solve problems with their current crops, or you can bring them *new* crops, the seeds to start rival industries."

The idea was steeped in history. It also carried the sort of American ambition common in the 1890s. Lathrop was suggesting that the key to their future success was in botany, and specifically foreign crops of economic value.

For most of America's hundred-year life, agriculture had been for subsistence, or, in the case of the Western states, for setting roots on the lands of native people. In the early nineteenth century, several major land deals had extended America's waistline. The biggest, the 1803 purchase from France, added almost a million square miles of its Louisiana territory—a bargain for just eleven million dollars. The United States got even luckier in 1848 when Mexico ceded its sleepy 155,000-square-mile California territory to its northern neighbor, along with enough land to make the modern states of Arizona, Nevada, New Mexico, Utah, and parts of Colorado and Wyoming.

Just over seven thousand Spanish people lived in the California territory, and even fewer in the other future states, so it wasn't a large loss. Except that nine days before the agreement was signed, a New Jersey carpenter found gold in a California creek bed. Despite his tiptoeing, the find became international news. The rush for gold subsided with time, but after that, the bigger claim to fame for the fertile and well-watered slice of land beside the Pacific would become its discovery as one of the most agriculturally productive pieces of earth.

In the tense days before the Civil War, Congress started discussing a large-scale giveaway of land to the people, both for economic growth and to make sure that America's new land stayed American. Under the Homestead Acts, anyone—except those who had ever fought against America—could apply for 160 acres, so long as they committed to live on it. And, came the implication, to defend it from Indians. The only other catch was that recipients had to occupy the land for five years before they owned it, which, to most people pursuing a new life in the West, didn't seem like a catch at all.

After the war ended in 1865, even former slaves were eligible for land, and not long after, Native Americans, too, the tracts given to families in an attempt to dismantle large tribes and reservations. Over the next thirty years, the government granted two million claims. Ten percent of all government property was given to first-time landowners, many who had no choice what to do with the land but to farm it.

The result was a flood of wheat, beef, and citrus that was sent east in such volume that supply eclipsed demand. In 1893, the same year that the world looked to the Chicago World's Fair for demonstrations of America's bright days ahead, the United States entered its first agricultural depression. Producing food had become a business, rather than a way of survival. Farmers needed to become competitive.

That competition didn't make for agricultural diversity. Attempting to grow new crops to outmaneuver your neighbor is simply too risky in farming, where uncertain environmental factors favor the familiar over the unknown. In the early 1880s, Joseph L. Budd, an American eulogized as "the highest authority on horticultural subjects in this country," had tried to import apple varieties from Russia. The plan might have worked if not for the lack of a central authority to act as a seed bank and help farmers troubleshoot—an authority like the Department of Agriculture or one of the land-grant colleges. Waves of blight had killed early apples, and America's humidity was stressful to Russian trees. What's more, apple reproduction is extremely heterozygous, with two parents that produce unpredictable offspring (much like humans), meaning the only way to guarantee consistent fruit is to clone a tree. Farmers who had spent their lives tending corn or cotton were largely oblivious about apples, so the novel fruit from a foreign land was neglected to death.

Lathrop believed that he and Fairchild were in a position to know better, not just about apples, but about thousands of other crops, too. Traveling gave them a view of rare fruits, but more than that, a reasonable understanding of growing methods they could relay to farmers back home.

The idea held the potential to kick-start a new era of agriculture in America. Bananas could grow in Florida; mangoes in California; avocados, perhaps, on the rainy shores of the American West. Even the mangosteen, the purple sphere from the Malay Islands no bigger than a baby's fist, could find fertile soil in the Southeast. Fruits that had never grown in North America and had only been tasted by a fortunate few would find opportunity to sprout on new land.

The contours of a plan were coming together, but there were still thorny logistics. Anyone who had shipped seeds back to America, as Fairchild had, knew that sending living plant material required someone to receive it. After a long ocean journey, seeds and cuttings would need to be planted quickly, in conditions as similar as possible to their comfortable habitat. Seeds and cuttings from the tropics that arrived in Washington would need to be carried down to South Carolina, or even farther, to Georgia or Florida, both barren lands where few people lived. At the fastest, the journey, start to finish, would take two months.

And what would happen when the seeds and cuttings arrived? Who would know how to care for them? The motley group of botanists at the Department of Agriculture spent their days researching old crops, not new ones. And the Department of Agriculture had one of the smallest budgets in Washington, reflecting its low regard. Even with Fairchild and Lathrop volunteering, pro bono, to complete the hard work of exploring and selecting, someone back home, likely someone who had never tasted a mangosteen or smelled a rancid durian, would need to complete the process of propagation, distribution, and, ultimately, marketing.

But the particulars would have to wait for another day. The hour was late and the world, at the moment, was preoccupied. It was December 31, 1896. In New York, where the sun was almost at its highest point in the sky, crowds of people began to assemble around Trinity Church at the south end of Broadway, waiting for a set of chimes at midnight. A new year meant a new day ahead, but before that, a raucous night.

At the same moment, Fairchild and Lathrop were floating in the dark, on a quiet ship somewhere near Singapore. The talk that began in the evening lasted late into the night. Their conclusion was vague and, in Fairchild's mind, ill-defined. But finally, they had an understanding and a collective vision that seemed to please them both.

Drifting in the Indian Ocean, the pair agreed to study plants useful to man, and with one providing the means and the other the brains, finding a way to bring them to America. While they talked, in the middle of the ocean and in the middle of the night, the ship's clock struck twelve, and 1897 began.

CHAPTER FIVE

The Listless Pacific

Lathrop took the last guest room, and so the only room left was the ballroom, wide open and boiling hot. An American named Edison had commercialized a heated glass bulb in 1879, but the technology had only recently come to Bangkok, delighting the hotel's owner so much that he kept his new electric lights on day and night, burning, humming, and radiating heat. After the hotel fell quiet, Fairchild constructed a tower of tables and chairs. He climbed to the top and unscrewed each bulb of the grand chandelier. He found his way down and dismantled his ladder in the dark, then fell asleep to the swishing sounds of cockroaches scurrying along the floor.

The early days of a new year brought another revelation for Fairchild and Lathrop. Washington wasn't prepared to receive cuttings of tropical plants, and even if it were, the land around the Chesapeake, which alternated between sweltering and frozen, would be a lousy place to raise plants accustomed to consistent warmth. It dawned on Fairchild first, who had little difficulty convincing Lathrop, that their collection expedition would need a tropical home.

Looking at a map, one could not have found a more perfect spot than Hawaii. The Pacific archipelago sat conveniently between Asia and North America, and in 1897, the islands were already American territory, if not in law then in spirit.

The United States had become the biggest trading partner for the Kingdom of Hawaii and its most abundant product: sugar. In exchange for the right to export sugar duty-free, Hawaii's monarchy in 1876 had granted the United States a military base at the small southern inlet of Pearl Harbor. Native Hawaiians, who numbered just under forty thousand, protested the agreement, fearful that any capitulation would lead to greater American presence. The people were right. United States marines stifled the protests and by the end of the century, a group of American civilians had begun living on the middle island, Oahu, home of the Hawaiian capital. In December of 1893, during his second term as president, Grover Cleveland publicly discussed annexing the islands to the United States. It would not have been difficult (his successor, William McKinley, eventually did it), but even the fact that people in Washington were thinking about it effectively opened Hawaii for any business America could dream up.

Fairchild and Lathrop agreed that for the next month, they'd hopscotch the South Pacific, stopping on islands as big as Australia and as small as Fiji. They'd survey worthwhile plants and collect cuttings and seeds. But the real goal would be to find them a tropical home. They imagined that in Hawaii they'd convince a landowner to donate soil for an experimental garden. A *donation* was crucial. Surely Lathrop could have afforded a plot of his own, perhaps an entire island. But an existing landowner was effectively a recipient, a willing addressee to receive packages from around the world and coconspire in a grand but vague plan of importing foreign plants.

The tensions between Lathrop and Fairchild were slowly becoming unkinked, a little every day as each assimilated more to the other's sensibilities. Lathrop's impatient outbursts were becoming less frequent and Fairchild reminded himself daily to make snappier decisions. Lathrop's style had grown more predictable, and Fairchild began to admire the man's demeanor, even his incessant storytelling.

"Uncle Barbour was a great raconteur," Fairchild observed of their early days together in the Pacific. "His seat was always at the Captain's table on shipboard and at whatever table he sat there was one continual round of fun and intellectual sparkle. His stories were always on a high level. He never indulged in off-color ones. I recollect how he burned up with sarcasm at a stranger in the smoking room once who prefaced a story he proposed to tell by saying, 'Well, as long as there are no ladies about . . .' He could make his audience listen to him without that low subterfuge. He never discussed such things with me and he never told or listened to such sex appeal stories.

"He was, in his time, the world's greatest reformer of those things that had to do with travel and he would spare no expense and stop at nothing if he thought there were graft or a lie hidden away somewhere in the makeup of anyone he met. If he suspected a steward or a purser of double dealing, he would hound him out of his position and spare no pains to do it. He considered this a plain duty to society."

One of Lathrop's helpful lessons to Fairchild was that peppering someone with questions could yield more plants than if he searched for them blindly. At a dinner party hosted by an American doctor one night in Bangkok, Fairchild passed around the table his name card, on which he had written, "What's the finest fruit in all of Siam?"

A scrawled sentence came back to him on a card he'd keep for the rest of his life: "It's the wampi."

This launched Fairchild on a quest for a wampi, or wampee, a small citrus fruit with rough, pale skin that would pass for a yellow grape if it didn't grow on a tree. It took less than two hours for him to find a grove and fill his pockets with cuttings, this time resolved not to ask for permission but, if caught, for clemency. Owing to this strategy, the wampi would one day live in California and Florida, although its botanical sibling the kumquat, less of a diva about soil

and water, would end up with more market share in the United
States.

In each part of the world he visited, Fairchild wrote to his friends
back home, regaling them with stories of Lathrop's peculiarities
and inscribing written portraits of the remote locales. In one letter
he described an "incomprehensible" scene in Bangkok. He witnessed a man fall into a river and then, unable to swim, splash
hysterically and beg people on the banks to pull him out. But as
Fairchild watched, himself too far to help, every person that was in
a position to save the man's life refused. According to the era's Bud-
dhist philosophy, anyone who rescued the man would be responsible for his future behavior, including crimes he might commit.
Saving him was too great a risk, and so, after a few minutes, the
man drowned.

Even in 1897, Sydney was a metropolis of wonder. The entire eastern
half of Australia had been parched by a winter drought. But in the
spring, buckets of rain turned dust into blankets of foliage, made
even brighter in contrast with the deep blue of the harbor. Lathrop
and Fairchild landed in Australia aboard a ship operated by North
German Lloyd, a line of such luxury, it once won Mark Twain's endorsement as "the delightfulest" way to travel.

Their steamer, the *Sumatra*, had smoking rooms for men and
drawing rooms for women and was so well built that in low water, it
could scrape the muddy ground and proceed undamaged. This Lathrop knew but Fairchild did not. When Fairchild shook him one night,
panicked that the vibrating ship must be sinking, Lathrop rolled
over. "Pshaw, I don't believe it," Lathrop said, half-awake. "We're
crossing the bar and the water is a bit low, go back to your bunk."

Australians had a habit of being short on words. If someone
didn't know how to answer a question, they stared straight and

walked away. It took considerable time for Fairchild to find his way to a grove of eucalyptus trees, the only species of plant he knew for certain existed on the expanse of land the British had once used to banish prisoners. The trees were bigger than he imagined, almost as tall as the great sequoias of the American West. As he looked up at them, a small lyrebird with the tail of a peacock passed by. Fairchild stopped to gawk at the bird.

While Lathrop spent his days reading in the hotel and entertaining guests with stories of his latest life-threatening triumphs, Fairchild explored. He took cuttings from branches of several different species of eucalyptus—there were more than five hundred— curious if they'd grow anywhere in the United States. They could provide shade, and in North America they'd lack natural predators.

A man in Australia stared at Fairchild, drawn first to the way he talked. Nathan Cobb was a Yankee, too, and in a far-off corner of the world, it was rare to meet a fellow American. Cobb was a specialist in nematode worms, but he had been lured down under by the newly created Australian Department of Agriculture, to figure out how to grow better wheat. Developing governments, especially those, like Australia, endowed with money from a foreign crown, had begun to consider growing food more efficiently.

As both an American and a scientist, Cobb found Fairchild and Lathrop's plan riveting. He quizzed Fairchild on all the places they had been so far. Then he brought Fairchild into his lab. He presented a small wheel that stood on a wooden stand. The wheel spun horizontally around a kernel of wheat, held in place by a sharp dental pick. A camera took pictures at eight different angles, which were then printed, catalogued, and studied to help farmers learn to recognize superior varieties.

So much was unknown about wheat in those days, and it had never been studied at a scale as small as this. No one knew why, of all the grains on earth, wheat, rye, and oats would make bread, and why other grains, such as rice, corn, and millet, refused to rise. Cobb had dismantled the cell of a grain of wheat. This revealed a protein that helped the dough hold bubbles of carbonic acid that let it increase in size before it was baked. By doing this, Cobb became the first man to identify gluten.

It would have been rude not to invite Cobb to dinner, so Fairchild informed Lathrop that the professor would be joining them at their hotel. On special occasions, Australians ate meat pies of mutton, curry, and lamb chops. The three sat with steaming bowls and full glasses, and for once, Fairchild directed the conversation while Lathrop sat silently and listened.

The people of Fiji had never met ice. For most of human history, frozen water had been a contemptible symptom of winter, and it hardly existed near the equator. In the nineteenth century, a Boston man named Tudor became a millionaire by introducing it to the tropics. But he never made it to Fiji, where cool breezes kept the climate more consistently comfortable than anywhere else on earth.

The first person to bring ice to a group of Fijian warriors was David Fairchild. He carried it from the ship's icebox as a token of goodwill.

"*Katakata!*" the chief yelled, the Fijian word for "hot." He dropped the piece of ice, then had to be persuaded to pick it up again. It wasn't hot, he realized, but extremely cold. Someone suggested he put it in his mouth, and when he did, he smiled. He passed the shrinking cube down a line of Fijian men; each held it on his tongue and then passed it along. Every one of them grinned; some even giggled.

Fiji's nickname, the Cannibal Islands, was given for the most literal reason. Far from a source of shame, eating other humans had become one of the islands' many cultural traits. On long stretches at sea, the Polynesians who settled there had turned to eating human flesh out of necessity, which continued when they reached the islands they later named Fiji. Eating human meat became as much a part of being Fijian as making fine pottery or woodcarvings. Lose a battle, and your bones would wind up under the victor's home. Upset the king, and you could end up in his stomach.

A Fijian defense of cannibalism—the oral history of how it started and why it continued so much longer than in other early societies—is a rationale largely lost to time. The clearest view of cannibalism comes from Westerners, several of whom visited Fiji during its nineteenth-century heyday and seemed to take great pleasure in demonizing a culture and its people.

"Murder is regarded as a gentlemanly accomplishment by them, and no young man is fitted to take his place in society until he has committed at least one homicide," the *Sacramento Daily Union* reported of Fijians in June of 1875. The wealthy partook most often. Common people received occasional invitations for the scraps from a human head or arms, known as *bakolo*. Flesh was so sought-after that the highest gastronomic praise one could give was to say, "It is as good as *bakolo*."

By this point in history, most cultures had moved on from the practice of eating other humans except in the most desperate of cases. But not in Fiji, a clear example of how culinary trends are intensely cultural and tied to morality. The running hypothesis at the time, which helped most of the world look at Fiji with resigned disapproval rather than moral outrage, was that cannibalism kept an island society stable. Problems created by a growing population with limited land required a drastic solution. Cannibalism, once a matter of food scarcity, became the culture's way of quelling tension between senior and junior males, both in pursuit of the same few resources—or more pointedly, women.

Alfred St. Johnston, an explorer who visited Fiji in 1883, reported to the world that Fijians really seemed to love the taste of human flesh. It tasted a bit like pork, but was more tender and flavorful, he was told. A man's absolute authority over his wife meant that he could slay and eat her. For ceremonial events such as the christening of a new canoe, a body would be sacrificed for each new plank, and then more corpses would be needed to roll the canoe to water. It turned into entertainment, Johnston reported:

> There used to be a regular display of slaughter, in a sort of arena, round which were raised stone seats for the onlookers. In this space was placed a large braining stone, which was used thus: Two strong natives seized the victim, each taking hold of an arm and leg and lifting him from the ground they ran with him head foremost—at their utmost speed, against the stone—dashing out his brains, which was fine sport for the spectators.

One run at the stone was usually enough, certainly for babies, although several dashes could be made for adults. After skinning the corpse, men filled it with hot stones to cook it evenly. The thumb and palm tended to be most sought-after.

There was little risk that Fairchild or Lathrop would meet this fate. Cannibalism had begun to fade as a cultural practice once the British landed on Fiji's shores, bringing with them Christian morality and cultural judgment, effectively introducing the notions of murder, shame, and repentance. By 1890, the practice was nearly wiped out, except for among a few elders who retained their taste for human flesh. But not for Fairchild's. His skin was white and known to carry unsavory flavors and the chance of disease.

Fairchild and Lathrop met the king of one of Fiji's largest tribes on Bau, an island one thousand feet wide that legend held had been artificially expanded by Fijian women who dumped baskets of debris onto shallow coral for decades until the island was enlarged. In the confusion of translation, the king was led to believe Lathrop was the president of the United States and Fairchild his personal secretary. The king, whose exposed belly shook as he laughed, was so honored at the audience, he ordered several women to prepare a kava ceremony so that his guests could drink the drink that made the mouth tingly and numb.

The women joined the circle, their breasts dangling as they chopped roots of the kava vine, and then chewed the roots into fibers. Fairchild's fascination turned to revulsion. "One by one," Fairchild recalled, the women "deposited their quids in the big bowl of water and walked out. The attendant then stirred the mess with his hands and dragged the coconut fibers through, partially straining the liquid." Fairchild dutifully drank. Later he learned that Lathrop poured his ration in the dirt.

As the two cruised the Fijian islands in a small launch, wild pigs regularly poached their supplies. Cuttings that Fairchild had taken of wild palms either decayed or disappeared in the blur of fast motion. The collecting part of the expedition had become an afterthought. Until there existed a place to plant them, Fairchild convinced himself that collecting plants didn't need to start in earnest.

It took more than ten days to reach Honolulu. Lathrop had been before, twice. For Fairchild, it was the farthest both east and west he had ever been.

The first to discover Hawaii had been Chinese sailors, enchanted by the crisscrossing grain patterns of the islands' sandalwood. But Americans and Europeans found a more practical benefit: agriculture, and mostly sugar. This discovery was the beginning of the end for the Hawaiian monarchy, which had lasted just shy of a full century.

Queen Lili'uokalani, the woman who would be Hawaii's last monarch, had reason not to like the Americans. She tried, with her limited military, to push them away, but the effort backfired. In 1893, a committee of thirteen men from America and Europe staged a coup to depose her. They argued that Hawaii wasn't reaching its agricultural potential. But the real reason was that everything about Hawaii—its soil, its weather, its strategic location—would benefit the United States. And unlike the spear-pointing Malays or Filipinos, the Hawaiian people were docile enough for the Americans to overtake.

As the rest of the world was fixated on the impending World's Fair in Chicago, the men barricaded Lili'uokalani in the royal Iolani Palace. Not long after, the Kingdom of Hawaii became the Republic of Hawaii, and the first president was Sanford Dole, an American whose snowy beard parted evenly into two white curtains. Dole would govern for the next decade. His cousin James would go on to build the largest pineapple company in the world.

Fairchild and Lathrop's reception in Hawaii was largely seamless because of the United States' incursion. Their goal in Hawaii wasn't to collect, but to find land and a botanically minded baron to receive cuttings. In theory, Lathrop and Fairchild would check on the garden every so often. Or better, someone else from the Department of Agriculture would, someone who could judge the plants and disseminate workable crops to farmers, and by doing so, allow Fairchild and Lathrop to stay in motion.

As the boat pulled into Honolulu, Lathrop explained their strategy. They'd visit all of his deep-pocketed friends, who, like Lathrop, might be compelled to participate less out of enthusiasm than boredom. If they demanded payment, Lathrop would oblige. But the cause would be more than a favor. They were asking on behalf of the United States.

The first man they visited was William Brigham, whose bald head and white beard gave him the visage of Charles Darwin. Brigham was a geologist who collected Polynesian artifacts, and he happened to be an oracle of plants. Inside his house just to the east of Pearl Harbor, Fairchild explained his and Lathrop's plan and fielded Brigham's many questions. How would the seeds get to American farmers? Who would want them? Does the Department of Agriculture even know about this?

Fairchild could offer little more than hypotheticals, and, once again, a retelling of his exciting work in Corsica.

Brigham declined to participate due to his advanced age of fifty-six, but he recommended a friend. The friend Fairchild met later that day was Samuel Damon, a politician. Damon didn't like the idea, either, or perhaps he couldn't be bothered. During a meeting in which he hardly looked up, he explained to Fairchild that he was more interested in tending his orchids than opening up land for other people's benefit.

The final person for them to ask lived on a different island, the biggest one and the namesake of the chain, Hawaii. Fairchild took a lengthy ride on a small boat, and again crawled off dizzy and sick, and lay for hours moaning in the shade.

He walked to the home of Claus Spreckels, a German horticulturist who had built great wealth and reputation growing sugar beets in California. He was also the chief force behind the downfall of Hawaii's monarchy—he didn't participate, but he owned enough Hawaiian debt to stretch its leaders impossibly thin.

There were a thousand reasons why Spreckels should have said yes. He had personally benefited from tropical crops, especially sugar. He was eager to learn about new crops that were beginning to appear in Hawaii, rare fruits like avocados and mangoes. Coffee, too, had qualities that seemed to fit Hawaii's climate. But he, like Damon, couldn't be bothered. Other matters of botany interested him more than waiting by the mail for urgent missives from a pair of travelers he hardly knew.

Before he left the island, Fairchild procrastinated boarding the small boat to return to Oahu. He tried poi, the flavorless mashed stem of the taro plant. He talked with a man who managed a leper colony on the island of Molokai. He wandered around the beaches, staring toward the endless reach of the horizon. And finally, a small indulgence, Fairchild took a horse-drawn cab to see the volcano of Mauna Loa. It was the largest active volcano on earth, having erupted nearly every half decade for the past three thousand years. Under it bubbled the caldera of magma that built the Hawaiian Islands. While Fairchild stood and scanned the landscape of hardened lava, it struck him that, in comparison, Vesuvius hadn't been that impressive after all.

Lathrop didn't speak. There was nothing to say. Securing land from one of several rich men was supposed to be easy, and yet Fairchild had failed. Lathrop's illustrious idea had been crushed by Fairchild's ineptitude, exposing lofty notions of plant exploration as little more than storybook fantasy.

Fairchild and Lathrop were given a ceremonial exit from Hawaii, during which they wore shirts of floral patterns and women placed plumeria leis around their necks. An orchestra punctuated the melancholy departure, and as the boat left the harbor, the musicians played the soft, slow notes of "Aloha Oe," the Hawaiian song of farewell.

Lathrop was eager to get home. He was a man whose joys didn't linger, and neither did his disappointments. He looked only forward, keen to return to the Bohemian Club, where his portrait hung on the wall. He would arrive in time to join the club's summer encampment in its redwood grove north of San Francisco. He had a new batch of stories, all ripe for embellishment.

Fairchild, however, saw his star fading. He had quit his job in Washington for Naples. He had left his work in Germany for the dream of Java. And he'd abandoned Java for a fanciful idea that materialized into a poof of air. Arriving in San Francisco, he spent several hapless days with Lathrop, distracted by the early-summer sundresses of the West ("I had never beheld so many beautiful and well-dressed girls in all my life as there were that day in San Francisco."). Lathrop bid him farewell with the detachment of a father leaving his son for a single day at school. He never said it, but Lathrop's demeanor betrayed his disappointment. "I felt that Mr. Lathrop was at times a bit doubtful about his 'investment,'" Fairchild would write. The plan hadn't failed for lack of money, but for lack of follow-through. That was a quality Lathrop never claimed to have, and all he required of his companion.

His far-flung travels now over, his ambitions sunk, Fairchild boarded a cross-country train with the intention of stopping halfway, in Kansas. Three years had passed since he had last walked American soil, and twice as long since he had seen his parents. After receiving word from their son in faraway Java, they found it hard to imagine he'd ever return.

His mother, Charlotte, at first didn't recognize him. George Fairchild greeted his son with the handshake of a fellow man. Their lives had taken dark turns. A decade prior, George had been named president of Kansas State University. Now a political movement known as Populism that brought a fear of establishment and corporate power had not only ejected him from the job but had driven him and his wife from their house after someone set it on fire. George was stoic, unmoved by his misfortune. He and Charlotte were preparing to move to Kentucky, where George could find new work.

After several dinners where Fairchild recalled stories of the Javanese durian fruit, the real-life cannibals of Fiji, and the idiosyncrasies of Barbour Lathrop, both George and Charlotte urged their son to return to Washington. Kansas wasn't a place for a boy of worldly ambition. They believed if he tried, he could get his old job back and rise through the ranks of the government.

As the train pulled away from the station, Fairchild smiled, seeing his parents wave at him for what would be the last time. As the steam locomotive picked up speed, he sulked in his seat, confronting the reality that awaited him in the capital. He would arrive in Washington, the city built between two rivers, at the height of humid August. He had only the money in his pocket, no place to live, and, most dismaying for an educated man of twenty-eight, no job.

PART II

CHAPTER SIX

One Cause, One Country

At the corner of Eleventh Street and Pennsylvania Avenue in Washington, D.C., was Harvey's Ladies and Gentlemen's Oyster Saloon. The capital city was known for its oysters, and Harvey's was the church of the shellfish. The restaurant was named by a pair of brothers who, following the Civil War, had experimented with ways to cook oysters—steamed, roasted, grilled, or fried—and concluded that steaming in lightly salted water was the superior method. The layout of the joint was as deliberate as the source of the oysters, which arrived daily on overflowing carts from the Chesapeake. The first floor was for men, the second for women, and the third a series of private dining rooms for the well-heeled. The fourth floor wasn't a floor but a facade, so the restaurant wouldn't be shorter than the two adjacent buildings.

Every president from Abraham Lincoln to Franklin Roosevelt ate at Harvey's. When David Fairchild returned to Washington in the summer of 1897, it was William McKinley's turn. Whispers that the major was in the building could travel from the third to the first floor faster than the plates of oyster shells down the dumbwaiter. McKinley, soft-spoken and reserved, had been president just six months, and his style appeared to be as a deal-making unifier, relenting to meet with anyone, even an enemy, who might be tomorrow's ally. The mystique of the president eating oysters did not last long. People returned to loud conversation, the ambient hum of men in suits, their ties loosened, drowned out by a piano.

Back in town, Fairchild spent his first few evenings at Harvey's, regaling his friends with stories of the Pacific. None provoked more interest than his descriptions of the girls in San Francisco in waist-tight dresses.

Fairchild's return to Washington wasn't as bleak as he'd expected. Despite being unemployed and homeless, he found the city relaxed and quiet. In less than a week he ran into an old friend, Walter Swingle, who had grown up on the same plains of Kansas. As boys, the two had been educated together, both taught by Swingle's mother. In the afternoons, when Swingle would help his father, a farmer, cut wood or drive cattle home from pasture, Fairchild sometimes tagged along. Those dirty-fingernail afternoons were a respite from life with his strict, academic father. They were also his first introduction to the physical work—not just the theory—of farming.

As they grew older, Swingle and Fairchild had followed nearly the same path. Both studied botany at agricultural universities before securing jobs at experiment stations for the Department of Agriculture. Fairchild, two years older than his friend, had recommended Swingle for the job, and Swingle's parents, on account of their son being too young, had had to give special assurance that Walter could handle the work. The irony now was that Swingle still had a job and Fairchild did not.

Swingle loved hearing Fairchild's stories, particularly about Barbour Lathrop. He had never met the man, whose description defied belief, but he enjoyed the caricature Fairchild drew with quotes and impressions. Fairchild would critique Swingle's mustache, clothes, and manners with Lathropian disdain. Twice in the past four years Lathrop had surprised Fairchild unannounced—once in Naples and the other time in Java—so one night at Harvey's, Swingle, feeling prankish, paid a waiter to deliver three glasses to

1893. Walter Swingle followed the same path as Fairchild, from the plains of Kansas to Washington, D.C. At the U.S. Department of Agriculture, he was given an office, a microscope, and the chemical elixirs to investigate how to keep crops free of pests.

the table, one of them, he said, for "a Mr. Lathrop," who would be joining them shortly. Swingle laughed as Fairchild fell pale.

Fairchild and Swingle found a boardinghouse on California Street Northwest, each renting a room from an old man who let only to young men. In the late days of 1897, Fairchild and Swingle managed to occupy the top floor. They discussed their travels and their futures late into the night. Swingle, who had studied in the classical laboratories of Bonn and Leipzig, was fascinated by the erstwhile plan Fairchild and Lathrop formulated in the Indian Ocean.

It made sense: America needed new crops. Swingle had believed for years, even as a teenager, that agriculture was a potent source for economic growth. After an 1891 trip to Florida, Swingle developed what would become a lifelong obsession with citrus. That year, at just twenty, he told a roomful of Florida citrusmen that a young man traveling around the world, especially to Asia, could yield incredible new varieties. Hell, even *he'd* be willing, and on a shoestring, just with his expenses paid. But his proposal was roundly dismissed. Travel was expensive, inefficient, and uncomfortable. Anyone who would want the job wouldn't be qualified. And all that time and energy, for what? The plan lacked guarantees that it would yield anything useful.

But sitting in front of Swingle was his friend who had actually brought the ambition to life, or at least had come closer than anyone else. Fairchild had spent several months acting as the kind of explorer Swingle had once imagined. Fairchild, for his part, seemed to revel in this elevation of his expertise. Travel with Lathrop had given him confidence and poise. In America's gilded capital, he found himself more knowledgeable about agriculture than anyone in town. If anyone was qualified for this type of work, he was.

Inspired by the possibilities, Swingle envisioned the two of them, and maybe a third, forming a coterie that would travel the globe and administer the introduction of plants. Two would search full-time, and the third—the three might rotate—would remain in

Washington to receive cuttings. They fancied their title as "agricultural explorer"—a term so whimsical, so obvious, that it came out of their mouths at the same time.

The brainstorming was based less on youthful naïveté than on a thoughtful budgeting of time, money, and human energy. They drafted a memo that alternated each man's handwriting, and they devised a hierarchy. The program would need structure. Both men understood how the world worked and knew the value of being sponsored by a government as powerful as America's. Rather than just send someone to travel aimlessly, they would make decisions based on fact, not merely hope. As botanists, they debated which families of crops would be the easiest to transport, and which could produce new crops the fastest.

One night, Swingle sat reading about Egypt. "My god," he said, "it takes date palms fifteen years to bear fruit. If this book tells the truth, we'll be old before we get anywhere in the date business."

Fairchild, without looking up, responded that the book was wrong.

On the evening of July 3, 1898, the street below Fairchild and Swingle's window filled with a raucous crowd. Newsboys yelled, "Extra *Star!*" hawking late-run broadsheets that reported the Battle of Santiago de Cuba, a naval clash just off the south coast of Florida.

On that very day, the eve of the anniversary of America's independence, the United States locked horns with a different colonizing superpower—Spain. Four centuries earlier, Christopher Columbus had claimed Cuba for the Spanish monarchy, which would eventually build an empire from the Colorado River to Tierra del Fuego. But gradually, the land was dismantled piece by piece until Cuba and Puerto Rico were the only Western Hemisphere possessions Spain had left. Now Cuba wanted independence. America was sympathetic to a colonized people hungry for liberty.

Americans had sided with the Cubans with surprising unity, not least because helping the island offered a chance to neutralize a Spanish perch so close to American shores. The conflict was the first major opportunity for America, not far past its hundredth birthday, to fight a long-standing bull of global dominance. If there was debate about the conflict, journalists didn't spend much time covering dissent. The *Chicago Tribune* included in each day's newspaper an above-the-fold etching of the American flag and the slogan "ONE FLAG, ONE CAUSE, ONE COUNTRY."

Even William Jennings Bryan, the man who lost the 1896 election on a platform of avoiding international skirmishes, supported the cause of *Cuba libre* with such enthusiasm that he publicly told President William McKinley, the man who beat him, "I hereby place my services at your command." More than freeing a colonized people, politicians also knew that siding with the Cuban insurrection would help protect trade routes for valuable commodities such as sugar and tobacco.

To flex its muscle in Cuba, the United States ordered the construction of a great battleship, the USS *Maine*. America's shipbuilding prowess fell far short of Spain's, so the top-heavy and poorly armed *Maine* was no match for vessels in the Spanish fleet, but that turned out not to matter. Its purpose in Cuba was to beef up America's image—effectively a pair of shoulder pads for the scrawny United States Navy. Yet not long after it left Key West in January of 1898, when the ship exploded with a window-breaking boom and sank to the bottom of the Havana harbor, it became a different kind of symbol.

What came next was one of the clearest examples of America's growing ingenuity, particularly the formation of the long-standing ethos that there was always money to be made, especially amid crisis. The journalism barons William Randolph Hearst and Joseph Pulitzer, locked in battle to outsell each other's New York newspapers, used the public frenzy for war—which each man's paper enflamed—to sell more papers. Both the *New York World* and the

New York Journal ran banner headlines above breathless reports of the fighting in Cuba, containing every detail except Spain's flat denial that it was responsible for the *Maine* explosion (a claim modern forensics have mostly held up). The hysteria made its way to Congress, which voted 311 to 6 to declare war on Spain, along with an allocation of fifty million dollars for President McKinley to spend how he pleased. Whether the war was warranted, or arrived at honestly, turned out to be irrelevant. Hearst would go on to serve in Congress. Pulitzer's name became shorthand for superb journalism.

Everyone in Washington was wrapped up in the war, America's biggest foreign conflict since its 1848 duel with Mexico. Politicians were at the same time delighted at the prospect of a fight—one American diplomat called it a "splendid little war"—and also wary at what they had started. Members of Congress worried they'd be foolish to send too many soldiers to Cuba, leaving Washington unguarded in case a Spanish warship sailed up the Potomac. In the days before radar, sonar, or reliable spatial monitoring, a surprise attack of this sort would have ended the war, and America not long after.

Fairchild seemed to be everywhere his fraught country needed him. After months of unemployment, he signed up to mine the Potomac with remote-activated bombs in case the Spanish invaded. He partnered with Frank Hitchcock—who would later become chairman of the Republican National Committee and, ultimately, postmaster general—and the two rowed around the river, stopping every few feet to drop a bomb and then activate it with a small wire that, when triggered, would blow apart the hull of a Spanish ship. Hitchcock struck Fairchild as featherbrained and clumsy, which worried him every time he connected the wiring to a bomb. Hitchcock always seemed to be the one holding the battery pack some distance away, not the one at risk of being blown to the clouds.

The Spanish never came to Washington. After the *Maine* explosion, Spanish officials tried to bypass America's overheating temper and sent a fleet directly to Cuba. When it got there, U.S. Navy ships blockaded Spain's incursion. On land, a volunteer horseback cavalry called the Rough Riders, led by forty-year-old Teddy Roosevelt, waged battle. The combination of land and sea warfare was a show of newfound American strength, so much that within days, much of Spain's fleet was either badly damaged or sitting underwater.

When Spain conceded defeat—after just 113 days—the United States, a nation on the rise, had for the first time eclipsed one of the world's top powers. Men like Hearst and Pulitzer, who had benefited from swells in newspaper sales, took the occasion to declare America an emerging force in its own right. They gloated that in just over a century, America had gone from mistreated colony to a nation of great confidence, military clout, and moral superiority.

The U.S. victory also turned out to be a victory for food. American soldiers had been sent to Cuba with rations of canned beef, a foodstuff so sordid and foul that after the war, Congress investigated why so many soldiers got sick. Sick soldiers might have lost the war for the United States, if not for the way they supplemented their diet with tropical fruits they picked up in Cuba. Soldiers marveled at new types of bananas, juicy limes and pineapples, and strange specimens many soldiers had never seen, such as the yellow carambola, also known as star fruit, with five perfectly symmetrical ridges. In a way, fruit had given America its edge in victory. And when soldiers returned, stories of these novelties awakened the American public, its palate stimulated by the diversity of new things obtainable in the tropics.

Secretary of Agriculture James Wilson was a tall, thin man whose gray beard, deep-set eyes, and receding hairline suggested constant concern over large matters. Behind his old desk, made of knotted oak with carvings of flowers and vines, he peered through wire spectacles at the three men who sat before him. Accompanying Fairchild and Swingle was Doctor A. C. True, head of the experiment stations and

Fairchild's former boss at the Department, who the young botanist hoped would add credibility to the request he was about to make.

James Wilson was a savvy man of politics who, owing to his character and shrewdness, had been President McKinley's choice to head the Department of Agriculture. A Scotsman, Wilson had emigrated to Iowa in 1852 in hopes of farming in a country that was economically ascendant. He hadn't sought out higher office; he was drafted by a neighbor who appreciated the way Wilson spoke, peppering his speech with biblical allusions. Wilson had built one of the strangest résumés in American history: he won a seat in Congress in 1882, was sworn into office, then learned after a recount that he had actually lost the election. Defiant, he used parliamentary procedures for two years to silence the other party's objection to his legitimacy. Then, with just minutes left in the congressional term, he resigned his seat to his opponent.

In Wilson's wood-paneled office at 1400 Independence Avenue, just steps from the Washington Monument, Fairchild explained that since the USDA was formed in 1862, its primary role had been to dispense seeds. But by 1898, the congressional seed program struck many people (farmers included) as laughable graft, a Gilded Age boondoggle that benefited politicians and no one else. It wasn't uncommon for packets specifying round pansies to yield horn-shaped foxgloves, and purple petunias came up looking like pink hollyhocks. When the packets were accurately marked, farmers were happy to take free seeds of corn and potatoes, but they didn't need them. The program, with an annual budget of two hundred thousand dollars, amounted to an entitlement relic from an era when farmers were starting their businesses, not expanding them.

But now farmers had a different kind of need. As fertile land was opening in the West and South, settlers were appealing almost daily, less for the Department of Agriculture's money than for its *wisdom* on what crops could be grown and how to fight pests. Fairchild had heard stories of farmers in the Upper Mississippi Valley who wanted hardier plants than the apples of the eastern states. Settlers in the Southwest needed drought-resistant plants and help with irrigation.

Fairchild argued to Wilson that the answers weren't inside the Department of Agriculture; they were across the oceans in places like China and Egypt where people had learned over millennia to farm in tough conditions. Fairchild told Wilson of his association with Barbour Lathrop, and of their attempts to introduce plants. He had become accustomed to describing the flavor of the wampi and the durian and the mangosteen, each enticing, worthwhile, and completely unknown in the United States. But beyond his personal tastes, wasn't it strange, Fairchild observed, man's propensity to be satisfied with so little when so much was available? Fairchild wrote a lengthy memo to organize his thoughts.

> To the most casual observer it must be apparent that the number of useful plants, compared with those of which man makes no use, is very small. The menu of an average American dinner includes the product of scarcely a dozen plants, and yet the number which could be grown for the table would reach into the hundreds. There are several reasons why the number of plants upon which we depend for subsistence remains small, and the competition between producers of the same plant product continues fierce, but the most potent one lies in a persistent conservatism of taste, which is both unreasoning and uncontrollable. That the German peasant should look on Indian corn meal as fit only for his live stock, or the inhabitants of some portions of Holland consider the sheep raised along their canals for the English market in the same light as Americans do horse flesh, are facts which must be reckoned with, however unreasonable they may appear, in any attempts at plant introduction.

Fairchild wasn't bold enough to think he could change human nature. But there was reason to believe Americans were more susceptible to expanding their palates than were people in other countries. As a symptom of its youth, he argued, the United States was impressionable.

Stretching some three thousand miles from coast to coast, from the cold winters of upland Maine to the sweltering summers along the Rio Grande, the United States enjoyed more climatic diversity than anywhere else on the planet. What if the Department started a pilot program to learn about those other crops? Fairchild asked. If it failed, the program could be killed. But if it worked, the benefits to American food could be infinite.

Fairchild wasn't asking to travel. He was suggesting that he run such a program from Washington. Swingle could go to Europe, and perhaps, he argued, they could fund the travels of another man, too. The whole operation could get by with a few thousand dollars and a little office space. Fairchild had even thought of a name to put on the door. He had scrawled it in his notes: *The Office of Plant Introduction.*

While Fairchild spoke, Secretary Wilson leaned back with an expression that betrayed he was impressed. His spectacles twirled between his fingers. He emptied his mouth into a spittoon.

Fairchild had come prepared. He also had good timing. The year 1898 was only half over, but it had already proved consequential—a year that revealed substantial stress on America's agricultural economy. Wilson's boss, President McKinley, had narrowly won election two years prior over William Jennings Bryan, whose populist campaign had riled farmers, especially ones who felt squeezed by advances in mechanization that they couldn't afford. McKinley was lucky, especially considering that Bryan's support had actually started as far back as the 1880s when farmers began to assemble into a group called the Farmers' Alliance. The group became fervent enough by the early 1890s to launch its own political party, the

Populists, which, led by Bryan in 1896, came within six hundred thousand votes of winning the presidency. If McKinley wanted to keep his job, he'd have to address farmers' angst. Not with tired old ideas, but with inventive new ones.

Wilson spat in the spittoon again.

He called for a man outside the office, who came in a moment later.

Wilson recounted the outlines of the idea.

The man, the Department's disbursing officer, thought for a moment, then admitted that, yes, if the secretary wanted it, money could be procured.

Wilson looked back at Fairchild. He'd be an employee again at the Department, giving him the credibility of government backing.

All Wilson wanted, however, were two changes to the plan.

One was to expand the plant-collecting team from a triad of young men to include anyone currently abroad on government business. They would be encouraged to contribute seeds, and, provided they be sensible, their expenses would be paid. Wilson believed this would widen the reach of the new section from a handful of hunters to potentially dozens.

The other change became apparent two days later. Wilson summoned Fairchild to tell him he had found office space. Fairchild and the secretary marched up four flights, to where the rafters nearly touched their heads. Wilson pointed to a small nameplate on the wall. The Office of Plant Introduction had become:

The Office of Seed and Plant Introduction

The title was obtuse. Seeds were part of plants. But Fairchild knew seeds were the currency of Congress, and if it helped convince Wilson and the Department's bean counters, Fairchild could look past the redundancy. Wilson had also procured an old carriage house for Fairchild to store plant material in—a pitiful greenhouse, but it would have to work. He walked outside with Fairchild to see it.

"Don't let them crowd you out, my boy," he said. The secretary stood for a moment, then turned and disappeared back inside.

Seeds began to pour in immediately. Durum wheats from Russia. Grapes, mushrooms, and pomegranates from Europe. Fairchild's initial ambition to start a plant introduction program was replaced by the urgency to find a place to put them all. The greenhouse, overflowing with papers and boxes from other sections, wasn't big enough.

Fairchild spent his days shuttling seeds to and from the greenhouse and returning in the heat of the afternoon to his desk to write. The majority of the job wasn't botany but correspondence. Explorers needed assignments; experimenters wanted samples; farmers were desperate for seeds.

To investigate how to expand the reach of the section, Fairchild decided to take a trip. Hawaii was too far, and his recent failure too fresh, so the only remaining place suitable for tropical botany was Florida, an area of remarkable heat and humidity and hardly any people. In 1898, there were just 1,600 people who lived on either side of the Miami River, which bisected the town of Miami like a pageant sash. No one prized Florida for its potential, least of all farmers. Salt-blasted land couldn't support wheat or corn.

This Fairchild knew. He was also aware that Florida's last experiment with food introduction had ended in spectacular failure. In 1829, Henry Perrine, United States consul in Campeche, Mexico, was one of the few men to answer Washington's request for useful plants. He became so interested in America's botany that he left his post to start an experimentation garden in south Florida. Perrine asked Congress for land in the region, but was denied due to hostility from the Seminole Indians. When he insisted that it was Florida or nowhere, Congress granted Perrine thirty-six square miles at the southern end of the peninsula. Cautious of the Indians, he moved his wife and three kids to Indian Key, a small island accessible only by boat.

The water, however, couldn't protect him. In August of 1840, a group of Seminoles raided Indian Key with torches and arrows. Perrine helped his family escape by boat to be rescued by the navy, and then he went back to battle with the Seminoles. Eventually, his limp body was discovered, charred by fire. After Congress passed a resolution honoring Perrine, the idea of plant experimentation went unmentioned for the next half century.

Another reason for Fairchild's visit to Florida was the rumor of a land donation on the south banks of the Miami River, where newly introduced plants might thrive. Florida hardly compared with the East Indies—its trees were short and their greens all the same hue. But it was dense enough to be jungle, and more important, it had tropical character. Plants like coconut palms and the occasional mango had already begun arriving, carried by birds, travelers, or soldiers returning from Cuba.

Near Miami, Fairchild met Henry Flagler, the wealthy cofounder of Standard Oil, and he was invited to stay at the rich man's new hotel, the Royal Palm, a five-story temple of modern luxury painted in Flagler's characteristic yellow. The resort was the first in Florida to have elevators, and its veranda, a wooden boardwalk almost a fifth of a mile around, circled Miami's first swimming pool. A perfectly circular driveway welcomed visitors in front, and out back, women in long, puffy skirts teed off rounds of golf. Florida had no one bigger than Flagler. In an empty landscape, the millionaire imagined a future of luxury hotels, grand estates, and sculpted gardens that would draw rich Americans. If there was a nineteenth-century disrupter, Flagler was it. After he financed Florida's first railroad, he transformed a sandy dune north of Miami into Palm Beach, the future home of American billionaires.

The upstart spirit may have been one reason Fairchild found south Florida so charming. But the region's potential for agriculture delighted him more. "I was thrilled to find tropical territory in the United States, and a love for southern Florida was born in my heart," he would write. And the more he thought about it, the more certain he felt that a flood of migration would one day fill Florida with thousands of people, maybe millions. A land in America with the potential to support coconuts, pineapples, and mangoes would be too irresistible to remain a ghost town.

At the time, however, Florida was a bust. Fairchild returned to Washington excited by the idea of starting an experiment garden in Miami, but was told the government didn't have the money to buy land, and Washington couldn't legally accept a donation. The early work of plant introduction came with regular disappointment of this sort. Trying to do something that had never been done, Fairchild met the institutional roadblocks that would forever hamper government efficiency. But Fairchild's work did become "thick and fast" in his judgment. When winter turned to spring that year, two things happened. Nursery stock had begun to sprout, which brought urgency to figure out where these samples could go. The facilities didn't exist to take adequate care of them, and more were sprouting each day.

Adding to his frenetic pace was Congress' endorsement of the program, and the insistence that more be done—and faster—to help American crop growers. Congress granted Fairchild's office a new appropriation of twenty thousand dollars—a sky-high sum for a new section run by a young scientist. Fairchild hired a secretary named Grace, who had a braid down her back and wore skirts that stopped at her knees. A decade his junior, she was the first female Fairchild encountered who was interested in plants.

And yet, despite the help, most of the work still fell to Fairchild himself. He worked evenings and Saturdays, frequently Sundays as well. Secretary Wilson made a habit of checking on him when he left for the day and upon arrival the next morning, chiding him that he ought to find proper housing. Yet with Swingle in Europe investigating table grapes, there was no one close to Fairchild to warn him to slow down. A nervous collapse was a real and dangerous condition brought on by overwork, and Fairchild seemed headed directly for one.

"By god you look awful!" said the man who darkened Fairchild's door one afternoon. Fairchild, in the middle of writing a letter, looked up to lock eyes with Barbour Lathrop, whose tall build filled the doorframe.

Lathrop hadn't gone completely silent after separating from Fairchild in San Francisco. Wondering what Fairchild was doing in Washington, he sent repeated missives, some cogent, some stream of consciousness. The occasional reply from Fairchild pleased Lathrop. Despite the failure of their original plan in Hawaii, the older man was impressed by the ingenuity Fairchild demonstrated in Washington. He had talked his way into a government department and built an office. And somehow, he had managed to keep it running.

But Lathrop hadn't come with accolades. In fact, after a year on his own, he had again grown hungry for purpose, and, judging by another surprise visit to Fairchild—this his third—renewed companionship. A blunt man who seemed incapable of giving a compliment, he made no effort to sugarcoat his assessment.

"David," he said, "you're no more fit to build up a government office of plant introduction than I am to run a chicken farm—and I don't know a thing about chickens."

Fairchild leaned back and smiled.

"You have no contacts with the rest of the world. How do you expect to secure your seeds and plants? You can't do that sort of thing by correspondence. If you try to run things from Washington, it will be a little pinchbeck affair."

The expression was new. Pinchbeck was a man who invented a cheap substitute for gold, a knockoff alloy made from copper and zinc. The sentiment, though, was an old one that Fairchild had come to expect. Lathrop believed Fairchild's botanical background was more useful on steamships and in foreign ports than in a poorly ventilated government office. Lathrop resorted to criticism to shroud his longing, even desperation, that the two might travel together again.

When he sat down to discuss details, Lathrop vowed that, as before, he would pay every expense, and that they'd visit different ports than on their last odyssey.

Two sleepless nights passed while Fairchild considered the proposal. His loyalty to Wilson, owing to the secretary's trust in him, was slowly overtaken by the realization that Lathrop was right. David Fairchild wasn't an office man.

"I do not approve of it at all" were Secretary Wilson's only benign words in a tirade of displeasure. Wilson accused Fairchild of running away from his responsibilities, and wondered who would take over the program Fairchild had lobbied so hard to create and that Wilson had expended political capital to support. Wilson didn't say it, but he resented Barbour Lathrop, whom he considered a reckless and irreverent influence on Fairchild. In Fairchild, Wilson may have seen a future secretary, a steady, inventive, and hardworking civil servant, who might rise through the ranks if he kept his head down. To Lathrop, such a fate was worse than being eaten by a walrus. Without arguing face-to-face, the two men were sparring over Fairchild's future. Would he be a man of methodical bureaucracy, or a capricious adventurer and gentleman?

The meeting ended with a grunt.

Ultimately, though, Wilson relented. Whether he fired Fairchild may have been a formality, but ties were severed. In exchange for his department receiving the future fruits of Fairchild's efforts abroad, all he offered was a formal letter with a gold USDA seal, which might help cajole stubborn foreign officials. Wilson stipulated that expenses would be paid by Lathrop, and, to procure plant material from foreign countries, he was granted a maximum budget of one thousand dollars. Even though Fairchild told the secretary that he would likely visit South America, India, and the dark continent of Africa, where unknown crops held millions of dollars of promise for America's farmers, and even though Wilson suggested that Fairchild look into cotton production in Peru, the cereal industry in Chile, and orange growing methods in Paraguay, the secretary of agriculture refused to pay Fairchild any salary.

When news reached Lathrop later that day, he, without blinking, agreed to cover that, too.

CHAPTER SEVEN

Crossing Countries

Silverware and crystal glasses flitted over a white tablecloth as the luxury train holding Fairchild traveled west from Washington, first through Chicago, and then through open prairie toward San Francisco. Taking a train west was a rare American journey in the late days of the 1890s, but it was a luxurious one. For every twenty East Coasters who voyaged to Europe, only one went to California. The novelist Charles Nordhoff made a grand display of riding a train across the country during the era and documenting every detail. "California," he reported, "is to us Eastern people still a land of big beets and pumpkins, of rough miners, of pistols, bowie-knives, abundant fruit, queer wines, high prices—full of discomforts, and abounding in dangers to the peaceful traveler." The rush of 1849 gold seekers had slowed to a trickle by the end of the century, the easiest nuggets presumed discovered. Now those heading west were pitied by their friends for the deluge of annoyances and dangers awaiting anyone with the audacity to leave the self-centered corridor between Washington and New York.

It would be years before Secretary Wilson would admit that Fairchild's decision to leave Washington had been the right one. Fairchild couldn't be caged; his talent exceeded the duties of a bureaucratic seed recipient. Other twenty-nine-year-old men might have been content with stable desk jobs, working for the United States government in the capital of the world's rising power with a typist of their own and an annual salary of eight hundred dollars. Perhaps that would've been enough for a younger Fairchild, too. But his ambition had grown, thanks to the influence and bank account of one man, for whom office work was a fate worse than death.

Lathrop, meanwhile, lacked the patience to wait for Fairchild to tidy his affairs in Washington. So Fairchild rode the Central Pacific Railroad across the country alone, passing hundreds of miles of corn, wheat, and oats in fields, all, in October of 1898, approaching the beginning of their slow-growing winter. The summer had brought excessive rains to the Great Plains, covering Midwestern corn and wheat with spots of bright yellow rust.

The voyage across America, east to west, left little impression on Fairchild despite the vivid look it offered of the country's transformation. The western frontier neatly embodied the progress of America's past—a nation scrappy and hungry. It also offered a portrait of the country's future. The concept of American superiority was born from revolutionary victory over the British. But as the country's ego grew, so did its energy, first in a second victory over the British in 1812, and then in exterminating the cancer of slavery in 1865. Each success brought bursts of new patriotism, and the frontier offered the best place to put it, effectively America's escape valve of ambition.

Europe, by comparison, had run out of land long before, which helped explain its wars and collapsed empires. But America could travel farther and farther west, until, in the 1890s, all the stakes of land had been claimed. If America's future could be foreshadowed, Fairchild would have seen it on the plains. A settled frontier meant no place left to put the excess enthusiasm of a growing country. America would have to expand in new ways: overseas, and in industries it had never before dominated, such as agriculture.

Fairchild was now traveling on Lathrop's dime, which meant an upgrade from the Nickel Plate Road menu of sliced tomatoes and baked beans afforded cargo-rate travelers. The Transcontinental

Railroad connected New York to Sacramento at the new, exhilarating speed of thirty-five miles per hour. Earlier railroad companies judged their success by simply running on time, with no additional frills. Seeing the inelegant way passengers brought their own food on board and how they relieved themselves in shanty huts inspired a man named Fred Harvey to start America's first restaurant chain, Harvey House, a series of railroad rest stops where young, unmarried women served quick gourmet meals to accommodate frenetic rail schedules. Eventually, by the beginning of the so-called golden age of travel, in 1890, the railroads had mastered onboard food service, which brought the luxury of calm and comfort. Delicacies like mutton chops, veal cutlets, and grouse could be washed down with endless glasses of bubbly French champagne.

An enviable menu, however, couldn't mask the endless squeal of steel wheels on steel track. When he arrived on America's foggy West Coast, Fairchild, well-fed but fatigued, was met in San Francisco by an irritated Lathrop, who announced before any greeting at all that the ship Fairchild had hurried across the continent to catch, the one that would take them to South America, had already left.

The next available boat taking passengers south would sail from New Orleans, a two-week train ride at least. Fairchild and Lathrop boarded a train heading south, hugging at times the Pacific coast. The train made a stop in Santa Barbara, where Fairchild spent a short layover with Dr. Francesco Franceschi, a long-nosed plant enthusiast who cut for his visitor a slice of a curious squash—"zucchini," he called it, emphasizing the full whimsy of the Italian name. Zucchini was new to Fairchild, and as a result of his tasting it in California, it qualified for plant introduction to farmers around the country. The squash had originated somewhere in Central America, yet its development as a food crop occurred in advanced laboratories in Italy and France. Nature's real intent was for zucchini to be eaten small, before its blossoms fell—its name Italian for "little squash." Chefs of the future would ignore this and value zucchini most for its size. Never mind that larger size brought diminished flavor, if any whatsoever. Nor was any botanist present to remind people that the vegetable zucchini, the enlarged ovary of the zucchini plant, was, in fact, a fruit.

Fairchild and Lathrop traveled south to Los Angeles, and then, for more than a week, east toward the Gulf of Mexico. A month after he had left Washington for the Pacific coast, Fairchild found himself in Louisiana. Fairchild and Lathrop reached the New Orleans harbor to learn that they had missed the Panama-bound boat by less than an hour. This time Lathrop was utterly disgusted. He bought tickets for the next train to New York, where he was certain a boat would eventually sail south.

After a month spent crisscrossing the country, missing a third boat might have entirely unraveled Lathrop's anxious resolve. For the best, on December 27, 1898, the men embarked from Queens, New York, hugging America's East Coast, bound for Jamaica. Ice covered the rigging of ropes and cables, all frozen solid by a cold wind. Each morning a passenger on board made a grand scene to ask the captain for the ship's latitude and longitude, a request with no practical purpose. Such a meaningless gesture annoyed Lathrop, who had long ago bored of the early novelties of travel.

Like train travel, ocean voyages in the 1890s had reached the height of glamour. Ships crossing the Atlantic bore names like *Mauritania* and *Majestic* and boasted expensive paintings and first-class libraries, lounges, and wood-paneled dining rooms. Routes servicing the Caribbean were more pedestrian, their ships outfitted more as shuttles than as floating hotels. Even so, on any given boat, Lathrop was always granted the best cabin. Fairchild slept with the masses, often sharing a small room or bunk bed with another passenger. Lathrop had a desk; Fairchild wrote on the floor.

Fairchild began to explore the moment he stepped off the boat.

"Kingston, Jamaica, was the first foreign port in which I began a serious study of the marketplaces," he wrote, "tasting the new fruits and vegetables, packing and shipping both seeds and cuttings of those which seemed desirable for introduction into the United States." At busy markets, he sampled everything for sale, including small red and yellow tomatoes that grew on a bush so large it resembled a tree. The fruit, he wrote in his pocket notebook, was *"Eaten after peeling off the thick rind, with sugar and cream or salt and pepper, or as an apple would be."* He also came across a lumpy, reddish fruit called an akee, originally from Africa but brought to the Caribbean on slave ships and adopted quickly as a side dish with fish. *"It has a fine flavor and is highly esteemed. For Puerto Rico and Hawaii,"* he scrawled.

After Fairchild's year as a Washington bureaucrat, his dispatches had acquired a new efficiency. If his first world tour was slowed by imprecision and uncertainty, to his second he brought the confidence of knowing what was worth his time and what wasn't.

His attention turned quickly to the brighter colors and sweeter tastes of mangoes, dwarf oranges, even cacao. Fairchild tasted them all, sometimes navigating through crowded markets as Lathrop sauntered behind, taking each sample and giving it a verdict. At this Lathrop was unusually helpful. "Mr. Lathrop had an extraordinary palate for flavors," Fairchild noticed. "Everything we introduced would have to run a gauntlet of sarcastic criticism when it reached Washington, but, when Mr. Lathrop had said that a food was 'good—delicious in fact,' I [would be] able to tell those who declared 'the stuff wasn't fit to eat' that evidently they had uneducated palates." More exciting than the new tastes was the logistical convenience that anything that grew in Jamaica, an island just over five hundred miles from the United States, could reasonably be expected to thrive in Florida.

The two were invited to dine with the governor one night, the high-water mark of any unannounced visit. And so the next morning,

Lathrop wanted to move on. He rarely missed the opportunity to re-mind Fairchild that if they wanted to see the world, they couldn't lin-ger anyplace too long. Fairchild convinced him to stay another few days so he could travel to the outskirts of Kingston, where small farms grew subsistence crops not seen anywhere else on earth. When he arrived at one farm, the fruit Fairchild observed was strange in shape, bulbous at one end and pointed at the other. Vegetable pears, people called them, a member of the cucumber family with crisp flesh and inoffensive flavor, akin to chomping an apple with a numb tongue. The vegetable pear would later be known in Washington as the cha-yote. "Mr. Lathrop was enthusiastic about the chayote," Fairchild said. He liked its taste and its versatility, like squash's, of being served either raw or cooked. Perhaps most compelling, the abundance of the chayote on hundreds of vines suggested they'd be easy to grow.

While Fairchild and Lathrop sailed south to Grenada and then to Barbados, a bundle of seed with written instructions made its way to Washington. With every new sample, Fairchild was con-stantly refining his packing method, alternating between potatoes and wet moss to keep cuttings moist. Swingle had experimented with wet cigarette paper, banana leaves, and sorghum moss. Fair-child tried all of these, and asked local people for advice on shipping plants. Most farmers were oblivious. Even botanical expertise couldn't overcome the fact that seeds had to move by boat, stop-ping at one port after another like a city bus. There was no express service, nor any assurance that the samples would stay alive in transit, if they reached their destination at all.

Even so, getting seeds to the United States was the easy part. Convincing Americans to actually grow the fruit, and then eat it, would be the bigger challenge. And this required volume. The work of food exploration wasn't solely to find crops in their original habitat. No one, not even Fairchild, whose academic knowledge and field experience exceeded that of most people on earth, could truly expect to find the world's most economically valuable fruits

by making short stopovers to small islands. Exploration, and especially food hunting, also required diplomacy. It required finding
researchers and enthusiasts around the globe who might serve as
correspondents, who might contribute seeds and cuttings as gifts
to America, or for the thrill of knowing they'd grow in United
States soil.

When he met these people, Fairchild would unfurl his introduction on Department of Agriculture letterhead, which identified him
as a culinary diplomat. No one's eyes lingered on the title "special
agent." The golden seal was shinier. Surprised at how well it worked,
Fairchild began to refer to the sticker, the embossed seal of the Department of Agriculture, as a "Dago dazzler."

Next was Trinidad. Fairchild knew that the island was the land
of mangoes, at least the most robust ones outside of the Eastern
Hemisphere. Though mangoes weren't unknown in the US, in
Trinidad he found an array of new varieties. At least a dozen grew
there, each one slightly different. Fairchild took three, and within
weeks the fruit turned up in Washington. His associates at the
USDA found the three mangoes to have insurmountable faults.
The Gordon mango was large but bland. The Peters No. 1 was
sweet but ripened unevenly. And the Pere Louis, while perfect in its
native habitat, couldn't be reliably grown from seed. All three were
discarded.

The rhythm of travel was becoming easier, and unlike on their
first voyage, Fairchild and Lathrop had a mutual understanding that
often required little discussion. The old kinks sometimes emerged,
but were less pronounced. Fairchild was happy, wishing he could
drag his feet and stay longer. Lathrop was less irritable than usual,
preferring only that the two could move a little faster.

As Fairchild and Lathrop crossed the small inlets between Caribbean
islands, back in the States the idea of plant introduction was taking

hold. One reason that Secretary Wilson had been so bitter to see Fairchild leave the Department was that he himself was energized by the idea of foreign plants. The secretary felt he was leading something historic, at least until Fairchild departed the office and left the effort in flux. Wilson's agricultural report for 1897, which came out in 1898, crowed about the exciting new effort. "A scientist has been appointed in the department to have charge of seed and plant importation," he wrote. "Our country has profited by introducing new seeds and plants, but much of this work has been done in the dark." The message was clear and boastful. Wilson continued. "The Old World contains many things that would be valuable to the New World."

This was news that needed to be proclaimed publicly. America was a country built on the idea that hard work and ingenuity would yield prosperity. Yet America's farmers were finding just the opposite, and they blamed the government. Newspapers crowed about the newest railroad, the newest oil discovery, and the newest boom on Wall Street. But farming seemed stagnant. "There is something radically wrong in our industrial system," the editorial board of the journal *The Progressive Farmer* wrote in 1887.

> There is a screw loose. The wheels have dropped out of balance. The railroads have never been so prosperous, and yet agriculture languishes. The banks have never done a better or more profitable business, and yet agriculture languishes. Manufacturing enterprises never made more money or were in a more flourishing condition, and yet agriculture languishes. Towns and cities flourish and "boom" and grow and "boom," and yet agriculture languishes. Salaries and fees were never so temptingly high and desirable, and yet agriculture languishes.

The frustration that poured into Washington from farmers tended to make clear that they weren't asking for money. Not that they were against a handout, but none were naïve enough to think that free money was a lasting solution.

What they wanted, instead, was acknowledgment that America's doctrine of expansion and reconstruction completely undercut farming. There was too much land, and on it, everyone growing the same crops. The nation was buried beneath great piles of corn, wheat, and cotton. In 1870, corn sold for 43 cents per bushel. By 1895, it had dropped to 30 cents, and less when sold in larger quantity. A bushel of wheat worth $1.06 in 1870 had lost almost 40 percent of its value by the time McKinley became president. Things got so bad that when corn became cheaper than coal, Kansas farmers began to burn their crop instead of sell it. In the Dakotas, the cost of harvesting and transporting wheat was more than it could sell for, so it was left in the field to eventually keel over.

A few decades earlier, the problem had been easy to solve. If things got bad, farmers could simply travel farther west, where land, opportunity, and start-over stories were still abundant. But by 1898, with land mostly occupied and risk-taking more expensive, farmers were stuck. And being stuck in a business that required new seeds, new labor, and expensive equipment meant constantly digging oneself into a deeper hole of debt.

America wasn't the first country to confront these problems. People in China had farmed for thousands of years before the United States first broke free of colonialism. Egypt's farmers had managed land since the dawn of civilization. The difference was that America's goal wasn't just to farm; it was to construct an industrial agriculture system bigger and more profitable than any group of people had ever built.

Few farmers could have realized that they were part of this grand experiment in human history. They were too busy being angry at their broken country. The promise that hard work would yield great reward was undercut by the reality that hard work was actually making people poorer.

As William McKinley took the presidency, a Wichita farmer named Mary Elizabeth Lease, a woman of thirty-seven years, four children, and a growing pile of unused corn, was building a reputation for her irreverence toward Washington. "What farmers need to do is raise less corn and more HELL," she often said. She flayed politicians and their profligacy in the face of suffering on the plains—at the cost of being ridiculed, dismissed, and reviled by those she assailed. But she didn't care. "The parties lie to us and the political speakers mislead us," she told audiences across the Midwest. "We were told . . . to go to work and raise a big crop, that was all we needed. We went to work and plowed and planted; the rains fell, the sun shone, nature smiled, and we raised the big crop that they told us to; and what came of it? Eight-cent corn, ten-cent oats, two-cent beef and no price at all for butter and eggs—that's what came of it."

On the morning his ship landed in La Guaira, the largest port in Venezuela, Fairchild touched the continent of South America for the first time. Lathrop, for all of his travels, had only sparsely visited the Latin countries that altogether constituted more than 10 percent of Earth's land. South America had been geographically inconvenient, isolated by oceans and far from everything, filled with forested swamps, mountains, and native peoples so unknown that Teddy Roosevelt himself, in the days after his presidency a decade later, hiked through the treacherous jungles of the Amazon on a journey so harrowing, American newspaper writers openly expected him to die. He didn't, but his later biographers were stunned to learn that the wicked conditions nearly drove him to suicide.

Venezuela had several culinary highlights, chiefly apio, a root vegetable that seemed like a mix between a carrot and celery. Another tuber, which appeared similar to a potato and had the taste of artichoke, flavored every type of Venezuelan soup.

But in the pages of his journals during his first trip to Venezuela, food and botany would not be the foremost things Fairchild would remember.

One morning after eating breakfast alone, he learned that Lathrop, still in bed, wanted to stay behind. Lathrop had woken feeling off, as though his muscles had slept themselves twisted. When Fairchild returned later that day, Lathrop was nearly dead. His head ached so severely that he fell in and out of consciousness. As he lay in bed moaning, the heat from his skin warmed the room. Somewhere in Barbados or in the mountains of northern Venezuela, a female mosquito had bitten him and transferred the virus that caused Caracas fever. The rest of the world knew it as yellow fever—yellow, because of the jaundice that corrupted red blood cells and lit the skin gold.

Fairchild had been at Lathrop's side for more than two months. The bite just as easily might have been his. "I was badly frightened, for I was totally inexperienced in medical matters," Fairchild recalled. Unusual for a man of the nineteenth century, he had hardly confronted death. Once, when he was nine, a neighbor boy got his foot stuck in a wagon wheel. Fairchild overheard the news so quickly—fracture, gangrene, funeral—that the occurrence felt removed. Only one other time had he seen a mammal die, and it was a horse.

Lathrop's panting attracted the attention of two other Anglophones staying at the same inn. Fairchild stood and watched as the men repositioned Lathrop. They forced fluids and soup and elevated the patient's head and feet. Fairchild sat vigil for two days.

That Lathrop did not die quickly was the clearest sign that he would live. And sensing that, Fairchild wondered whether he might still have time for crop collections. Even if Lathrop died, Fairchild thought, the older man would bristle at an expedition squandered.

The two Englishmen provided such good care that in less than a week, Lathrop, once near death, could stand on his feet. A few days later, his temper returned, bringing immense relief to Fairchild.

Having spent a week longer than planned in Venezuela, the country that nearly took his life, Lathrop was ready to leave immediately.

Fairchild helped him hobble from a flimsy wheelchair to a horse cart to a waiting ship. As they traveled west toward the Panama isthmus, Lathrop's only request was fresh milk. When the boat stopped for provisions at Maracaibo, the final port in Venezuela before moving on to Colombia, Fairchild set off to find some. Cows covered hillsides like patches of carpet, yet no one sold milk. Fairchild found a man willing to deal, provided Fairchild milk the beast himself. The price was exorbitant—five dollars per bottle, or nearly a hundred today—but the milk was warm and fresh.

The north coast of South America was neither man's favorite, and as a result of such episodes, they never returned there together.

As their steamer hugged the coast, the small shanty huts on shore looked like festering pools for yellow fever and malaria. Lathrop's continued convalescence and Fairchild's fear of catching something similar left them both happy to remain on board until a train would take them across Panama to the Pacific.

Happy, except when considering their accompanying cargo. As days passed, Fairchild and Lathrop sat on deck with fifty moaning bulls. The ocean breeze, long in its gusts, proved no match for the growing piles of manure, which covered the ship's deck and grew taller each day.

CHAPTER EIGHT

Alligator Pears

The Andes, sharp and protruding, were striking at first sight. But even their peaks, which poked through the clouds, couldn't mask that the mountains presented a large problem. Fairchild spent his days in Lima at markets, polishing seeds of fruits grown nearby and judging which could be suitable for American fields. None were qualified. Crops that thrived five thousand feet up in the Andes would never grow in America's low-lying plains. Agriculturally, the Andes stood alone: an icy ridge adjacent to a warm ocean; strewn with active volcanoes and geologic faults that could trigger landslides and floods. Other than building mountaintop civilizations like Machu Picchu, the Incas' most notable accomplishment may have been living with the planet's most fickle climate, where temperatures could oscillate fifty degrees in hours.

For all of its glamour, food exploration was, as Fairchild was learning, a process not prone to wild success. Finding workable crops demanded educated guesses about growing conditions, but even in favorable environments, the guesses still amounted to gambles. "A pinch of seed may come half around the world for a cost of only five cents," Fairchild wrote about the tedious process, "but growing the seed will probably require a flat in a hot-house, followed in sequence by a bench of two-inch pots, a greenhouse of six-inch potted plants, half an acre of rich soil in a nursery, and an orchard."

Provided all of that aligned, the biggest unknown remained

people's tastes. Food, like fashion, tended to appear in trends. An item debuted either with a burst of popularity—like the hamburger in the 1870s, making steak portable and quick—or with a great flameout, like the nineteenth-century delicacy of broiled eels. Even if food producers could preordain innovation, truly transformative popularity came from individual eaters. Early adopters would need to feel ownership, as though they were leading others into a more enlightened future.

This inconvenient reality would be clear to Fairchild in the Andes with a crop called quinoa. It was, by any botanical measure, a crop of dramatic versatility. It began with the Incas on the shores of Lake Titicaca, and the Incas built their entire diet around it until the Spanish brought cereals like barley, wheat, and oats that all seemed better. Now, in 1898 Peru, quinoa struck many outsiders as more novel than practical. "A Scotchman told me that he considered a porridge of quinoa better than the finest oatmeal," Fairchild wrote, before listing all of the reasons it would never work. Samples of quinoa had once circulated at the Department of Agriculture, but it had been quickly dismissed. It was crunchy and fine, and had a confusing glow. No one knew what part of the plant one should actually eat: its leaves—as with its botanical cousin spinach—or its grain, which were its seeds (thus making quinoa a fruit).

Microscopes and refractometers weren't yet advanced enough to measure a food's complete nutritional content, which would have revealed quinoa not as a grain but as a protein, with the rare quality of having all nine amino acids the human body can't produce on its own. That, and not a trace of gluten. Its global popularity today, especially among vegetarians, is based on that finding, which seemed to surprise Peruvian and Bolivian farmers more than anyone. In the years after 2005, when quinoa was granted the highest honor in agriculture—the title of superfood—the global price tripled.

But Fairchild had been too early. Other than pointing out that the Andeans had put quinoa in cakes and beer, and that it might be tested in the South and the mountains of Colorado, all he could suggest to his Washington colleagues was that quinoa could be useful "as a medicine . . . to remedy catarrh," a great buildup of sinus mucus the world would come to know as the common cold. And so quinoa remained local and indigenous for another ten decades.

During Fairchild's visit, Peru's global claim had been over potatoes, which sprouted between the Pacific and the ridge of the Andes with more genetic diversity than human beings. Seven millennia of potato evolution had yielded variety unimaginable in most serious parts of the world, where farming was a business, subject to rules and regimens. If two villages were isolated from each other, the potatoes each village produced turned out as different as snowflakes. Any visitor to the region would have found small potatoes and big ones, varieties with smooth skin and ones with deep eyes. Farmers had bred types that grew on mountains, on hillsides, and close to the sea. Some grew best under harsh sun. Others demanded shade.

To an agricultural explorer like Fairchild, potatoes were old news. The tubers had supposedly already made their way to Europe in 1586 in the satchel of the English circumnavigator Francis Drake. They became such an easy and reliable crop that by the eighteenth century, nearly a quarter of all people in Ireland, the Netherlands, and Belgium based their diet almost entirely on potatoes. British colonists brought potatoes back west to their new colony in North America, first to the Jamestown, Virginia, settlement, and from there, the tubers spread across the continent. By 1899, almost an entire century had passed since Thomas Jefferson had served at the White House fried potato sticks sprinkled with salt— a lasting delicacy curiously named after the French, even though the Belgians are believed to have made them first.

As a result, Fairchild's hunch may have been that potatoes, bland in flavor and agriculturally boring, wouldn't be surprising or useful to anyone back home. Red corn and yellow squash filled the seed sacks that Fairchild prepared for Washington. Both were uncommon varieties with few redeeming traits—but the colors were novelties, good for, if nothing else, attracting bemused onlookers in pavilions of agricultural fairs. They also had the benefit of being easy to trace. If Fairchild ever passed a field of red corn, as he did in the 1920s in the American South and West, he could know the seeds grew in the United States because of him. For now, the colors would delight his desk-based colleagues back in Washington, and that alone was reason enough to send them north.

Fairchild's curiosity was overshadowed by Lathrop's unbearable discomfort. His symptoms of yellow fever had faded, but in their place rose a deep distaste for Peru. The place held bad omens, and bad memories.

All this time that Lathrop was depending on Fairchild to be the brains of the expedition, Lathrop in fact had botanical experience of his own. Just one episode, really, and of all the stories Lathrop repeated at length to anyone who would listen, this one he retold so frequently that Fairchild had memorized every detail. It wasn't only boastful; it was personal, indignant, almost rueful, as though the man endowed with stratospheric wealth had in some way been slighted by the universe.

When Lathrop first visited the Andes, sometime in the 1880s, he had been struck by how his mountain guides carried heavy loads up steep hillsides without ever growing tired. Their muscles and diet seemed common, as did their environment. The only difference he could tell was a plant called coca that the men chewed as they climbed.

Lathrop was intrigued by whatever miraculous component in the leaves made this possible. He sent several samples to the Academy of Sciences in San Francisco to be chemically tested. If the leaves hadn't been ignored, Lathrop might have been the man who introduced cocaine to the United States. Instead, Lathrop never heard back from the academy and no records showed the parcel had ever been received.

Lathrop being Lathrop, he claimed omniscience anyway, retelling the tale with a self-satisfaction that he had known something brilliant from the start. But in fact, coca was well on its way to popularization already, thanks to a German chemist named Albert Niemann who in his PhD dissertation described the way he isolated coca's potent properties—research that required ample sampling—and came to the conclusion that coca instigated "a flow of saliva and leaves a peculiar numbness, followed by a sense of cold when applied to the tongue." The suffix "caine" was added for its anesthetic properties, as with procaine or novocaine, leaving unmentioned coca's effects as a powerful stimulant.

This modesty for cocaine was short-lived. Within a decade, cocaine found allure as a sizable upgrade from other stimulating plant extracts, such as coffee or tea. The large pharmaceutical company Parke-Davis sold cocaine in smokable, edible, and liquid forms, the last of which came with a needle for easy injection into a user's veins.

Around the same time, a morphine-addicted pharmacist in Georgia developed a formula for a drink that was, in its earliest versions, 2.5 percent cocaine. The product had only one obvious name, in homage to the coca plant: Coca-Cola. The world benefited from this, and many people, their brains full of distracting dopamine, welcomed the amusement. But not Lathrop. All he saw was a missed chance for glory as the patron saint of hyper human efficiency.

After the wild topography of the Andes, Chile offered a return to predictable climates and fertile soil. The land also brought a coincidence of geography, particularly to someone doing the work of American plant exploration. Chile was almost exactly as far south as the United States was north, its capital, Santiago, at the precise inverted latitude of Los Angeles, California; Lubbock, Texas; Atlanta, Georgia; and Charleston, South Carolina. No two regions on earth can be climatically identical, but if there was anything Chile could contribute, it was that its time-tested crops were ready to grow in many regions of the United States. The only delay would be that they'd have to go through Washington first.

So it would be curious for Fairchild to learn later that of all the crops that he sent from Santiago, few would ever grow in the United States. There was a mountain bamboo known as *chusquea*, toned with a blush that colored the stalks red. He carefully packed saplings of a low-growing tree with no common name—just its Latin name, *Persea lingue*—that seemed a promising candidate as a street tree along avenues in New York or Washington. His favorite was an ornamental tree, called mayten, with lazy tentacles that succumbed so much to gravity that it appeared to be weeping. It never made it to Washington.

The problem may have been more bureaucratic than botanical. With all the ornamental trees he sent, plus the new varieties of squash and watermelon, and even some collections of strange Chilean beans, there simply wasn't capacity for such abundance. Food exploration was new, and Fairchild knew that the experimental stations to which much of this material was entrusted were not in shape to receive it.

But there was one sample that made it. History tends to favor successes, not the failures. The crop he was about to find would be mentioned in his obituary as a high achievement, perhaps the greatest of his life.

As he bit into the oily green flesh, Fairchild couldn't have known he was holding in his hands the future crop of the American Southwest. But he had a hunch. It was a black-skinned fruit, a variety of alligator pear, or as the Aztecs called it, "avocado," a derivative of their word for testicle. It grew in pairs, and had an oblong, bulbous shape. The fruit had the consistency of butter and was a little stringy. But unlike the other avocados he had tasted farther north, in Jamaica and Venezuela, this one had remarkable consistency. Every fruit on the tree was the same size and ripened at the same pace, rare qualities for anything that grew in the consistent warmth of the subtropics.

In Santiago, where a boat had deposited Fairchild and Lathrop, the avocado had an even greater quality. Fairchild listened intently as someone explained that the fruit could withstand a mild frost as low as twenty-three degrees Fahrenheit. Such a climatic range suggested a perfect crop for America. From central Mexico, the worldwide home of the first avocados, centuries of settlers had carried the fruit south to Chile. David Fairchild mused about taking it the other way, back north. "A valuable find for California," he wrote. "This is a black-fruited, hardy variety."

Lathrop tagged along on the daytime expedition when Fairchild tasted that avocado. He agreed that a fruit so hardy, so versatile, would perfectly answer farmers' pleas for novel but undemanding crops, ones that almost grew themselves, provided the right conditions. Fairchild didn't know the chemical properties of the avocado's fatty flesh, or that a hundred years in the future it would, like quinoa, find esteem, owing to its combination of fat and vitamins. But he could tell that such a curious fruit, unlike any other, must have an equally curious evolutionary history. No earthly mammal could digest a seed as big as the avocado's, and certainly not anything that roamed wild through South America.

History could wait, as it often does. While a cart with a horse idled nearby, Fairchild bought every avocado he could, emptying his pockets of Chilean pesos. He hoped within the bins was piled sufficient diversity to sustain the crop in faraway soil. Most of the avocados were solid as a stone, but by the time they were packed into small boxes, some started to soften, a signal that they ripened off the tree, rather than on. Only when nearly a thousand avocados were packed was Fairchild confident that at least a few would survive the lengthy ocean voyage. On each box, he wrote in large block letters, "Washington DC, Department of Agriculture, Division of Seed and Plant Introduction," and he watched as the crates were carried away.

On June 10, 1899, the day Orator F. Cook opened one of the boxes back in Washington, the first indication of Fairchild's eager endorsement of this particular shipment was its size. Cook was the man unlucky enough to replace Fairchild as the office-based recipient of hunted plants. More than ten boxes sat in Cook's office. He pried one open, picked up an avocado and bit into the rind, then peeled back its skin to inspect its flesh. The fruit was clearly rotten, emitting a putrid smell of brown mold. But the important part, the seed and its genetic material, was alive.

Cook had seen an avocado before, but not like this—so smooth, so green. The fruit took an express route to the greenhouse, where workers propagated the seeds, first in soil, and then suspended slightly in water. Fairchild had included written instructions that only mature trees would fruit, after several years, not months. He advised that as soon as the seedlings grew reasonable roots, they should be shipped to experiment stations in California to be shared with farmers interested in experimental crops.

Cook complied, and then mostly forgot about the avocado.

In California, that single shipment helped build an industry. Other avocados turned up as well, from travelers or tourists who packed the oversized seeds as souvenirs. There were one-off stories that avocados had been spotted in America before, in Hollywood in 1886 or near Miami in 1894. But none were as sturdy as Fairchild's Chilean variety, prized for its versatility, color, and flavor—a résumé of strong pedigree. Fairchild's avocado would turn out to be a mix of a Guatemalan avocado and a Mexican avocado and to have been only a short-term tenant in Chilean soil before Fairchild picked it up. But as with most popular fruits, the true geographic origin faded into irrelevance.

Farmers and early geneticists dissected this sample and ones that came after it to create newer cultivars attuned to more specialized climates or tastes. This work yielded a twentieth-century variety called *Fuerte*, Spanish for "strong," growable in the coldest conditions ever tested on an avocado. It fell from favor after proving unable to ship even modest distances without bruising.

A different descendant of Fairchild's shipment of avocados would endure as the lasting variety. A quarter century after Fairchild tasted his first Chilean avocado, a mail carrier in Fallbrook, California, foresaw dollar signs in the fruit and managed to collect seeds from every available avocado—from fields, from neighbors, even from the trash bins of restaurant kitchens. He wasn't a botanist. He had dropped out of high school and had little academic training. He was simply an early enthusiast.

The man kept a garden behind his house, and in 1926, when one of the seeds sprouted completely vertical, unlike other varieties, his kids were the first to notice. Within a few months, when the small tree formed walnut-sized nuggets of fruit—at a rate of maturation far faster than any other variety—the man knew he had something different. He knelt next to the small tree, fourteen inches tall, and had his wife take a portrait, a pose later memorialized in a painting.

A decade later, on the afternoon of August 27, 1935, a full thirty-six years after Fairchild collected the Chilean ancestor avocado and ten thousand years after humans first domesticated the fruit, the man applied for a patent. He hired an artist to sketch his avocado from every angle, including the one most true to its original namesake, hanging from a tree like a drooping testicle. When it came time to name the variety that would become the world's most popular avocado, accounting for more than 80 percent of the global market, he didn't name it after his wife, Elizabeth, whom he was

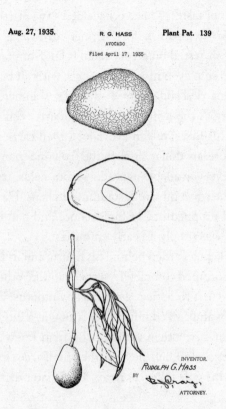

Aug. 27, 1935.   R. G. HASS   Plant Pat. 139
AVOCADO
Filed April 17, 1935

INVENTOR.
RUDOLPH G. HASS
BY
ATTORNEY.

Fairchild's avocado shipment from Chile helped launch an industry. In the following decades, avocado enthusiasts in Southern California used the fruits of Fairchild's shipment, along with others, to incrementally develop new avocado varieties. Until one day in 1935, when a postal deliveryman named Rudolph Hass, who had poured his life savings into growing avocados, filed a patent for what would become the world's most popular variety.

said to have met at a church picnic, or after his neighborhood of La Habra Heights in East Los Angeles, where the first seedling once grew. Lacking imagination more than vanity, he thought only to name it after himself, Rudolph Hass.

To journey from Chile to Argentina meant crossing more than 150 miles of jungle and mountains while riding, much to Lathrop's disgust, atop the back of a mule. He had no desire to linger in the Andes. He wasn't above nights in the wild—although he enjoyed camping about as much as he enjoyed drinking cheap brandy. What worried him were the rumors. He heard the stories about gangs of thieves who rifled through travelers' bags while they slept. The guides who arranged the passage assured him protection, but he was wary of them, too. His posture and attire and the coif of his mustache betrayed his affluence.

But having little choice, Lathrop packed with a deliberate notion of defense. He assembled his valuable letters and credentials in a small package, which he placed at the center of his trunk, tucked among his soiled laundry and hardcover English novels. To find it, someone would have to rummage through everything, and if that happened, he and Fairchild would either be tied up somewhere, or dead.

Fairchild, in his usual contrast to Lathrop's sour mood, was excited to cross the world's longest mountain range, whose peaks climbed four miles into the sky. As the party's mules trudged up narrow, rocky inclines, Fairchild held tight and took in the view of colossal condors that swung overhead. Their bodies, rotund and awkward, nearly four feet from head to tail, glided in careless arcs, as they took advantage of wind patterns to stay aloft while peering down for prey. Fairchild's vertiginous fascination with the birds came partly from the coca leaves he had chewed—a remedy to distract the brain from reduced oxygen high above the sea.

His mule slipped on a patch of ice at the edge of the trail. Its front legs buckled, shifting the animal and its rider forward. Fairchild tensed as he slid.

Lathrop yelled before he could find the words, but there was nothing anyone could do, least of all Lathrop, who had tied himself to his animal so he could avoid paying attention. Everyone watched Fairchild approach the thousand-foot abyss. The animal kicked to regain its step. Then it kicked again. Fairchild grabbed at the mud, at the ice, but there was nothing to grip as he slid further. It was, he would later describe, "a horrid moment of suspense."

Fairchild lived, but no thanks to his efforts. The mule kicked a third time, a desperate last attempt, with such force that it would either fall to the side or stand up. In one motion, it found its footing and picked its body up. Fairchild rose with it.

The moment had passed too quickly for Fairchild to comprehend such a swift and unmerciful end. No one talked for a full minute, silenced by the seriousness of the episode. The animals continued on, climbing and descending ridgelines and narrow trails, breathing heavily. Fairchild pulled his mule in from the unguarded edge.

Eventually, Lathrop broke the silence with a stream of stories about his travels, his encounter with coca leaves, and the souvenirs he sent back home for the amusement of the Bohemian Club. The journey from Santiago to Buenos Aires had started on April 16, 1899, and would take twelve days. If it meant arriving alive, Fairchild was comfortable letting his companion talk until the end of the century.

After crossing the Chilean Andes, the party entered Argentina and continued all the way to the Atlantic coast. Near Buenos Aires, Fairchild collected cuttings from a fast-growing and soft-wooded evergreen tree named *bella sombra* for its beautiful shadow. The cuttings from the tree would eventually make their way to California, where *bella* would be cultivated as a shade tree. A more culinary discovery was a strange mountain papaya no larger than a small plum and amenable to temperatures below freezing. Years later, Fairchild would try to merge this papaya with a more tender species. Hybrids, he would conclude, were easier to imagine than to actually make.

From Buenos Aires he and Lathrop boarded a boat—Lathrop's choice—rather than prolong the discomforts of their overland journey, and steamed north, up the coast toward Brazil. It was dawn when they arrived at the mouth of Guanabara Bay. Low clouds hung over Sugarloaf Mountain, standing majestically above the city of Rio de Janeiro. For visitors to stay in Rio was verboten, not by law but by taboo: to spend a night was to risk yellow fever, which permeated the low-lying city like a heavy mist. As the most dangerous times for parasite activity were dawn and dusk, Fairchild and Lathrop opted to stay at the United States' diplomatic residence in Petrópolis, a mountain municipality forty-two miles to the north.

To investigate plants in Rio's botanical garden Fairchild had to ride a small cog railroad down the mountain, followed by a short boat ride to central Rio, a trip of nearly four hours. In an era when traveling across oceans took weeks, few people could be bothered by mere hours. But the commute restricted Fairchild's plant surveys to the hot midday after ten A.M. At four P.M., the train would climb the mountain again and deliver its foreign passengers to their safe perch above the clouds.

Fairchild managed to get his hands around just one species that interested him, a distinctive dwarf mango called *Itamaraca*. He described it in his notebook as "flattened like a tomato and with a very delightful aroma and a golden color." Dozens of mangoes had already been sent to Washington and hundreds more would follow. The competition was for the most reliable variety. The Itamaraca wasn't it. Notable for its small size and abundance on the branch, it would prove better as a backyard novelty than something that could support an entire industry.

But Brazil wasn't a bust. One of Lathrop's cousins, who was living in the country, took Fairchild and Lathrop to São Paulo, where he promised to introduce them to the greatest coffee growers. Even in 1899, Fairchild knew that coffee was a futile fantasy for the United States. America had become the biggest customer of Brazil's coffee, which would have made acquiring the plant strategic. But Fairchild knew a rival industry would never sprout back home. No part of the United States could offer the warmth and humidity the coffee tree demands, which originated in the East African tropics of Ethiopia before migrating on colonial ships to balmy Brazil.

Instead, Fairchild's final days in Brazil centered more on matters of diplomacy than diet. Around a large table in São Paulo, he listened as half a dozen men representing different governments discussed the politics of America's rise. The Spanish-American War, a victory for the United States, had ended the year before, bringing a pause to the fight over global hegemony.

But those around the table had the suspicion that America's ascent was not yet complete. Things were changing, in some ways disconcertingly, revealing a decisive disruption of the world order. There, in the waning months of the final year of the nineteenth century, as red dust from coffee fields blew like powder through the air, the group of educated men of politics, diplomacy, and warfare talked long into the night, agreeing on little except that the next century would belong to the United States.

CHAPTER NINE

Grapes of a
Venetian Monk

Barbour Lathrop had yet to recover fully from his bout with yellow fever. Aboard a ship that departed Brazil, his moans and complaints attracted the attention of a fellow passenger, and by the time the vessel pulled into harbor in London in June 1899, the man had persuaded Lathrop to head directly to Karlovy Vary, Czechoslovakia, for a treatment known as the alkaline-sulfur water cure. Taken in a warm bath, the treatment was to drink alkaline water while fully stretched out to reduce stomach acidity. Lathrop became a "crusty person" when forced to consume anything he deemed distasteful, Fairchild recalled, but if it brought an end to the vomiting, Lathrop would oblige. Besides, the cure beat other rumored remedies, including one that called for repeated enemas of tea infused with cayenne pepper and petals of the flower lobelia.

Fairchild had written off London and didn't care to stay long. He couldn't imagine any crop that, in several hundred years of colonial and political association, Great Britain hadn't already shared with America. What's more, the country was agriculturally unenviable, handicapped by a cool climate that was good for beans, tubers, and little else.

But the short layover did yield one surprise. Late summer was peak season for Windsor broad beans, also known as fava beans, and at the market the day he and Lathrop left for Czechoslovakia, Fairchild deemed the oversized legumes, each as wide as an American quarter, suitable to send back. His package to Washington contained a handful of beans with explicit directions that they required a long, cool spring, like that in the Rockies or Adirondacks. A woman had offered him a puree of the bean, one of his early experiences with the delightful, salty mortar known as hummus.

After Lathrop sipped alkaline water in Czechoslovakia, he and Fairchild journeyed to Venice. By now he had learned that plants turned up in bizarre places, and there was no place more peculiar than Venice, a city built upon canals, whose tides took perfect turns flooding the city twice each day, leaving life so stunted and strange that the city's zoo had a single horse to allow children to know what an animal looked like.

Venice's agricultural bounty was in its restaurants, where earlier food explorers had dropped delicacies from their worldly travels. Near the Bridge of Sighs, Fairchild watched gondolas haul monstrous squashes, onions, cauliflowers, and tomatoes to Venice's famed chefs. Taking in the scene, he raised his camera at the same moment several people lifted their eyes for the rare sight of a man taking a picture.

Dining by himself one night amid boisterous shouts in Italian, Fairchild tried for the first time a curious, stalky vegetable that resembled a small tree. Its crown was full and bumpy, and its young seeds, he noticed, were buried deep in the bushy branches, making them nearly impossible to extract and unlikely to survive the lengthy voyage back to America. But he paid the café's chef for a handful of them, along with a pile of sweet peppers and a flat squash he didn't like but tucked into his pockets anyway.

The vegetable's name, he learned, was *broccoli*, pronounced with emphasis on its last syllable. Broccoli turned out to be a cool-weather cousin of the cauliflower and cabbage. All three of them had their origins in northern Europe, benefiting from the frosty climate that Fairchild had dismissed. Ultimately, Fairchild wouldn't be the one

1898. On the Grand Canal in Venice, fresh fruits and vegetables were the products of centuries' worth of faraway foods brought back by travelers and explorers returning to Italy. Items such as tomatoes, squashes, and onions were slowly incorporated into Italian cooking.

credited with officially bringing broccoli to America. That would be his friend Walter Swingle, who several months earlier in France had picked up a form of primitive pseudo-broccoli that consisted of more leaf than anything else, and shipped samples back with a note that it needed *"more extensive trial."*

Now that the childhood friends were both botanical explorers, Fairchild and Swingle exchanged postcards documenting their exotic travels. To bemuse each other, they attempted to write in the language of the country they were visiting. As both men moved about the globe, the postmarks were covered with a series of forwarding addresses. Until eventually, the messages that had started as mysterious became indecipherable completely.

In Venice, Fairchild wandered for days on his own, which offered, in addition to time to think and explore, the extra benefit of a break from the war brewing between Lathrop and Secretary Wilson.

Lathrop's donations, measured in time, money, and plants, had so far been met with ungrateful silence by Wilson, who considered Lathrop eccentric. He blamed the millionaire for Fairchild's decision to leave the Department to ramble around the world in a way that appeared to him haphazard and unfocused.

In fact, Wilson's disappointment and anger at Fairchild were signs of how much he liked the young man. Wilson and Fairchild were both sons of the Midwest who came to Washington for important government work. Lathrop, by comparison, had only money, which he had not earned. Wilson feared Lathrop's swollen ego might rub off on Fairchild, an earnest young man corrupted by the haughtiness of luxury.

Meanwhile, Lathrop acted as though Wilson's lack of respect caused him as much discomfort as his recent bout of fever. He grew upset each time he recalled that the secretary had refused to see him when he visited Washington to liberate Fairchild from the bureaucratic doldrums. In the months that followed, Lathrop had

underwritten an entire government research program that required
expensive travel for two. A thank-you note would have been nice, or
reimbursement for the purchase price of the plants, altogether
$338.50 after twelve months in transit. Yet Lathrop had received no
recognition, zero. He wrote a pointed letter to Washington, attention anyone at the USDA who might care. "It has puzzled me that no
one in the department sent me a line of acknowledgement of services rendered, money expended and plants shipped, to say nothing
of any appreciation shown for the subsequent work expected of me."

The letter, too, was met with silence.

His resentment boiled over in Venice. After an informal accounting of his expenditures on nearly every continent, Lathrop angrily
came to the conclusion that until Washington acknowledged his
contribution, he would refuse to fund any more plant shipments.
The decision threatened to kill the project.

Discreetly, Fairchild wrote to Orator Cook at the control center of
the Office of Seed and Plant Introduction, urging that someone, *anyone*, recognize Lathrop in some small way. Cook never responded,
but several months later the Department published its annual yearbook, which included a list of 450 new plants sent by Fairchild from
the West Indies, South America, Europe, Asia, and the East Indies.
Included in the official document was an unsubtle disclosure:

> Through the generosity of Hon. Barbour Lathrop, of Chi-
> cago, the Department of Agriculture has been made the re-
> cipient of a large collection of seeds and plants. . . . Some of
> the many importations of seeds and plants made through the
> efforts of Mr. Lathrop have already proved to be of decided
> value to the farmers of the United States. The warm thanks
> of the Department are due to this public-spirited citizen.

The shipments never actually stopped during Lathrop's tantrum.
But they had appeared at the Department unsigned—an indication

that Fairchild had sent them behind the older man's back, on his own dime. After Lathrop's accolades had been published, however, the shipments returned to their regular size and frequency. Except now, in the usual note Fairchild wrote with each shipment detailing each crop and who'd picked it, he credited not just himself, but Lathrop, too.

For five days Fairchild wandered Venice's dark backstreets, as visitors had for a hundred years and would for a hundred to come. Riding in a gondola that wound through the Grand Canal, he stared at the black smoke rising from chimneys and at the fresh flowers on the windowsills. As the tide rose, seawater from the canal lapped up onto Piazza San Marco, driving away the lazy pigeons. The rising water brought in slow-moving swirls of straw, eggshells, and cabbage stalks.

A white-bearded monk at a Venetian monastery smiled with full teeth when Fairchild said he had come searching for plants. The monk escorted him to his small garden barely bigger than a man lying down. Fairchild took his portrait in front of the only peach tree in Venice.

As they spoke, the monk told him of a seedless grape variety not far away in Padua. Grapes weren't unusual in America, but seedless fruit was a growing fad. To be without seeds is to be sterile, and sterile plants can reproduce only by cloning. The seedless grape variety the monk spoke about would be a genetic replica of grapes grown by ancient Romans.

Grapes were sweet and delicious, but being seedless held potential beyond a single fruit. Could the same method that produced the grape produce a seedless peach? A seedless lemon? A California horticulturist named Luther Burbank was pursuing answers to these exact questions. Fairchild would later meet Burbank, and not particularly like his mad-scientist ramblings. But Burbank enjoyed the fantastic potential of tweaking genes. He imagined that a plum with no pit would be a delightful ball of juicy flesh.

Fairchild hardly slept the night before he left Venice to track down the seedless grape. Due to Lathrop's status as a frequent traveler, Fairchild was able to secure a room in the Hotel Bauer-Grünwald, a posh Venice guesthouse rumored to have once housed Marco Polo. Fairchild bedded in what he was told was the room the explorer once occupied, its ceiling so low he had to stoop when he stepped inside.

Around two in the morning, he awoke to beautiful music that floated into the room like moonlight. Peering out the window, he watched the blackened outline of a man in a gondola, a flute extending from his face. "To my delight, the gondola turned into the side canal almost directly under my window," Fairchild recalled. "The musician was dressed in black from head to foot and was alone except for the gondoliers."

As he stared out the window, Fairchild considered his good fortune. On assignment for his government, for the second time in Italy, a land of glamour, charm, and grace. "Those moments," he wrote of the minutes he spent looking out the window, "still live in memory as an exquisitely perfect experience." He watched the flute player pass beneath his window and float away, the music growing softer with distance, until all he could hear was the melody in his head.

The first train left Venice at seven in the morning, and by ten, Fairchild was knocking on the large metal door of a monastery in Padua. A monk answered, and after taking one look at Fairchild, summoned the head father who explained in sharp staccato how to walk to a small nursery nearby. The man promised that a single vine flush with grapes would catch Fairchild's eye.

He spotted it from several feet away, fluffed abundantly with rose-colored grapes growing on a wooden garden arbor. The bunches, broad shouldered and heavy with fruit, extended sixteen inches to the ground. Fairchild placed a grape in his mouth to confirm the fruit's sterility, then another, and then a handful. Adding to the pleasantly sweet taste, the lack of pits lent itself to the convenience of volume.

Seedless fruits had no seed for Fairchild to collect. Instead, he sliced the vine's stem diagonally and wiggled off several saplings, enough for a sample. He carried them in his pocket back to Venice, along, as was his custom, with a handful of fruit.

Lathrop's face stayed motionless when Fairchild showed him the sticks. But his eyebrows rose at the sight of half a dozen purple pearls of sweetness. The older man smiled as he ate one.

Before Fairchild could send them off to Washington, the cuttings needed two more days to sit in a rooting concoction that he received at the monastery. Preparing his shipment, Fairchild scrawled his impressions:

> This grape should be given the most serious attention, both by raisin growers and breeders of new varieties, as it has remarkable possibilities. That it has not become more generally known in Italy may be explained by the fact that no raisins to speak of are made in this part of the country and the Italian vine grower is bound by tradition and will plant no new sorts. The Sultanina vines thrive in rich, sandy soil, receive only stable manure, resist drought very well, and are pruned and trimmed in the ordinary ways. An abundance of sunlight is required.

The grape, of a variety known as sultanina, would ultimately grow best in the wet and temperate soil of California, America's region most climatically similar to the Mediterranean. Fairchild's sample from Italy was the *Sultanina rosea* seedless raisin grape, which was a stronger specimen than a green sultanina that had already made it to California as nursery stock. Regardless of who was first to lay eyes on the sultanina, the variety took little time to grow into the most popular grape in America, adored by winemakers, raisin producers, and people who ate grapes by the fistful.

Egypt was the birthplace of civilization, the first location where humans gathered under a central government and built some of the world's first cities. This led to dramatic advances, including written language, the wheel, and eventually, beer. People had never assembled like this before, and it was all because of farming. Farming in a group brought new efficiency and scale. When people worked together, they could dramatically increase their production of wheat, barley, and domesticated animals. Mesopotamia, the early civilization, thrived thanks to lush soil and overflowing water.

This was assuring news for a plant hunter. Crops in Egypt had to be old, and to be old meant they were hardy. There would be no anomalies, only strong agricultural specimens, tested by time and chosen for their strength.

Fairchild was as eager to see the place where farming was invented as a matador might find a pilgrimage to Spain. On October 31, 1899, Fairchild and Lathrop registered at Shepheard's Hotel, a grand six-story palace in Cairo that attracted deep-pocketed travelers from the United States, Europe, and Russia. The crème-colored building, boxy and modern with a luscious veranda that allowed diners and drinkers to peer down at the dusty street, was flanked with manicured gardens and palm fronds that pointed upward toward the symmetrical steeple, which was monogrammed with the hotel's initials, "SH" that were designed to look unsubtly like a dollar sign.

Considered the greatest outpost in the world, Shepheard's was known among wealthy tourists as the place to see and be seen by the world's most interesting people, and to watch Eastern life on display. From the wicker tables covered with white tablecloths on the veranda, guests witnessed Egyptians ride donkeys so small that the riders' feet dragged on the road, and water vendors who hawked sips from bloated goatskin canteens. Turkish soldiers passed by in gold-embroidered uniforms, and dervishes strolled under large, red headdresses.

For once, Lathrop consented to a lengthy stay. Egypt was among the world's most fashionable destinations, a rare land that mixed ancient history with modern gusto, the midpoint where East met West. Lathrop couldn't deny the region's importance, even if he was still fatigued by his recent illness. If the goal of their odyssey was botanical discovery, the lessons of the Fertile Crescent couldn't be rushed.

Unencumbered, Fairchild felt his curiosity piqued not just by Egypt's crops, but by the roots of agriculture itself. Their expertise in farming also led to Egyptians being first to experiment with irrigation, and their system, which took advantage of slight slopes in the land, worked swimmingly. The biggest concern in farming—*when will it rain?*—could be circumvented by digging basins that would fill when the Nile River overflowed. The basins, in turn, emptied into canals, which trickled the water on fields in a steady, consistent stream.

Over thousands of years, this method yielded a multitude of crops, which now found their way to Fairchild. Someone offered him sesame seeds, which few Americans had ever seen. "The seed is used as a medicine," he wrote. "Put in water (soaked eight to ten hours) it becomes mucilaginous, and when sweetened to taste and with a small quantity of lime juice, is said to be a refreshing drink." The same day, he made acquaintance with the chickpea, also known as the garbanzo, also known as the Egyptian pea. The red bean was roasted like a nut and tasted like popcorn. The Spanish used the garbanzo as a substitute for coffee, and a lucrative one: an Egyptian landowner reported to Fairchild that an area known as a *fedan*—roughly an acre—would yield a bumper profit of twenty American dollars every year. Fairchild built a stockpile of seeds, beans, and cuttings, along with notes, for an eventual shipment.

Of all of Egypt's ancient crops, there was one that seemed new, and it was cotton. Over the country's six-thousand-year history, Egypt had had little experience with the crop. It had originated sometime around 3000 BC in Pakistan, or perhaps Mexico—no one knew for sure. Upland cotton, the yellow-flowered relative of hibiscus, came to the United States in 1790, and by the 1820s it had become America's most valuable export, thanks entirely to slave labor in the South. That, and Eli Whitney's creation of a machine called a cotton engine, a "gin" for short, that separated cotton fiber from seeds.

Egypt only started planting cotton in its rich soil around 1800, but over the century cotton alone would allow Egypt to grow from an economic infant into a global force. Its dynastic leader, Muhammad Ali, had been given cotton seeds by a Frenchman who promised they would yield a cash crop easy to plant and cheap to harvest.

He was right. After Ali died in 1849, his successors tried to grow the cotton industry bigger with loans from Europe, which taught the country's leaders lessons in foreign economics and debt. The next lucky thing to happen to Egypt was America's Civil War, which stalled American cotton exports. Distracted Americans meant Egyptian farmers could meet the global shortfall and become a major producer. In the 1840s, America had been exporting cotton to Egypt. A generation later, the direction reversed.

With money pouring in, the new ruler of Egypt commissioned the construction of a railway throughout the country; it would be the most extensive in the world. He expanded the bounds of Alexandria, Egypt's port city on the Mediterranean. Even more bullish, he decided to turn Cairo into a culture capital by emulating another one: Paris. He widened the city and built a new neighborhood known as "Paris on the Nile." It had large verandas, cafés with sidewalk seating, and Parisian-style buildings. Visitors to Cairo would be pleasantly surprised to find English bookshops and fashionable boutiques.

The cotton boom built Cairo into not only an economic hub but an intellectual one, attracting top minds to the renewed capital. And this would lead to innovation, the kind all developed countries enjoy once they've figured out how to feed their people. In 1897, Egyptian farmers interbred a cotton from Georgia and a cotton from Peru to produce, as Fairchild noted, "a variety with a long, very silky and crinkly fiber of a light-brown color."

This new cotton, he learned, was known as Jannovitch cotton. It was easy to grow and its seeds were easy to reproduce, the perfect combination to satisfy recovering Southern growers short on money and labor. The long fibers were so much softer, and so easy to distinguish from the coarse cotton traditionally grown in the American South, that only a few years after its creation, Jannovitch cotton, which was neither native to Egypt nor there for long, became known as "Egyptian cotton," a name that grew to be global shorthand for exotic luxury.

"If you think it is such a good thing, why don't you send more of it?" Lathrop asked one day as Fairchild obsessed over the latest shipment he was preparing for Washington. It would be his biggest yet, and he deliberated how much of each crop to send. For a month, he built a mountain of seeds and cuttings, and then took three days to pack them with precision to ensure airflow, moisture, and minimal stress on the journey across the Atlantic. He knew what it was like to receive large shipments at the Department of Agriculture and how well-curated seed parcels could languish if too big or confusing to unpack, as had been the case a few years prior when he had received a bulging package of Russian wheat seeds that died before able hands could plant it all.

He packed and repacked, and repacked again. The final parcel contained forty-three types of crops, from cantaloupes to peppers to okra, his notes as colorful as the foods themselves. There were seeds of Egyptian pumpkins (*"superior, both in amount of flesh and in sweetness"*), cucumbers that *"ripened for the table twenty days earlier than the ordinary cucumber,"* and onions that he *"recommended for irrigated Western lands."* He included forms of beans, corn, and squash that he believed could outproduce native varieties in the United States.

He took particular delight in the strange names—names no one in his country had ever heard. There was a small seed called "flax" that produced oil (*"grows in regions which are dry"*). There was red strawberry spinach (*"gives a brilliant color to vegetable dishes"*) and something called the edible jute, whose leaves, when dried, could be turned into a thick gluey soup (*"It forms a favorite dish of the Egyptian peasants, probably because of its cheapness"*).

Finally, at the top, he placed seeds and samples of Egyptian cotton. Following Lathrop's advice, he sent two bushels of seed instead of one, seed that on the open market would have cost an exorbitant forty dollars if a generous grower hadn't enjoyed Fairchild's charm and offered it for free. Both Fairchild and Lathrop were surprised when they learned the shipment would cost one hundred dollars, the monthly salary of a well-paid American. Yet with this price came the guarantee the crate would arrive safely in Washington. Unlike shipments from non-English-speaking ports that would be transferred from ship to ship, some delayed by weather, others by indifference, Fairchild's shipment would sail directly from Cairo to New York, stopping only in Mediterranean ports, to amass a bigger transatlantic haul.

The investment turned out to be worth the price. Plant breeders in Washington had already begun experimenting with cotton, and their varieties were shipped west to California and Arizona, where growers had the optimal conditions—hot and damp—to build a new hub for high-quality cotton. Fairchild's cotton from Egypt was the best they'd ever seen.

In Arizona, a man named A. J. Chandler was at the time working with cotton, trying to demonstrate whether it would grow well in the desert soil. Fairchild's shipment from Egypt supplemented Chandler's efforts, which proved more successful than he could have imagined. A new, long-staple variety raised the quality of American cotton, and thus boosted demand in a growing market. One use for cotton particularly helped: lining the insides of automobile tires, which couldn't be made fast enough.

Jannovitch cotton was the first of Fairchild's earliest finds to illustrate that the idea of plant exploration for the purpose of starting rival industries in America was economically valuable—and geopolitically strategic. As cotton farmers in Arizona and California increased their output, Egypt's dominance waned. British buyers turned back to the United States, whose exporters were easier to deal with, and where large expanses of land allowed the price to stay low.

Cotton, as with any crop, continued to evolve. The early Egyptian varieties transformed into new and hardier strains that grew more easily and reliably. By the time fighting began in the Second World War, Arizona's test plot of long-grain cotton had yielded a hundred-million-dollar industry, enough money to fuel the state, and enough cotton for every American to have a pair of britches.

From Shepheard's Hotel, Fairchild loaded his and Lathrop's trunks onto a camel and rode next to Lathrop to a waiting ship in the Gulf of Suez. As he watched the green hills of Egypt recede behind him, he pulsed with the confidence of a man hitting his stride, of feeling well suited for the work of a globe-trotting botanist.

And he would be, for a time. In Egypt, however, Fairchild couldn't have known about the growing number of people back home who had begun to believe his work was unnecessary, even dangerous, and that the world, awash with new opportunity, was changing too fast.

CHAPTER TEN

Citrus Maxima

Fairchild stood in a Javanese market surrounded by oddities and trinkets as a woman strung his arms with bracelets and garters. He usually avoided these types of souvenir fairs, each an awkward chance to be ogled as a rich Westerner. Nor did he need kitschy junk to remember his travels.

But here he was, every inch of his extremities covered with yarns and gold-plated bracelets, his pockets bulging with mirrors, beads, and patches of sparkling fabric. A crowd had gathered around him, murmuring with confusion and mockery. When the woman asked him if he was finished shopping, Fairchild looked around and pointed to two small cat statues. He gave the woman a few more coins and then slipped through the crowd, the figurines in his hands.

It was impossible to know how many people he'd barter with, so he scooped up as many items as possible. The island tribes in the Indian Ocean had little exposure to anything from beyond their shores, which made strange shiny objects a sort of currency to goad tribespeople into giving him plants.

After leaving Egypt, the pair had steamed south and west aboard a luxury British steamer. So close to India, any ordinary traveler might have stopped in Bombay, a city in constant explosion. But Lathrop had no interest in the exceptional crowds, the filthiness, and the way culture burst at one's face. Fairchild might have protested if Lathrop hadn't promised he could visit India another day on his own (on Lathrop's dime). Lathrop also proposed that, instead of India, they steam quickly to Java and embark on a forty-day cruise of the Malay Islands, the same islands where Alfred Russel Wallace had come to discover the mechanism of evolution. This, he knew, Fairchild would not protest.

While Fairchild shopped for items to trade, Lathrop handled the arrangements, which included visits to more than a dozen islands, many completely unexplored. The final stop would be Papua New Guinea, the bulky isle that had become Germany's early experiment in colonialism. The Netherlands India Steam Navigation Company had begun charter service through the islands, which was previously impossible due to unpredictable danger. Rumors of the islanders' bloodlust for white skin were easier to assume to be true than actually finding out for oneself, so they continued to circulate for decades. Even Lathrop, one of the nineteenth century's few cultural relativists, couldn't tell if the Steam Navigation Company had deemed the group of islands newly safe, or simply profitable.

Neither man was scared—extreme wealth had a way of ensuring a measure of security. Yet still, American tourists weren't warmly welcomed anywhere in the Dutch East Indies except Java, a policy more to protect against encroachment than outright violence. Fairchild suspected the Dutch "sensed the unavoidable effects that have come from our towering pyramid of wealth which scatters over the world like locusts"—or in other words, American travelers' reputation for snooty entitlement, and America's hot streak of taking over other peoples' colonies. He and Lathrop were technically researchers, not tourists, but still, when he had to talk to an official, Fairchild's words came out with the slightest tinge of an Italian accent.

The small boat, long and slender, was perfect for the voyage ahead, able to slip narrowly between islands and pass over coral reefs. As it left Java, Fairchild drank in the blueness of the water and moistness of the air. Even though he had been to Java once before,

the islands of the Java Sea enchanted him anew, a paradise of mar-
velous plant life, insects, and bizarre animals. These were the result of active volcanoes, which kept the already-warm tropics in a
perpetual hot bath that bred diversity in ways the mid latitudes
were too fickle to accommodate. There were coral atolls in the water and purple mountain peaks high above, all surrounded by a
stretch of blue sea smoother than glass. Despite the danger ahead,
he enjoyed thinking he knew the region well.

It was an afterthought if Fairchild or Lathrop noticed that, as the
boat left Java, the world inaugurated the twentieth century. Early
January of 1900 felt like any other time; the ship bobbed in every
direction as it rose and fell between swells.

Under the tropical sun, Fairchild and Lathrop were granted a
pair of deck chairs and spent the first few days of the voyage giggling about a man they had met months before in Chile with the
name *Señor Izquierdo*, or Mr. Left. They'd banter in colloquy, one as
Mr. Left and the other Mr. Right, thoroughly confusing themselves
until they'd slap their knees and double over laughing.

Lombok was the first stop on the forty-day itinerary. Steep volcanic
hills arranged in a lazy horseshoe cast a shadow on the ship as it
approached the shore. The Dutch had only recently pacified Lombok's people, then claimed the sooty volcanic soil as their own.
Large cliffs and subpar farming conditions—except close to the
shore, where thirsty palm trees grew—meant there weren't many
indigenous people to begin with, maybe a few hundred. Still, colonization hardly meant harmony, and so the indigenous lived apart
from the Dutch in strict separation, both by custom and by choice.

Fairchild returned to the ship with only a black-and-white lima
bean and a new variety of peanut. "The native market yielded little
in the way of interesting plants, and altogether our days . . . were a
disappointment." He found the same on two more islands, Bali and

Sulawesi, where he believed the wondrous tropical crops he had seen in Java were hiding deep in the islands' interior, requiring weeks of travel that Fairchild didn't have, and a fearlessness of ornery islanders that he lacked.

In Fairchild's diaries, notebooks, and memoirs, as in the writings of so many people in his day, there are frequent ruminations of this sort of racial insecurity, equating danger with things unknown or poorly understood. Many island civilizations at the time were indeed angry and violent to outsiders, but for reasons that were largely lost on Fairchild. As a white American of the nineteenth century, he had never known life with the indignities of colonization, and he couldn't comprehend what a formerly free people thought about being invaded by a foreign power. As a result, he frequently judged such unfamiliar people, even pitied them. "At each place we met different types of natives who had grown up on their respective islands knowing nothing of the world beyond the waves breaking on their white beaches," Fairchild asserted.

The natives' knowledge of the world was, in fact, more complex than Fairchild realized. The people of these Indian Ocean islands understood they had been invaded by Europeans who had brought violence and disease, and raped the islands' women so frequently that babies began to appear with caramel skin. Contrary to Fairchild's opinion, the fact that the islanders didn't kill white visitors was a sign of the islanders' racial progress, a reluctant admission that they couldn't keep white men away with comparatively impotent weapons like arrows and knives. Even more racially aware was the way island people were resigned to their fate of colonial subservience—to the point that when a pair of American plant explorers dropped anchor, the group of native islanders whose only possession was the island they stood on wouldn't fight off the American visitors, but would humbly help them explore.

The best example of this came at Ceram Island. Off the eagle-shaped outcrop west of Papua New Guinea, the shallow sea at low tide moored the boat in soft sand a quarter mile from the beach. One by one, the island's men, bare chested and with stained sarongs around their waists, sloshed through the water toward the ship, aware that fully clothed men on board wouldn't want their trousers dampened by the waves, and would rather be carried ashore.

One had ugly red spots on his chest, and as he approached, Fairchild realized that the sickly-looking man would be, as he described the arrangement, "my horse."

As he rode toward the shore on the spotted man's back, silver fish jumped from the water around them and onto the thin pencil branches of mangroves. Fairchild, wearing long pants and a collared shirt, tried not to touch the man's skin, fearful it could convey the contagious ringworm fungus. When the man dropped his cargo on the firm sand, Fairchild gave him a nod. The sand around them was light brown and looked alive, moving toward the water and away from it, shells of hermit crabs scurrying from the waves. A dog with no hair other than a single knot of blond on its head ran toward Fairchild, and right before the expected bite, the animal rubbed its face on Fairchild's leg. He laughed, and the island men did, too.

As he waited for the other men to be ferried ashore, Fairchild couldn't help but steal glances at the nearly naked brown bodies, all around him drowsy penises, sagging breasts, fickle clumps of hair. An American could grow up in those days without seeing a naked body, unless in an artist's studio. For a thirty-year-old bachelor, gawking was less from deviance than from plain curiosity. Excusable, in Fairchild's case, so long as he wasn't caught staring.

Twenty-four hundred miles separated the beginning of the Java Sea voyage from the end, and within that distance were strewn thousands of islands, some a just-swimmable distance apart. Proximity united the islands, but the people divided themselves. Fairchild remarked that the squabbling seemed childish and petty, a little like "the feuds of poor whites of the Kentucky Mountains. . . . Both are evidence of the insanity of mankind at this level of culture." On one island, several warriors escorted Fairchild to the home of their chief, where they showed him an old iron cannon that had been a conquest of a long-ago battle. The artillery didn't work without the powder to shoot it, but their enemies coveted it, and that alone gave it value.

Farther along, the island of Dobo would offer the most vivid and tragic demonstration of violence. The boat that preceded Fairchild and Lathrop's had sent its engineer and boatswain ashore to meet the Papuans and perhaps trade. But as soon as they touched the sand, a storm of arrows rained on them. The boatswain managed to row away, but the engineer was stranded on the beach, and his sprint into the brush amounted to accidental suicide. The captain sent a second officer in official uniform to negotiate the engineer's rescue, but when arrows fell on his boat, too, he turned back.

If a military escort had been available, Fairchild might have made another attempt at the rescue. He knew that the military uniform of the prior man had looked threatening, and the best strategy would in fact be a slow approach, followed by exaggerated gestures to demonstrate that a white man's presence brought respect and not a threat, and that he considered the islanders equal partners in cultural dialogue. But any remnants of Fairchild's boyhood hubris had been replaced by the cultural wisdom that some people are not to be bothered, and so he didn't object when the captain announced they'd move along.

The next day, at the island of Sekar, a rock barely big enough to sustain a hundred people, the situation was only slightly less fraught. As Fairchild prepared to board a rowboat to cross the pristine blue water toward the white sand, he noticed the scowls of the men standing on the shore.

"Laugh," the captain told him. "Joke and do comic ridiculous things. Don't look serious or one of the ugly fellows may run a spear through you, too."

Fairchild pulled the boat ashore. He maintained a permanent smile and held his arms in the air, looking a little like the clowns of his youth who had come to Kansas in the traveling circuses. He spoke in a high-pitched voice and opened his eyes as wide as they'd go.

The Papuans stared at him unmoved. By 1900, they had become bored by the antics of white men, and especially by the mirrors and beads they brought as oddities.

No one laughed, but no one killed Fairchild, either. And when his act had gone on long enough in front of the *radja*, the princely ruler of Sekar, Fairchild said the only thing he could think of: that he was interested in plants.

As he rowed the small boat away, next to him sat a citrus fruit shaped curiously like a pear, and nearly the size of his head. The rotund fruit was green and obese, and on the inside, as everyone on board the ship would soon learn, pink and orange. It was a pomelo, also known as a shaddock, a citrus of such girth it commanded the scientific name *Citrus maxima*, partly for its size and partly because of its reign as one of Earth's few original citrus ancestors.

In many ways, though, the world had already moved on from the pomelo. Grapefruit orchards had sprouted in America, thanks to English colonizers, who brought the fruit with them and grew it as a novelty in northern Florida, the only place where the climate was suitable. By 1885, Floridians had begun to ship grapefruit to Philadelphia and New York. Its popularity would rise, both in the United States and around the world, which made the pomelo, especially in 1900, rather old news.

Still, Fairchild thought an original pomelo specimen could be valuable breed stock. There was also the value in a fruit so large and oblong, it almost defied belief. And so he felt lucky to have one, even if it required extra attention to ensure that his only specimen stay alive. *"Seeds of a large and very sour variety,"* he noted while the taste was still fresh in his memory. The seeds separated from the flesh easily. He placed them in a damp cloth and wrote a reminder to keep the cloth wet until he could pack them with soil, and after that, send them to the other side of the world.

When the forty-day cruise of the small Malay Islands ended, Fairchild turned his desires to the Philippines, which were newly relevant in 1900, because they were newly American.

The people of the United States, empowered with victory over the Spanish in 1898, had developed a growing hunger for expansion. The spoils of the war included the islands of Puerto Rico in the Caribbean, Guam in the Pacific, and the Philippines, a territory nearly as far from Washington as someone on Earth could possibly be. The Philippines belonged to the Spanish for so long the very name for the islands had come from Spain's King Philip II, who, by 1898, had been dead for three hundred years.

Now Manila was American territory, which seemed like a convenient stepping stone to the East and the five hundred million Chinese who could become customers for American products. Rationalizing the ethics of something so nakedly self-serving, American politicians concocted elaborate explanations that it was America's *obligation* to maintain control of helpless Filipino people who couldn't "uplift themselves," as President McKinley claimed. Albert Beveridge, an Indiana candidate for the United States Senate, argued that leaving the Filipinos to self-rule would be "like giving a razor to a babe" or "giving a typewriter to an Eskimo."

Rhetoric like Beveridge's did little to persuade Filipino insurgents that they should be grateful for American supervision. Instead, they swiftly turned their arms from their Spanish occupiers to their American ones, with even greater force. Filipinos escalated

small battles into great acts of brutality. After an American soldier
was found murdered with his stomach slit open, an American com-
mander ordered the death of every Filipino in the village, over one
thousand people, according to a young soldier who wrote home
relaying the story. Americans back home largely sat back and allowed the military to figure things out. There were opponents, and
none more largely named than the deep-pocketed Andrew Carnegie, who offered to buy the islands from President McKinley for
twenty million dollars and set the Filipino people free. His offer
was declined.

When Secretary Wilson learned that Fairchild was in the region, he sent a letter asking him to survey the agricultural potential
in the United States' newest colony. "An American military presence might work in your favor," Wilson wrote to Fairchild.

Despite Fairchild's credentials as an American in an American
territory, Wilson's speculation was wrong. The islands weren't mol-
lified. Continued uprisings by Filipinos against the Americans had
left Manila constantly on the edge of violence, leaving agriculture
the furthest thing from anyone's mind. Fairchild's arrival coincided
with monsoon season, which transformed roads into quagmires of
mud. He managed to find some mango varieties on the outskirts of
Manila that he thought people might appreciate in Florida. His instinct turned out to be sharp when the carabao mango, as sweet
as candy and not too fibrous, became known as the "champagne
mango" in warm states that could grow it. Its slender body and but-
tery flesh shocked American taste buds that had never tasted anything so saccharine aside from pure sugar. The mango left such an
impression on growers and breeders that its genes found their way
into almost every American mango variety for the next century,
the stuff of plant breeding dreams.

Fairchild, of course, was oblivious to this future success, another
of his most significant contributions to American farmers. All he

saw while visiting the Philippines was that Filipinos weren't ready for him. The pipe dream of pacifying the islands through agriculture turned futile when Fairchild learned that the Dutch had tried with coffee, and the Spanish with farming equipment, and both efforts had ended in failure.

On the ship that took them away from the hotbed of the Philippines and, for the first time, to mainland Asia, Fairchild sat to write Secretary Wilson. "The time is not yet ripe for any comprehensive agricultural survey of the Philippines inasmuch as they are not yet sufficiently pacified," he wrote. "What would require at the present time a year to accomplish can be done later in less than a quarter of the time and at far less expense to the country. Any explorer who might be sent out from the Department would be in constant danger, would find themselves blocked continually by the movements of the insurgents and would be able to do very little in return for the outlay of money which would be necessary to maintain them."

Fairchild's message was received in Washington and, through a series of emissaries, made it to the desk of President McKinley. If violent Filipinos couldn't be pacified with force, McKinley thought they might be tamed by democracy. After consulting Fairchild's report, McKinley sent a portly federal judge named William Howard Taft, a man oblivious about the Philippines but with the legal know-how, to set up a civilian government, wherein Filipinos could rule themselves, or at least hold the illusion that they were.

Taft tried to calm people by offering protected markets for Filipino goods in the United States. But this had the effect of even further enflaming the Filipinos, insulted at faux generosity. Upon seeing the red-hot anger of the Filipino people, Fairchild believed that nothing short of the American military leaving the island country to itself would truly pacify its people. But his opinion was either never shared or never heard. From start to finish, America's costly entrenchment in the Philippines would last forty-eight years.

There was nowhere to move, nowhere to step, nowhere even to look without catching someone's eye. People surrounded Fairchild's every latitude. Even getting onshore had required a series of minor collisions with other boats, in them men filling net bags with fish and wearing hats as pointed as their shouts. "One's most overwhelming sensation is of the unbelievable congestion of the mass of human beings," Fairchild thought upon arriving in Canton, China, on his first visit to the most populous country on earth. For forty centuries, China had gone through cycles of boom and bust, of economic rise and decline, births and deaths of religious sects and governments. The only thing that hadn't declined was its population, which seemed to rise daily with the sun until, in 1900, Chinese people accounted for almost one-third of all humanity. Such shoulder-to-shoulder volume had brought a sense of discipline and order, and Fairchild believed that such order would make seed collecting a breeze.

So much about China was surprising to the senses. Chickens hung, often alive, under shop awnings. Smells of rice and seaweed wafted with the scent of steaming vegetables. The smell that wafted heaviest was of sewage—"an overpowering stench" to Fairchild—which men with large sticks across their backs carried in pairs of buckets. One shining example of China's ingenuity was in fertilization; no phosphorus was lost, not from humans or dogs, or even from the excretions of silkworms. Human corpses, rich in nitrogen and phosphorus, were returned directly to the soil, buried under small mounds of dirt, where the deceased had lived or died. This efficiency also extended to food; butchers wasted no part of a sheep that could be used, down to its unwashed intestines.

The only superfluous commodity in China was human energy, which existed in such wild abundance that it stood in the way of any innovation that might make people's lives easier. Backbreaking work carrying sewage or directing the cacophony of carts and

1901. Fairchild found fertilizer abundant everywhere he went in China. Near Canton, earthen pots full of dung made an orchard of star fruit trees "smell to heaven," he wrote.

animals provided jobs, and with those jobs, the guarantee of keeping people occupied.

Luckily for Fairchild, the thickness of people seemed to be matched by the same thickness of crops. A farmer at one small market allowed him to try guava, which he had experienced before, but not like the one in his hands, which perspired with luscious pink flesh. He found a round, yellowish fruit called a Dutch eggplant and peaches so sweet he imagined them perfect for preserves. There were small citrus grapes that grew on trees ("loquats," an Englishman told him, although they were likely kumquats instead), and peppers of varying sizes and kinds. He inquired one evening about the crunchy white disks in his chop suey. A man told him they were tubers called water chestnuts, although they weren't nuts. They were an aquatic vegetable with the rare culinary quality of never getting soggy, even when cooked. *"Worthy of consideration as a plant for cultivation in the swamps of the South,"* Fairchild scrawled.

His shipment of water chestnuts indeed made it to the South. But they never caught on. They had to be grown in muddy swamps, which wasn't a fatal flaw, but it was inconvenient and dirty, all for a small food with little flavor. If the United States had had more land or been at a point in its history when it valued more efficient use of land, farmers might have begun producing water chestnuts just because. But as with many of Fairchild's crops, the timing just wasn't right, and thus, water chestnuts remained an Asian food. The best evidence of this may be that in America ten decades later, water chestnuts tend to play little more than a humdrum role as supporting actors in Chinese takeout.

Instead, the top value of being in China was its rice. No one grew more rice—or grew it better—than the Chinese. Their methods had proved unmatchable. Fairchild walked through rice fields, sometimes ankle-deep in water, pulling up plants where permitted, and then later, he'd attempt the same in fields where his presence wasn't sanctioned. He sent six rices back to Washington, including one that would eventually sprout in the Carolinas and several others that grew better in California. No country could topple China's rice dominance, but the United States had its own contributions to make with rice. America's limits on land, water, and labor resulted in innovations of its own. The typical American spirit of finding new and better ways of doing old things eventually yielded machines capable of planting rice, and hybrid seeds that drank less water.

It was just as difficult to leave China as it had been to arrive, and as the boat traveled back to Hong Kong, where Lathrop, who didn't care to visit China, was waiting, Fairchild's head spun. "Surely only a nightmare could fill my brain with such fantastic people, practices, and customs. Everything which I had experienced during my days in Canton seemed utterly unbelievable." China had been an astonishing mix of wonder, oddity, and risk—a future superpower, one might think, if it could harness the incredible energies of its people.

From Hong Kong, Fairchild and Lathrop traveled to Bangkok, where the captain, wary of a coming monsoon, permitted only a single overnight stay. On the boat, Lathrop made acquaintance with an English couple who stood out among the Chinese immigrants and laborers on board. The man, Mr. Farnham, exchanged pleasantries with Lathrop about travel and the pride of being Anglo amid so many foreigners. Mrs. Farnham said nothing, but smiled politely, holding in her arms a baby whose skin glowed crimson.

Disease had chased Fairchild and Lathrop all over the world on every habitable continent. So far Fairchild remained healthy, untouched by illness, and Lathrop was feeling better with time. Yet he frequently noted that never before had illness so depressed his functionality. Only now, at fifty-two, was he feeling his age. And in an era when life teetered on the edge, a healthy body never more than one unwitting step from ruin, health was a common topic of discussion.

"I believe the baby has cholera," Lathrop said to Fairchild later that evening. "I'm going to give them my cabin."

He moved his luggage into Fairchild's room, occupying the bed while Fairchild was left with an upholstered chair. In the subsequent days, the infant's cries from the other side of the wall grew louder, then stopped. The Farnhams became absent in the ship's dining room. Lathrop arranged for a small coffin to be delivered to the grieving couple, a gesture Fairchild noted "which so well illustrates Mr. Lathrop's warm heart."

With disease having already claimed one life, the passengers were eager to leave the boat when it docked in Ceylon, the British colony that would one day find the name Sri Lanka. Lathrop was the first to disembark, and soon the two traveled by coach quickly away from the boisterous activity of the port, into the mountains toward a resort near a botanical garden where more tropical crops might be found.

Fairchild had felt tired when he left the boat, and throughout the journey to the resort, he sulked in his seat, fatigued and light-headed. To reassure Lathrop—and himself—he claimed he was simply tired and in need of rest on firm ground, outside the rolling sways of the boat. But Lathrop eyed him suspiciously as Fairchild's head drooped. By the time they reached the resort, Fairchild could hardly stand; an attendant helped him to his room.

The symptoms seemed to indicate typhoid fever, a bacterial infection spread from human to human, and likely acquired on the boat where the little girl expired. Typhoid had been among the most debilitating diseases of the nineteenth century, causing millions of deaths, until a British scientist developed a vaccine in 1896. But here in Ceylon, inoculation was impossible. At first a victim would become tremendously tired, and when he wanted nothing but sleep, great headaches and muscle aches would set in, followed by sweating, coughing, and alternating episodes of constipation and diarrhea. By the time the delirium began, the victim would

1902. Fairchild's case of typhoid in Ceylon made his visit to the island uncomfortable, unproductive, and almost fatal. Either when he arrived or just prior to departing, he overlooked a beach in Mount Lavinia, near Colombo.

usually lie on his back with eyes half-open and loudly moan in what was known as "the typhoid state."

At first, Fairchild slept half the day, and then didn't leave bed at all. Lathrop could do little but sit at his side as he slept, but Fairchild would awake frightened and sweating, which frightened Lathrop as well. For Barbour Lathrop, a man with no children, the person lying before him had become kin, the closest he would come to having a son, and perhaps the only person alive he could tolerate as a long-term travel companion. Out of affection he had begun calling Fairchild "Fairy," and in return was called "Uncle Barbour." All of Lathrop's frequent upbraiding during their first tour had been remarkably successful, for before him lay a young man worldly in experience and confident in intellect. Moreover, their economic pursuit of plants rested on Fairchild's expertise, effectively the rudder to their botanical adventures. Lathrop's usual mechanism for coping was to project apathy. But as he watched the clock on the wall, he waited, anxious and scared, a feeling that anyone else, anywhere in the world, might have called love.

"He'll have to be moved immediately," the hotel manager announced one morning while Lathrop ate breakfast.

"Moved to where?" Lathrop asked.

"To the hospital."

The manager had heard a rumor that a boarder might have typhoid. When he noticed that the young man who had checked in with Lathrop hadn't come down for breakfast in several days, he realized who it was. Unlike cholera or malaria, typhoid was believed to be contagious, and the manager believed that Fairchild's illness threatened everyone in the hotel.

Lathrop's tenderness couldn't check his usual bluster.

"I've seen that fetid hospital," he said. "He won't be going there."

"Sir, with respect," the manager answered, "I cannot have a case of typhoid in my inn."

Saying nothing, Lathrop reached into his coat pocket and pulled out the shiny revolver that he carried everywhere, the tool of pre-caution for a traveler—at least that's what the man down the street from the Bohemian Club had told him when he sold him the weapon. This was the first time Lathrop found it necessary to use it.

He placed the revolver on the table, then locked eyes with the hotel manager.

"He will not be moved."

Indeed, no one moved Fairchild, nor did anyone fuss about it again. Eventually, he began to sit up, and then stand up. When Fairchild could walk unaided across the room, Lathrop decided it was time to find a more agreeable place for his companion to convalesce.

Lathrop had London in mind, and he paid a pair of men to carry Fairchild by stretcher from the hotel to a train, and a boy to accompany him to the port. The boy had never ridden a train before, and Fairchild had to throw shoes for attention as the boy hung his head out the window.

Lathrop had secured cabins on a steamer called the *Prinz Hein-rich* that had two smokestacks and Western accommodations. For only the second time in the half-dozen years Fairchild had known him, Lathrop surrendered the first officer's cabin. For the twenty-five days to England, Fairchild lay on a large white bed, his novels and catnaps interrupted only by the savory arrival of omelets peppered with salted ham, stews with tender chunks of beef, and a teapot refilled at what felt like every hour, all of it consumed in luxurious solitude.

PART III

CHAPTER ELEVEN

Lemons, Leaves, and the Dawn of New Light

Secretary Wilson studied Fairchild's face for an uncomfortably long time. After nearly two years on assignment—trekking across the sea to South America, Europe, Africa, and the islands that dotted the Indian Ocean—the botanist-turned-explorer was back in Washington, D.C., sitting before his former boss, and for the first time, he had come to confront the mess he had left behind at the Department of Agriculture.

Wilson had agreed to see him only reluctantly. Any satisfaction the secretary might have felt at Fairchild's success was overshadowed by the grudge he still held about Fairchild's untimely and undignified departure. In his absence had come a string of men with poor qualifications to take his place, and thus, the program of seed introduction that Wilson had once crowed about to the president lurched along as Fairchild meandered the globe with Barbour Lathrop.

In reality, Wilson had every reason to be pleased with Fairchild. In two years, Fairchild had visited every arable continent, shipping back the seeds of an estimated one thousand plants, including foods, shrubs, and trees. Some had been propagated, and others had already been shared with regional experiment stations and given to farmers. The plan to hunt globally for crops and introduce them to the United States was showing unquestionable signs of success. But the Department's chief, still nursing resentment over Fairchild's desertion, was loath to admit it was true.

Wilson's temper tantrum in Washington had followed Fairchild in letters around the world complaining about the disarray of the Department, until finally, in June of 1900, Fairchild wrote to Walter Swingle that the petulance was unbecoming. "Think what the effect of this petty squabbling among we botanists must have upon a businessman like Mr. Lathrop!" he wrote. Fairchild could take the blame for his hasty exit, but Lathrop's ego needed nourishment, especially if the pair were to continue their travels. Fairchild cautioned that denying Lathrop ongoing respect would be like killing a goose preparing to lay a golden egg.

Lathrop's pride bruised easily. But Fairchild's annoyance wasn't unreasonable. The two had traveled together for four years, and in that time, Lathrop had spent thousands of dollars to fuel the operation that was enriching the United States with plants from parts of the world few Americans had been to. Lathrop covered Fairchild's travel expenses and a small salary, thereby freeing the Department from any cost except that of shipping plant material to Washington, which amounted at most to a few hundred dollars. Granted, it was enjoyable, and Lathrop liked Fairchild's company, but making a donation to one's country still came at a cost of money and convenience.

Even if Wilson didn't thank Fairchild and Lathrop directly, there were signs that he appreciated Fairchild's work—and more pressing, that he wanted him to continue hunting for plants of culinary and economic value.

Fairchild had been in Washington just two days, but when Wilson finished harrumphing in their meeting, he suggested that Fairchild immediately embark for Germany. Fairchild booked passage on the next boat to Europe.

His assignment was to infiltrate a group of German hops farmers, who held the key to superior beer. Beer had been around for thousands of years. By 1500, Germans were honing their brewing methods, and by 1900, Germany's ingredients were the envy of beer makers everywhere, particularly in the United States. Master brewers in Saint Louis and Milwaukee were beginning to scale their recipes and were eager to bring high-quality but low-cost beer to millions of people by using better ingredients.

Hops—which are technically fruit—probably originated somewhere in Mongolia, but the Germans took initiative to grow them best. Over centuries, Bavarian and nearby Bohemian breweries, many with adjacent hops fields, improved their varieties by drawing out and strengthening the smooth, tangy notes that give beer its body. American beer, by contrast, was full of harsh bitterness, a result of inferior hops and barleys. Hops grow best in cool, rainy climates, much like in the Pacific Northwest, where few people lived at the beginning of the twentieth century, let alone visited.

Bavarian growers knew of America's troubles with beer making. In fact, all of Europe knew American hops were laughably inferior. An 1892 article in *The Edinburgh Review* gloated condescendingly, "American hops may be dismissed in a few words. Like American grapes, they derive a course [sic], rank flavour and smell from the soil in which they grow. . . . There is little chance in their competing in our market with European growth, except in season of scarcity." European fields, however, were sage and worn, their plants honed for centuries to accentuate the smooth bitterness and spicy florals they would bring beer. The harvest method was on equal footing with their taste. After they were picked, the fields were left empty, the vines left dormant, for a full season to repopulate their branches. Ever aware of their crops' value, Bohemia's top brewers were known to hire young men to guard the fields at night. This would complicate Fairchild's assignment. But he'd still find a way to acquire top-tier hops—if not diplomatically, then by outright theft.

The beer hall was the gathering center for Bohemian hop growers. That's what the innkeeper said when Fairchild checked into a two-room guesthouse in Polepy, a village so small its people numbered in the dozens. Even the man, a garden sitter with a pipe between his lips, eyed Fairchild suspiciously. The nearby growers had formed a cartel of sorts to prevent one of the region's most popular hops, the Semš red hop, from spreading, and here was a foreigner with an American accent who had come to learn about beer.

Most types of German hops had been grown for centuries, yet the Semš hop was new, the product of a man named Wenzel Semš who grew hops with the help of training poles. In 1853 Semš saw sprouting in his yard a heavy-yielding variety, its hull covered densely in flowers, which turned into cones full of hops. Wenzel Semš took a cutting and propagated it, and then again, and then so many times that within four decades it became the eminent hop of Bohemia. Fairchild learned this history over beers, laughing with the growers in his thick American-accented German, a ploy, albeit genuine, to earn their trust without ever mentioning his motives on behalf of America's rival industry.

It wouldn't have been hard for Fairchild simply to pilfer a few hops, perhaps in the middle of the night when the watch boys dozed off, and leave town immediately, before anyone noticed. He had the skills for such a heist, and the confidence to get away with it. Without DNA or genetic testing, even a well-documented paper trail couldn't prove American hops had been acquired dishonestly from Europe.

But Fairchild had a different idea—a plan that reveals as much about his character as it does about the attitude of calculated restraint America would eventually develop. In lieu of espionage, he wondered how to win the men over. "How could I hope to convert them to my philosophy of a free exchange of plant varieties between

1901. Bavarian hop growers guarded from foreigners the secrets of their superior hops. Fairchild befriended his innkeeper in Polepy—a man known as Herr Wirth—to obtain information to plot a strategy. Fairchild flattered Wirth by taking his portrait.

the different nations of the world? It seemed that the best thing was to . . . make friends with the growers. Possibly they might then be willing to let me have some cuttings."

One night in the beer hall, when empty glasses covered the table, Fairchild mentioned that he'd enjoy seeing the house where Semš, the prized son of Polepy, was born. Semš was long dead, but his legacy permeated the village as though he were royalty. Flattered by the interest of a visitor, Semš' son received Fairchild the next day at the house where his father had once lived. Fairchild laid on thick charm. He told the junior Semš how unfortunate it was that no formal record existed of the hop's discovery, and wondered what would happen to the memory of the Semš' origin story after several more generations, when younger growers would forget the history completely. "I suggested that a tablet be placed on Semsch's house, and offered a generous contribution towards the expense," Fairchild would later write, phonetically spelling out how "Semš" was pronounced.

The junior Semš was struck by both the idea and the gesture. News spread, as Fairchild suspected it would, creating in one small town and with a few dozen dollars more goodwill toward America and its inventive and generous people than might've been accomplished in a century of German-American trade and diplomacy.

Whether Fairchild was conniving or earnest is hard to know, but it didn't matter. One rainy night, he answered a knock on the door of his guest room to find one of the growers soaked to the bone. When the man asked if he wanted cuttings of the Semš hop, Fairchild, feeling bold, said yes, and explained why. The man laughed, then relented.

"There are some members of the society who won't approve, so I cannot do this openly, but I will ship you one hundred cuttings to a station down the line," the man said.

A few days later, the hops arrived at a small inn several miles away where Fairchild waited. Exactly three weeks after that, on December 18, 1900, the Semš hop was on American soil.

This was either good timing or bad, depending on who you asked. Hop growers reacted with predictable jubilation at news that a long-elusive European variety was newly theirs—in the sense that what the government owned was effectively their property, too—and that government officials had begun testing it for distribution.

Owing to this success, as well as to the confidence of a country starting to do things right, American hop growers began to produce better hops, and eventually, better beer. This was the business that brought people, money, and attention to Oregon's Willamette Valley, a future ganglion of American hops.

But to a group of outspoken women, the Semš hops, and all hops, were unwelcome. The Woman's Christian Temperance Union had spent decades arguing that there was corrosive power in alcohol. The women's group urged schoolkids to take the so-called Blue Ribbon Pledge, swearing off alcohol for life. The fight against alcohol was part of a larger struggle over civil rights. Alcohol was consumed mostly by men, in saloons where women were excluded, and in meetings of local government, where women weren't welcome to vote.

It's easy to see temperance as a crucial and meaningful movement in American history, when an oppressed group pushed painfully but successfully for empowerment and inclusion. Yet one of the temperance movement's lamentable effects was that, as the country crept toward the full Prohibition of the 1920s, fields of prized hops, including the ones that Fairchild acquired through espionage, were plowed up and replaced with crops few could protest, like tobacco, corn, peaches, and pears.

The eventual devastation of world war, however, yielded other opportunities. Temperance eliminated the need for many hops, but not all. The American hops that European growers ridiculed in 1900 became the best hops on the market two decades later when fighting

left Europe's fields in ruins. Europe's wartime thirst for suds provided American farmers a much-needed bridge to keep their operations running through Prohibition. For when Prohibition
whimpered to a close in the early 1930s, Europe's pause amounted
to a lucky head start for an American industry that would one day
produce the top-selling beers in the world.

As a country, America was changing, slowly, but with the quicken-
ing pace of a waltz giving way to a rumba. By 1900, the giants of
American innovation, the visionaries who would put people in automobiles, in airplanes, and on television—the Henry Fords and
the Wilbur Wrights—had already been born, and were showing
their imaginations to be proportional to their country's swelling
pride. The United States entered the new century with the largest
industrial economy, the largest agricultural economy, the highest
per capita income, and the highest level of education humans had
ever seen. The days after January 1, 1900, had been filled with news
of firsts: the magic of telephones began to trickle to normal people
with nickel-in-the-slot public telephones in drugstores and hotels; a
growing number of moviemakers began to populate a town in California called Hollywood where, if they violated New Jersey pat-
ents held by Thomas Edison's motion picture company (which they
intended to), they could abscond to Mexico; and the Washington
Monument, the erect symbol of America's upward spirit, was up-
graded with an electric-powered elevator that crept at a single mile
an hour for a thrilling five-minute ride to the top.

The presidential election of 1900 had shown the biggest leap of
all—the campaigns had collectively spent an astounding three million dollars. The widespread feeling that everything was getting
bigger delivered immense pride, as Chauncey Depew, a senator
from New York, proclaimed. "There is not a man here who does

not feel 400 percent bigger in 1900 than he did in 1896," Depew crowed in Philadelphia at the century's first Republican National Convention. "Bigger intellectually, bigger hopefully, bigger patriotically, bigger in the breast from the fact that he is a citizen of a country that has become a world power for peace, for civilization and for the expansion of its industries and the products of its labor." To excite the crowd, organizers arranged for an enormous elephant to shuffle down the aisle, a motif of the Republican party and indication that, truly, the old bounds of reality no longer applied.

The man those Republicans were there to see, William McKinley, would end up winning a rematch that year against his 1896 rival, William Jennings Bryan, this time by a wider margin than four years prior, thanks to the country's victory, on his watch, over the Spanish and, if one held his nose, America's new ownership of the Philippines. McKinley had much to take credit for, including America's progress with plants, led by the most seasoned and senior agricultural explorer for the USDA. In his State of the Union address in December of 1900, McKinley gloated, "The Department of Agriculture has been extending its work during the past year, reaching farther for new varieties of seeds and plants," as though tipping his hat to Fairchild himself.

James Wilson, whom McKinley had asked to stay on for another term as agriculture secretary, read the speech the next day in his office, aware that he had made the president look good. Wilson could be a grumpy man but he was an honest one, who must have admitted to himself that the idea of food exploration, and credit for its success, weren't entirely his.

The first sign Fairchild had of the past giving way to an unrecognizable future was a telegram that reached him in Europe with news that his father was dead. He had acquired some disease, gone in for surgery, and died on the operating table. George Fairchild had been a product of the nineteenth century, a nearly perfect metaphor for its sorrow and antiquity. George had grown up in a strict atmosphere of Puritan dogma, in which dancing, smoking, swearing, drinking, cards, and theaters were all taboo. Even though George had been fired from his job, had watched his house destroyed by arson, and had seen his five offspring leave his home, in the final year of his life, he finally saw his life's work published, a tome on life in America's center, monochromatically titled *Rural Wealth and Welfare*. With the growing excitement for days ahead rather than those behind, the volume was outdated almost the day it was published.

David Fairchild was struck by the news, by the "grief and loneliness" of sudden loss, of ascending from his family's second generation to its first. But the sadness natural in any man who loses his father didn't slow him. If Fairchild, now thirty-two, had developed a philosophy, it was that life, no matter its pleasures or misfortunes, requires the constant work of "pushing on."

The sunshine fell on his face, glaring and golden with opportunity. And so, with telegram still in hand, he stood up to find something new.

He found a boat bound for Italy, where, like last time, he took quick cuttings of wine and table grapes, almost all seedless. He gazed at a towering carob tree, attractive as a shade provider in gardens and for its pods of seeds that tasted as sweet as honey. A botanist near Trieste helped Fairchild acquire superior filberts, or hazelnuts.

The coast of Austria-Hungary yielded what people called *capuzzo*, a leafy cabbage. It was a two-thousand-year-old grandparent of modern broccoli and cauliflower, that was neither charismatic nor particularly delicious. But something about it called to Fairchild. The people of Austria-Hungary ate it with enthusiasm, and not because it was good, but because it was there. While the villagers called it *capuzzo*, the rest of the world would call it kale. And among its greatest attributes would be how simple it is to grow, sprouting in just its second season of life, and with such dense and bulky leaves that the biggest challenge of farming it seemed to be how to make it *stop* growing. *"The ease with which it is grown and its apparent favor among the common people this plant is worthy a trial in the Southern States,"* Fairchild jotted.

It was prophetic, perhaps, considering his suggestion became reality. Kale's first stint of popularity came around the turn of the century, thanks to its horticultural hack: it drew salt into its body, preventing the mineralization of soil. Its next break came from its ornamental elegance—bunches of white, purple, or pink leaves that would enliven a drab garden.

And then for decades, kale kept a low profile, its biggest consumers restaurants and caterers who used the cheap, bushy leaves to decorate their salad bars. Kale's final stroke of luck came sometime in the 1990s when chemists discovered it had more iron than beef, and more calcium, iron, and vitamin K than almost anything else that sprouts from soil. That was enough for it to enter the big leagues of nutrition, which invited public relations campaigns, celebrity endorsements, and morning-show cooking segments. American chefs experimented with the leaves in stews and soups, and when baked, as a substitute for potato chips. Eventually, medical researchers began to use it to counter words like "obesity," "diabetes," and "cancer." One imagines kale, a lifetime spent unnoticed, waking up one day to find itself captain of the football team.

After this find, Fairchild, too, was feeling the growing confidence of a man well-traveled, well-read, and learned. Conversations with strangers brought the pleasure of learning something new, and occasionally, showing off the sheen of worldliness he'd acquired from Lathrop.

One night in Trieste, he joined a group of street men, so-called "boulevardiers," drinking coffee and gossiping about women. Fairchild judged their lives provincial and sad. "I could not understand why they were content to live such utterly aimless lives," he wrote later. He must have showed his hand, because when one of the men asked Fairchild what was so exciting about *his* life, Fairchild wagered that he could cram more romantic glamour into a week of travel than the small-minded man could find in a year of late-night prattle.

It would take less than two days for Fairchild to win the bet. A storm struck the steamer Fairchild boarded to leave Italy. The wind battered the hull and, in the fog of night, another boat nearly crashed into it, its bowsprit sweeping over the steamer's deck. Fairchild jumped to avoid being mauled and when he sought shelter in the dining room, a pretty woman fainted into his arms. Rarely did Fairchild find the occasion to behold a woman, and particularly one so vulnerable. What came next was so novel and pleasurable that it remained salient in his memory for decades, a vignette in his abridged memoirs of his lengthy travels. The woman would turn out to be an Austrian countess, young and with turquoise blue eyes. He would learn their color later, as he laid the listless woman on a sofa, sat beside her, and fanned her gently back to consciousness.

In February of 1901, the prospect of dried table grapes led Fairchild to Greece, where he watched, repulsed, as grapes were laid on slabs of dried manure, believed to be more absorbent than dirt, and baked under the sun until they became raisins. Large melons hung in greenhouses. Fairchild tasted one and was underwhelmed, but when someone assured him a sweet winter melon would last until spring, he arranged a shipment to Washington.

In Greece, Fairchild met with the German botanist Theodor von Heldreich, who showed him tiny green beans known as lentils, and beige pistachios, the most tender of nuts (even though they're not nuts but, in a convoluted way, fruits). Pistachios had already been tasted in America, their delicate taste finely suited for confectionary flavoring in foods like ice cream. But all pistachios in the States were imported. Fairchild hesitated before buying the trees—a stunning fifteen dollars apiece—but he plunked down one hundred dollars to send half a dozen fully grown pistachio trees across the Atlantic. No one objected back at headquarters, for the simple reason that, as far as the Department knew, the trees were the first budded pistachio trees ever to exist in America.

Heldreich, a week away from his seventy-ninth birthday and a year away from his death, saw in Fairchild the same youthful energy he once possessed when, with the influence of his scientific friend and mentor Charles Darwin, he first moved to Greece in the 1850s to study plants in a place more fertile than Germany. Now it was Heldreich's turn to pass wisdom of scientific exploration, and it would be to Fairchild.

Like an Arabian genie, he offered Fairchild three paths. "[He said that] I would find seedless lemons on the island of Poros; walnuts with shells almost as thin as paper on the island of Naxos; and the famous Valonia oak on the island of Crete," Fairchild recalled. He only had the authorization to continue in a straight line, and in the direction of Egypt. Walnuts were grand, and Fairchild loved the imposing grandeur of oak trees. But a seedless lemon had the potential to be transformative back home.

He found the precise orchard Heldreich had mentioned on the island of Poros, near the southern tip of Greece, and there, holding his suitcase, he sunk his teeth into the tart, seedless fruit. Unlike the haste and angst he felt stealing citron from Corsica, he now felt the indifference of confidence. He tasted one lemon after another, inspecting each for seeds, the juice running down his chin until his mouth stung with acid.

Fairchild operated with the professional demeanor of a man now granted government funds to do crucial work. But for a rare occasion in his work as an agricultural explorer, he considered picking fruit for himself, simply to enjoy, whether it helped anyone or not.

So he filled his suitcase with lemons. Some would make it back to America. The rest would be the small and tart pleasure of the man, alone in the orchard and alone in the world, who had picked them.

The new man in Washington, Jared Smith, was overwhelmed by the pace at which seeds were arriving, even though he couldn't have been surprised. In addition to Fairchild and Swingle—who was hunting for figs in Algeria—there were now three other explorers in the field. One searched for stronger forms of wheat in Russia, another man for rice in Japan, and a third explored the South Pacific on the off chance that the Philippines were finally pacified and could start growing sugar for the United States. When the South Pacific explorer discovered the fighting was still fierce, he turned instead to Chinese ports and collected seeds of cucumber, squash, and eggplant.

More than ten new plants were arriving in America each day, a jarring pace and quantity. The ones marked "urgent" had come from Fairchild, who knew how to win attention amid an influx of botanical competition. One of his time-sensitive parcels yielded a yellow fruit called a cashew. The fruit looked like a mix between a mango and an apple, and Fairchild cautioned in all capital letters that the fruit was very poisonous. But from the cashew fruit grew an elbow-shaped nut. If smoked to remove the poisonous oil coating, cashew nuts were suitable to eat. And indeed, Americans have Fairchild to thank for what became a beloved confectionary treat, the demand for cashews rising steadily through the twentieth century. Fairchild was responsible for bringing cashew nuts to American eaters, but not to American farmers, who couldn't handle the crop. Cashews' genetic similarity to mangoes left them unable to withstand even a minor frost, and thus suitable for Florida only. But farmers there just shrugged. The fruit demanded too much land, buckets of water, and relentless labor, all for a small nut. It was

David Fairchild introduced thousands of crops to American farmers. These watercolors, commissioned between 1899 and 1919 by the U.S. Department of Agriculture, portray new fruits that had come into, or were newly growing in, the United States, as a result of Fairchild and other food explorers.

17314
Corsican
from Chas J Lott
Oroville, Butte Co Calif.

D. G. Passmore
3.2.99

Citrus medica, Corsican citron

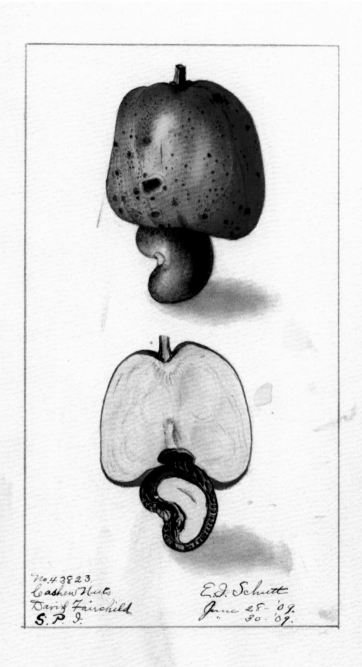

No. 43823.
Cashew Nuts
David Fairchild
S.P.I.

E.J. Schutt
June 28 - '09.
" 30 - '09.

Anacardium occidentale, cashew nut

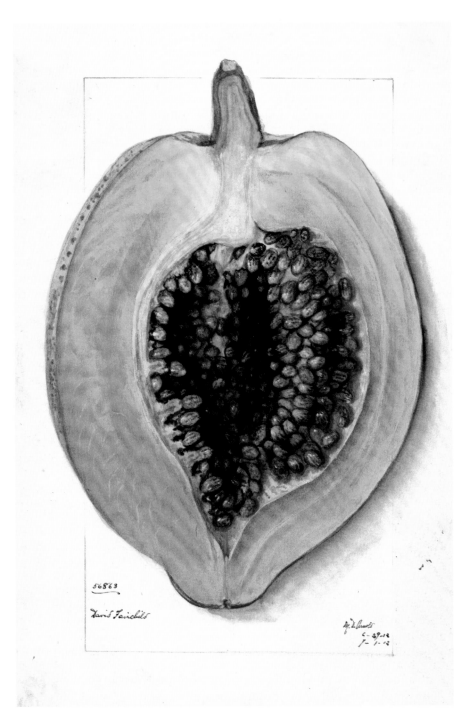

Carica papaya, papaya

Garcinia mangostana, mangosteen

No. 88451.
"Wagner"
C. F. Wagner.
Hollywood. Calif.

R. C. Steadman.
5-16-'16

5-18-'16

Persea americana, avocado

23014
Sultanina rosea
John Rock
Niles Alameda Calif

G. G. Passmore
Oct. 14 1901

Vitis vinifera, grape

38498
Peters No. 1
A. J. Pettigrew,
Manatee,
Manatee Co.
7-18-'07   Fla.

M. A. Newton
7-26-'07

SANDERSHA MANGO

Mangifera indica, mango

No. 88882.
"Tom Watson."
Dr. Shoemaker.
Bought in Center Market.
⅓ size.

R.C. Steadman.
7-1-'16
6-28-'16

Citrullus lanatus, watermelon

cheaper to import cashews from places like India, which became (and remains) America's long-standing supplier.

Cashew nuts, however, did illustrate an important lesson in plant espionage. And not because Fairchild acquired them, but because people *liked* them. Food introduction has two distinct phases. The first is farming: Will people with land agree to grow a new crop and produce it at a large-enough scale to make it a viable food? But the second phase—the one that questioned whether people would actually *like* a new food—was beginning to occupy more and more of Fairchild's thinking. In fact, anyone involved in food introduction in 1901 had started to see the transition from exploration and cuttings to markets and consumption.

Buffalo, New York, wasn't anyone's first choice for a place to answer the question, What would Americans want to *eat*? But Buffalo would end up being the host of the 1901 Pan-American Exposition, where visitors could drink in the sight of Niagara, the grandest of all waterfalls. The fact that America was willing to host a world's fair so soon after its success in Chicago in 1893 showed that the nation was a lasting player of ingenuity. And at the center of the 1901 fair stood two large pavilions, each showcasing America's proudest industries: electricity and agriculture.

A Boston architecture firm designed the seventy-five-thousand-square-foot palace of agriculture flanked with semicircular arches and cylindrical columns. If visitors could be lured away from the bright lights of the electricity pavilion, they found hanging above the doorway of the agriculture palace plaster moldings of the United States' new acquisitions like grapevines and coconut palms. Inside was a cornucopia featuring fruits like watermelons, cauliflowers, and new varieties of tomatoes that were stacked on tables. It was the biggest agricultural trade show America had ever held, and every day, farmers and their helpers brought armloads of celery, potatoes, cabbage, and onions to replace the five thousand crop samples on the tables. Whether the discarded ones were old, or simply ugly, was irrelevant. How the items looked mattered most, followed close behind by the burst of their flavor.

Farmers took turns wandering the rows, stopping to grope squashes and tomatoes, and jotting down the names of the men who grew them, for later correspondence. Mary Bronson Hartt, a food reporter, watched this activity for hours before penning a dispatch for the popular *Everybody's Magazine* about the free exchange of crops and ideas, all in the pursuit of growing American agriculture to a scale that could benefit everyone. A tour of the pavilion of crops, Hartt wrote, "serves to deepen your faith in the enterprise and progressiveness of the great American farmer."

Fairchild had helped build an appetite for this display of new crops. A world's fair accentuated such excitement for novel crops, particularly when one compared the United States to Europe. In 1900, the other side of the Atlantic was entering a steep agricultural stall. Global shipping—especially since the invention of the steamship in the 1870s—had opened new routes to Europe, and with them, an influx of grain, meat, and fruit from overseas that undercut European prices year after year. New refrigerator ships made the problem worse; bananas sent daily from the tropics demonstrated that Europe was simply too rich to compete with more upstart countries.

It wasn't that France, England, Germany, and Spain couldn't use their wealth to experiment. For centuries explorers had delivered to these countries foods from the most remote places on earth. But self-sufficiency had eclipsed innovation. Europe's patchwork of small countries separated by different laws and governments left little land to experiment on. That, and little energy for reinvention. Countries that built themselves as social democracies offered less incentive for their people to create things new and dynamic. At least compared to a young nation like the United States, whose past was far less interesting than its future.

Unfortunately, Fairchild never made it to the Buffalo exposition. He was in Europe at the time, which left him oblivious to what these farmers were saying about his crops, and about their appetites in general. This information would have been exceedingly valuable in helping him choose where to go next and what kinds of crops to prioritize.

Even more unfortunate: news of the agricultural bounty in Buffalo would not be the most-remembered part of the fair.

One warm day in early September, as the summer slowly turned to fall, President McKinley visited the fairgrounds in Buffalo. He wanted to see the agriculture hall for himself, and to crow in a grand speech about America on the rise. "This country is in a state of unexampled prosperity," he said, and then rattled off all the ways the railroads, the telegraph, and the steamships were connecting America to the world as never before. As it happened, it was the last speech McKinley would ever give. While shaking hands afterward, McKinley came face-to-face with a man who fired two bullets into the president's chest. The man was a disturbed anarchist who believed America was benefiting only the rich, and that McKinley was as good as anyone to blame.

The president lived for another week, alert and joking ("How did they like my speech?"). But when the gangrene set in, the first president of the twentieth century, a man enthusiastic about American prosperity and unapologetic about whom it clobbered along the way, fell asleep and never woke up.

CHAPTER TWELVE

On the Banks
of the Tigris

Fairchild took several months off from traveling after McKinley's death. The country was in grief, and he needed rest. He had been in near motion for three years.

The majority of those years he had spent with Barbour Lathrop. But his last trip to Germany and through Europe had been entirely on his own. Fairchild didn't seem to mind the solitude, but the sudden absence of companionship had stung Lathrop like a ripped-off bandage. Lathrop practically demanded that Fairchild return to the United States via Maine (rather than Washington), where Lathrop's sister, Florence, owned property in Bar Harbor. The town had grown into one of America's most stylish resorts, the summer home of J. P. Morgan and Joseph Pulitzer, the latter of whom built a hundred-thousand-dollar "cottage" there with modern plumbing. Fairchild obliged, and he and Lathrop spent a week together on Florence's land in a bungalow beside the water. The two had developed a habit of talking late into the night—sharing travel stories and jokes. One evening, sometime between when the sun went down and when it came up, they planned another jaunt to the other side of the world.

Not long after, Fairchild left for Los Angeles. The Office of Seed and Plant Introduction had grown into a premier government office, so important that more people—eventually twenty-four—had been hired to do the work, receiving and distributing seeds, that Fairchild once did alone. He was in demand.

The hunt for plants started as philanthropy. But by 1902, finding ways to help farmers had become a top government priority. Still, despite the impressive display in Buffalo, people whose livelihoods relied on growing food weren't entirely content. Seeds had helped diversify fields and raise incomes, but farmers were facing new problems. In Washington, groups of farmers protested at the Capitol against mechanized farm equipment that saved time and reduced labor, like the combined harvester-thresher (also known as the combine) and the gasoline-powered tractor. So what if they made farming easier? New machines cost money, eliminated jobs, and gave early adopters a leg up. Everyone else wished such innovations didn't exist.

These types of advances in farming, crops, and equipment pushed people out. When Fairchild was born in 1869, one in four American workers farmed. A generation later, it was one in five. What would normally be good news instead laid bare a pesky side effect of innovation: greater efficiency requires fewer workers, leaving rural communities with little to support themselves. The irony was that the fewer people who remained on farms were producing more food of greater variety than any generation before them.

The Los Angeles where Fairchild arrived was a city of dairy and citrusmen. Before movie stars or pop musicians, the most notable people in Los Angeles seemed to be land developers, who had visions for how Southern California could take advantage of its temperate climate and more natural resources than one hundred thousand people could possibly need. The 1890s had revealed, miraculously, that there was oil under Los Angeles.

The real estate developers were in the business of marketing land, and that required endorsements. Southern California newspapers had publicized the government's plant-hunting success, crediting

Fairchild, Swingle, and his colleagues with new strains of wheat, barley, and dates.

This made Fairchild a sort of celebrity. He wrote of his arrival, "They were soon at my heels begging for favorable comparisons between the fertility of the Nile Valley and the fertility of the land which composed their particular holdings, notwithstanding the fact that much of their land was white with alkali." To someone trying to sell land, the Nile Valley in Egypt meant soil fertility the same way Paris stood for love and Bavaria for beer. Fairchild explained repeatedly that fertility isn't innate, but a product of regular flooding that renews nutrients. When the Nile floods, the influx of water brings new phosphorus and nitrogen, both fuel for plant growth. But he left with the impression that the developers either didn't understand, or didn't care to.

From California, Fairchild crossed the Pacific. His ship stopped briefly in Hawaii, the island kingdom that, since his last visit, had become a territory of the United States, taken by force against the wishes of forty thousand native Hawaiians, who signed two petitions—one for men and the other for women—protesting United States annexation. A Nevada congressman responded to the documents by introducing a resolution declaring, dishonestly, that the Hawaiian government wanted to cede its rights of sovereignty to the United States. If Guam and the Philippines were examples of America humbly supporting the abandoned lands of a former colonizer, Hawaii was evidence of America's brash bullying, taking something valuable without bothering to ask anyone's permission.

History remembers this era as a period of national bombast, when America's polar political parties united to make bold demands of the world, and if denied, to press forward anyway. But that attitude wasn't shared by everyone. In pockets of America's large and small towns, it wasn't hard to see irony in how the United States, a former colony that rebelled against mistreatment, seemed eager to act as a colonial bully itself. And as much as Fairchild benefited from a world suddenly open to America's hunger, he found deep discomfort watching indigenous people steamrollered by imperial lust. "I cannot but be sad that such a happy people, living in peace and plenty, should ever have been discovered by the white man and decimated by his diseases and civilization," Fairchild later remarked about the Hawaiian Islands. "I am glad that I saw a few of the quiet places of the world before the coming of automobiles and jazz."

Fairchild secured lines of communication in Hawaii, which was easier this time (with his government endorsement) than his last attempt, when he was a free agent. On account of Fairchild's success, Secretary Wilson had ordered a new experiment station on Oahu and another in Puerto Rico, to receive tropical plants deemed too fragile for a detour through Washington. Wilson was especially interested in coffee, spices, and rubber, all tropical products Americans were increasingly using, but that no American farm had yet been able to harvest at scale.

As the boat continued farther west across the Pacific, Fairchild used the long voyage to ask questions of fellow passengers. He would often ask, "What is the most remarkable fruit you've ever eaten?" and then scribble furiously as the person pulled up some recollection from their childhood. A Chinese minister's wife told him about two new fruits, the Chinese bayberry and the longan, both walnut-sized fruits that, thanks to this conversation, would end up growing in Florida.

Unexpectedly, the ship stopped in Japan on account of an approaching typhoon, and then again in Hong Kong, where Fairchild rode a small boat upriver to Canton. This was his second visit, but this time he looked for peaches. The Chinese ate them green, so he sent unripe specimens to Washington, where they were used for breed stock with the more popular peach varieties arriving from Persia. He also collected samples of persimmons, ginger, and olives.

Rarely did Americans visit India at the turn of the century. It was faraway, unknown, and rumored to have violent clashes between untamed Indians and the noble British. On paper, India belonged to the British Empire, but there was no way anyone could have constrained India's cultural force, a hurricane of life, energy, and enterprise. "Look where one will, whether by day or by night, everywhere he will find men living, and trying to live and making the most of their earthly career," Rajendralal Mitra, one of India's top cultural scholars, once said of Bombay; the description seems to transcend all time. Fairchild sat in a place where women in long yellow and red robes, their wrists covered with imitation pearls and emeralds, danced before him to earn a few coppers. Still, India, like most places outside of America and Europe in 1901, was moored in disease. Cholera and bubonic plague seemed to feast on the squalor of human density, where houses were built atop other houses with little circulation of air—"an insanitary labyrinth," a British doctor called it. Fairchild's visions of his earlier battle with typhoid likely contributed to his not wanting to stay in Bombay long, especially when he noticed that the boys preparing food in even the most Western hotels had dirty hands.

Fairchild knew, however, that disease kept people away. In places where it lurked was also the possibility of plants few Westerners had seen before. "The best Indian mangoes grow on this side of the peninsula," said a man named Douglas Bennett, a Scot, in response to Fairchild's questioning. Hundreds of mango varieties were to be found in India, but the Alphonso mango was the most popular. It was also the best example of early globalization— the fruit was introduced by the Portuguese, who had picked it up somewhere in South Asia in the sixteenth century and named it after a Portuguese general, Afonso de Albuquerque.

"I'll give you some cuttings of the finest strain of Alphonso, on one condition," Bennett said. "You must name it after me."

The Alphonso was indisputably best. But Fairchild was skeptical that there could be an even *better* subspecies that was sweeter and less stringy. He was used to such grand endorsements for fruit that turned out to be mediocre. Still, he indulged the oddness of the request.

"I must see the tree myself," Fairchild said. "If it is indeed superior to mangoes Europeans and Americans have tasted, then yes, you have a deal."

The fruit checked out. Its sunset yellow flesh was tender, its flavor fruity and tropical. What made it distinct was the thinness of its shiny skin, and its slim stone, not much thicker than his finger. The Douglas Bennett Alphonso mango landed in the United States along with about eighty other mango varieties that Fairchild sent. His shipments became bigger and bigger, and he fashioned the abundance and selection of mangoes as an insurance policy for the growers in Florida, who could surely find one they liked among dozens of varieties. The Douglas Bennett Alphonso would turn out to be good for Florida and Hawaii, but not great, at least when compared to the mangoes that arrived over the next decade. Its flavor became average in a country that demanded dynamic.

Fairchild could know none of this. All he knew was that he needed to work fast. One of the stories that would follow Fairchild through the rest of his life was of the day a steamer was sounding its horn at Bombay's busy port. A captain told him his overflowing baskets of mangoes were too large to take on board. So, with minutes to spare, Fairchild hired a group of children to eat more than a hundred mangoes, stripping them of their worthless flesh. He piled the centers into a small basket of wet charcoal as the kids chomped, giggled, and licked the stones clean.

Fairchild would find Baghdad captivating, perhaps in part owing to how difficult it had been to get there. A military ship was the only transportation he could find up the Persian Gulf, but before he could board, an officer told him he'd have to be vaccinated for plague. Fairchild rode a squeaky rickshaw into Karachi, to the home of a man known for vaccinating; the man tipped a young calf infected with smallpox on its side and scraped a scab on its belly with a rusted needle, then brought the needle to Fairchild's arm. Straining to be polite, he let the man continue, but quickly after, Fairchild rubbed the wound with disinfectant, which reversed the inoculation and left him open to diseases far worse than any transmitted by the calf.

The border officials knew none of this, and Fairchild was granted permission to continue north. But two days later, there was a commotion on the ship about a case of plague, a Shiite pilgrim, one of five hundred who were going to visit the birthplace of Hussein, the grandson of the Prophet Muhammad. The plague on board would have prevented the ship from entering any new port, leaving it floating in purgatory. Fairchild was not devastated when he learned the man had "fallen" and broken his neck, thus allowing the ship to remain uncontaminated ("It certainly is a good way out of the mess," the captain said). The man's body was tied to a block of coal and thrown into the Persian Gulf. So little care was given the corpse that it somersaulted and splashed headfirst, which brought shrieks from his fellow pilgrims on board who saw the sloppy burial as a sign of mortal disrespect. Fairchild and another man helped calm the pilgrims and prevent a mutiny. Not long after fish started to investigate the new body on the bottom of the Gulf, all talk about the man stopped. The episode rattled Fairchild enough that he decided to sleep on the deck of the boat, where ocean air blew in gusts.

Thinking the trip couldn't get more uncomfortable, he was awoken at dawn by pilgrims who prayed loudly each morning, their prostrated bodies facing Mecca. As the ship approached southern Iraq, Turkish authorities, who had somehow learned of the case of plague, ordered the vessel quarantined. Fairchild was lucky—he had white skin, which limited his quarantine to only one week. He spent seven days sandwiched between pilgrims, passing time with a handmade slingshot constructed from two forks and an elastic band, which he used to target chirping sparrows. He refused the quarantine food and ate only boiled onions.

The final insult, once he was released from quarantine, was that as soon as the outline of Baghdad was in sight, the small boat puttering up the Tigris River ran aground. Someone told Fairchild it was an old Mississippi steamboat that somehow found a second life as an unreliable water shuttle seven thousand miles away. Fairchild finally ran out of patience. He tossed his tripod and trunk over the side of the ship, dragged them ashore, and, making deep footprints in the riverbank, completed the final stretch to Baghdad the way people had for thousands of years—on foot.

If there was a silver lining, something to make the hellish voyage even partly worth the effort, it was that somewhere between the vaccination, the boats, the quarantine, and the long walk, Fairchild met a man who mentioned a smooth-skinned peach known as a nectarine that could be found in the city of Quetta, a part of modern Pakistan. Considering the hardships of the hot desert landscape, where at every mile lurked a new danger, he declined to investigate. Instead, he asked the man to send him seeds, and the man eventually did. The close, fuzzless relative of peaches was first mentioned by American botanists in 1722. But Fairchild's Quetta nectarines took less than four years to become the most popular variety in America, a country hungry for novelty. Farmers in Iowa, Texas, and California later sent Washington deeply grateful letters for such a large yellow fruit, splashed with yellow and carmine, with a tart sweetness, and deemed a terrific candidate for shipping. ("This we believe to be the best of all nectarines . . . its large size, firm skin, and flesh make it particularly desirable," one horticulturalist in Chico, California, wrote.) This appetite for better fruit, however, was in every way insatiable, and so not long after the Quetta's rise came its inevitable replacements. But genealogy has secured the Quetta's presence for the long term—parts of the Quetta can still be found in nearly every nectarine grown commercially in the United States.

Meanwhile, Baghdad lived up to its allure. For thousands of years, the city had been the biggest intersection of the world, a bazaar containing great riches of a lush era of Islam. The palaces that had housed caliphate leaders for eight centuries still stood, yet the city had begun to change with the opening of new markets that received goods from ports around the globe. Iron from England, wood from Sweden, spirits from France, and porcelain dishware called china—which took its name from its origin—were all traded daily, their exotic provenance earning high prices. Consolidators assembled bulk shipments of wheat bound for London and sheep hides for America.

Sand flies bit everyone, regardless of status. But Baghdad residents could be identified by the volume of bites on their foreheads. Over time the bites would bleed, scab, and then scar into dime-sized marks known as "Baghdad buttons." Fairchild gawked openly at the customs of Muslim people. "Women in black gowns and masks instinctively turned their backs for fear that I might see their faces," he wrote. "A camel caravan passed—a family moving from one desert place to another, its women hidden from public gaze by an enormous basketlike arrangement covered with gay cloths. I even saw whirling dervishes, whom I had always believed to be inventions of Barnum & Bailey."

Elbowing his way through crowded bazaars, Fairchild amassed hundreds of dates, some dry, some sticky with hardened syrup. The place where humans had farmed for centuries was also a good place to pick up new strains of wheat, millet, barley, chickpea, and even maize. Unable to read Arabic, Fairchild almost certainly collected seeds and samples that had come to Baghdad from far-flung parts of the world—perhaps even North America—without knowing, only to send them back home with a foreign postmark.

His stays were becoming shorter, both for efficiency and because of his wariness of stigma toward Americans. Foreigners tended to view early-twentieth-century America as a paragon of modernity—a stable government, a creative population, a buoyant economy.

1902. In Baghdad, the intersection of world civilizations, Fairchild visited bazaars in search of the novel and exotic. On the outskirts of the city, men covered their piles of barley and wheat with large mats to protect them from hungry sparrows and the heavy morning dew.

But much like China's rise in the twenty-first century, America's also brought an air of skepticism.

Few people knew the United States' intentions, or how it would wield its growing power.

Fairchild left Baghdad with arm muscles bulging under the weight of fully formed fruit. He might've found it easier to acquire suckers, the base offshoots of date trees, yet Fairchild knew suckers could die on a nine-week ocean voyage, so he decided to take both fruit and suckers, an insurance policy in hopes one would live.

He spread mud on the deck of the boat that carried him away. The captain watched bemused while Fairchild laid down the suckers, doused them in water, and then rolled them through the mud. When the dirt dried hard as clay, he wrapped it all in sackcloth to retain the moisture. Because of either Fairchild's ingenuity or a simple stroke of luck, the suckers made the ocean voyage alive.

In the years following shipments like Fairchild's, the date industry elevated the American West. Dates came to populate Southern California in a way no crop had before. By the 1910s, growers were taking the next step in agricultural innovation by selecting the dates that grew best in the microclimates of Southern California. One of those dates, the Deglet Noor, infused life and economic vitality into California's Coachella Valley by exploiting soil and climate nearly identical to the Arabian Peninsula's. The influence was so appreciated that in the 1930s, Coachella Valley High School named its mascot "the Arab," not from cartoonish racism but, officials argued, in honor of an agricultural gift as meaningful to Coachella as Lady Liberty had been to New York.

The Indian Ocean, azure and clear with clashing calm, passed by without any remarkable thought from Fairchild. Despite the perception of global travel as the height of glamour, the actual demands of spending long voyages on boats and docking in cities full of diseases were beginning to show signs of wear on a man who had by now circled the globe nearly three times. In his journal, in place

1905. One of the first date palms in Walters, California, an area so enriched by Arabian dates that, ten years later, officials renamed the town "Mecca" in tribute to the Muslim holy city.

of his earlier boyish fascination with discovering new things, he started to dwell on the hardships of travel. "The food was bad on the boat and everybody was very tired of it" was all that he wrote on the ship from which he departed the Persian Gulf. He was not only wary of disease, but in the diversity of all he had seen, he had become sensitive to items of low quality and the distracting drama of people fighting. Because of his aversion to violence, he avoided Karachi, where he was told he would have needed a personal guard, and instead entrusted a few dozen dollars to two fellow travelers and asked them to send more date suckers to the United States. The travelers complied, but their naïve efforts proved worthless when the plants, their roots cut too short, arrived dead.

From India, he could have gone anywhere, but he moved quickly toward Japan. Barbour Lathrop was on an adventure of his own and had suggested they meet in Yokohama, near Tokyo, a destination requiring twenty-eight days of transit.

When his boat laid over in Saigon, then a French colony, Fairchild came across a French botanist as eager to introduce new plants to France's colonies as Fairchild was to bring them to America. Plant exploration had become more common, especially for countries with colonies to support with new crops. The Frenchman helped Fairchild find mangoes and mangosteens, two unrelated fruits. In all his travels, Fairchild would come to describe the mangosteen, with its purple rind and wedges of white flesh, as "the queen of tropical fruits. . . . It has a beautiful white fruit pulp, more delicate than that of a plum, and a flavor that is indescribably delicate and delicious." He speculated that "its purple brown rind will . . . bring fancy prices wherever it is offered for sale."

This prediction proved flat wrong when American farmers found the mangosteen's skin too thick, its flesh too small, and its shape too oblong to produce at large scale. That would be especially disappointing to Fairchild. For a man who had seen dozens of countries and thousands of fruits, he would go so far as to call the mangosteen his favorite.

The port of Yokohama was strewn with small fishing boats and straw-hatted men, who all looked up at the site of a steamer pulling to dock. Having spent a month on a boat, any passenger would burn with desperation to escape the rocking and rediscover his balance. Fairchild knew to stand at the gangplank to be the first to disembark the ship. The air was heavy with the odor of fish. As the passengers left the steamer, the boatsmen returned to their nets, alive with twitching silver. Fairchild made his way to Lathrop's hotel, as eager to see his friend as he was to hear English again after a month at sea.

"Don't move!" Lathrop shouted. He was sitting up in bed, newspapers covering his lap. He had a cold, and doctors, fearing something serious, had ordered him to stay horizontal. With Fairchild frozen, Lathrop clutched a paper funnel and with two fingers tapped tiny brown shavings into a beer bottle.

"I had a hell of a time getting this seed and since those fellows in Washington want it for breeding I don't propose to lose it now," Lathrop said, still without looking up.

While Fairchild had been exploring India and Iraq, Lathrop had hunted tobacco in Southeast Asia, stopping in Singapore and Java. He chatted up local gardeners and farmers in hopes of finding the valuable Deli strain of tobacco, which northeast American farmers wanted as a replacement for their inferior varieties. He finally struck gold in Sumatra. Lathrop flattered Sumatran growers with lavish praise for their agricultural wisdom, from which America could learn, but when he eventually asked for seeds in a "peaceful exchange" between the two peoples, he was laughed out of the room. Rebuffed, he let loose with his usual candor about the stupidity of the tobacco growers. One grower saw opportunity in Lathrop's desperation and later visited him with an offer to secretly sell him a small sample of seed at a steep price, more than thirty dollars. The wealthy Lathrop happily accepted and the man sent the seed. In Lathrop's later retelling of this story, the man apparently died before receiving his payment, thus allowing Lathrop, in his own estimation, to emerge victorious.

"What kept you so long?" he asked Fairchild after the tobacco dust was packed. "You missed the Japanese flowering cherry trees. However, I suppose you got a lot of date palms. I would like to have seen Baghdad with you but I knew you would collect more stuff if I were not along. Besides, I imagine the food was pretty bad, wasn't it? Anyway, I've missed you. I've been laid up in the hotel for a couple of weeks now. . . . I'm in no shape to go around with you. You can do better work alone anyhow."

Traces of the former senior-junior relationship had dissipated, as made clear by Lathrop's eagerness to see again the younger man with whom he could indulge the most bombastic and grandiose versions of himself without fear of being ostracized or judged.

Indeed, the reason that Fairchild had rushed to Japan, without stopping for any additional exploration, was to glimpse the Japanese flowering cherry trees. Lore of the trees was known all over East Asia, and some horticulturists in Washington knew of the trees' great springtime beauty. Fairchild wondered if the cherry trees, which didn't produce actual cherries but only pink blossoms, would be attractive to farmers.

Probably not, was his conclusion, and so he sent only a few dozen cuttings to officials in California, who were so confused when the branches and roots turned up in 1903 that they neglected them in the broiling sun of California's Central Valley. Only years later would it dawn on Fairchild that the United States' *East* Coast would be best for flowering cherries, and specifically Washington, D.C.

For most of the stay in Japan that summer, Lathrop was too worn-out to explore, so Fairchild continued the type of solo adventuring that he enjoyed. Of all the countries Fairchild had visited, Japan struck him as the most advanced on matters of horticulture. He learned about Japanese miniature gardens, the art of Japanese papermaking, and the superior qualities of Japanese fruits and vegetables that didn't grow anywhere else in the world. Wealthy people introduced him to foods of affluence, like raw fish, seaweed, and a bean cheese they called tofu. He thought it impossible to eat with two narrow sticks held in one hand, but after a few tries, he got the feel for it.

It was in Japan that Fairchild picked up a yellow plum known as a loquat and an asparagus-like vegetable called udo. And a so-called puckerless persimmon that turned sweet in sake wine casks. One of the most unrecognized discoveries of Fairchild, a man drawn to edible fruits and vegetables, was zoysia grass, a rich green lawn specimen attractive for the thickness of its blades and its slow growth, which meant it required infrequent cutting.

And then there was wasabi, a plant growing along streambeds in the mountains near Osaka. It had edible leaves, but wasabi's stronger quality was its bitter root's uncanny ability to burn one's nose. Wasabi only lasted in America until farmers realized that its close relative the horseradish root grew faster and larger and was more pungent than the delicate wasabi (which tends to stay pungent only fifteen minutes after it's cut). Small American farms still grow Fairchild's wasabi, but most of the accompaniment to modern sushi is in fact horseradish—mashed, colored, and called something it's not.

As weeks fell by, Fairchild found that he enjoyed the horticultural lessons Japan had to teach. Not to mention the social discipline lacking in the hurried avenues of the United States. The quietest days of Fairchild's life were spent in bamboo gardens near Tokyo. One afternoon in the late golden light, amid tall green stalks and the soft rustle of leaves in the wind, Fairchild took an hour, maybe even two, to sit silently and meditate.

CHAPTER THIRTEEN

Bell's Grand Plan

In August of 1903, upon his return to Washington, Fairchild's reputation preceded him and he received an invitation to speak to the National Geographic Society. Fairchild had heard of the elite club that fancied itself the headquarters of well-traveled and adventurous men. He had offhandedly written a story in 1898 about his travels in Java for the society's struggling journal. But to be invited into the lion's den filled with the country's most learned, wealthy, and well-connected men was an honor extended to few. The invitation came from Gilbert Grosvenor one evening in the parlor of the Cosmos Club. Grosvenor remarked that, considering all he had heard, he thought Fairchild would have a white beard. It was a polite way of saying Fairchild looked young.

Grosvenor, with slick black hair parted on his left, wasn't old, either—just twenty-eight—nor was he worldly. His job as editor of the *National Geographic* magazine had come from a series of nepotistic favors. Alexander Graham Bell, the famed inventor and one of the bearded men who unquestionably belonged in the Geographic's marbled meetinghouse, had gotten Grosvenor the job. Grosvenor had married Bell's daughter Elsie, and not long after, Bell lobbied the society's council to secure his new son-in-law a stable income. Grosvenor had no experience running a magazine, but he was given the keys to the publication with the imperative to build it, or at the very least, to keep it alive.

Fairchild had a healthy ego by now, letting his head grow with his reputation as "one of the most extensively traveled men in the world," according to a 1904 profile in *The Houston Post*. He spent evenings in all-male clubs, chiefly the Cosmos, which one historian later called "the closest thing to a social headquarters for Washington's intellectual elite." He was regularly quoted in newspapers and fielded frequent questions as a horticultural authority.

One reason for Fairchild's inflated confidence may have been his obliviousness about social Washington. Except for a few weeks of respite, Fairchild had been absent from the city nearly half a decade, during which Washington bloomed with the youthful energy of Teddy Roosevelt. Roosevelt approached governing with the same force he once brought to battle in Cuba, evading any attack thrown at him. He courted members of Congress on long horseback rides. He built a briefing room near his office to curry favor with journalists. He renamed the executive mansion the "White House" and got rid of its passé Victorian décor. Then he started to invite young people inside for dances and social events.

Fairchild missed all of it and knew virtually no one. If the sage men of the National Geographic Society had wide renown, Fairchild knew almost nothing about them.

That was especially true of Bell, the burly and whiskered Scottish-American inventor. Even in 1904, Alexander Graham Bell was a household name, the kind that made audiences applaud and cheer in appreciation for his magical creation that transmitted a human voice by electrical current. Three decades after its invention, very few houses had a telephone, but everyone knew about it.

Standing before a roomful of white beards and puffed mustaches, Fairchild hadn't the slightest idea what Bell looked like. Every man in the audience looked the same. So he tailored his speech to no one in particular.

Fairchild delivered the pitch that he had by now refined over thousands of conversations. "The government enterprise of Plant

Introduction [is] to introduce and establish in America as many of the valuable crops of the world as can be grown here. [It's] to educate the farmer in their culture and the public in their use—to increase by this, one of the most powerful means, the agricultural wealth of the country." He detailed the greatest successes—the Japanese rice, the Corsican citron, the tropical mango. He explained how importing dates had created a new industry in California, with millions of dollars at stake. His presentation demonstrated the kind of political awareness that most men never find, the clairvoyance to understand when the government must invest before profit-driven companies can rush in and improve.

> [Acquiring plants and producing food] are problems that private enterprise will not naturally undertake; they are problems that concern the wealth-producing power of American soil; they are problems that the government has shown its ability to solve in a manner involving an insignificant outlay of the public funds. They encourage the production of food and other products that we now import from other lands, and they concern the establishment of farm industries which, for generations to come, will support hundreds of thousands, perhaps millions, of American citizens.

When he finished, the men lined up to shake Fairchild's hand and tell him how their lives once intersected with the contents of his remarks. The line slowly grew shorter until, at the end, Grosvenor approached him with news that Bell had invited Fairchild to his weekly Wednesday gathering at his home in Dupont Circle. "Wednesday Evenings" were shorthand for Bell's private salons, which some believed held more prestige than a visit to the White House. In the moments after he accepted the invitation, Fairchild had the impulse to buy a new suit and visit a barber.

Fairchild's return to Washington was different this time, primarily in how it formed a punctuation mark at the end of his lengthy travels. He was tired and longed for consistency. He wanted to sleep in a bed where the horizon didn't shift. Almost penniless, he needed a regular salary. And at thirty-four, he wondered whether he might spend less time searching for plants and more time finding a wife.

Fairchild didn't cower when he visited Secretary Wilson. It was his third return to Washington, his third time unemployed. Wilson had so benefited from Fairchild's fearless and pro bono work on behalf of the Department that he couldn't possibly refuse Fairchild's request for a job. But he did reveal his slight but still unquenchable resentment for Fairchild's unprofessional departure in 1898. When it was time to discuss Fairchild's salary, Wilson offered one thousand dollars per year, the equivalent of a paltry fifty thousand dollars today for a man of lofty education and worldly experience. Even less flattering, Wilson assigned Fairchild the cumbersome work of compiling an inventory of all plants imported into the United States since 1900.

The Department of Agriculture had ballooned since the early days when Fairchild was a junior botanist. A few dozen employees had become four thousand. "This branch of our government had become one of the greatest research centers in the world," Fairchild noticed. The Department had outgrown its offices so frequently that agriculture officials overflowed into the Treasury and State offices. At this pace, the Department of Agriculture's modest redbrick headquarters would be demolished and replaced in the 1930s with a vast marble complex, sprawling in its reach and purpose, with more than four thousand rooms. It was, at that time, the largest office building in the world.

Four months passed before Fairchild could arrange the scattered memos and mailing labels for the inventory, which together amounted to 4,396 introduced plants. In his introduction to the inventory, Fairchild thanked everyone who had contributed seeds, eleven people in all. Yet he also puffed his well-formed ego. He made clear that most items tallied had come from "the writer" of the document—himself.

Meanwhile, the enduring feud between Wilson and Lathrop, now just embers from an earlier flame, still left Lathrop unpaid the full recognition he thought himself owed. Fairchild's new position provided him the full means to thank his benefactor himself. "Of the nearly 4,400 new introductions, a very large number represent work accomplished by the explorations of Mr. Barbour Lathrop of Chicago, with whom [I] had the pleasure of being associated as Agricultural Explorer," Fairchild wrote in the report—a copy of which was sent to the president. "Mr. Lathrop's explorations, which have required about four years of travel abroad, were carried out with the one practical object of making a reconnaissance of the useful plant possibilities of the world, and have successfully covered every continent and touched every important archipelago." He called Lathrop a "public-spirited man," further tipping the government's hat to Lathrop's philanthropy, and knowing how satisfying Lathrop would find it.

The assertion of "every continent" made Fairchild especially proud. No one counted Antarctica—barely had Ernest Shackleton even embarked south of the eighty-second parallel—but the boast did include Africa. Despite having visited, Fairchild knew much remained on the vast continent to be explored. Egypt was a cosmopolitan meeting place, yet below the Sahara Desert, the land remained largely untouched except by European colonists. Lathrop had urged Fairchild to visit Africa before settling down, not only because he believed it would have new plants, but because Lathrop was a man known to do things solely to brag about them later. So Fairchild's final trip before he returned to Washington, before he spoke to the National Geographic Society, and before he met a woman who would captivate him, was, as he put it, to "circumnavigate Africa."

Visiting Africa was indeed boastworthy. Few Westerners went, most kept away by racist caricatures of uncivilized tribespeople. In 1898, the Royal Geographical Society had sent the British explorer Ewart Grogan to walk from Cape Town to Cairo, along the way exploring what he called the "pygmies" of uncontacted tribes. "This obviously entails a great risk," Grogan wrote. His widely published dispatches compared the tribal men to "dog-faced baboons." Grogan, himself neither an anthropologist nor a biologist, showed little shame in questioning whether the "savage" people of Africa were in fact the missing link of Darwinism, the bridge between wild primates and modern humans.

Fairchild avoided drawing this conclusion—which he would have found scientifically suspect if not intuitively far-fetched—in part because he didn't venture too far inland. An ocean-based voyage wasn't the best way to discover a wide piece of land, but it did allow expedience and safety. "I was much disappointed, for I had hoped to find something worthwhile, and felt sure that there would be many things if we had time enough to get into the interior," Fairchild recalled. The coast was made even less remarkable by the fact that most shoreline had been colonized in Europe's power struggles between Britain, France, Germany, Italy, Belgium, Spain, and Portugal, which were really a fight over the continent's commodities, including palm oil, rubber, and cotton. The bickering over land had become so heated that in 1894 the German chancellor Otto von Bismarck convened a summit in Berlin to divide up Africa and its resources. Everyone was invited, except for any Africans themselves.

There were other barriers to plant collecting in Africa for Fairchild. East Africa had few harbors, and landing required an unreliable

1903. Undeveloped harbors on the east coast of Africa meant large steamships couldn't dock. Passengers venturing ashore, like Fairchild, had to be loaded into wicker baskets and lowered into smaller boats.

method of being lowered in a clothes basket into a small dinghy next to a ship—which was especially perilous in choppy seas. In Mozambique, Fairchild picked up a small, perfectly round fruit. It was a Kaffir orange, named for the pejorative term for black Africans who ate it. Only one orange made it back to the ship, where it hardened like a rock; Fairchild had to use a hatchet to break open its dried-solid skin. Inside was brown flesh with the taste of a ripe banana.

Farther south, Durban yielded the carissa plum, deep red in color and with white leaves that resembled those of a tropical plumeria. Fairchild sent a case to Florida, believing the mix of foliage and fruit would prove an attractive combination (he was right). A chef in Cape Town delighted Fairchild with an outlandish fruit—a personal-sized pineapple, no bigger than a drinking glass—that he believed could change the world. "We tore the pineapples to pieces with our forks, and, to our astonishment, found scarcely any core. Also they were far sweeter than any we had ever tasted, and had practically no fiber," he wrote. He saved the tops and sent them in.

Wouldn't every American want a pint-sized pineapple all to themselves, the way they were used to eating a banana or apple with no need to share? No was the answer. Growers in Florida and Hawaii weren't interested in small; the people wanted big, even bigger pineapples than already grown, no matter the weight or the cost of shipping. So Fairchild's giddiness, the kind a grown man could find only from a personal-sized pineapple, was brashly extinguished.

Alexander Graham Bell's home was located just south of Dupont Circle, at 1331 Connecticut Avenue. One of the most elegant in Washington, it was a house befitting a man of Bell's prestige: a bespoke three-story redbrick mansion, angular and boxy, with a circular staircase, a grand parlor lined with fine oak, and pregnant windows that swelled out toward the street on every floor—all in the precise taste of Bell and his wife, Mabel, for an immodest thirty-one-thousand dollars. Money flowed freely in the years after Bell demonstrated the telephone, which contributed to America's growing reputation as a land of opportunity for immigrants. The inventor had risen from tragic circumstances: tuberculosis killed his two brothers, which spurred the family to move from the United Kingdom to Canada, and then to America. The move to North America opened a path for young Bell to soar higher than Great Britain would allow. The most remarkable thing about Bell wasn't his famous inventions, but that in thirty years he rose from frazzled immigrant to denizen of the highest level of America's intellectual elite.

In a way, Bell was one of many. In the years around the turn of the century, men of science found Washington to be a city in renaissance, a place where casual conversations among a roomful of men could yield dramatic expansions of government. One effect of reconstruction after the Civil War had been the government's eagerness to rebuild, which it did by funding scientific associations. Around the same time men were inking the charter for the National Geographic Society, other scientific societies sprouted, including the American Biological Society, the American Chemical Society, the American Anthropological Association, and a society for entomology enthusiasts. By 1900, there were too few men to sustain the profusion of societies, on whose rosters, one after another, often appeared the same names, leaving one to wonder if the few hundred men needed an excuse to escape their families two, three, even four nights a week.

Each Wednesday evening at seven o'clock, twenty men in three-piece suits would gather in Bell's downstairs parlor, where they would mingle until their host escorted his aged father, Alexander Melville Bell, a man born in 1819, to a chair in the center of the room. Bell would make opening remarks, perhaps giving the evening a theme such as "exploration" or "curiosity." Then he'd invite one man to speak about science or the arts. The senior Bell was unquestionably proud to see his son the nucleus of such cerebral energy. Melville had provided the inspiration for his son's inventiveness, even though Alexander's father-in-law provided the push. Gardiner Hubbard wouldn't permit his daughter Mabel to marry the scatterbrained inventor until Bell got serious about a single project. Only after Bell patented the telephone in 1876 did Hubbard allow the wedding to proceed.

Bell, in his high-minded scheming, had a similar plan for Fairchild, whom he had only observed once, and had never formally met. But Fairchild reminded Bell of his younger self, ambitious yet capricious, established but with much still to accomplish. Fairchild didn't know this. He sat in the corner hoping no one questioned whether he belonged. As he tried to follow the discussion, he became distracted by the titles on Bell's bookshelf. He later described the scene that delighted him:

> Mr. Bell was at his charming best on these occasions, for he enjoyed his guests, drawing them out with courteous and interesting questions. You were conscious of his dominant personality the moment he entered a room; his thick grey hair curled back from a high, sloping forehead, and he had a full beard and extraordinary eyes, large and dark, under heavy eyebrows. Mr. Bell was tall and handsome with an indefinable sense of largeness about him, and he so radiated vigor and kindliness that any pettiness of thought seemed to fade away beneath his keen gaze. He always made you feel that there was so much of interest in the universe, so many fascinating things to observe and to think about, that it was a criminal waste of time to indulge in gossip or trivial discussion.

Bell loved the discourse, but the real purpose of the salon was to forge bonds between different disciplines, where overlap could yield new discoveries. A chemist meeting an entomologist, or an environmentalist brainstorming with an engineer. Fairchild's first Wednesday Evening salon brought about two lasting relationships of his own.

The first was with Alford Cooley, the government's civil service commissioner, who had enviable status as a member of Theodore Roosevelt's "tennis cabinet." The group, as Cooley explained to Fairchild, was informal, a friendly alternative to Roosevelt's stuffy panel of serious advisers. A profile of the tennis cabinet in *The New York Times* described the group thus: "The President joked, they laughed; the President talked, they listened; the President played tennis, they lost." Cooley, whom the paper described as "the strenuousest of the strenuous," and the four other members of the faux cabinet were so close to the president that they advised Roosevelt on matters ranging from statecraft to spelling, and were the influential force behind adding "In God We Trust" to American coins.

It was through Cooley that, one day in April of 1903, Fairchild first came to meet Roosevelt. Little is recorded about their interaction except that the president, skilled at putting people at ease, congratulated Fairchild for the work he had done on America's behalf. Roosevelt made an offhanded suggestion that planted itself in Fairchild's mind, that a man of such worldly knowledge and experience could be useful if he stayed still for a while, and particularly in Washington.

The second person Fairchild came to know at Bell's salons was of a different sort. She was his age and fair skinned with long brown hair and slender fingers.

Bell's plan lurched into motion. After several Wednesday Evenings at the Bell mansion, Fairchild received an invitation to Gilbert and Elsie Grosvenor's house for an intimate dinner. It was Bell's idea, and he asked his daughter to arrange it. When the places were assigned, Fairchild found himself next to Elsie's younger sister, Marian Bell, who, at twenty-three and with her hair in a bun, was worryingly unmarried. Marian was still young by any standard, but her family's high status drew attention to what might have been unre-markable in any other family.

Marian knew about the setup on account of her loquacious sis-ter, Elsie, but Fairchild did not.

Elsie and Gilbert served dinner, and then stayed quiet. Marian was fascinated by art the same way Fairchild was by science, and for two hours, Fairchild listened as she described her love of sculp-ture and her trips to New York. Fairchild imagined that a girl so articulate was certainly spoken for.

But before the group disbanded for the evening, as if according to plan, Elsie Grosvenor worked into the conversation that her sis-ter was not yet engaged.

An earlier Fairchild, obtuse and birdbrained, may not have picked up on such an unsubtle disclosure. But now he had a well-formed social awareness, an instinct he had honed over years talk-ing with all kinds of people and in all kinds of situation. Elsie's aside was all it took.

"I left the house, my mind in a whirl," Fairchild wrote of the evening. It's conceivable that Fairchild believed he'd never find himself coupled, that he'd begun his adult life a bachelor and would end it that way as well. He once carried on a cursory engagement with a woman in Maine, to whom he was reasonably attracted, but not enough to curb his constant travels. His greatest influence had been Lathrop, who demonstrated in their years on steamships that life could be exceedingly well lived without a wife.

Fairchild's reaction to Marian, however, suggests that he simply hadn't met the right woman, one who could both challenge his in-stincts and put him at ease. And then, as if someone answered a prayer he hadn't prayed, here came someone as engrossing as she was radiant, who oozed poise and a charisma so pure it nearly drowned Fairchild's attention. "Concentration proved difficult," he wrote, describing his walk home. Plant introduction was no longer his sole object of affection.

CHAPTER FOURTEEN

A Brain Awhirl

Fairchild toiled for days about how to talk to Marian. He wasn't so much intimidated by her well-regarded family as he was baffled by what to say. Among all the things Barbour Lathrop had taught him in their years circling the globe, how to speak suggestively to a woman hadn't come up. With his hairline beginning to recede, Fairchild considered himself not particularly handsome—an assessment Marian later confirmed ("his intellect" had caught her attention first). But he had already demonstrated his strong upbringing and heightened sense of manners. And perhaps most important for a man seeking the affections of a woman, that he could be interesting by being interest*ed*.

He now lived at 1440 Massachusetts Avenue in another boardinghouse, this time squarely in the center of social Washington. It was one block from the National Geographic meetinghouse, six blocks from the White House, and four blocks from the Bells' mansion, where Marian lived with her parents. Even amid wisps of winter, it was an opportune distance to express his affections in hand-delivered letters.

A week passed before Fairchild decided his first move. At the Grosvenors' dinner, Fairchild had mentioned that he had amassed a personal collection of Javanese batik cloths, pieces of material with geometric designs made by molds of hot wax. Marian showed a hint of interest in the artistry she had only read about and never seen, so Fairchild sent over a small parcel of sarongs, which, in a breathless letter he rewrote twice, he clumsily offered to give her as a loan, not quite a gift.

> Miss Bell,
>
> The plain colored sarongs are from Siam and seem of mixed silk and cotton but the figured ones are from Java—that fairest of all Earth's islands—and they are Manchester cottons only. But how transformed they are by those soft browns and yellows from the tropical forests. . . . Please keep these as long as you like, they are for your study. If you want Java, yes, I will be delighted to get them for you. Isn't the weather gorgeous among the trees?
>
> With best regards.
> David Fairchild

Marian sent a cursory thank-you note.

After several more days, the best plan Fairchild could concoct was to invite her to visit his office. Fitting with the times, but perhaps not his intentions, he suggested she be accompanied by a chaperone.

Courtship in the early 1900s proceeded at the pace of a groggy house cat, nimble in ways but overall slow and unsure. Only recently, in the waning years of the 1890s, had courting begun to change from a transaction to a pleasurable activity—an innovation so meaningful it took on a new term: "dating." This was largely the effect of gender imbalance, which allowed a smaller pool of women to be selective among an abundance of men.

Had Marian lived a decade prior, her parents might have matched Marian her with a suitor based on their compatibility: a man to support a household and a woman to run it. But now, in 1904, a year when half the population of the United States was under twenty-three, burgeoning couples wanted more, and women could afford to be choosy. It wasn't uncommon for a woman to feign illness, play hard to get, even end a relationship prematurely to test a man's true devotion. Physical attraction hadn't arrived as a top priority, but it still mattered. The Reverend Joseph Bush had written a manual on marriage and courtship circulated widely in the United States. "If, in marrying, you get nothing but a pretty face, you make a bad bargain," Bush wrote. "Beauty wears out, but breeding is in the bone and, in choosing a partner for life, regard should be had to what will last." His recipe for a lasting union was to seek someone with a refined soul, a large heart, and a noble mind. The opposite of all of these qualities should be avoided.

On Thursday, January 5, 1905, Marian visited the Department of Agriculture with her grandmother Gertrude Mercer Hubbard, who at seventy-seven retained an aura of pearled glamour even after having been widowed for seven years. An awkward hour passed as Fairchild toured Marian and Mrs. Hubbard around the building, at one point taking them to the high-altitude attic that once housed the fledgling Office of Seed and Plant Introduction. One imagines him nervous and stiff, reduced to an insecure teenager, avoiding eye contact and the natural flow of conversation to kick himself mentally for the inanities exiting his mouth. The three stood in front of a planter box growing a woody climbing vine just beginning to show tender white flowers. He explained that it was from West Africa and a candidate for a new American garden shrub. He was, however, too modest to mention that just months prior he himself had been on the coast of West Africa in Sierra Leone. Even if he had wanted to boast, he seemed to lack the capacity to know how.

A few days later, Fairchild learned from mutual friends that Marian would be attending the Washington Charity Ball hosted by the Washington Junior League at the New Willard Hotel. Fairchild's age, just shy of thirty-six, put him on the upper end of beaus, but he decided to go anyway. When he tried to fill his dance card for the twenty waltzes and two-steps, he found only five women willing. He danced with the first four—one of whom was married—and then stood at the wall watching Marian be spun around the room by other men. When his turn came, the band played Strauss' "Wiener Bonbons" waltz, the longest song of the night. The way Fairchild mixed up his steps made Marian laugh. And by the end of the song, he had worked up the courage to ask her to dinner. He wrote "supper" in his dance card next to Marian's name, as if he'd need the reminder to remember.

Marian wasn't prone to falling in love. She had reached her midtwenties with only one young man making suggestive advances, which had annoyed her so deeply that her parents wondered if she was interested in men at all. The only man who had captivated Marian's attention was the sculptor Gutzon Borglum, a New York artist who would one day be asked to carve the faces of four American presidents into a granite mountain in South Dakota. Borglum's studio was in New York, and after being granted an apprenticeship, Marian made regular trips north to see him.

Marian had been drawn to the way Borglum's hands moved over the medium, be it rock or clay, and she particularly liked the moment the subject began to reveal itself—a nose, a face, a smirk. Marian watched him build busts of saints and apostles for the Cathedral of Saint John the Divine near Central Park. In 1904, with her eyes wide, she watched him work on a sculpture of seven stampeding horses that would later end up in the Metropolitan Museum of Art. She delighted at Borglum's brilliance, the explosive way he was never satisfied. Once, he shattered a collection of finely sculpted angels when a critic off the street innocently suggested they looked "feminine."

Clearly, it was the right side of Marian's brain that lit up with creative amusement. This confused her family, no one more than her left-brained father, a man whose every action tested hypothesis after hypothesis via the scientific method. Even so, Marian thoroughly admired her inventive father, and he her. "I think [she] is going to develop into a self-reliant and beautiful woman," Bell wrote his mother in 1892, a few weeks after Marian turned twelve. And she did, largely thanks to her mother's influence each summer in France or Italy, where Mabel Bell would bring her daughters to concerts, galleries, and museums.

For all the credit granted Bell, the famous inventor had a deficit of affection for his daughters that in later years could be deemed overt sexism. Bell didn't hide his disappointment that having two daughters would leave no one to carry on the family name (the Bells had had two sons, but both died as newborns). He repeatedly skipped family vacations in Europe with Mabel and the girls to stay home and work on a new idea. In 1898, Clara Barton, the Civil War nurse who founded the Red Cross, invited eighteen-year-old Marian to accompany her to Cuba to treat soldiers fighting in the Spanish-American War. Her father thought it would only "wound" Marian and "accomplish no good," so she didn't go.

Her father didn't find out about the apprenticeship with Borglum until Marian had already accepted, which was the only reason she was permitted to do it. And to Marian at twenty-one, New York felt like the center of the world. The more she became engrossed with Borglum's work, the more she fell in love with the energy of the city. She attended concerts in the apartments of young musicians, often unchaperoned. She mingled with sculptors and architects in Greenwich Village. Twenty years before the arrival of jazz, her parents worried about the raucous, liberal, and undisciplined influences of New York. Alexander and Mabel Bell wanted their daughter to find a husband as much for social appearances as because they hoped it would settle her down.

David Fairchild seemed to be that calming influence. But he

wasn't boring. He was a man of science, a traveler of terrific adventure, whose work was reasoned, methodical, and yet had an element of art, at least to the extent that the work he was doing—brightening the color palette of American agriculture—had never been done before.

The letters kept arriving at Marian's house, delivered early in the morning during out-of-the-way detours Fairchild took by the Bells' house to the office. Marian would respond, enamored by the attention, but she was unwilling to equal Fairchild's more poetic, often unedited pronouncements.

For their first official date, on January 13, 1905, Fairchild took Marian to the Washington Symphony Orchestra to see the Scottish pianist Eugen d'Albert. Fairchild took her hand as d'Albert played Beethoven and Tchaikovsky. And when they left, he tucked the program in his pocket to remember the occasion. He wrote her later that night.

> That music was so deep and took such a hold that my
> brain is awhirl. . . . You were very good to let me hear
> it and I do like the intoxication of it though it seems
> very showy and leaves one a bit weak.

> David

Marian enjoyed responding with tantalizingly little, but enough to invite more missives.

> I like the way you write—it's very simple and direct.

> Marian

There was a lot Marian began to like about Fairchild, and eventually his demeanor became part of his charm. At a party hosted by the Grosvenors, Fairchild flailed his hands while he told a story. He knocked over a candle and spilled hot wax all over his coat, ruining it, but Fairchild continued the story as though he had made the same faux pas dozens of times before. Marian would later note, in longhand, how she enjoyed his resilience in the face of setback, however minor.

In February of 1905, a month that brought blankets of snow, they both took trips away from Washington. Marian left first for Detroit on art business. The collector Charles Lang Freer wanted to donate to the Smithsonian Institution a portion of his personal collection, and Marian, on account of her father's connections and because she had studied art, was asked by the Smithsonian to inspect the gift. Fairchild, not long after, took the train to Florida. He wrote to her from his Department of Agriculture office, and then once he departed, on any stationery he could find, at each stop feeling more comfortable with himself, more flirtatious, in the way an uncertain lover finds his footing.

January 31, 1905

Department of Agriculture of the United States

Marian,

Did you ever look at a friend's photograph through a big microscope? I'm going to look at you through mine—my new one for there is something real about the image that the delicate fashioned lenses cast. This letter shall reach you earlier than the others for it will catch the last delivery. I hope it will find you in the sunshine and not the shade. I send a leaf from a winter's day which I spent years ago in the Adriatic, with a dear old Italian monk, looking for a new sort of

grape which is now growing in California. You will
excuse this letterhead note paper will you not? It is
some left from the last trip. Now come the letters,
more of the artificial moonlight and a tramp home in
the snow.

> Good night
> David Fairchild

Several days later he wrote from Wilmington, North Carolina,
on hotel letterhead.

> February 13, 1905

There is no use in my trying to deceive myself—each
day seems to make your image more and more a part
of my life. All day long the rain clouds and the twigs
against the sky have been the only things of beauty
worth watching and in the beauties of these things
your presence has been so fully and so real that I
cannot tell you of it.

> David

Fairchild wasn't eager to introduce Marian to Barbour Lathrop,
who he feared could undo all of the delicate groundwork he had laid
with a single remark, exposing Fairchild as churlish by association.
In his letters to her and on their dates together, Fairchild had described Lathrop in terms more cutting than flattering. The nuance
of his relationship with Lathrop, the man who both enriched and
annoyed him, often simultaneously, was difficult to put into words.

"My friend—you know who—by forty years of travel became
like a naughty child among a host of presents," Fairchild had once
told Marian. "He wanted fresh personalities all the time. Yet we

traveled year in and year out through all sorts of lands and when last we parted our eyes were moist. . . . Between us there never was nor could there ever be such a bond of sympathy, such similarity of tastes, as have brought him and me together."

Fairchild's warning aside, nothing could have truly prepared Marian to meet Lathrop for the first time. When he brought Marian to call on Lathrop in a Washington hotel room in the early days of 1905, the discussion started worse than expected:

"Uncle Barbour, this is Marian."

Lathrop studied her.

"Well, she has fine eyes."

Then he turned to Fairchild.

"My God, Fairy, what has happened to your hair? It looks as though it hadn't been cut for months. You had better go right down to the barber shop and get a cut. You are a fright!"

Lathrop turned back to Marian, his voice raised.

"You think you can make him look like your father, do you? But your father has a great leonine head. He can wear his hair long. Fairy can't."

Marian ran from the room crying, likely more embarrassed than actually stung. Fairchild followed her. In the hallway, Fairchild consoled her.

Lathrop had criticized Fairchild hundreds of times, about his hair, his clothing, his sluggishness, his lack of manners, his lack of respect, his shallowness of intellect, and any number of other things that entered his mind and left it just as quickly. Fairchild had become immune to it all. Yet when he was insulted in front of a new lady, *his* new lady, the critique cut deep. Why couldn't Lathrop understand the high stakes of this first impression, of being polite to someone important to Fairchild? Lathrop's petulant outburst suggests he may have been bitter that Fairchild had found the companionship that had eluded Lathrop for so long. Or worse, that Lathrop lacked the self-awareness to know he had said anything wrong.

"Good Lord, what have I done?" Lathrop said when it became clear he had offended Marian.

It wasn't Lathrop who repaired the uncomfortable encounter, nor was it Fairchild. It was Marian. After she stopped crying in the hallway, she suggested that perhaps Lathrop was right, that Fairchild could use a haircut. Faced with an opportunity to stand up for himself, to demonstrate stiff resolution after a stinging insult, Fairchild chose differently. He knew that battles should only be fought when they have a reasonable chance of being won, so he obeyed.

When he returned from the hotel barbershop he found Marian and Lathrop giggling together over a story Lathrop was telling, a botched first impression granted a second chance.

"There," Lathrop said to Marian. "You must admit that he looks better." Whether she thought so or not, she agreed.

The climax of Fairchild's courtship with Marian came one day in February, just three months after they first met. Their dating had been steady and passionate, cresting with dozens of letters, sometimes many a day. Marian traveled north to New York for an art show. Fairchild, now so devoted he was prone to theatrics, followed her secretly.

The plan wasn't only to casually bump into her in Grand Central Terminal. The plan was to take the same train back to Washington with her. Fairchild studied the timetables and memorized the path Marian would take to her train. The glimpse of a stunned Marian must have left Fairchild exceedingly self-satisfied.

The plan worked. Marian gasped as Fairchild stood with a toothy grin and a bouquet of carnations. Somewhere between Trenton and Baltimore, David Fairchild asked Marian a question. And there on a moving train, as it hurried south through the rain, he and Marian Bell agreed to spend their lives together. Instead of a ring, Fairchild gave her an engagement necklace made of Mexican

1903. In the months before his 1905 wedding, Fairchild took a break from traveling with Lathrop (pictured seated). One of their last excursions together had been a visit to Sweden.

gold and attached to an antique Roman coin with mystic characters. If the characters had a secret meaning, it remained secret between them.

Their attraction for each other was a potent factor in their decision to wed. But what mattered more was the opinion of Alexander Graham Bell, whose sole authority could approve or deny his daughter's marriage.

By now the permission was largely a formality. Bell liked Fairchild; the setup had been his idea, and their engagement a logical extension. Yet still, Fairchild spent three days composing a lengthy letter to detail his pedigree.

"My dear Daddysan: for Marian says I may call you so," he started his long-winded essay. He described his family and upbringing, his lineage of university presidents, professors, and other academics. He said that his mother once told him that he might be related to Oliver Cromwell, Britain's first lord protector. He explained his full education and the path he had taken from Kansas to New Jersey to Washington, and then the association with Barbour Lathrop that opened his world to Java, Australia, and the islands of the South Pacific. He employed the names of scientists, both famous and obscure, with whom he had worked. Fairchild wasn't so much trying to impress Dr. Bell as he was penning a formal petition of his worthiness to join the esteemed Bell family.

Unsurprising to everyone, Bell agreed to the marriage. He may have been uneasy about Fairchild's modest family—none of whom Bell had met, on account of their being distant or dead. Yet he had always valued adventure, and here was his daughter, in love with an adventurer scientist, a rare specimen in 1905, or any era.

East Coast newspapers enjoyed the story of an artistic daughter of a famous inventor marrying a government scientist. Sensational reports spread the rumor that Marian's dowry could be as high as one million dollars, an incredible fortune. The confidential reality was undoubtedly smaller, likely around fifty thousand dollars—a sum still astronomical for a future son-in-law with less than five thousand dollars to his name.

The engagement was short, only eight weeks. And by pure luck, the period coincided with a new wave of exuberance in Washington for the arrival of Teddy Roosevelt's second term, which brought a gaiety of parties all over town. Fairchild found himself with two tickets to Roosevelt's inaugural ball at the Pension Building in the neighborhood that would eventually neighbor Chinatown. He was reluctant to fill his dance card with any name but Marian's. And when the dances stopped, the revelers gorged themselves on creamed oysters, French peas, chicken croquettes, and deviled ham. Dessert was the most memorable part of all: a tutti-frutti salad made of candied raisins, cherries, and pineapple, a culinary safari of worldly fruits.

On the day of their wedding, April 25, 1905, the procession of the extended Bell family to Twin Oaks, a white mansion on Woodley Road, was so hectic, Fairchild almost forgot to give Marian the corsage he had ordered specially with flowering cherry blossoms. The blooms were Marian's favorite flower from her favorite story of her fiancé's travels. He made himself a matching boutonniere.

Before the ceremony he gave her one last letter, which he had written late the night prior in the moonlight, kept awake by the timeless nerves of a man before his wedding:

April 24, 1905

My Marian, my own darling, let's not forget that like
two leaves adrift together we are in the stream of life
and let us hope no bars no shallows, no eddies nor
currents are to drive us apart, but we shall reach the
open sea.

Let's live dear girl and get from life what she holds
in store for those like you and me, who've learned that

all the world wants is a smile and a caress. It's now our
wedding day. I love you with the fullness of a heart
that's longed to love for years but has not found what
now you've given. You're the sweetest, dearest, girl of
all. I love you, yes, I love you.

David

The wedding proceeded in the spring of Washington, forever its
best season, between trees and surrounded by Marian's abundant
family. The estate was known to be the most beautiful park in
Washington, where Fairchild and Marian were only granted their
nuptials because the property belonged to Marian's grandparents
Gardiner and Gertrude Hubbard, who traded seasons between the
estate and their Dupont Circle home, just two miles apart.

Alexander Graham Bell, his beard blown lightly by the wind,
walked his daughter down the aisle. Everyone noticed her white accordion chiffon dress with pompadour silk, her flowing veil, her
bright smile. No one realized that she had forgotten to wear the corsage of cherry blossoms she had been gifted, least of all Fairchild,
who stood with a stupefied smile as his bride shuffled forward.

They laughed after the ceremony about how she forgot the flowers. And then, figuring the story would make a nice souvenir, they
plucked the flowers from Marian's corsage and from David's boutonniere, stuffed them into two envelopes, and sealed them shut.
The mementos from their wedding would be passed down through
generations of their descendants, each a product of their marriage,
until one hundred years later, when the erosion of time would dis-
integrate the petals into dust.

CHAPTER FIFTEEN

Cherry Trees with No Cherries

Fairchild's first choice for a best man to stand beside him at his wedding was his closest boyhood friend, Walter Swingle. But Swingle was abroad, searching for something, somewhere. Barbour Lathrop, his globe-trotting companion, was difficult to pin down, and unable to attend the wedding. And so, with his dearest friends unavailable, he turned to Charles Marlatt, the man who had the bare qualification of having grown up next to Fairchild in Kansas.

Marlatt had once been the strange neighbor boy obsessed with bugs. Now he was a fully credentialed entomologist devoted to the study of American insects. Many insects were immigrants to America the same way that Fairchild's fruits were, but Marlatt saw a more ominous future for the country if it was negligent of what was crossing its borders. With his own eyes, Marlatt had seen the damage insects could do. In the 1880s, he watched the San Jose scale, an ugly yellow insect, infest and suffocate fields in California. He took an expedition to Asia that was as desperate as it was fraught with danger to hunt for the scale's natural predator.

When he found a candidate species to demolish the scale, he brought an entire colony back. The predators were red and black beetles, each so graceful and feminine they became known as lady-bugs (also ladybirds). Marlatt's were thought to be the first ladybugs in America, which was a remarkable accomplishment, considering that the full colony he tried to introduce had almost fully died en route, except for two of its inhabitants—"Mr. and Mrs. Ladybug," newspapers called them—who, with only their kinetic energy, rebuilt the population and eliminated the pesky San Jose scale. If Marlatt was born with any patience, watching this tense episode had consumed it all.

Marlatt liked Fairchild—he was six years older and tended to see Fairchild as a younger brother. They both had a deep love for science. In a way, Marlatt was responsible for Fairchild's love of Java. In the 1870s, it had been Marlatt who first alerted Fairchild that the famous Alfred Russel Wallace would be visiting their town. Fairchild informed his father, who then invited Wallace to stay in the Fairchild home for an evening, during which the biologist fascinated George Fairchild's son with vivid descriptions of the Malay Archipelago.

But in Washington, a town more professional than personal, Marlatt's feelings toward his childhood friend had grown as lukewarm as a tight-lipped smile. To Marlatt, Fairchild enjoyed enormous privilege, first in his family connections that landed him his first job with the USDA, and then in his association with Barbour Lathrop, who financed his travels around the world. Marlatt hadn't had it so easy. In Kansas he served as an apprentice to a government entomologist, and then did fieldwork in Texas cotton fields and Virginia orchards, delaying his opportunity to set roots and start a family. When he finally did marry, he took his wife on his scale-hunting trip—part honeymoon, part official business—to China, where Mrs. Marlatt was attacked and killed by intestinal parasites. Four years later, in 1905, Marlatt had worked his way back. He was named head of the Division of Entomology at the USDA. If Fairchild's story had been one of good luck and hard work, Marlatt's was a combination of bad luck and the need to work even harder. For him, fighting against invasive insects had become personal.

In his earlier days, Marlatt believed that insects and fungi were as unstoppable as the climate, undeterred by national borders. But in 1898, he had the type of revelation that makes one sit up in bed. He realized wormy apples and mildewed grapes were just as dangerous as people infected with cholera. Plant diseases could spread quickly over large distances and wipe out entire industries. In the first few years of the twentieth century, amid all the excitement about new travel and a world open to America, Marlatt tried to explain to anyone who would listen that the same trains, ships, and canals that brought new nursery stock also brought pests, weeds, and diseases. He pointed to the infestations of periodical cicadas on his native plains of the American Midwest. The clouds of humming grasshoppers, he said, were as debilitating as the plague of locusts in the story of the Exodus.

Even more alarming, the federal government had left pest inspections to the states, each constrained to only the area within its borders. This patchwork system handicapped the federal government's efforts to deal with outbreaks across state lines, or worse, maladies imported from abroad. An entomologist sees the world through the prism of insects, and everywhere Marlatt looked were examples of states spreading diseases while Washington sat, watched, and did nothing.

This was the type of dread that motivated Marlatt for more than a decade. And in 1905, at exactly the point Marlatt and Fairchild were both rising in the circles of social Washington, attending the same parties and society meetings, the one crop they would clash over—the one that would come to be known around the world as the tree of Washington, D.C.—was slowly making its way toward America's shores.

After their wedding, David and Marian Fairchild decided they weren't city people. They wanted space and some land, at least enough to have a garden of their own. Fairchild's affinity for plants had rubbed off on his artistic-minded wife, and so, with the free-dom of being a newlywed couple, and the windfall of a generous dowry from Mr. and Mrs. Bell, David and Marian bought a ten-acre patch of heavily wooded land just outside of Chevy Chase, Mary-land. To help their daughter and new son-in-law sustain life in the suburbs, the Bells gifted them an automobile with an enchanting top speed of twelve miles per hour. Marian, who would later be employed as a wartime ambulance driver, became the first woman in Washington, D.C., granted a driver's license.

They both loved the property so much, they camped on the bare land the first day they owned it. "Like children, we waded in the brook, chased the squirrels and built a fire of twigs beneath the oaks," Fairchild wrote. After they constructed a feeble wooden structure, their mornings were filled with the baking of chickpea muffins. With the extra garbanzos, Fairchild made soup.

Finally, after all his travels, Fairchild had his own land, his own canvas to fill with the trees and shrubs that in all his travels had emerged as his favorites. He planted an entire bamboo garden and ordered rootstock from the foreign botanical offices he had visited. He imported ornamental trees from Europe, bitter Chinese mel-ons, even the kudzu vine he had found in Japan, which took great effort to get to root, and then, when it smothered part of the gar-den, required even more energy to kill it.

All Marian wanted, however, were Japanese flowering cherry trees, which she referred to simply as "cherry blossoms." Fairchild ordered 125 of them from the Yokohama Nursery Company in Yo-kohama, where he had spent that recent resplendent summer. The nursery owner, a man named Uhei Suzuki, was so pleased to hear from Fairchild again—and to have an American customer—that he nearly gave away the trees for free, just ten cents apiece.

Six months later, in the spring of 1906, the trees showed their pink blossoms for the first time, and with them came buzz—the type of buzz, in days before major movie stars, that only horticulture could

THE

Yokohama,

Nursery,

Co., Ltd.

Nos. 21–35,

Nakamura,

YOKOHAMA,

JAPAN.

1901

The Yokohama Nursery Company was the only Japanese seller of sakura flowering cherry trees. The company's catalogue in 1901 featured its premier product. Fairchild wrote directly to the owner of the company to order more than a hundred trees, his first of many orders that would lead to American demand for more.

produce. Fairchild spent the early mornings walking amid the budding trees, their petals speckled with dew drops against the gray sky of dawn. He carried his camera, a new one that could magnify the blossoms, filling the full frame with the delicate beauty that had so taken him in Japan. Word of the Fairchilds' exotic pink trees brought so many onlookers to their front yard that Fairchild ordered three hundred more as a gift to the city of Chevy Chase.

This was especially notable for a suburb of Washington. The capital city itself wasn't terribly good-looking in the early twentieth century. The most impressive part of Washington was its design, its streets clean and angular, wide and efficient. But you couldn't put a city plan on a postcard. Nor could one gloat about the new Washington Monument, impressive but clumsily placed. The Potomac lapped near the obelisk, encasing the area in a perennial field of mud. Thomas Nelson Page, the man married to Barbour Lathrop's sister, gave a speech to the Washington Society of Fine Arts on May 4, 1910, calling for someone to do something to beautify Washington. "We are much given to claiming that Washington is now the most beautiful city in the country, and one of the most beautiful in the world; in fact we are much given to claiming that whatever we are, we are the 'most' of that," he argued. "But if I may say so, without giving offense, this mental attitude, which is essentially that of the provincial who knows little of the standards by which comparison is made, is unworthy of a great people."

Page's larger point—that a city's capital is symbolic of its stability and aspirations—had for years distracted the ego of America's proudest supporters, none more than Teddy Roosevelt. In his second term, Roosevelt prioritized giving Washington the stately facade afforded the shiny capitals of Europe. He urged Congress to fortify the raw land around the Washington Monument with sediment to transform it into a park. Ideas poured in from visionaries who imagined a future of beaches, polo fields, baseball diamonds, paths for walking and bicycling, and a separate road for automobiles to pass at greater speed. This area would come to be called the speedway, and it struck several people that the flowering cherry trees could lend the tidal basin an elegant visage.

Fairchild wasn't the first person to think downtown Washington and the cherry trees could make a dignified pair. Eliza Scidmore, a journalist and Washington networker, one of the few women involved in the National Geographic Society, had been enchanted by flowering cherries for years. Her brother was a consular officer in Japan, which brought her regularly across the Pacific, most memorably in 1887, when she first saw the trees. But in Washington, her exuberance was lost in translation. It was perhaps because the political environment wasn't right, or because she was an eccentric woman in a town of self-admiring men, that her pleas were answered with cynical questions. People wondered, "Why bother with cherry trees that don't produce cherries?"

Fairchild's trees, however, had proved the draw of cherry blossoms, not for their fruit but for their annual pink bursts. Every tree Fairchild imported brought demand for two or three more. For a time, he nearly became a plant importer filling personal orders. Still, delighted by the interest, Fairchild saw the cherry trees as an opportunity to inspire young kids into botany. On Friday, March 27, 1908, which happened to be Arbor Day, he invited one boy from each school to visit his home, which he and Marian had begun to call "In the Woods," to receive a tree and planting instructions for his school yard.

The next day, a Saturday, Marian drove Fairchild into town to give a lecture to students and parents from all over Washington at the Franklin School at Thirteenth and K streets. Fairchild invited Scidmore, whom he introduced as "the most noted writer on Japan." He described his travels, as had now become a popular part of any speech he gave, and recalled his first view of the sakura in Japan. He ended his lecture by displaying a photograph of the unsightly speedway near the Washington Monument. What an excellent place, he mused, to plant cherry blossom trees.

The next morning in the *Washington Star*, Fairchild's parting thought was given front-page treatment. If the trees were planted soon around the tidal basin's speedway, they could bloom the following spring, and not long after, the newspaper reported, "Washington would one day be famous for its flowering cherry trees."

Here was an example of Fairchild's suddenly high standing as a member of the Bell and Grosvenor families. What Scidmore had tried to accomplish for decades, Fairchild influenced with the lightest of touches. It wouldn't be long before the United States had a new president, William Howard Taft, and as the people of Washington were starting to like the idea of bringing cherry blossom trees to the capital city, America's first lady, Helen Taft, was warming to it, too.

While Mrs. Taft marveled over their beauty, her husband saw a diplomatic tool. America was a Western country born from the influence and customs of Europe, and Americans saw Asia as foreign, in both distance and concept, and had long rejected elements of its cryptic culture.

It would be easy to dismiss this attitude as ethnocentrism: Americans shunning foreign people less for who they were than how they looked, faulting them for taking American jobs, as labor leaders did in San Francisco in 1905. In 1907, Japanese and Korean people in some cities were forced into segregated schools, and elsewhere, attacked on the street. Japan had been at war with Russia over land in Manchuria and Korea. Giddy newspaper editors in New York ran headlines about the prospect of war in the Pacific if the conflict escalated.

To defuse this tension, Taft's predecessor, Roosevelt, had thought a truce was the most sensible solution. In the agreement, America would stop mistreating Japanese people and Japan would stop sending immigrants to America. The agreement was childish, effectively a time-out separation that reflected poorly on everyone, most of all the United States. It was clear to anyone who bothered to look that the country that had built its foundation on being open to everyone had become racially selective in deciding who was welcome.

But President Taft knew the Japanese better. As secretary of war in 1905, the same year Fairchild got married, Taft had visited the imperial country, where he was welcomed to the harbor of Yokohama with a fireworks display in his honor. Now as president and motivated to smooth over relations, Taft quickly realized that the cherry trees could be the perfect way to quell the antagonism. Importing trees was more palatable than importing people, especially ones vying for jobs. To Japan, it was an opportunity to show off a beautiful piece of itself in America's capital. Japanese officials also enjoyed the tacit admission that despite America's larger size, population, and economy, the countries were, in a way, equals. An editorial in *The New York Times* saw planting Japanese trees in the heart of America as an extraordinary opportunity for Japan.

> There is nothing in the American life to illustrate just what the cherry means to the Japanese people. But suppose we had some symbol of nature that would embody all that Plymouth Rock, all that the Declaration of Independence, all that the Emancipation Proclamation means, of liberty, patriotism, union; and then, suppose our President should on some occasion, with the greatest care, select 300 of the choicest specimens of this emblem and officially send them as representing the felicitations of the American people to a friendly power, at the time of some important celebration— can you imagine what such a gift would mean?

So when the mayor of Tokyo was tasked with finding the three hundred finest cherry blossom trees in the city to be uprooted and shipped to America, it became his top priority. The agreement, it appeared, had something to please everyone.

Everyone except Charles Marlatt, who didn't want foreign plants in the first place, and would see to it that even one damaging insect would leave him no choice but to march up the steps of the White House and make it his mission to undo everything his childhood friend was trying to accomplish.

The initial plan for three hundred trees turned into two thousand. Tokyo's mayor, Yukio Ozaki, was so excited about playing a part in high-level diplomatic relations that he continued selecting trees until the steamer that would sail across the Pacific was so full it couldn't hold another twig. The trees were selected young to ensure a long life in Washington, and their roots cut short to conserve space on the ship.

A year had passed since Fairchild brokered the gift between the State Department and Kogoro Takahira, the Japanese ambassador to the United States, and the paperwork had involved the extended bureaucracies of both governments. Fairchild had begun the negotiations, but when they rose to the highest levels of government, the lead person became James Wilson, now in his twelfth year as secretary of agriculture. On November 13, 1909, Wilson notified the plant industry office in Seattle that a shipment of high importance would be arriving on December 10. There were many reasons to be excited about the shipment. There was the diplomatic success politicians imagined when the trees would be photographed near the Washington Monument. For ordinary people, there was the anticipation of something new and beautiful coming to town. And for the botanically minded like Fairchild, there was the promise of biological exchange enriching both countries.

The trees reached Seattle as expected. Port workers packed them onto temperature-controlled railcars and cleared the track ahead for the thirteen-day trip to Washington.

Fairchild saw little reason to worry about something as innocuous as cherry trees. Hundreds had already been planted in the United States, most on his personal orders. Compared to the invasive plants and animals that had wrought damage on United States soil—honeysuckle, water hyacinth, tumbleweeds—flowering cherry trees seemed as harmless as field mice. But this exchange wasn't his alone to handle. While Fairchild had helped generate support and excitement for the exchange, Marlatt had visited the same government officials to caution of the dangers. Marlatt had even walked across the National Mall to the State Department, where he argued to Secretary of State Philander Knox that the whole idea was poorly thought out. The trees hadn't yet arrived, which to an ordinary person might have granted them the benefit of the doubt that they were clean. But to Marlatt, the fact that no one had yet *certified* the trees clean was almost definitive proof that they were dirty. Secretary Knox believed the diplomatic benefits outweighed any biological risks, but to be safe Knox took Marlatt's warning to Taft anyway.

Taft was the kind of man who had trouble making up his mind. Broad shouldered and powerfully built, Taft had been the hand-picked choice to succeed Roosevelt, who left office so popular his endorsement for president could have gotten a fern tree elected. The support allowed Taft to avoid the slugfest and maneuvering required in a typical election, which might have proven to the public—as it did four years later when he lost in a historic landslide—his shortcomings as an executive.

In some ways, Roosevelt and Taft were similar, both progressive and averse to corporate power, but Taft was cautious and careful, less out of thoughtfulness than nerves. He doubted his decisions and, when challenged, allowed his mind to be easily changed. He had enjoyed the nitty-gritty of being a lawyer who served as solicitor general, governor of the Philippines, and secretary of war, all positions that allowed him to obsess over fine points of policy and law. He hated granting interviews or being photographed, in part due to his three-hundred-pound heft. Roosevelt had once offered Taft an appointment to the Supreme Court, but Helen Taft had urged her husband to finish his work in the Philippines and leave open the prospect of his own presidency. Roosevelt liked that idea better and began to tout Taft as the torchbearer for a third Roosevelt term. Taft, however, showed that to be an imperfect promise. While Roosevelt had been a charismatic barnstormer eager to create new things, Taft was a stodgy introvert, burdened by the demands of the presidency and insecure in his capacity to fill it.

Marlatt, by way of Secretary of State Knox, had not been able to change Taft's mind. But the prospect of catastrophe did give Taft some pause. He ordered the trees inspected thoroughly at the garden storehouse near the Washington Monument before they were planted. Fairchild, who was by now America's leading expert in Japanese flowering cherries, was asked to complete the initial inspection. Marlatt insisted on being present, too.

When the two pried open a crate, Fairchild's first thought was that the trees were too big and their roots cut too short. This left them vulnerable to corrosion on the monthlong voyage from Japan.

The Japanese had sent large trees not out of spite but out of generosity, for mature trees would show vibrant blossoms the fastest. Fairchild believed they could be salvaged. Perhaps the tops could be pruned to reduce stress and allow the trees to recover from the trauma of transport. "Young stock would undoubtedly be in a much more healthy condition, and the importation of it would have been accompanied with much less risk," Marlatt would later write.

But Marlatt had bigger concerns than the health of a single shipment. The trees didn't look right. And when he closely examined the roots, he noticed small insects, "serious infestations," he wrote, his words almost dripping in I-told-you-so glee. The roots were plagued with root gall, two kinds of scale, a curious new species of borer, and six other dangerous insects. Marlatt could make out the Chinese *Diaspis*, a white scale insect known to kill trees by ruthlessly feeding on fruit. He spotted the wood-boring *lepidopterus* larvae that survive by gnawing on trees' leaves and their woody insides. And there was the well-known and unwelcome San Jose scale, which Marlatt noted, despite its name, originated somewhere in China.

In spite of his enthusiasm, Fairchild was forced to agree with Marlatt that insects could present a risk to American soil. He was accustomed to unusable crop. Not every seed or cutting had to be treasured. But what worried him most was how to break the news to the president that the trees, the symbol of friendship in a fraught diplomatic relationship, were faulty. And that America, which had already rejected so much about Japan, would have to reject its trees, too.

There was no delicate way to handle this. And the situation brought Fairchild anxiety. "Every sort of pest imaginable was discovered, and I found myself in a hornet's nest of protesting pathologists and entomologists, who were all demanding the destruction of the entire shipment," he wrote.

It wasn't hard to foresee a surge of support for people like Marlatt, the nativists who wondered whether it was worth it to import plants at all. Farmers across the United States had enjoyed the benefits of plant exploration, but newspaper reports tended to focus on the hazards. The same kind of hysteria that pushed the United States into Cuba, the Philippines, and the Pacific Islands now fueled frenzy over the costs of imperialism. Were the benefits of a few novel fruits worth the possibility that new pests could take down America's entire agricultural system? Editorials quoted past examples of the Hessian fly that "demolished" cereals or the rude English sparrow that "fought" native bluebirds for space and food. All did damage, but the implication was that their biggest sin was that they *sounded* foreign, unwelcome in an ego-boosted country that fancied itself superior and, in every way, exceptional.

Really, though, this sort of country-to-country contamination was largely inevitable, particularly amid globalization. Doors were open, and it was better to deal with invaders that entered the United States in government labs than on the shoe tread of future travelers. The United States couldn't build a wall to keep out unwanted things any more than places like Egypt or China could prevent their prized crops from being taken by David Fairchild.

But what made this unfortunate situation worse was the potential for agriculture to affect other issues of diplomacy, like trade, tourism, and military alliances. A foreign country could easily interpret the American aversion to natural diseases not as a prudent protection of its natural assets, but as hardened xenophobia.

Marlatt's report about the trees' infestations gave Taft little choice, and on January 28, 1910, the president ordered the trees burned. Fairchild thought of making one last attempt to save the trees, to prune them himself and spend several days tediously combing the roots of six-legged intruders. But it was no use.

Everyone familiar with Japan's sharpened sense of cultural pride braced for Tokyo's reaction, and the likelihood that America's attempt to bridge relations with the Japanese had been sullied, perhaps forever. As Marlatt and his team propped the trees together like a teepee, someone invited reporters to watch them be lit aflame. A news item appeared on the front page of the next day's *New York Times. The Washington Post* ran a two-page article about foreign plant danger. *See?* Marlatt and his henchmen effectively told the public. *Thank goodness we were on the case.*

And yet, the overall reaction wasn't one of satisfaction. America may have sharpened its ego, but it hadn't lost its sense of decency. Did the destruction have to be so public, so transparent? Couldn't America with its outsized creativity have imagined a way for everyone to save face? Someone wrote an anonymous letter to several different East Coast newspapers questioning what good the rebuke to the Japanese had done.

To destroy the cherry trees, to tell the . . . Japanese government that it had been done and why, and to let the story get out—well, that, to transpose a familiar phrase, was more wise than nice. Perhaps it wasn't even wise. The thing to have done was to have some carefully arranged accident happen to those trees before the time came for setting them out—an accident of the obviously unavoidable sort, a clear "act of Providence." Then the needful number of departmental Secretaries could have told Japan how sorry we all were, and the incident would have passed without embarrassment or humiliation for anybody.

The letter might have been written by Fairchild, angry and sad, yet with enough scientific sense to know there wasn't much choice. More stinging was that the blaze of trees had granted fuel to those fearful of the unknown. An unfortunate mistake by the Japanese gardeners offered American xenophobes something to point to as proof that the world really was out to contaminate the shiny armor of the great United States. The trees and their crates burned for a little over an hour, and when their embers died, so did much hope of patching relations with the most developed country in Asia.

Yukio Ozaki, the mayor of Tokyo, happened to be visiting Washington when word got out about the bonfire of cherry trees. He had come several weeks prior to witness the reception of Japan's prized symbol in America's capital.

Not long after the trees were burned, Ozaki received David Fairchild in his hotel. Fairchild had come to apologize, or in a less dignified way, to grovel for the biological blunder. No one was at fault, he explained, even though a man of his experience could certainly have packed the shipment from Japan with more diligence and finesse to improve its chances of arriving healthy.

But Ozaki had a different reaction than anyone expected, illuminating just how little American leaders understood foreign relations and cross-cultural diplomacy, particularly with the poorly understood Far East.

In reality, Fairchild's apologies were dwarfed by Ozaki's. While Washington cringed at the insulting gesture of burning a gift, Tokyo had apparently viewed the problem as having given a faulty present, as though its token of kindness had turned out to be a bouquet of disease. "We are more satisfied that you dealt with [the trees] as you did, for it would have pained us endlessly to have them remain a permanent source of trouble," Ozaki explained.

Of *course* the trees had to be burned, Ozaki said. And if President Taft would still entertain the exchange, Japan would like to send over another shipment of trees immediately. Better trees this time, packed by experts.

No one felt happy about the course of events, but it surprised American officials how deferential and apologetic Japan had been in response. One could have easily interpreted this deference from Japan, long proud and polite, as a sign of America's stature, an admission that Japan needed America's respect more than America needed Japan's. Mayor Ozaki's wife, in a fawning letter to Helen Taft, apologized again for the mishap and then characterized the second shipment of trees as a "memorial of national friendship between the United States and Japan."

Gardeners and chemists from several of Japan's islands were brought to Tokyo to help select another batch of sakura, the expectations higher this time to get it right. A famous Japanese chemist named Jokichi Takamine was tapped to oversee the process and was told the second shipment could not be mishandled. Three thousand and twenty trees for Washington were selected as an insurance policy, and to hold them, a bigger boat that could cross the Pacific faster. The trees were raised in virgin sod, and their roots wrapped in damp moss. The trees were fumigated twice with hydrocyanic acid gas to asphyxiate any insects, and then placed in cold storage to slow the trees' metabolism.

Charles Marlatt wasn't pleased upon hearing of a second shipment. But he considered it a small victory that the first shipment, with its faults on display to the public, had proved his point. Biological imports couldn't be left to chance. The incident had successfully undermined the pipe dream that everything that showed up on America's shores would come exclusively with benefits, and no risk.

Fairchild, too, had been encouraged by the arrival of the second shipment and the verdict, after they received a "minute and careful examination," that the trees were clean, young, and healthy.

Four years to the day after Fairchild's 1908 gift of the trees to Washington's schools, on March 27, 1912, Mrs. Taft broke dirt during a private ceremony in West Potomac Park near the banks of the Potomac River. The wife of the Japanese ambassador was invited to plant the second tree. Eliza Scidmore and David Fairchild took shovels not long after. The 3,020 trees were more than could fit around the tidal basin. Gardeners planted extras on the White House grounds, in Rock Creek Park, and near the corner of Seventeenth and B streets close to the new headquarters of the American Red Cross. It took only two springs for the trees to become universally adored, at least enough for the American government to feel the itch to reciprocate. No American tree could rival the delicate glamour of the sakura, but officials decided to offer Japan the next best thing, a shipment of flowering dogwoods, native to the United States, with bright white blooms.

Meanwhile, the cherry blossoms in Washington would endure for over one hundred years, each tree replaced by clones and cuttings every quarter century to keep them spry. As the trees grew, so did a cottage industry around them: an elite group of gardeners, a team to manage their public relations, and weather-monitoring officials to forecast "peak bloom"—an occasion around which tourists would be encouraged to plan their visits. Eventually, cuttings from the original Washington, D.C., trees would also make their way to other American cities with hospitable climates. Denver, Colorado; Birmingham, Alabama; Saint Paul, Minnesota.

Considering the trees were at first rejected and then accepted, Marlatt and Fairchild both had grounds to claim an element of victory. But the philosophical clash between them would grow bigger. The fight between men who had started as boyhood friends would wind up winner-take-all, the victor to define whether America would embrace the unknowns of the world or run fearful from them for the entire century to come.

PART IV

CHAPTER SIXTEEN

The Urge to Walk

Being a husband delighted Fairchild. Marian never tired of asking questions about his travels and botanical interests, and either genuinely or out of wifely duty, she adopted Fairchild's boyhood fascination with Java. The two would have a son together in 1906, Alexander Graham Bell Fairchild, who later in life joked that David's vow to take Marian to Java was the only reason she married him.

The domestic harmony, however, came at a cost. In just three years Fairchild had transformed from bachelor to husband to father, and with the obligations came restrictions on his travel. In the days after Fairchild had cabled word of his marriage, Lathrop, in Egypt, responded with a lengthy letter conveying a measure of resigned congratulations from an old stag. He seemed to see Fairchild's happiness as his own, and at fifty-seven, he watched his protégé acquire something that, either by choice or by fate, he had never been able to.

Despite his inexperience, Lathrop couldn't help but offer advice for marriage, revealing that he fancied the idea of being a superior husband and imagined, in another life, the type of spouse he'd be.

Shepheard's Hotel, Cairo
March 18th, 1905

My dear boy—

Your letter telling of your hope—or yearning rather,
reached me three days ago—the cablegram arrived
last night—telling me of your happiness.

After dancing around the room, in a highly
undignified manner for one of my years—and giving
several cow-boy whoops, I immediately cabled you. . . .

I am made happy in the belief that you have found a
woman whose tastes will agree with yours—and that
the two of you will be better mated than single. You
have an honest, affectionate nature—but to your credit
be it said, woman is even more of a mystery to you
than to a mere worldling like myself. Your years of
hermiting left you a more earnest man but also a more
ignorant one. . . . So take heed to this advice from a
battered old bachelor, one who, as you know, holds
good women in the highest respect. Don't bore your
lady love to a too incessant attention. Give the other
men a chance—and she will enjoy your talk all the
more after their empty prattle.

Don't be stilted in writing or speech with her—
naturally you write an excellent letter and talk
intelligently and entertainingly—but when you put on
social frills you are a failure. Your education and
association have been on thinking lines. When you
leave those you are very apt to flounder—where a city
ass would gaily prance along. God forbid you should
talk to anyone on scientific subjects only—but don't
try to be kittenish. Few women can stand a

dullard—but not one worth knowing can long care for
a man who tries to appear what he isn't . . .

So my advice to each one of two experimenters in
the marriage game can practically be summed up as
follows—

Be natural—but not insistent.

Be more anxious to give than to take.

Be comrades.

. . . You ought to be a married man, and I am
delighted to learn that all the chances for a happy life
are in your favor. God bless you, boy . . .

My one regret is—no more tramps together.

> Yours affectionately,
> Barbour Lathrop

The poignant letter with exceptional honesty betrayed the depth
of Lathrop's affection. And yet, of all Lathrop had written, the last
line held the greatest weight, the indelible mark of something irre-
versible.

Indeed, the tether of an early-twentieth-century marriage effectively clipped Fairchild's wings. He had become like a shipwrecked
boat, happy in its location but immobile nonetheless. While this normally wouldn't be a problem in bigger government offices with a
diversity of ages, Fairchild wasn't only the head of the Office of Seed
and Plant Introduction; he was the brains and thrust behind the entire operation. For more than seven years his travels and shipments
had brought the largest quantity of new fruits, flowers, trees, and
shrubs to America. He had spent years arguing that plant hunting
was important work. Now, anchored, he needed more people to do it.

Three men were already on assignment for the Department,
one looking for alfalfas in Russia, another for dates and olives in the

Mediterranean, and the third in Cuba hunting the best tobacco on earth. *The Strand*, a monthly magazine famous for being the first to publish Arthur Conan Doyle's mystery stories, would put Fairchild's team on equal footing with Sherlock Holmes, calling them "envoys of agriculture." But Fairchild was unmoved by breathless reports. He knew from experience that what all three men lacked was the burning curiosity for newness, the instinct to feel around in the dark and stumble headlong toward the unknown.

Sitting in his office day after day, Fairchild fixated on China, a land still full of hidden treasure that no Westerner had fully explored. His written inquiries to botanical authorities there were misunderstood or ignored. One letter from an Irish friend of Lathrop's living in Szechuan contained the unhelpful advice, "Don't waste time and postage; send a man."

A younger Fairchild, the one who bumbled through Corsica on a shoestring, might have gone himself, unaware of the risk and willing to confront challenges. But that was before he was married, and before he had been spoiled by Lathropian luxury.

Who else was suited for such dangerous work?

"He's a strange fellow," said one of Fairchild's assistants one day. "A bit erratic perhaps, for he doesn't seem to care about staying in one place."

The man under discussion was Frank Meyer, a Dutchman working in the Department's greenhouses, who seemed antsy and unfocused, as though yearning for an adventure—a man qualified, if not perfect, for the open position of China explorer.

Frank Meyer was indeed spirited and peculiar. He had gravitated toward horticulture out of childhood curiosity. He was also idealistic: he grew up in an aspiring utopian society modeled after Henry David Thoreau's *Walden*. Before coming to America in 1901 he had been the assistant of the renowned Dutch geneticist Hugo de Vries, who had first published the theory of "genes."

Yet Meyer was also impatient. After he had immigrated at age twenty-five, he planted trees at the Missouri Botanical Garden, propagated saplings at an experiment station in California, and then worked as a junior gardener for the USDA in Washington, D.C. At each job he became so restless being stationary that he eventually quit.

Meyer had an obsessive lust for plants. At the age of twelve, when his parents had asked what he wanted to do when he grew up, he said he wanted to travel the world studying edible plants. His father replied that they were too poor for him to study science, so he had better learn something practical, like making musical instruments.

Meyer left Holland to escape this fate. He wanted to touch and taste trees and shrubs, to subject every plant to his senses. His feelings bordered on familial: he looked at plants with compassion, patience, and a sense of devoted affection. This oddity, one that most people would have dismissed as the quirk of an uncultured man, deeply impressed Fairchild as the unteachable skill required for discerning among plants. "It was a characteristic sight to see Meyer quickly pick off and chew a fragment of a dried plant," Fairchild observed, "or smell furiously some plant material in order to bring to bear on it all of the powers of his remarkable memory."

Curious to size up a man hungry for discovery and adventure, Fairchild invited Meyer for an interview. He came sweating so profusely, his clothes were soaked through. Withholding judgment, Fairchild noted, "His eager face was sparkling with the real light of a born traveler."

Meyer's credentials were sterling even in a field occupied by few. But there was something eccentric about him. He sat with eyes wide open, transfixed on the wall behind Fairchild. He asked questions in deep, Dutch-inflected speech and then answered them, like a one-sided interview. "What don't we know of the world, well

1905. Fairchild immediately liked everything about Frank Meyer (pictured)—his love of walking, his compulsion for collecting plants, his apathy toward danger—and found him perfectly suited for long and treacherous travel in China, alone and on foot.

there is so much," Meyer said quizzically. His mastery of plants was savantlike.

And an even more remarkable and valuable characteristic: he loved to walk. Several days before his meeting with Fairchild, Meyer had walked to Mount Vernon, twenty miles south of Washington. He had once walked across the Alps to explore orange groves in Italy, and had marched hundreds of miles across Mexico. Now, if given the chance, he wanted to walk across China, a territory known to have so few roads, the only way to cross it was on foot. "Better small and fine than large and coarse," he would say about crossing China, even if no one quite knew what that meant.

Here was a man perfect for the task. A botanical explorer uninterested in money, glory, or luxury, who would march across one of Earth's most dangerous but botanically rich regions.

If Meyer wasn't qualified for Fairchild's roster, there wasn't a man alive who was.

The first question was how to introduce Meyer to Marian and Marian's famous parents, the Bells. Fairchild took Meyer shopping and bought him a green dinner jacket. The Bells loved him immediately. Never mind his wafting body odor, or scruffy cheeks, or his aversion to eye contact, or his tendency to become unfocused by lengthy tangents; in an instant, Alexander Graham Bell could tell that Meyer was endlessly interested in learning. That alone made a man worth knowing.

Meyer left on his first trip on July 27, 1905, with papers to remain in China for three years. Red tape and bureaucratic obstacles had become so arduous that Fairchild might have called off Meyer's mission, if not for the agricultural largesse Fairchild knew would be waiting in the faraway country's interior. The same way Egypt offered the most advanced farming methods, central Asia promised

actual crops that had benefited from several thousand years of human selection to work out kinks.

At Fairchild's request, Meyer's first assignment upon arriving in
Peking, the city one day to be known as Beijing, was to find the
grindstone persimmon, a swollen seedless variety, which Fairchild
remembered from his own initial visit to southern China, that
"makes its appearance on the Peking market and has become a favorite with many Europeans there." After that, Meyer was to follow the wind, guided by only his taste and intuition.

Meyer met Charles Marlatt one time before he left—in passing
and in a hurry. The same instinct that gave Fairchild confidence in
Meyer's capability filled Marlatt with suspicion. Not only was
Meyer, a Dutchman, a living embodiment of untested foreign
things in the United States; he was going to a region festering with
the unknown. The same plants Fairchild had called "plant immigrants" Marlatt called "plant enemies." To Marlatt, Meyer was like
a spy crossing enemy lines in an oblivious act of betrayal.

Marlatt couldn't stop Meyer's trip. The Bureau of Entomology
that he oversaw didn't have the jurisdiction. Nor, in 1905, could he
have put up bureaucratic roadblocks for all imported plant material. Marlatt did, however, decide to turn his outrage over Fairchild's recklessness into action. And as Meyer prepared to depart
the country for a long voyage across the Pacific, Marlatt began to
formulate his plan to make sure people like Meyer wouldn't be able
to contaminate the homeland with his and Fairchild's fanciful delu-
sions of biological harmony.

This animosity was lost on Meyer, who instead found himself
showered with excitement and praise. *The Washington Post* would
splash Meyer on the front page, calling him "the Agricultural Department's Christopher Columbus." The *Los Angeles Times* began a
long-running series on the dangers facing Meyer—"Chinese outlaws,
murderous thieves, rampant disease." "This is what agricultural explorers are doing," the paper wrote. "Going to all parts of the world

in search of new and hardier varieties of grapes, grains, alfalfas, and all other products of the soil which might be imported to America and add to our farm and orchard wealth."

The reports of Meyer's bravery (and later his heroism) were clearly embellished, but even Fairchild, the seasoned plant explorer, knew little of what Meyer might confront. Both of Fairchild's stints in Canton had been in luxury; he had stayed in Western hotels and ridden in wicker chairs on men's shoulders. Meyer carried only papers to confirm his identity and enough money for food and postage. He brought a chunk of silver to shave off for bribes, along with chemicals for preserving seed, drugs in case of illness, and several surgical instruments. "In these trips a man must be his own doctor, preacher, and devil," the *Post* reporter wrote prophetically.

This treacherous solitude is what Meyer craved most. "I am pessimistic by nature," he had once told his friends. "I withdraw from humanity and try to find relaxation with plants." Now the moment had come to feed his recluse spirit.

A pessimistic Meyer looked optimistically over the rails of his steamer bound for China. Just days before he left, Meyer had written his family in Holland how lucky he was to get such "a beautiful job." He wrote to Fairchild that he was committed to "do all I can to enrich the United States of America with things good for her people."

And so, when the ship reached Shanghai, Meyer wanted nothing more than to pick a direction, and walk.

Three years had passed since Fairchild last occupied the cabin of an ocean liner with Barbour Lathrop. Their tour around Africa had been their last together. When Fairchild returned to America and entered a new phase of life, Lathrop lost his rudder, the person who gave purpose to his constant motion. Lonely and anxious, he simply continued globe-trotting in luxury. For what he knew, it was all he was good at.

He picked up young men here and there, trying with each to re-create the magic of his partnership with Fairchild. One came close, named Drummond, the son of a friend from the Bohemian Club. Drummond had the wide-eyed ineptitude of an earlier Fairchild but lacked the spark and promise.

Fairchild's life was on an incline during his years with Lathrop, but Lathrop saw his own peak during their jaunts together, and afterward, begin to peter off. He wrote to Fairchild not long after their travels together ceased:

> I . . . never dreamed I'd so sadly miss the daily plant
> talk, the collecting, the shipping and the news of
> success or failure. Before these plant trips began, sight
> of quaint places and peoples made travel an
> unwearying pleasure. Now, it fails to satisfy me as it
> did—and during the year past I have been in some
> measure blasé—as I never was in all the years past. I
> don't acknowledge it, or permit myself to show it—but
> much of the keen interest is gone and I begin to
> wonder as to what the future has to offer one of my
> restless spirit. However it ends, it will be all right—and
> I'll not whine—for I have lived at least two lives in
> one—as compared with those other garden-wall-snail
> men—and can spice my mental gruel with memories
> of past feasts.

Such melancholy missives show just how much Lathrop had changed since their first meeting on the SS *Fulda*, the Atlantic steamship where Fairchild encountered Lathrop's peacocked ego, then big enough to fill a dozen steamships.

Fairchild remembered their years together wistfully. But he had little time to dwell on such memories. "The work of plant introduction is going on at such a frightful pace that I have been pretty nearly snowed under," he dictated to Marian to send to Lathrop. He made no mention of the glory days or Lathrop's malaise, either because he didn't miss them or because he was too occupied with the present to consider the past.

Fairchild had other things to think about, and not all of them botanical. Every day America was changing, in ways large and, often, even larger. Every year between 1903 and 1908, a miraculous period kicked off by a pair of Ohio brothers realizing man's supernatural dream of flying through the air, had been a sort of annus mirabilis in American history.

Fairchild knew Orville Wright. The younger of the two brothers visited his and Marian's house in Chevy Chase to see the cherry blossoms, and Fairchild had dined with him at the Cosmos Club, the networking hub where Fairchild met Gilbert Grosvenor, the man who introduced him to *National Geographic*, and ultimately, his wife. Fairchild was one of many people who asked why Orville and his brother kept their early flights so secret. The mystery had cost them credibility, especially as others were making public attempts at extended flights. The answer, as both Wrights repeated often, was to protect their design from being viewed and stolen— even though, with the hindsight of history, this precaution was mostly unnecessary.

Still, Orville struck Fairchild as smart and ambitious, even if his appearance—baggy pants, oversized jacket, and dirty cap— lacked crispness. They also had a mutual friend, an army lieutenant named Tom Selfridge, whose father was an acquaintance of Lathrop. In 1905 Selfridge was a young man, age twenty-three, who received permission from President Roosevelt to pause his military service to join a group of men investigating flight. His eagerness to see man airborne, and eventually glide through the air himself, had made him, incredibly, the protégé of Alexander Graham Bell, Orville and Wilbur Wright, and an engineer named Glenn Curtiss, despite all competing against each other to demonstrate a heavier-than-air flying machine. None of the men minded Selfridge's dueling associations, except for the Wrights, who suspected him of spying for Bell. "I don't trust him an inch . . . but he makes a pretense of great friendliness," Orville told Wilbur. Selfridge's "great friendliness" eventually won over Orville, who in 1908 granted Selfridge the chance to become history's first airplane passenger during a test flight at Fort Myer in Virginia. (When the plane holding Orville and Selfridge dived unexpectedly, Selfridge also became the first person ever to die in a plane crash.)

Fairchild was partial to Bell out of family loyalty, and also for his father-in-law's proven record for earth-changing invention. Moreover, Bell envisioned that the elusive secret to suspending man in the air would be tetrahedral kites, an idea that seemed more plausible than the oblong biplane the Wrights were developing in Ohio and North Carolina. Bell created a large board of tetrahedral cells, then affixed a single seat for a man to sit in; the only restraint would be the tightness of his grip.

History awards the Wright brothers credit for the first manned flight, just twelve seconds, in North Carolina in 1903, even though a shortage of witnesses led to widespread skepticism. As the Wrights were refining their design, Bell, Curtiss, Selfridge, and a host of other aspirants were doing the same to theirs. By 1907 *Scientific American* was offering a silver sculpture of an eagle with spread wings sitting atop a globe to anyone who could fly a full kilometer in the presence of a representative from the magazine. The contest had the effect of reducing the field from many aspirants to just two: the scrappy Wright brothers and the more established and better-funded union of Bell, Curtiss, Selfridge, and a Canadian engineer named Douglas McCurdy. The Bell team spent the summer of 1907 experimenting with every imaginable way to get off the ground—biplanes, kites, it hardly mattered. The year's most valuable currency was time.

After each test, the men would gather to compile notes and observations, discussing necessary adjustments before the next flight. Bell, in his characteristic knickerbockers and beret, always requested more information from the group. A man motivated by grand visions of innovation had an equal hunger for detail. He would stay up all night examining measurements, plotting physics equations, and troubleshooting failures. The rising sun signaled his bedtime, after which he'd sleep until ten, and then rise for more tests and measurements, the more minute the better. He believed large discoveries were the sum of small ones put together.

That same summer, Fairchild and Marian were visiting the Bells at their estate in Baddeck, Nova Scotia, on a sprawling peninsula that had taken Dr. Bell decades to amass. A little parcel here, another there, until it all added up to six hundred acres, which Bell had named Beinn Bhreagh, Gaelic for the "beautiful mountain" that rose at the end of the landmass. At the peninsula's tip, nearly touching the water, was the mansion of all mansions, a redbrick palace with more than a dozen rooms for the grandchildren (and future great-grandchildren) to explore.

Fairchild watched from a hillside, near where bald eagles nested and swooped for fish, as the group made one flight after another, each for longer time and greater distance, yet all short of a kilometer. The hill was littered with kites, some more than thirty feet long, discarded after failing in some way. "I sensed vaguely in 1907 that I had arrived at Baddeck at a critical period in the development of the heavier-than-air flying machines," Fairchild later wrote.

Bell's group made meaningful progress. The next summer, in June of 1908, Glenn Curtiss invited the Fairchilds to watch him attempt the *Scientific American* challenge in Hammondsport, New York, in a new biplane called the *June Bug*, named by Bell in tribute to the delicate flight of the June beetle. On America's birthday, July 4, 1908, the Fairchilds arrived for the attempt, the weather overcast and windy. The plane wasn't much to look at, in Fairchild's words, "frail but trim, with its struts, wires and white canvas surfaces mounted on bicycle wheels." But Curtiss had been a maker of motorcycle engines, and the main requirement of an early flying machine was a powerful engine with enough thrust to leave the ground. Curtiss showed the confidence of a man who had it figured out.

After a thunderstorm delayed the attempt, judges used a lengthy string to measure a full kilometer, along an abandoned racetrack, over a potato patch, and beside a vineyard with sharp fence posts capable of piercing a falling man.

The engine roared. Curtiss, his long brown hair blowing in the wind, guided the plane thirty feet in the air. The flight was so loud, people covered their ears. But no one covered their eyes. Curtiss touched down with an ungraceful bump that bordered on a crash. He was unhurt, as was the plane. But he had landed short.

Though running out of daylight, Curtiss was determined. Fairchild and the rest of the crowd helped push the plane back to the track where it had moments ago lifted off. Curtiss lifted off for a second time, flew over the crowd and over the mark, and then a little farther. People squealed when Curtiss emerged from the plane. Even the grouchy skeptic from *Scientific American* acknowledged that the feat had been accomplished and the trophy won.

Curtiss' achievement was notable in that it was documented. Man had flown, people had seen it, and a magazine of scientific repute had confirmed it was true. Yet this was a stunted achievement compared to the aviation milestones still to come: the hours-long test flights by the Wrights, Charles Lindbergh's 1927 transatlantic odyssey, and the great jets that would one day drop bombs on the other side of the world.

But men of science, like Fairchild and his father-in-law, Bell, had great respect for the first breakthrough, the proof of a concept. A glass ceiling could be shattered once; after that, latecomers could only break the pieces into smaller and smaller shards. "That brief afternoon at Hammondsport had changed my vision of the world as it was to be," Fairchild wrote. "There was no longer the shadow of a doubt in my mind that the sky would be full of aeroplanes, and that the time would come when people would travel through the air faster and more safely than they did then on the surface of the Earth."

The future had come, and Fairchild, again, had a front-row seat.

Exactly three days after Curtiss' famous flight, on July 7, 1908, Frank Meyer returned from China. His beard was longer, his eyes sunken, his skin worn like the leather of his boots. He had grown his fingernails so long over three years that they curled upward. The excitement around the office wasn't as much because of the arrival of Meyer as it was the story behind the seeds and saplings he had sent from China, and also from Manchuria, Korea, and eastern Siberia, which he had decided to walk across, too. People wanted to know the story behind each one.

From Shanghai, Meyer had sent seeds and cuttings of oats, millet, a thin-skinned watermelon, and new types of cotton. The staff of Fairchild's office watched with anticipation each time one of Meyer's shipments was unpacked. There were seeds of wild pears, new persimmons, and leaves of so-called Manchurian spinach that America's top spinach specialist would declare was the best America had ever seen. Meyer had delivered the first samples of asparagus ever to officially enter the United States. In 1908, few people had seen a soybean, a green legume common in central China. Even fewer people could have imagined that within one hundred years, the evolved descendants of soybeans that Meyer shipped back would cover the Midwest of the United States like a rug. Soybeans would be applied to more diverse uses than any other crop in history, as feed for livestock, food for humans (notably vegetarians), and even a renewable fuel called biodiesel.

Meyer also hadn't come empty-handed. He had physically brought

1907. Meyer wrote regularly from China, sometimes attaching photos he had developed. The letters described his work and the entourage he assembled to help him navigate, communicate, and collect.

This note reads: "5260 caravan on road from Peking to Wu-tar-chan [Wutai Shan]. Our caravan consisting of 8 mules and 7 men slowly creeping through the now dry bed of a river, the rivers become broader and broader on account of the deforestation of the mountain and all arable land is washed away. F. N. Meyer near Wu-tar-chan [Wutai Shan] Shansi [Shanxi], China, 1907."

home a bounty, having taken from China a steamer of the Standard Oil Company that, unlike a passenger ship, allowed him limitless cargo and better onboard conditions for plant material. He arrived with twenty tons, including red blackberries, wild apricots, two large zelkova trees (similar to elms), Chinese holly shrub, twenty-two white-barked pines, eighteen forms of lilac, four viburnum bushes that produced edible red berries, two spirea bushes with little white flowers, a rhododendron bush with pink and purple flowers, an evergreen shrub called a daphne, thirty kinds of bamboo (some of them edible), four types of lilies, and a new strain of grassy lawn sedge.

And his grand finale, two rare white-cheeked gibbons for the National Zoo, which attracted reporters in a way plants couldn't, and generated handsome publicity for Fairchild's office.

It was clear his voyage hadn't been easy. Nor had it been glamorous the way Fairchild's high-end odysseys with Lathrop had been. Meyer relayed how Chinese villagers eyed him as a "western devil." People watched him wash his naked body in bathhouses, sometimes full audiences gawking at the sight of a white man. Rumors spread regularly in 1906 that foreigners could be massacred at any time. He avoided death, but in February of that year, he was mugged and beaten bloody. His only defense, which allowed him to cheat death dozens of times, was a heavy sheepskin coat he wore during all seasons and that projected a strong man underneath. It was big, bulky, and irreversibly stained with layers of dirt. He wore heavy boots and a round wool hat, and let his brown beard grow untamed—altogether presenting a portrait of a frightening-looking man who may harbor fighting skills, or worse, contagious diseases.

He was beaten several more times and nearly strangled to death at least once. He confronted hungry bears, tigers, and wolves that he managed to either outrun or outsmart. In all, over three years, he regularly marched twenty miles a day. The man who loved to walk had found his adventure, a continent as filled with danger as it was unending.

Meyer had proved even more adept at plant hunting than Fairchild expected. His packing was meticulous, his seeds perfectly clean, all laid on beds of wrung-out peat moss to prevent drying out or molding in transit. Meyer rejected the trappings of fancy hotels and guest-houses for modest inns and local food, saving the Department—and the United States government—thousands of dollars. Even more impressive, he had come in early and under budget. He had written his itemized plant lists on thin paper to save postage. The accountants didn't scrutinize his receipts; they marveled at them, all orderly and with angular Chinese scrawls.

Fairchild held a barbecue at his home to celebrate Meyer's success. Around a bonfire, Meyer regaled the office with stories of the Orient, the fashionable term for where he had been. He described Chinese quirks like when villagers were awestruck at "the candle" inside his flashlight. He recounted how people tugged his boots and pants and stared at his blue eyes. He imitated the bandits and recreated the beatings in Siberia and described how he slept on brick beds swarming with vermin and hung a mosquito net to protect himself from the locusts falling from the ceiling. During at least one winter, he said, he withstood temperatures of twenty-five degrees Fahrenheit below zero.

The cold was especially inconvenient when he came to an inn where a foreigner had written on the wall, in French, *"Hotel of 1000 bedbugs."* Meyer had to choose between sleeping outside in the cold and building a fire that would fill the room with smoke and activate the bugs. He chose the warmth, and constructed a makeshift bed by pushing together three small tables. Another discomfort, he recalled, was the stench. "When I tell you that chamber pots and water closets are unknown, you may imagine the rest."

Still, the hardship had been worth it, both for Meyer and for America. It wasn't yet clear, but one of the greatest successes of Meyer's life had occurred on his first expedition. A world-changing find that he had almost missed.

Several weeks before he left Peking, Meyer visited a small village and noticed, in a house's doorway, a small bush with fruit as yellow as a fresh egg yolk. Meyer ignored a man who told him the plant was ornamental, its fruit not typically eaten but prized for its year-round production. The fruit looked like a mix between a mandarin and a citron (which later genetic testing would confirm). It was a lemon, but smaller and rounder—its flavor surprised him as both sweeter than a citron and tarter than an orange. And its price, twenty cents per fruit or ten dollars per tree, suggested that people with an abundance of other citrus valued it greatly.

Meyer had little room in his baggage, but he used his double-edged bowie knife to take a cutting where the branches formed a V, the choice spot to secure its genetic material.

That cutting made the voyage to Washington, and then the trip to an experiment station in Chico, California, where it propped up a new lemon industry grateful to receive a sweeter variety. The lemon became known as the Meyer lemon, and from it came lemon tarts, lemon pies, and millions of glasses of lemonade.

For this contribution, Meyer wasn't paid much. The government sponsored his travel and his postage. His modest salary—just 1,200 dollars per year—seemed low for a man of such esteem and growing fame. After Meyer's first expedition, Fairchild quietly increased his salary to 1,400 dollars. Fairchild also saw to it that Meyer would return to China and its surrounding areas, and then again after that, with each expedition coming the reasonable expectation that Meyer would turn up an incredible new cache of plants.

This style of exciting and exhausting plant hunting vaulted Meyer from obscurity to national renown. Fairchild sent a telegram to Gilbert Grosvenor at *National Geographic* reporting, "Frank Meyer is back from three years in Northwestern China, he could give an interesting account of agricultural explorations." Fairchild also arranged for Meyer to meet Teddy Roosevelt, a man in the sunset of his presidency but with increasing energy, and on a lively streak of environmental conservation. Fairchild thought Roosevelt might be interested in hearing about the deforestation Meyer witnessed in eastern China, and the ghastly effects of hillsides cut naked of their trees.

Meyer grudgingly accepted the invitation, only because Fairchild insisted. He visited Roosevelt in his Long Island home in Oyster Bay, where the president spent the summer of 1908. Meyer brought photographs of the Wutai Shan mountain east of Beijing, where he had witnessed such devastating deforestation that it triggered landslides that cut off rivers, suffocated farmland, and washed away entire villages. Few men in those days said no to the gregarious Roosevelt, and so when the president asked Meyer if he could include the images in a report to Congress, Meyer, marveling at his trajectory from poor immigrant to a man asked permission by a president, agreed.

For all this he remained humble—often soft-spoken and reluctant to accept credit. But in rare moments of guarded comfort with Fairchild, Meyer exhibited a healthy sense of self, an ego that had powered him through cold, dark, and thankless months, amid fights with attackers and arguments with translators and rumors of his impending death at the hands of lawless gangs. He kept his confidence hidden, but inside, he had grown proud of his growing record as botanical daredevil. "I will be famous," he once said. "Just wait a century or two."

CHAPTER SEVENTEEN

Outlaws, Brigands, and Murderers

Frank Meyer's success wasn't enough to appease Charles Marlatt. In fact, it made him even more suspicious. By 1909, Marlatt had converted his wariness of Meyer into outright disdain.

If not for his childhood friendship with Fairchild, Marlatt might have taken Meyer to court, or worse, a dark alley. His anger often verged on spite. When government entomologists discovered a new Chinese insect in America, Marlatt, whose government duties also included naming new things, vindictively tagged the pesky bug *Dynaspidiotus meyeri*.

Marlatt felt only slightly warmer toward Fairchild. Their wives were friendly—they took weaving classes together—and outwardly, the men were cordial and polite. But in the private conversations they shared with close colleagues, each complained about the other's ineptitude. Marlatt's crime was hysteria, and Fairchild's naïveté.

Marlatt's stubbornness was a sign of panic, not reason. It was based on fear and on the idea that the very act of exploring opened oneself to unnecessary risk. Organisms perfectly normal in their natural setting could be dangerous somewhere else, and with no warning. "The greatest danger is often from something you do not know about," Marlatt warned. "It is the unknown things that you cannot find that we have to protect this country from." The best example he offered was the chestnut blight fungus that was stran-gling American chestnut trees, great icons of the frontier. The blight originated somewhere in China, where it was innocuous, but became dangerous when it entered American borders.

This was insane to Fairchild. To be scared of unknown things based on a few cherry-picked examples wasn't a policy; it was an im-pulse, and a foolish one. For every evil that Marlatt illuminated, Fair-child found something good that had come of it. The Chinese chestnut blight that apparently kept Marlatt awake at night had also brought Americans new varieties of Oriental pears and Chinese chestnuts, both resistant to the rust, and thus, advantageous for America to produce. "It would be eminently unfair to assume that because we do not know that little apple seedlings from the old world or from Japan are as clean and free from disease as any which we can produce in America, they represent undesirable immigrants and should be excluded from the country," Fairchild argued one day to a group of forestry officials, some of whom sympathized with Marlatt.

Still, Marlatt banged his drum louder and more forcefully. The threat of insects was growing more dangerous every day. The boll weevil, which had come to the United States ten years earlier and tended to feast on cotton flowers and buds, was now beginning its eventual wipeout of the cotton industry, which had just barely re-gained its footing after the Civil War. Marlatt claimed the invasive insect was responsible for the spread of typhus, yellow fever, and ma-laria. These claims weren't backed up by science, but that hardly mat-tered. Marlatt was simply raising awareness and, in the process, taking little pain to drop frightening words—"dirty," "destroy," "dangerous." If he could have changed government policy himself, he would have. But he and his like-minded colleagues knew that in a representative democracy, lasting change comes not by personal fiat but from Congress.

One of the reasons Marlatt was so angry during the cherry blossom episode was because his first attempt to shut down reckless plant imports by legislative vote blew up in his face. He had drafted a bill for Congress that called for inspection of all nursery stock at all American entry points. It wouldn't have ended plant imports, but would have made the process so onerous that Fairchild and his band of explorers would be driven to quit. Marlatt found a sympathetic congressman from Kansas to introduce the bill—quietly and during the lethargic lame-duck session of 1910. It passed through committee, then through the full House of Representatives, and then through a committee on the Senate side. The penultimate step, before the president signed it into law, would have been passage by the full Senate. But the night before the vote, a group of legislators sympathetic to the nurserymen caught wind of Marlatt's idea of "national safety." Marlatt's proposal, in addition to slowing the activities of Fairchild's office, would have tightened a noose around an entire industry of people who grew plants with imported rootstock. The lawmakers blocked the bill, and Marlatt lost.

Marlatt's boss told him, "Now that you have had your fingers burned, drop the effort." But Marlatt refused, vowing that he would immediately engineer a new bill.

Four months after the first defeat, he tried again, this time with another bill, and, rather than attempt in secret, he decided to act in full view of the public. In April of 1910, Marlatt testified in front of Congress that the United States needed a "Chinese Wall" of its own to keep out so-called "plant enemies." The testimony was almost theater. Marlatt dropped scary terms and chilling statistics, to the point that William Pitkin, Fairchild's friend who happened to be head of the American Association of Nurserymen, called his bluffs distortions or, even worse, pure lies.

The rationale that fueled the nurserymen—and Fairchild, too— was that America shouldn't act in fear. Most incoming plants from around the world were fine, and responsible inspections of suspicious loads were sufficient. What the nurserymen didn't say, but was certainly true, was that Marlatt's quarantine proposal would cost nursery growers billions, plus the incalculable loss of American economic growth. The nurserymen had a powerful voice, but not as powerful as the Ladies' Garden Clubs of America, with membership in the thousands. The women opposed any change in the plants available for their use, many of them from abroad.

Perhaps as a result, Congress didn't act that year, nor the year after. Impatient, Marlatt instead took his zeal for change to state governments. States had the power to police anything entering their borders, and no state had more plants coming in than California, mostly owing to the Hawaiian Islands. After the islands' 1898 annexation to the United States, ships shuttled between Honolulu and San Francisco, carrying sugar, pineapples, and the occasional crate of guavas. Marlatt asked California officials in Sacramento if they were aware that the Mediterranean fruit fly—also known as both the West Australian fruit fly and the Bermuda peach maggot—had recently been spotted on Oahu. And did they also know that steamships from Hawaii were arriving weekly, almost entirely uninspected, in San Francisco?

Technically, it was illegal for California to act on its own. Its jurisdiction extended *to* its borders, not over them; only the federal government could regulate *between* states. And yet, Marlatt's fear campaign had whipped up such frenzy on the West Coast that California's governor, Hiram Johnson, the man who would be Teddy Roosevelt's failed running mate a year later, decided to act unilaterally.

Governor Johnson was a grouchy, impatient man. He had no interest in waiting for Congress to protect his state from impending attack. His administration created a Quarantine Division, which, almost overnight, began to prohibit the shipment of all fruits from Hawaii, inspected or not. When it came to travelers themselves, who were guaranteed a measure of protection against searches of their shoes, bags, and bodies, Johnson leaned on the steamship companies that operated between Hawaii and California. Faced with the threat of losing access to California ports, the companies forced passengers to sign a waiver consenting to a body search. If it meant a safer country, travelers were glad to oblige.

Fairchild, however, was incensed. Marlatt had drummed up overblown fear. And then, in an affront to Thomas Jefferson's framework of a federal republic, egged on a state to thumb its nose at the federal government. Fairchild took this personally. He marched to Marlatt's office, where the two got into a shouting match.

Both men yelled past each other, as though arguing over a wide ravine.

But that wasn't the worst part. The worst part hadn't happened yet. The worst part would wait until Frank Meyer began sending plants from his second expedition, in 1911, not long after California instituted its new policy. Meyer shipped material from eastern China while he continued to walk across the Caucasus, Russian Turkestan, Chinese Turkestan, and a new part of Siberia.

Fairchild had mostly shielded Meyer from the public feud with Marlatt, so Meyer couldn't have known what would happen when his heaping pile of cuttings, suckers, and seeds finally landed in San Francisco.

Meyer's shipment contained thirty tons of Asiatic plants, meticulously packed, labeled, and organized. The contents may have yielded the key to a new industry of citrus, new apple varieties that would one day be American heirlooms, or grapes that would elevate America's wine producers decades ahead of schedule. The world would never know.

Even Meyer, a man who had faced the gravest indignities on a continent that seemed to ooze with disease, crime, and death; even Meyer, who had seen all the horrors humans were capable of, froze in eye-bulging disbelief when he learned that as soon as his crates reached San Francisco, they were seized, fumigated, and burned to ashes.

That summer, Fairchild took a break from the feud. He wanted to escape the tension, and the scorching heat of Washington. The ill-ventilated Department of Agriculture was only habitable in the early morning, so Fairchild had adopted the habit of arriving at dawn and staying inside the steamy building as long as he could bear it, dashing off correspondence by hand to save the time it would take to type. When he'd had enough of it, he suggested to Marian that they go see her parents in Nova Scotia.

Mr. and Mrs. Bell always loved seeing the Fairchilds, and particularly the pair of rascals known as the Fairchildren. David and Marian now had two; their second, a daughter, had come that spring. To the great delight of Barbour Lathrop, they named her Barbara Lathrop Fairchild.

When the Fairchilds landed in Canada, Mrs. Hubbard, Marian's grandmother on her mother's side, urged David and Marian to extend their trip to come visit her in England, where she summered each year. The Fairchilds didn't object to traveling even farther from Washington. The same type of transatlantic steamer that once shuttled Fairchild across the ocean on his first overseas trip now carried him, his wife, and their two young children. The voyage was unremarkable compared to the life-changing ocean crossing when Fairchild met Lathrop, their arrival left them perfectly punctual to have tea with Mrs. Hubbard at her English estate near the border of Scotland.

Fairchild and Marian wandered through the cool, damp air visiting the gardens of Mrs. Hubbard's neighbors. He marveled at the large conifers, many of which had not long before been introduced to the United States. He visited Murthly Castle, constructed in the fifteenth century. He was in a daze from the piercing debate in Washington, and in a sort of denial that plant introduction, to which he had devoted his life, was at risk of withering away.

The fight over foreign plants didn't stop while Fairchild was abroad. But it did escalate when he returned. What had begun at the

Department of Agriculture and had then risen to the halls of Congress and the California statehouse would now be brought to the people—a war for public opinion.

Fairchild mapped out a plan. He proposed speeches to the scientific societies in Washington. He submitted an article to the *Youth's Companion* magazine of his childhood, hoping inspired kids could convince their parents that exploration was good and exciting. He asked his friend Edward Clark, a writer, to contribute an article for the influential *Technical World* magazine, a feeder of news and commentary to newspapers across the country. Fairchild provided Clark with the stacks of letters Meyer had written from Asia, each of which had come with a new shipment of seeds and cuttings. Fairchild couldn't believe that anyone who learned of Meyer, a man cheating death for farmers he didn't even know, could oppose the type of plant introduction that, for over a decade, had enriched America.

"Explorer Meyer," Clark would write, "has frozen and melted alternately as the altitudes have changed; he has encountered wild beasts and men nearly as wild; he has . . . been the subject of the always alert suspicions of government officials and of strange peoples jealous of intrusions into their land—but he has found what he was sent for." In the package of materials Fairchild sent Clark, he included articles that demonstrated the popular appeal of Meyer's work, including one from the *Los Angeles Times* in 1908 detailing how Meyer, with just "coolies and carts," set off to cow a region of "outlaws, brigands and murderers."

Fairchild urged Clark to underscore the success of plant introduction, many exciting foods made possible by Fairchild's hands and virtually all under his watch. The thick alfalfas from the Andes that had "radically" extended the range of American alfalfa. The dates from the Middle East that had yielded, just that year, "five tons" of fruit in Southern California and Arizona. The mango industry in Florida that had grown from nothing to a commercial behemoth. The list continued with the same pace as one imagines Fairchild banging his head against a wall. Seedless persimmons, new cherries, ten forms of olives, apples, pomegranates, wild peas, hardy oranges.

None of this was to diminish the danger of invading pests. But Fairchild lobbied Clark—and anyone else who would listen in a country increasingly fearful of the outside—that there were protection measures already in place. Rooting out the threat of foreign invaders should be the work of government scientists, not of untrained port workers around the country. As Fairchild expected, Clark's essay would run in many newspapers, in agricultural hotspots like Duluth, Minnesota; Sandusky, Ohio; and Corning, Iowa, where agricultural sympathy could go far.

Marlatt, meanwhile, had decided on a different strategy for his campaign. Why kowtow to farmers when the people making policy decisions were on the locomotive corridor between Washington and New York? The better strategy was the undemocratic one: to lobby the influential eggheads in Washington, who could then push Congress to pass a law for plant quarantines. Who cared if farmers liked it?

Mostly out of strategy and a little out of spite, Marlatt hit Fairchild in the most sensitive of places: his family. Marlatt pitched an article about the dangers of plant invaders to the *National Geographic*, the same magazine that listed Fairchild and Swingle as associate editors. Gilbert Grosvenor, the chief editor, and Alexander Graham Bell, the society's erstwhile president, were partial to Fairchild, but neither could deny that Marlatt had the credentials to make his argument. The magazine was a journal of science, not a family mouthpiece.

In May of 1911, one month after Clark's essay defending Fairchild (and glorifying Meyer) was published around the country, Marlatt's article was awarded top billing in *National Geographic*, the lead story with a forceful cover line.

PESTS AND PARASITES
WHY WE NEED A NATIONAL LAW TO PREVENT THE IMPORTATION OF INSECT-INFESTED AND DISEASED PLANTS
By Charles Lester Marlatt

Marlatt's report was breathless and hysterical. But it was compelling. The magazine, which now regularly published photographs, ran thirty-one images with Marlatt's story, nearly all of them showing trees crawling with colonies of vermin. These pests had caused great damage, Marlatt said. The Argentine ant was "destroying" citrus in Louisiana. The alfalfa-leaf weevil had already decimated "hundreds of fields of alfalfa in Utah, and is spreading to adjacent States." To say nothing of all the diseases still to be discovered—ones that could kill the sprawling fields of potatoes, corn, and wheat.

> Fully 50 per cent of the important injurious insect pests in this country are of foreign origin. Among these are the codling moth, the Hessian fly, the asparagus beetles, the hop-plant louse, the cabbage worm, the wheat-plant louse, oyster-shell bark louse, pea weevil, the Croton bug, the Angoumois grain moth, the horn fly of cattle, and in comparatively recent years have been introduced such important pests as the cotton-boll weevil, the San José scale, the gypsy and brown-tail moths into New England, the Argentine ant into New Orleans, and the alfalfa-leaf weevil into Utah. . . . A properly enforced quarantine inspection law in the past would have excluded many, if not most, of the foreign insect enemies which are now levying an enormous annual tax on the products of the farms and orchards and forests of this country.

Without providing evidence, Marlatt claimed the annual loss due to pests could be as "inconceivable" as one billion dollars. The number made Fairchild's small-scale boasts of industry growth (five tons! dozens of trees!) look quaint by comparison. Marlatt also laid blame for the obstinacy. "This effort has been blocked very largely by a small body [of people] who, careless of the consequences to the country at large, feared some slight check on freedom of their operations," Marlatt wrote, speaking squarely at those who imported plants, like Fairchild and his star explorer, Meyer.

The story made valid points. A changing world had spread disease faster than ever in history. The golden age of travel had also been the golden age of transport, moving everything—good and bad—across oceans with unprecedented volume and speed. Moreover, Marlatt's photos weren't doctored. They were taken with the intention to shock, but all were based on things that were in fact happening in the United States. Swarms of moth larvae or blister rust were real problems, causing towns in some places to chop down full groves of pine.

Yet Marlatt's argument fractured where it assigned blame. If small-scale imports of lemons, apricots, or cherries could be linked to outbreaks and field wipeouts, Marlatt couldn't show it. He bore the burden of proof to rationalize a new law, and he fell short.

This nuance wasn't lost on Fairchild, who was himself guilty of having an overly idealistic view of nature, believing that diseases could be stamped out easily and that the benefits of research always outweighed the risks. But Fairchild's opinion fit within the idea of globalization—building a wall of isolation wouldn't give America an advantage; it would hamstring its efforts to remain competitive. "The whole trend of the world is toward greater intercourse, more frequent exchange of commodities, less isolation, and a greater mixture of the plants and plant products over the face of the globe," he would argue. Closing America's borders would render the country a little like the cannibalistic tribes of Fiji, isolated from the world and forced to adopt unseemly habits to sustain itself.

When Fairchild saw Marlatt's essay in *National Geographic*, the first impulse for a man not prone to impulsiveness was to resign from the board. It surprised him that Bell and Grosvenor, who ran the magazine, would give unsubstantiated hysterics such a high platform. But Marian, who was befuddled that the dispute had become so personal, and so quickly, urged her husband to combat words with better words. A bit like Lathrop in earlier days, she encouraged Fairchild to continue the argument, to win at any rhetorical cost, rather than walk away pouting. Resigning would have turned Fairchild into a small scientist, she believed, easily dismissed as a man of ego over fact.

So Fairchild lobbed the shuttlecock back. Five months after Marlatt's 1911 essay in *National Geographic*, Fairchild penned the October issue's leading story. With it, Fairchild attempted to soften the debate, to remove the drama he sensed was putting off the casual reader, and to reframe a scary topic as something almost humanitarian.

NEW PLANT IMMIGRANTS
By David Fairchild

Plant exploration, he explained, had "barely touched the fringe of its possibilities." Thirty-one thousand different plants had come into the country by now, and that quantity represented only a small fraction of the bounty still waiting to be discovered. Together, he said, they demonstrated the "greatness of the possibilities which progress in agricultural research is creating."

A point of particular pride was that, compared to Marlatt's thirty-one photographs showing gruesome scenes of vermin, decay, and neglect, Fairchild's photos showed delectable specimens. Robust forests of bamboo. Bunches of ripened dates. Swollen alfalfa. A bulging persimmon. It was subtle, and perhaps no one but Fairchild noticed, but there were thirty-three in all.

In reality, dueling magazine articles amounted to small megaphones at a time when it seemed like everyone was shouting. For in the early months of 1913, the earth shifted again for plant introduction. Woodrow Wilson became president on March 4, and with his arrival came the end of James Wilson's sixteen-year stretch as secretary of agriculture. It was (and remains) the longest tenure for any cabinet secretary in American history. Counting the days he spent clearing his desk after Woodrow Wilson's inauguration, James Wilson held the office under four presidents. In that time, he expanded the Department of Agriculture's staff and expenditures sixfold.

Secretary Wilson wasn't sad to go. Rising from a poor Scottish immigrant to United States secretary of agriculture had been one of the world's most meteoric paths, living proof that America was committed to building itself with the best people from around the world. Once a ruthless political manipulator, Wilson in his later years had mellowed, even humbled. It genuinely surprised him that each president had decided to keep him in the job, a sign of his capability and how little McKinley, Roosevelt, and Taft had trusted their own expertise on matters of food and soil.

President Wilson's victory had come largely on domestic issues. Campaign contribution limits were too high; the federal government was too poor not to levy an income tax on every person; the weakest Americans needed help. The implication had been that foreign policy could wait, or, depending on the day someone asked, it didn't matter. The imperialist policy that men like McKinley, Roosevelt, and Taft had built for decades, the one whose centerpiece was a world for America to exploit, now seemed foolish in a world full of danger and mistrust. While McKinley, Roosevelt, and Taft had spread America's reach by collecting colonies (Hawaii, Puerto Rico, the Philippines) and protecting others (Cuba, Panama), Wilson believed America could make do with its assets at home, not expensive and hard-to-reach ones abroad. Part of his platform called for the independence of the Philippines, less out of moral responsibility than because of a *why bother?* approach to a territory that had soaked up so much American treasure for a decade and yielded little in return.

And so, with his right hand raised, Wilson's oath of office ended America's fourteen-year stretch of imperialism.

Fairchild found 1912, the year of Woodrow Wilson's election, lamentable in other ways, too. The president's inward-not-outward policy about America's place in the world would also extend to agriculture. Wilson believed that the future of American farms wasn't in novel foods but in "efficiency." Farming more by farming smarter. It was a worthwhile goal for a country trying to build itself, but Fairchild was as familiar with large-scale farming as he was with Parcheesi. His expertise was in botany, not running a farm, and this ineptitude cost him—and his office—relevance.

Worse, one of the last acts of Congress before Wilson's election had come at great cost to Fairchild. The long-standing feud between him and Marlatt boiled over on August 20, 1912, when one of them was declared the winner. Marlatt prevailed when Congress passed the Plant Quarantine Act, a name as blunt as the action it required: to regulate the entrance of all foreign plants into the United States.

After years of advocating for America to close its doors, Marlatt had bested Fairchild. The law wasn't the "Chinese Wall" Marlatt once proposed that America build around itself. But the Quarantine Act halted the unrestricted flow nonetheless.

Even having won, Marlatt couldn't stop fighting. When he learned that the secretary of agriculture would have the power to clear plants for entry, he argued that such discretion was too specific for a man of such generalized power. The bill was eventually amended to give authority to a new agency called the Federal Horticultural Board, which, conveniently, Marlatt controlled.

Despite Secretary Wilson's former jousts with Fairchild, the outgoing secretary would have been a robust ally of Fairchild's now-widespread program of plant introduction. Wilson had bene-fited from Fairchild's success; it was at least one reason he kept his job so long. And Wilson had loved Frank Meyer, reading with en-thusiasm the letters that came from China. The James Wilson skep-tical of plant introduction in the 1890s had become a devoted apostle of adventure and horticultural modernity. Secretary Wilson's de-parture meant a less sympathetic new secretary would take the job, one who shared President Wilson's view that America didn't need foreign things.

If there was a bright spot among the disheartening prognosis, it was that Frank Meyer kept exploring. Even though Meyer had to subject his findings to more and more inspection and scrutiny, there remained at least one narrow avenue still open for importing plant material. The new secretary of agriculture, David Houston, a uni-versity president with no farm experience, asked Fairchild to turn Meyer into something of a double agent—exploring to find useful plants (that would have to pass inspection) *and* to investigate plant diseases infecting the United States whose antidote could be found abroad. The mandate allowed Meyer to depart on a third expedi-tion, a proposed journey through northwestern China, through Gansu Province to the border of Tibet.

Houston asked Meyer to investigate whether the blight poisoning America's chestnut trees was of Chinese origin, and if so, how the Chinese people, with their centuries' worth of farming experience, had stopped it.

To find out, Meyer sailed first to Beijing. He found the fungus and, to everyone's surprise but his, that the Chinese had long before bred trees resistant to the fungus. Meyer took cuttings of these trees. When his shipment was received, a group of pathologists told Fair-child that Meyer's work was the most meaningful accomplishment in a decade of pathology research. This pleased Fairchild, who had grown accustomed to Meyer working miracles. It also showed in one example how plant exploration offered not only problems but solutions.

Fairchild was satisfied seeing Meyer's eventual shipments home, all inspected carefully. He sent new varieties of walnuts, hazelnuts, and chestnuts, and new seeds of jujubes, pears, apples, peaches, and a small, red, berrylike fruit known as haw. His shipment set a new record for quantity of plant material ever shipped from China to Washington. All of it passed quarantine.

When Meyer was in the field, this type of abundance was normal. But it had a side effect that Fairchild couldn't have expected.

The dispatches that *The Los Angeles Times* had been publishing about Meyer's adventures, the ones that detailed his harrowing tales of near-death encounters and Hollywood-style evils, had attracted the attention of a young man in Altadena, California, who had grown up gardening and then run a commercial nursery.

Wilson Popenoe, twenty-one years old and easily excited, wrote to Fairchild that he had a particular fascination with avocados and wanted to explore like the gun-toting, road-hardened, danger-seeking Meyer. Popenoe said in his letter that he had already been around the world once, hunting for dates for his father, who ran a commercial nursery. But now Popenoe wanted to be a real plant hunter, a government agent. The job would bring an upgrade in budget, adventure, and, if he could emulate Meyer, glory.

Fairchild wrote back to Popenoe and explained that plant exploration was detailed and tedious work, newly subject to rules and obstacles, and even during the best day exploring still required substantial expertise and immeasurable danger.

Popenoe assured him he had what it took. He explained that he had wandered the same streets of Baghdad Fairchild had once risked his life to reach. He had caught malaria in a foreign port, and had been holed up with dysentery for weeks. Wilson Popenoe, at just twenty-one, knew what seed hunting entailed. And after he gave it some thought, Fairchild, now forty-four, agreed. Finding skilled young men to continue the burdensome job of plant exploration had now become his life's work.

CHAPTER EIGHTEEN

Fly the Coop

Under the new rules of the Quarantine Act, introducing plants wasn't illegal, just much harder. Any plant that entered the United States had to be brought directly to Washington, D.C., no detours like the cross-country trips that Meyer was making with cargo from the West Coast. Fairchild was ordered to build a receiving center on the National Mall and was given five thousand dollars for it, a sum large enough for only a modest shack one fire away from wiping out the entire program. Entomologists would pick up the new samples every week, put them in a queue for testing, test them, and if they passed, return them to Fairchild's scientists, who would propagate them into seeds and send them out to farmers. Introducing plants was still possible, but the new obstacles effectively covered what was once an open highway with red lights and stop signs.

Fairchild couldn't restrain Meyer even if he wanted to. Meyer continued to explore, but with increasingly erratic emotions. He was everywhere, all at once, and accelerated both his collecting of plants and his intensity for the world. He showed up in places nobody suspected. He visited his family in Holland, and then Saint Petersburg, and in the months that followed, ventured to Chinese Turkestan and remote Mongolia. His letters to Fairchild showed the miraculous way Meyer cheated death, sometimes daily, as he was continuously robbed, threatened, and warned not to enter areas rich in useful crops that he visited anyway. He covered icy terrain and emerged atop mountains only to keep walking down the other side. He truly hated staying still.

On this, his second expedition, he clipped cuttings of wild apricots and asparagus that he would send back to Washington. Both found their way into the hands of nurserymen, and eventually farmers; this had become the usual process for Meyer's findings. He mailed back the newest and most durable varieties of plums and cherries that grew abundantly in high temperatures. He picked up soybeans, which he now had studied in volume so great he could spot tiny nuances in their appearance and how they grew. Constantly afraid of being poisoned in a culture where he stood out, he ate only bread and sausage, and drank only tea, the only vitamins he consumed coming from the fruits and vegetables he chewed for study.

Very few things could have stopped Meyer. He was reckless and ruthless, and had seen such horrors that warnings of mountain gangs or animal attacks were as good as fiction to him until they actually happened. But Meyer had heard reliable reports about fighting in the Chinese territory. There was a rebellion afoot in 1912 that had started a year earlier to overthrow the Qing Empire, China's last imperial dynasty. Despite the setbacks and institutional roadblocks, the threat of revolution and the new rules that covered his work in Washington, his luck never ran out. "It seems as if the good wishes from so many people who take an interest in my work keep some sort of protective atmosphere around me," he wrote to Fairchild in the months before he came back.

Indeed. Meyer returned to Europe before crossing the Atlantic. Again he averted tragedy with the blind luck that had become his signature.

In April 1912, Meyer held a ticket to return to America on a majestic new ocean liner, the RMS *Titanic*, the most impressive and durable ship ever built. If he hadn't become ill the day before the

Around 1911. Meyer covered thousands of miles on foot, constantly looking for clues that might yield new foods. In the town of Aksu in Chinese Turkestan, Meyer marveled at a strange sunken valley carved by the Aksu River. "It would be strange indeed if in so peculiar a civilization as this there should not be found new food plants," he wrote. He asked the owners of these houses if he could inspect their kitchens. He sampled their foods and collected seeds of the ones he liked.

voyage and traded his ticket for one on the next ship, the RMS *Mauretania* departing four days later, he, a grown man unqualified for a lifeboat, would have perished in the cold Atlantic.

Meyer lasted just a few months in Washington before he itched to return to Asia. Something about the continent and its endless plants called to him, and with such ferocity he quickly forgot about the fighting that had only months before driven him away.

His short stay in Washington, however, meant he could meet Wilson Popenoe, the young man who looked at Meyer with such fawning admiration it left Meyer speechless. He was used to people eyeing him suspiciously and threatening to break his neck, not admirers staring glassy-eyed with a goofy smile. Meyer didn't want to mentor anyone. He had too much work to do. "I wish I had seven bodies," he would later tell Fairchild, complaining that he didn't have enough time to complete the work he found so urgent.

Indeed, if Meyer had had six assistants, he could have used them. Because what Meyer lacked most wasn't money or energy; it was time. China's unrest was only a small matter compared to the larger war the world was poised to fight. America hadn't yet entered the conflict that would be known as the Great War, the first war to drag together all of the globe's major powers, but it was heading in that direction, and the prospect of a changing world effectively put Meyer on a deadline.

Before returning to Asia, he decided to make a tour of the United States. It wasn't for tourism but for research. He wanted to go to Gansu Province, an area believed to be insulated from much of the fighting. It also stood to reason that, being so scarcely visited, it was full of plants that no Westerner had seen. If this was true, it would be impossible for Meyer to bring them all back. He needed to understand which kinds of things farmers wanted, and what kinds of growing conditions they could provide. He visited farms along the

Around 1916. Popenoe followed the advice and the literal footsteps of Fairchild, including making an early trip to Guatemala to search for better avocado varieties. Popenoe came to like avocados so much that he spent the next decade on assignment in Central and South America devoted solely to avocados.

northern United States, traveling from Boston nearly to Seattle, popping in on men in their fields. Often, they emerged from their barns curious why a sloppy, bearded man was chewing on their plants.

Meanwhile, back in Washington, having been rebuffed by Meyer, Popenoe became the protégé of David Fairchild instead. Fairchild was his boss, and also his landlord. Popenoe rented a room in the Fairchilds' home in Maryland and paid for it with the generous eight-thousand-dollar-a-year salary that Fairchild granted him. Such a large sum likely reflected Fairchild's former budget, designed to sustain a dozen plant explorers. The new quarantine rules and bad publicity had made the work so arduous and prone to inducing hysteria that many of the former contractors had quit. By 1915, Fairchild's best hopes had almost entirely narrowed to Meyer and Popenoe alone.

Popenoe was eager to return to traveling after the trip to Baghdad he'd described in his pitch letter to Fairchild. He had a singular focus to board a boat, to go somewhere unknown. He wore the same pair of torn pants day after day and only barely combed his hair. He was, in almost every way, like David Fairchild had once been, full of passion but empty in direction, a man who wanted to go somewhere but oblivious to how to get moving. The only difference was that Popenoe lacked self-doubt, the crippling overanalysis that kept Fairchild away from Java long after Lathrop had given him the means to get there. Popenoe was ready to leave at a moment's notice, provided someone first told him where to go.

This imbalance of knowledge and experience fashioned Fairchild a little like Lathrop, the mentor wise in the world who had seen and experienced all that the young man before him dreamed of. Fairchild seemed to relish the opportunity to pay forward what Lathrop had once given him, a leg up in a world where not having one would've spelled a dramatically different fate. "The chief tried always to help me as 'Uncle Barbour' had helped him," Popenoe would later tell people. Fairchild egged Popenoe on, he chastised him, he urged him to get his hair cut. Just as Lathrop had done at the beginning of their travel together, Fairchild, only half joking, made Popenoe promise that as long as he was doing the work of plant introduction, he wouldn't get married. "Keep away from the girls," Fairchild told the junior explorer. "Wait awhile and you can have anything you want. If you settle down now it'll greatly interfere with your career." Even so, Fairchild remained worried that Popenoe would become restless and, as the boss put it, "fly the coop."

Lathrop, meanwhile, continued to reappear on occasional visits to the office or in letters from around the world. Without Fairchild, Lathrop was aimless, wandering tropical ports, drawn to warm locales where his arthritis wouldn't flare up. When bored, he would talk up nursery growers in the tropics and ask questions Fairchild had given him, or convince them to send stock to Washington, attention David Fairchild. In exchange for Lathrop's efforts, Fairchild granted him the title "special agent" for the Department of Agriculture, with an annual salary of one dollar, although Lathrop would never cash the checks.

When it came time for Popenoe's first assignment, Fairchild thought of a task with relatively low risk and high potential. He wanted Popenoe to investigate the popular navel orange and scour Brazil, where it was rumored to have originated, for a better variety to boost farmers in a flooded citrus market.

Fairchild deemed the mission worthwhile because the navel had been one of the few plant introductions to have occurred by accident, by a series of such lucky coincidences it almost defied belief. In 1869, William Saunders, the American government's chief horticulturist, asked American consuls to contribute valuable seeds from their countries. One consul in Brazil sent twigs from a sweet seedless orange that grew near the port of Salvador, but the cutting died en route. He then sent a shipment of buds from Brazil, which

Saunders propagated onto rootstock and then sent to Florida, where they, too, died.

By a stroke of incredible luck, Saunders had also given two trees to his former neighbor in Washington, a woman who had moved to California. She planted the trees "in her doorway," lore would relay, and then watered them by hand (her husband was too cheap for formal irrigation). In 1879, she entered into a state horticultural contest a seedless orange with an odd indentation in its bottom—a navel, someone would call it. It won first prize and carried the humble orange from obscurity to ubiquity.

Fairchild was skeptical that it happened so conveniently. Having made plant introductions for decades, he knew the road was paved with pitfalls and failure. He knew what kind of expertise, growing conditions, and gardening finesse were required to recreate the precise fruit someone saw in a faraway country. A dominant orange grown by accident seemed as far-fetched as a man one day walking on the moon.

But if the navel was, in fact, a stroke of luck from a charmed consular official, Fairchild imagined that even better fruit could be found by a professional trained to know what to look for. Fairchild paired Popenoe, the adventurer, with two citrus experts for a three-man expedition to Brazil. In the weeks before they left, Fairchild was impressed to see Popenoe studying Portuguese, preparing himself with the skills and knowledge to do a thorough job.

Popenoe and the pair of citrusmen departed New York on October 4, 1913, aboard the SS *Vandyck*, which, to their surprise, was also carrying Theodore Roosevelt. The former president, out of office and bored with his post-presidency, had decided to embark on a punishing and dangerous adventure.

Popenoe, ever the opportunist, stood next to Roosevelt as reporters on deck yelled questions and flashed bursts of light. Roosevelt and his son Kermit would leave the boat at the Amazon to explore the River of Doubt. Popenoe wrote in his trip report that while standing next to Roosevelt, he put on "a dignified look" and tried to appear like he was meant to be there all along.

In the spring of 1914, Fairchild had never been busier. The Quarantine Act constrained the work of plant introduction. The new law had made it impossible for private nurseries to import their own plant material. His office had become a bottleneck, in many ways drained by the imperative that all American plant activity was subject to his office's oversight.

When he wasn't in the greenhouse supervising the receiving and unpacking of material, his office overflowed with visitors, many unannounced. A man who had once enjoyed the meditative silence of weeks-long sea voyages and wandering alone from field to field, he hated the constant activity. "Carrying on profound research in the hubbub that prevails in most government offices is as difficult and rare as composing good poetry on a noisy street corner," he wrote.

Fairchild was putting in the same long hours he had as a young bachelor when he had no one waiting at home. But now he had three children; his third, Nancy Bell Fairchild, was born in 1912. He sometimes slept in his office to avoid the long commute to Maryland and back. For this, his mother-in-law, Mrs. Bell, complained he was neglecting the kids. She had a way of using generosity to cloak her nagging. If money was the problem, she offered innocently, she could help.

Money wasn't the issue. The issue was that Fairchild could feel the pyramid that had taken his entire life to build slipping like sand through his fingers, rejected by an oblivious nation that didn't understand what effect its ignorance was having on its agricultural growth. He stayed in his office long into the night devising ideas. As he saw it, the way the law was implemented was costing enormous sums of money that might otherwise have gone toward research on plant diseases, or better yet, means of disinfecting contaminated crops. Fairchild became angry every time he thought about how the law would deter young people like he had been, who might choose a career in botany or horticulture if the road were smoother.

Moreover, Fairchild could see ways that the Quarantine Act was beginning to hamstring farmers. They didn't need novel crops quite like they did in the 1890s, but now, a generation later, they needed better versions of their existing crops. "I . . . felt strongly that when the quarantine . . . discouraged private initiative, the government was obligated to develop its own methods of introduction and dissemination for their benefit," he wrote. By this he meant breeding seeds together. Hybridizing. Creating new forms of fruits and vegetables in labs. This was supposed to be private-sector work, the type of research that gives one farm a leg up over competitors. As the United States marched toward war, there would be more ill-conceived efforts by the government—rather than private companies—to solve societal problems. Many of the directives would land on the desk of Fairchild, now by default one of the country's most senior food experts. People asked him how to grow more food on a fixed amount of land, how to conserve food that already existed, and how to create drugs and oil in case of disruptions to foreign supplies.

The biotechnology America developed over the next century could have easily solved these problems, particularly how to grow more corn per acre, ship bread longer distances, and create canned fruit that would last months on the shelf. There would be large agribusiness companies to research these questions, first motivated by the threat of war, and later by the promise of profit. The Monsantos, Syngentas, DuPonts. On the eve of world war, however, America, largely unprepared for a global conflict, didn't have time to experiment or to hope that men like Meyer or Popenoe could solve sweeping problems on their faraway expeditions.

One early idea found its way to Fairchild's desk and seemed so simple, so obvious, that he was surprised he hadn't thought of it first. If fruits and vegetables could be dehydrated, they could be stockpiled with no risk of spoiling. They would be lighter to transport and edible for years. Soaking them in water would allow them to be "brought back" overnight, as if nothing had happened to them. Would people even notice?

Advances in this field had come from George Washington Carver, a black man who had been born into slavery in Missouri but rose to become a respected botanist and inventor. Carver visited Fairchild's office one afternoon in January 1918 to discuss vegetable drying. Carver was a pioneer in the same way as Fairchild: both men empowered farmers to diversify. Fairchild's strategy had been through exploration; Carver's was via research. Carver wanted to find other uses for common foods like peanuts and sweet potatoes, in hopes they would expand the market and help farmers sell more. He demonstrated how potatoes could be turned into flour, and thus, a substitute for wheat. At the USDA, he baked a loaf of bread using potatoes. The method required dehydrating the potato before grinding it into fine dust.

The next day, Carver returned to the Department to talk details with Fairchild, specifically about starting a pilot project to dehydrate ten thousand bushels of potatoes. At the end of the meeting, Fairchild was so impressed, he slammed his closed fist on the desk. "We must do something now, we have fooled [around] long enough," he declared.

The logic was sound. But the culinary implementation was not. Fairchild should have known by now that people wouldn't eat something new just because someone suggested it. Food introduction required cajoling and persuading, and a generous helping of luck.

Despite Carver's grand plan, and even though Fairchild built a kiln at home to personally experiment to find the optimal temperature and duration to dehydrate foods, and even though he and Marian enjoyed seeing which type of dried and rejuvenated vegetables would pass muster with the kids, few people found the idea appetizing, and even fewer ate the vegetables. Least of all the soldiers who might have benefited from the culinary convenience as they prepared to fight in Europe. The War Department shielded them from the unsavory indignity.

One day, Fairchild schemed with an old friend, Emil Clemens Horst, to convince military leaders that dried vegetables weren't as bad as they sounded. Horst brought twenty-six types of vegetables, including dried corn, potatoes, beets, carrots, spinach, and more—enough for forty people to sample—from California to Washington. Stripped of their water, the dried vegetables were light enough for him to carry on the train.

At the Willard Hotel, where Fairchild had a decade earlier first courted his wife, he and Horst watched from the side of the room as an assembled crowd of army men, chemists, dietitians, and Red Cross officials politely chewed the samples with pursed lips and squinting eyes. "Most of the guests politely lied about it," Fairchild remarked later. "But some of them disappeared without saying anything."

That included one senior official for the United States Food Administration, who would give her official report of dried vegetables to the agency's chief, Herbert Hoover. After the luncheon, the woman returned to her apartment, and vomited them all out.

CHAPTER NINETEEN

Sad and Mad and So Utterly Unnecessary

The day Popenoe and his citrusmen returned from Brazil was not a happy occasion. Fairchild tried to mask this fact with a barbecue at his house in Maryland to honor their homecoming, and he described their return as "thrilling," but still, anyone could easily tell that after months of walking, Popenoe ended the Brazilian expedition with little more than a shrug. He had collected several odds and ends, including Brazilian cherries, cashew wine, guava jelly, translucent apricot-like fruit, and Brazilian grapes known as jaboticaba. Even though the men packed their cuttings meticulously and took great pains to ensure they were clean, only a fraction passed inspection.

The navel orange that monopolized California soil apparently had no equal, and there was nothing better to be found. In a country where the introduction of *new* plants was becoming harder and harder, confirming the superiority of an existing one was reason enough to celebrate.

While Popenoe had been gone, his small office at the Department had been turned into a quarantine station for the entomology department, another step in the slow creep to extinguish plant hunting entirely. Fairchild schemed for several months to arrange a new assignment for Popenoe, perhaps one on his own where he could emulate Meyer. But few options remained in a world becoming skeptical of outsiders, and with America wary of the unknown.

Two months after Popenoe's return, events that unfolded across the ocean trivialized the hand-wringing in Fairchild's office, and it happened faster than anyone could've foreseen. In Sarajevo on June 28, 1914, a Serbian dissident pointed a gun at a man in a car who was in line to be the head of the Austro-Hungarian Empire, a man named Franz Ferdinand. Such an event normally wouldn't have made international news, except that the bullet was fatal, and another bullet killed the man's wife, who was riding next to him. The incident led to riots, and then crackdowns in the streets, and then a diplomatic crisis that devolved so quickly that militaries around the world either rushed to declare neutrality or readied for battle.

The event that sparked the Great War, later known as World War I, was only a surprise to anyone who hadn't noticed the rising tides of nationalism, xenophobia, and cultural insecurity brought on by a more connected world. Within five weeks, German troops began crossing the border into Belgium for the first battle in what would amount to the biggest and deadliest global conflict in human history.

The United States wouldn't enter this war until 1917. The country lacked a strong military—in numbers and passion. Americans were divided, almost equally, about whether to get involved in Europe. The most consequential opinion belonged to Woodrow Wilson, who explained that war would distract the country from all of the progressive advances it had made: breaking apart monopolies, leveling a modest income tax to strengthen the government, creating a government bank called the Federal Reserve to manage the country's money. Wilson vowed, "Every reform we have won will be lost if we go into this war." War wasn't glamorous, either. Older Americans still reliving Civil War deaths didn't want another round of loss, nor were younger parents moved by the promise of valor.

This was demonstrated by one of 1915's most popular songs, "I Didn't Raise My Boy to Be a Soldier": "Who dares to put a musket on his shoulder / To shoot some other mother's darling boy?"

Popenoe was one of those darling boys. He didn't want to fight. His hunting career was only just beginning. Fairchild put him to work collecting avocados in Guatemala—a part of the world that, at least for the moment, remained safe. Popenoe spent three years there, riding thousands of miles on horseback, living on beans, avocados, and chayotes. He wandered from field to field, and when he found avocado varieties he liked, he would take notes and return again and again to taste them in minute detail. After studying thousands of trees, he returned with twenty-three varieties ("the best ones") to introduce into America. He sent them in tin tubes with oiled paper, having inspected each meticulously to ensure they'd clear quarantine.

Considering the circumstances, Fairchild was pleased with the work. So was Popenoe's father, Fred, who gloated that between his selling and his son's hunting, avocados had become the Popenoe family business.

And yet, only one opinion truly mattered to Popenoe, and it came in a letter to Fairchild in early 1917. Wilson Popenoe had "captured the field," Meyer wrote from China. He conceded that the young man who once fawned over him now shared the same stage. "It will be a race between [him] and me to see who will leave to posterity the greater number of introductions."

It was a race an aging Fairchild was proud to see his explorers compete in. So long as Meyer could stay hunting, or at the very least, remain alive.

Frank Meyer had started as a happy man, eager to have a job that let him walk and explore. But after three expeditions, he was becoming despondent. Each successive trip had resulted in more drama and fewer plants, cresting with his third expedition, on which he shoved an interpreter down a flight of stairs after the man suggested Meyer was crazy for continuing to walk into rebel-held territory. He was drawn into a fistfight with Chinese officers who suspected he was smuggling opium in his trunk of seeds and plants—a charge Meyer's response didn't disprove. One guard roughed him up, then spit in his face.

On the other side of the world, Charles Marlatt was escalating his assault on Meyer's work. Marlatt watched as one of Meyer's shipments, on its way from China to Washington, was hit by a hurricane and destroyed in Galveston, Texas. That shipment had been in Texas because of the quarantine. If not for Marlatt's laws, the seeds could have gone straightaway to experiment stations. Meyer was shocked and riled. To Marlatt, it was a righteous stroke of luck.

The only thing Frank Meyer really enjoyed was walking across landscapes and hunting plants, and in 1915 that was becoming more arduous every day. If the Washington fights and the conflict in Asia weren't enough, Meyer felt the weight of loneliness after so many years hiking alone through mountains and barren fields. He admitted to a case of *Heimweh*, the German word for homesickness. He once promised himself—and Fairchild—that at forty, he'd retire and slow down, but he had already ceased being thirty-nine. "The specter of a lonely old age looms up larger and larger, and the spectacular office of an agricultural explorer does not hold it down any longer," he wrote. "At eighteen one thinks that one can see everything. At forty, you know that the world is too big and life is too short. You reduce your plans and wishes."

Fairchild's response to Meyer's despondence was that it might be good for him to keep exploring, or at least, to spend some time with a fellow Westerner. His entire identity was defined by plant exploration—the hunt, the chase, the conquest. People had read his name in newspapers and his work had inspired a younger generation.

Perhaps what he needed most was to keep moving through fields, perhaps in the wild pear forests in the region of Jehol, north of Peking.

Meyer agreed, but he had come to resent Fairchild's tone. It was more often nagging than friendly. An earlier Meyer would have let it roll off his back. But he had grown bolder and into a man who urged his boss to "put a little less officialness in your letters and a little more warmth, for I am all alone here and am not much in conversation with my fellow men so one needs a little sympathy in his letters."

Fairchild replied that he understood, that he, too, had experienced that loneliness. Although Meyer's circumstances, amid hostility, mistrust, and extreme weather, were undoubtedly worse.

One reason Fairchild pushed so hard for his beleaguered explorer to return to the job may have been that Fairchild was pleading for Meyer's sanity as much as for his own. Meyer's slow breakdown was coinciding with a similar collapse of plant introduction, dragged down by Washington drama. Whether to comfort Meyer or himself, Fairchild wrote his explorer a motivational screed in hopes of reminding Meyer what he had signed up for, the job he had loved, and the service to his adopted country, whether anyone thanked him or not.

"We have only one life to live and we want to spend it enriching our own country with the plants of the world which produce good things to eat and to look at," Fairchild wrote. Fairchild insisted to Meyer that if he didn't feel well, he should return to America. But it came across as insincere. Fairchild filled the rest of the letter with plant talk and suggestions for Meyer's route.

The harder Fairchild pushed, the deeper Meyer sank. Fairchild requested that Meyer acquire one hundred pounds of opium poppy seeds. Securing them would provide an opportunity for American farmers, given China's crackdown on the crop, and the threat to behead any farmer growing it. This assignment would require permission from the president of China himself, whom Meyer couldn't get to, let alone convince. On this and Fairchild's other requests—to get fifty kilos of mustard seeds, dozens of samples of papeda citrus, and scores of shade trees for American cities—he began to fall short, hampered by limits on access and his own energy. "The loneliness and the hardships of life here are beginning to be more and more distasteful to me," he wrote to Fairchild.

This distaste began to manifest into physical symptoms. He experienced digestive trouble, insomnia, and bouts of fever. The immediate cause was his "nervous sleeplessness." Between the civil war in China and the larger war raging in Europe, Meyer's larger problem was "the paralyzing effect of this never-ending horrible war." He openly wondered if humanity had hit its peak in 1914, believing that so much fighting had set off the slow collapse of the world.

Leaving China and returning to Washington wouldn't have been difficult. Meyer could have caught a steamer down the Yangtze to Shanghai, and then to Hawaii or California, effectively aborting his trip. No one could've blamed him, considering the circumstances. Meyer even wrote to Fairchild that he had imagined soon leaving plant collecting to younger men.

But for some reason, Meyer couldn't let himself quit. It was an indication that despite his sorrow, the quest for plant exploration still burned inside him, however dimly. He also pondered the notion of what he might return to in America. He could expect safety in Washington, but the threats of world war couldn't guarantee security anywhere. Instead of following the Yangtze to Shanghai, he decided to go the other way, deeper into central China, in search of wild peaches.

Fifty pieces of mail were waiting for him when he reached Hankow, a city in central China on the Yangtze River. Many of the missives were from Fairchild and had been delayed months by incessant forwarding. Fairchild seemed oblivious to Meyer's hardships, and his mental state. "It is difficult to imagine just what conditions surround you, and I imagine it is more difficult even for you to imagine what changes are taking place here in America," Fairchild wrote Meyer on May 2, 1917.

It was. And as several months passed, the chasm between Meyer and Fairchild continued to grow with the distance and time it would take for letters to be delivered. If Meyer was crying for help with his anxiety or state of hopelessness, Fairchild missed the request completely, repeatedly filling letters with botanical suggestions and chatty encouragement.

Limits on Meyer's ability to move freely began to fray him. "I tried to write for a few nights and days in succession, so as to finish all of this troublesome correspondence." But, he continued, "nature stepped in and I got an attack of nervous prostration and could not sleep, rest or eat any more."

A doctor told Meyer the ailments were caused by overwork, loneliness, and worry. Added to that was the fact that a man prone to boundless wandering had been given constraints, and that the voices in his head had no escape valve. He began to refer to himself in the third person, feeling removed even from his own body. He observed, "The change from 'roughing it' to sedentary work seems harder and harder to over-bridge as a person gets older. . . . If one only could have a congenial fellow white man with one, it would not be so hard on one."

The letters piling up only added to Meyer's deepening anxiety. If he had kept moving as he had on his prior expeditions, he could have outrun them. But as he stayed still, they caught him and delivered more requests than he could handle. A millionaire farmer in Beijing wanted his advice. American experiment stations wanted help with crops Meyer had picked up years earlier. One letter in April 1917 broke the dismaying news that the United States had entered the Great War. The news was especially troubling to a man who had grown up with dreams of utopia and harmony.

Around this time, when Meyer was running out of hope, he was also short on paper. One evening in a moment of introspection, one of many with no one around to talk to and with his anguished mind retreating to a place of darkness, he taped three envelopes together to make a list. He titled it "Proposed Resignation" and filled it with ten reasons why he might finally quit:

1. Not feeling as well as formerly—sleeplessness—less energy
2. Mentally soon tired: not being able to do as much work as formerly
3. Paralyzing effect of this terrible everlasting war
4. Loneliness of life and very few congenial people to associate with
5. Travel with all this enormous amount of baggage
6. So much squalor and dirt in China
7. The destruction of my one and one-half years' work over herbarium material has given me a much deeper blow than I ever admitted
8. The new plant quarantine laws; the difficulties of shipping
9. No garden to study the plants one has collected
10. Assistants have no real interest in this work

All of these factors weighed on him like a ship taking on water. He thought one evening, "Is it strange that a man at times gets very tired? And the more so now, since my adopted country has seen fit to join in with others in this monstrous world war and we will get our lists of wounded and killed from now on regularly in our lop-sided and misinformation-giving daily and other papers."

Meyer spent his lonely nights thinking about the war, his days so empty that his thoughts routinely turned macabre. When Fairchild asked him to brainstorm new ways for the United States at war to produce more food, he responded that America might kill all unnecessary animals, and put incurable criminals and insane people "out of the way."

To anyone reading these thoughts on the other side of the world, this seemed highly unlike Meyer. A man who had overcome so many physical evils had been weakened by vague events far away from him. People shown Meyer's letters thought they came from a different man. Fairchild again dismissed the gravity of Meyer's deterioration. His response to Meyer, while gentle, reflected an era before depression meant more than temporary sadness or had a clinical diagnosis as a mental disorder.

June 29, 1917:

We are all much grieved to hear that you have had a nervous breakdown. We can none of us believe but that with your unusual physique you will rally from your nervousness and get back on your feet in a short time, providing you can shake off your worries with regard to things to be done, responsibilities that have come as a result of the war, etc. . . . Do not forget that we consider the knowledge which you have accumulated a most valuable asset. You have begun a great work, and it would be a tremendous pity not to carry it further, particularly during these strenuous times. . . . Everyone in the Office sends hearty greetings to you and warmest sympathy. I remain,

Very sincerely yours,
David Fairchild
Agricultural Explorer in
Charge

The reason for increasing pressure on Meyer was that the war had begun to fill Washington with anxiety across every federal agency. President Wilson increased the war budget, which brought nearly fifty thousand new residents into the capital, many in automobiles that congested the streets with black clouds and traffic. In August of 1917, a month normally dormant, with congressmen fleeing the humidity, the city buzzed with frenetic energy. Few people knew how to help but everyone bounced around anyway.

Attention to the war took top priority. To make room for military planners, the Department of Agriculture moved its offices up the street to an office building with more space but less light. Meyer, when he received this news, called this "a bad piece of business" that took the staff "further away from plants and the out-of-doors than ever before." Fairchild, however, saw the move as a positive, likely because he had no other choice. A new office would shield his work from visitors, at least temporarily, to let him get back to "the serious questions of plant introduction work."

In truth, however, there wasn't much work to do. Marlatt had sown concern about the unknown, but the war brought fear of death and destruction—specifically in anticipation of a German invasion. The media fed these fears. In 1915, a bestselling book, *Defenseless America* by Hudson Maxim, the man who invented smokeless gunpowder, fictionalized a German attack on the United States. The same year, it became a motion picture, which showed Washington laid waste by German bombs. Government posters urged people to buy as many war bonds as they could manage.

In April of 1917, the same month Meyer was emotionally breaking down in Yichang, President Wilson ordered the creation of a Committee on Public Information, charged with demonizing the enemy and whipping up patriotic obligations to convince people to fight the war however they could. The Department of Agriculture created its own propaganda, including posters calling people to help harvest corn, and another to cut waste:

FOOD

- Buy it with thought
- Cook it with care
- Serve just enough
- Save what will keep
- Eat what would spoil
- Home grown is best.

DON'T WASTE IT

Trying to introduce plants amid the flurry of war was like trying to sell petunias in a hurricane. People's interest in new foods, or foods at all, had to do only with whether they were cheaper than before, or whether they lasted longer. "No one can adequately describe the confusion of those early days [of the war], nor can I look back at them without a shudder," Fairchild later wrote.

In the winter between 1917 and 1918, while Fairchild paced around the office considering the latest harebrained schemes to feed American soldiers in Europe (grow more beans! eat cornmeal to preserve flour!), Marian started driving an ambulance. She was qualified because she could drive. The woman who had once been forbidden by her father to assist Clara Barton in Cuba now worked for the Women's Red Cross Motor Corps of Washington, taking shifts around the clock.

The Fairchilds' Maryland estate, meanwhile, became a retreat for peaceful thinking. Woodrow Wilson used the Fairchilds' property to escape tightly wound Washington and occasionally brought his secretary of war, Newton Baker, for frank and classified discussions about the war. While Mrs. Wilson and Mrs. Baker admired the cherry blossom trees, the president and Baker wandered the estate discussing plans for America's entrance into the war.

At least until they sat on a bench fastened between two trees. The flimsy board snapped, dropping the two men on the ground. They might have laughed in a different context. Baker later told Fairchild, "I thought for a moment we had been bombed!"

During all this, Frank Meyer sat alone. His only news came from Fairchild in Washington, and occasionally, from his friends in Holland. Fairchild had become too stressed to attend to Meyer's increasingly erratic emotions. He also admitted he didn't know what to say.

> You speak in one of your recent letters of wishing you
> had someone to advise you. My dear Meyer, these are
> times when we all need advice, but unfortunately
> there are times when those who try to advise feel
> peculiarly incompetent to do so. I might easily advise
> you to come back to this country and take up the
> breeding of plants, but I do not feel sure that a man of
> your restless disposition will be contented with the
> necessarily quiet life of a plant breeder. . . . I must now
> stop and take up other pressing duties. Hoping that
> you are recovering from your temporary indisposition,
> and with kindest regards, I remain,
>
> David Fairchild
> Agricultural Explorer in
> Charge

It seemed as if Meyer couldn't deteriorate more. But he did. His interpreter in Hankow, where he stayed amid the ongoing fighting, quit after becoming impatient with the hot climate and the food.

"What would become of our social structure if we all did the same?" Meyer asked, utterly frustrated. This incident had been the final test of Meyer's racial tolerance. He wrote to Washington to describe unabashedly how difficult it was to deal with a "non-intellectual race":

> I have become so calloused to opinions of Chinese, that it matters but mighty little what they think, the whole race has become too weedy for lack of healthy contact with outside people during all of these past centuries. With the exception of a few they are quite satisfied with the ways their forefathers did things . . ."

Like the West, China was marching further and further into troubling times, with new rebellions that fueled the bands of robbers and outlaws that tormented Meyer. Rebels looted and started fires. Soldiers stormed towns indiscriminately to impose martial law, often shooting machine guns loudly into the ground. Floods from the Yellow and North rivers washed out fields and displaced people, exacerbating confusion and chaos.

Meyer was at particular risk. An outsider could be easily accused of trying to quash the rebellion, or worse, trying to help it. His movement remained slow for the following months. His mood changed with the weather. At times he'd find the energy to return to spurts of plant hunting, but with a sluggishness as though wearing cement boots, constantly paranoid and suspicious of his surroundings.

He tried to put this sentiment into words for Fairchild. He described how food supplies were running low and fighting raged around the clock. "As I am writing we hear the rickety noise of rifle fire, for the Northern and Southern troops are at battle only a mile or so north of the city," he wrote Fairchild. "That we do not live 'at ease,' you can easily imagine." In the Yangtze Valley, a sense of depression hung in the air, which affected Meyer so deeply, he began to question his life.

"I feel the evening of life slowly descending upon me," he wrote, "and the fearful sorrow which hangs all over the earth does not make life the same it once used to be."

Meyer kept receiving letters from Washington, many delivering the dispiriting news that his earlier seeds had arrived in poor condition, or worse, not at all. Fairchild checked in with him periodically. Mail service was already slow, but the war made it even slower, delaying letters up to three months by the time they'd reach China and chase Meyer from inn to inn.

In March of 1918, nearly a year after Meyer's nervous breakdown, Fairchild wrote him a long letter about plants. Its length revealed as much about Fairchild's esteem of Meyer as it did about Fairchild's loosening grip on his own work. He closed it with a tender sentiment shared between two men whose worlds had been shaken beyond recognition.

> Do not become despondent in any case, for,
> regardless of the fearful sorrows and the horrible
> features of the life which is around us, we must push
> on to bigger and grander things before life really
> closes in on us.

In the heat of war, and amid his ongoing collapse, Meyer summoned the strength for one more bout of collecting; the resulting crops his final contributions to his adopted country. Near Hsing-shan-hsien, he came across a ginkgo biloba tree with edible seeds that Americans would later find useful for boosting brain function and treating high blood pressure. A few days later he filled his trunk one last time, with Ichang lemons, a hardy type of citrus from the region where citrons and papedas originated. He sent them to Swingle, who was back in Washington studying how to make citrus hybrids stronger for farmers, shippers, and eaters.

Once that was finished, Meyer entered a tailspin. Sleeping went from difficult to impossible. Revolution filled every street with looting and burning. Soldiers fired guns into crowds. When the bullets killed people, Meyer watched as the soldiers mutilated the corpses, digging out the hearts and passing them around for bites of courage. His inns, which began to host the dirtiest people lacking anyplace else to seek refuge, were filled with lice so thick he could see them scurrying across the sheets. "China is surely in a sad plight now" was all that he concluded, as anyone might have. "Oriental character and republicanism do not seem to agree."

On Thursday, May 30, 1918, Frank Meyer fell asleep with a pain in his stomach. He had been vomiting for two weeks. His journals revealed that he dreamed of his friends in Holland, who had once urged him to immigrate to America to find its glowing spark of prosperity. He had lost weight and could hardly keep food down, and when a servant boy asked if he was okay, he lied and said he felt fine.

He and the servant boy boarded a boat, the SS *Feng Yang Maru*, bound from Hankow to Shanghai, where his ordeal would finally end. Meyer paid for a cabin in Chinese first class, a cheaper alternative to foreign first class, to save the government money.

He shuffled around the boat for two days, drinking tea and eating porridge and murmuring to himself.

Just after midnight on Sunday, June 2, 1918, Meyer left his cabin and wandered to the ship's railing, looking into the dark Yangtze below. He wore a white undershirt, gray trousers, and yellow shoes. There were no suspicious people on board, no one with a motive to attack a sickly foreigner on a luxury boat. Just a despondent man who held little hope for a fractured world.

The next day, a man near where the boat had passed found Meyer's body. It was black with dirt. He brought it to a local hospital. While everyone stood around staring at the lifeless creature, the man who found the corpse asked if he could keep Meyer's shoes.

A telegram reached Shanghai, which relayed the news to

Washington. Someone at the State Department who had followed Meyer's adventures responded that the man who had given America so much deserved a dignified burial.

Samuel Sokobin, an American consular official, hurried to the village and paid a pair of Chinese men to help dig up Meyer's body, which, in keeping with local custom, had been buried in a shallow pile of mud on the banks of the Yangtze. Sokobin put Meyer in a coffin to be taken to Shanghai. He wondered if Meyer might be Jewish and would want a Jewish burial. He wondered if Meyer's father in Holland wanted to bury his son, or if the Department of Agriculture wanted its prized explorer to be honored in Washington. But lacking evidence for any of these possibilities, and with a decomposing body on his hands, he buried Meyer in a Protestant cemetery in Shanghai. When it came time to prepare his headstone, the consul in Shanghai summed up Meyer as best he could: "In the glorious luxuriance of the hundred plants he takes delight."

Several weeks later, Meyer's final letter arrived in Washington. Hundreds of Meyer's letters had been delivered to the Department of Agriculture, but this time, the envelope seemed like an artifact. "It often seems that we do not live ourselves any longer but that we are being lived," he wrote. The closing salvo, of the letter and of his life, diagnosed the world with stirring accuracy that would be forever relevant: "Times certainly are sad and mad and from a scientific point of view so utterly unnecessary."

Fairchild's sadness, brought on by his own loneliness as he watched his work slowly drowning in Washington bureaucracy, prevented him from comprehending what had happened to Meyer. Every bit of evidence pointed to Meyer's suicide, to a man unequipped to silence the demons brought on by war and suffering. But Fairchild, either in denial or blinded by his own angst, wondered if what killed Meyer was vertigo or another nervous reaction. Could he have fallen over the rail? Was he pushed? For the rest of Fairchild's life, he considered Meyer's death a mystery.

Fairchild held a memorial for Meyer at his house in Maryland, where the staff somberly celebrated Meyer's work with stories and photographs of his plant conquests. Fairchild paid tribute to the man whose plants would forever be growing on American soil—in mountains, in fields, in backyards and orchards of little cottages. Wherever they are, Fairchild said, "they will all be his."

In his will, Meyer left one thousand dollars to the Department, to be divided among the one hundred men he had worked with. The men might have each taken ten dollars. But they agreed, unanimously, to create a medal in his honor. The Meyer Medal would be awarded annually for virtuous acts of plant introduction.

That Meyer had given his life to introduce plants set a high bar for anyone qualified for this honor. But Fairchild could think of one. A man who had encouraged the work of plant hunting, who gave years of his life and thousands of dollars to the only work he ever found fulfilling, useful, and important. In 1920, Fairchild saw to it that the medal's first recipient would be Barbour Lathrop.

CHAPTER TWENTY
Wij Zijn Amerikanen

The bird squawked and squealed, writhing with wild insanity. It was caged, its wings clipped, its hunting prevented by its confinement. The bird was a monkey-eating eagle, named literally for its most noteworthy skill, and Fairchild watched the animal struggle against the metal wires.

Fairchild had escaped the dining room of the hotel to stare at the bird, its delicate gray feathers in contrast to the fury on its face. His boyhood fascination with wild things was now accompanied by the patience of an older man. It was 1940, he was seventy, and he was in the Philippines. For at least an hour, he had nowhere to be.

After the war ended in 1918, David Fairchild mostly gave up. He was calm and composed, with the self-awareness to recognize that he had been pushed ceaselessly back. Meyer's death had hamstrung Fairchild's efforts to introduce novel plants, and as the war ended, tired Americans had little appetite, and even less money, for the program to rev up again. The popular *Plant Immigrant Bulletin* that once circulated to farmers and nurserymen around the country was terminated. David Houston, the secretary of agriculture at the time, also instituted a new regulation, Quarantine #37, which ended all private importations of plants and bulbs. The Department was exempted from this provision, but it tarnished the reputation of Fairchild's office as a source not of valuable material but of ominous disease.

Confrontations with Marlatt had cooled, but the radioactive embers of earlier battles were slow to decay. Any chance that Fairchild and his childhood friend would reunite and chalk up their squabbles to the fog of impending war vaporized in 1921. Still not satisfied with the laws he helped engineer, Marlatt took to the pages of *National Geographic*, again to celebrate his success, penning a rhetorical victory dance. His claim that quarantine measures had kept out hundreds of pests was built on data that was impossible to confirm, but it stood to reason that diligently inspecting rootstock would occasionally uncover invaders. He relegated the honest disagreement with Fairchild to a place beneath the intelligence of the American people. "If the average American knew as much of plant diseases as he does of human and animal diseases, the necessity of a quarantine against infected plants would not need to be sustained by argument," he wrote. Fairchild might have responded, but he was tired and decided not to. He thought it'd be a better use of time to give his son, Graham, age fifteen, "the most tremendous of all experiences": a visit to a tropical jungle. So he took him to Panama.

As the seed collection program deflated, the part of postwar Washington that most irked Wilson Popenoe wasn't the heated rhetoric but the budget. In 1919 and 1920, he watched his commissions dwindle. Fairchild tried to keep the office afloat by trying out new explorers, but none proved qualified for such fraught work. The new explorers spent lavishly and regularly requested new commissions for greater and greater sums. Popenoe finally had enough in 1925. He traded plant hunting for easier money—and more of it—and took a job as chief agronomist for the United Fruit Company, a corporation growing in value and prestige. Not long after he turned thirty-one, Popenoe signaled to Fairchild in the subtlest way possible that he wanted to resign. He met a smart and pretty bamboo researcher, and married her.

Fairchild attempted to halt the losses, to reduce the office's expenses, and to convince Popenoe to stay. Still, Fairchild's efforts amounted to one man trying to change the currents of the Atlantic. In 1923, for the second time in Fairchild's life, a wealthy man, this time one named Allison Armour, asked if Fairchild would consult on a series of expeditions to collect plants around the world for private buyers. Fairchild accepted. Just as he had done in 1898, he explained to the secretary of agriculture that he needed to leave the program he had created. He told his staff—and himself—that he'd be gone just a short while. But this time, he didn't go back.

One thing that made private life more palatable for Fairchild was that he and Marian had begun to escape more often to Florida. The swampy mess Henry Flagler once imagined a future metropolis was expanding, its population booming 50 percent in the seven years after the war. New economic growth left people with more money, along with paid vacations, retirement pensions, and automobiles, which turned Florida into an attractive place to vacation. Not long after the war, the state repealed income and inheritance taxes, which brought even more people (and money) south. Property values boomed; people even bought land underwater in hopes that landfilling would turn it into beachfront property. The twenties would be a time when Americans judged one another by what they owned, and Florida became a new frontier for status and luxury.

The Fairchilds weren't drawn to Florida's vogue. They liked the weather, the calm, and most of all, its tropical breezes. Only in Florida could an American feel the warm sun and midday rains and be surrounded by the crawling vines and towering palms that Fairchild loved in Java. Only in Florida could an American feel as if he actually lived in the tropics. So in 1916, when the Fairchilds came across a piece of land in Coconut Grove next to the lapping waters of Biscayne Bay, they bought it.

On his first visit, Barbour Lathrop named the house "the Kampong," the Malay term for a family compound. Lathrop had ceased his overseas travel in the early twenties, his health failing and arthritis flaring. The steamships of earlier days were replaced with

Around 1920. Barbour Lathrop **(left)** and Alexander Graham Bell both spent part of their final years with the Fairchilds in Coconut Grove, Florida. Bell died in 1922 at his Nova Scotia estate, Beinn Bhreagh. Lathrop died five years later in Philadelphia, Pennsylvania. He never had a formal home or any descendants, which left no obvious place for his body to be sent. He was buried in the closest cemetery.

private cars, which shuttled him from San Francisco to Chicago and Florida, where he stopped to visit friends, or to convalesce from bouts of bronchitis or laryngitis in hospitals.

Fairchild often hosted Lathrop at the Kampong, along with the Bells and their scientific friends Thomas Edison and Harvey Firestone, who sought Fairchild's opinion on matters of botany and chemistry. Firestone, a tire magnate, was especially interested in growing rubber trees. To Edison, Fairchild told the story of the inn owner in Bangkok who left his electric chandelier burning all night. It's hard to imagine that the "investment" Lathrop made in Fairchild could have yielded any greater return than seeing his protégé visited and consulted by the era's most renowned scientific minds.

After a lifetime of moving, Lathrop, nearly eighty, logged his last steps into a Philadelphia hospital room. Fairchild was in Europe when he heard the news, heartbroken not to have been at Lathrop's bedside on May 17, 1927, the day the old man expired. His remaining wealth had secured him a plot in a cemetery on the outskirts of Philadelphia. But his having no direct descendants, along with his lifelong disinterest in writing much down, allowed death to sweep away much of the story of his extraordinary life.

Fairchild was left the primary steward of Lathrop's legacy. He described their thirty-three-year friendship, highlighted by eight years of travel together, as "an intimate comradeship" and "the major romance in the story of my life." No one—not even Lathrop—truly knew how many times he had actually circled the world. One obituary would say thirteen, another twenty-five. Lathrop told people eighty-three.

Fairchild filled his own advancing age with the same curiosity of his youth. "His blue eyes sparkle with a deep, unquenchable interest and enthusiasm for all things," a pair of friends observed of him. He would pepper his grandchildren with questions, particularly during long drives he and Marian would make from Miami to Nova Scotia, where they built a summer house of their own at

Beinn Bhreagh. "What's the most interesting thing you learned today?" Fairchild would ask.

He was known to offer a quarter to any youngster who could
conduct an interview with a stranger and return with a previously
unknown tidbit. He advised, "If you can't be useful to someone or
they can't be useful to you, move on."

The voyage that Fairchild would recount most to his grandchildren
wasn't his first crossing of the Atlantic, or his adventure in Corsica.
By the time his kids had kids of their own, Fairchild's first sighting
of Java and his visits to the Kingdom of Hawaii seemed to have occurred in another life.

His favorite trip of his life, he would tell them, was an expedition to the Malay Islands with Marian and a group of their friends.
It was luxury travel aboard a private yacht, as Fairchild had been
accustomed to with Lathrop. And its pace was sufficiently slow for
a man in the sunset of his life.

The trip, in 1940, was part adventure, part philanthropy. A
wealthy accountant, Robert Montgomery, had offered to donate
land in south Florida, as much as eighty-three acres, to create America's first botanical garden devoted solely to the flowers, vines, and
fruits of the tropics. It was the kind of place Fairchild had visited in
Buitenzorg, Tokyo, and Rio de Janeiro. Fairchild resisted when
Montgomery wanted to call it the Fairchild Tropical Garden. But
when someone pointed out that no one alive was a more qualified
authority on tropical botany, he relented.

Having a garden required filling it. An aging Fairchild might
have sent other people to collect, younger enthusiasts to travel on a
private research mission to build this biological museum south of
Miami. But once more in his life, Fairchild had the itch to leave the
confines of land and see the illustrious Malay Archipelago. Alfred

1935. Marian and David continued to make annual trips to Beinn Bhreagh, Nova Scotia, their pace of life slowed by their advancing age. But David remained enchanted by his wife (pictured) and tropical plants, including the bowl of mangoes in front of her. Several years later, in 1939, the two would decide to embark together on one last plant-hunting expedition.

Russel Wallace, now long dead, had lit in Fairchild a lasting spark that endured like the brightness of the equatorial sun.

The world was again at war, again spurred by the Germans, and again threatening to engulf the planet. The aftermath of the Great War had led to another great war, particularly because Germany left the first war humbled. In a treaty signed at Versailles, German leaders were forced to admit fault, relinquish some land, and pay war debts. This was, in a nationalistic sense, humiliating. A German veteran of the war built on this vulnerability a campaign to be chancellor, giving well-attended speeches about how Germany should march forward defiantly. He won office by vowing to restore Germany to its former greatness and purity.

Germany's hubris didn't threaten an expedition in the Malay Islands. Holland, which still held legal ownership of the Indies, declared itself neutral in 1939, just as it had done in the First World War. And the Philippines were still, technically, American. The bigger threats were from Japan and China, at war since 1937 over land and labor. Japan had become richer and stronger, a combination that fueled its own imperial lust.

But Fairchild deemed the risk worth taking. He knew his own expiration loomed. "Besides," he would write, "in our philosophy dangers to health lurk everywhere, and the majority of folk seem to die in their own houses of some accident, perhaps from slipping on the bathroom mat, or from contracting some one of the diseases which spread through civilized society possibly even faster than through the scattered societies of the more primitive world."

In his lifetime he had seen humanity become more guarded, more filled with fear and prone to war. And so there was, at any moment, no safer time than the present.

He and Marian left for Los Angeles on a train much faster than those of the 1890s. Ocean travel had advanced, too, although it was now becoming antiquated. People confident enough to fly in metal airplanes could cross oceans not in weeks but in hours. Seeds no longer had to be stripped of moisture or shipped in potatoes; they could be carried as cargo through the air, resting on nothing but damp peat. Even the inspection process had been streamlined. Officials inspected plants at seaports and airports, bypassing Washington completely.

A typhoon hit their ship heading across the Pacific, rocking their boat so ferociously that chairs in the dining room fell over, emptying their occupants on the floor. Marian wrote to her three children, describing how surprised she was at the dangers of their voyage. "Two or three times a wave hit the boat with such a stunning blow that my heart missed a beat or two." Fairchild tried to distract everyone by telling funny stories.

The ship for the voyage through the Java Sea was called the *Chêng Ho*. It was a junk, an ancient Chinese-style sailing ship custom built in Hong Kong for the expedition. The ship was decorated in classic Chinese style, with hand-carved porcelain, a glowing sun, phoenixes, and dragons over the portholes. This time the person who underwrote Fairchild's expedition wasn't a man, but a woman, Anne Archbold, the heiress of John D. Archbold, who had helped start Standard Oil. Archbold offered to cover every expense; all the Fairchilds had to do was meet her in the Philippines. America had granted the Philippine Islands a measure of independence in 1935, which began its decade-long march toward full sovereignty. Long after his earlier visits, when Fairchild wondered if botany could cure the fierce antagonism between Americans and the islanders, Manila had become a quiet but functional town where automobiles brought people to jewelry stores and movie theaters.

So, it was in the small town of Davao, not long after the expedition got under way, that Fairchild gawked at the eagle in the cage. While he watched its struggles, he may have considered how lucky he was to find himself again in the Indian Ocean, so many years after his first visit and still with the strength for a new adventure. He might have thought about all the wealthy benefactors he had

found to fund his exploits, nearly all through happenstance meetings that yielded thrilling opportunities. He could have fixated on
the notion that, amid a constantly shrinking and interconnected
globe, there still remained plants undiscovered by the Western
world. But most likely, even for an old man who had seen so much,
an eagle that ate monkeys proved, yet again, the bizarre wonder of
the tropics.

The *Chêng Ho* stopped in Sangihe, on an island a dozen miles
wide with a four-thousand-foot volcano rising above the clouds.
Children who may never have seen visitors squealed as they surrounded Marian and other members of the party. Fairchild wandered off to "botanize," as he called it, to collect palms. The Malay
he had learned in Java had rusted by now. With hand gestures and
props from the boat, he convinced the islanders to show him their
rarest palms, one deep red and another with a spineless trunk. He
studied mangroves along the shore, their roots stretching to reach
muddy soil. He watched a colony of weaver ants secrete silk from
their glands and then pass it around to form a nest stronger than a
man's hands could rip.

More children, singing and chanting at the tops of their voices,
awaited the boat as it pulled into Siau. The island was still smoking
from an eruption and leaned to one side. Forty kids followed Fairchild as he collected seeds from one tree and shrub after another.
He met the chief of the island, joyful at being called upon by an
American. When the chief ate leaves of the papaya plant, Fairchild
asked if he could take the chief's picture when he was midbite. If
people at home learned that faraway people ate papaya leaves—
later shown to balance blood sugar, boost immunity, and even
weaken cancer cells—they might try them, too. His cynicism about
people's stubborn tastes had grown strong. "I know there are many
people who will shy at the idea of even tasting the leaves of the papaya," Fairchild wrote of the encounter. "But as they shake their
heads they will reach for a cigarette."

Aside from the plant hunting, which continued at Fairchild's now leisurely pace, the high point of the trip was when someone brought a coconut crab on board, alive with great weight. The women shrieked as Fairchild and the crew tried to train it backward into a jar. The animal complied, but only after its powerful pincers broke a mop handle in two. To preserve the creature, Fairchild filled the jar with formaldehyde.

The low point would come several months later when Ned Beckwith, the expedition's photographer, was arrested, suspected of spying, perhaps for the Germans, or working for the Chinese, since the *Chêng Ho* had all the appearances of a Chinese boat. Dutch soldiers confiscated his camera and inspected his film.

"Wij zijn Amerikanen," Fairchild insisted when he rescued Ned from the lockup. "We are Americans." A cablegram from the Dutch East Indies' capital, Batavia, confirmed this, and Ned's captors allowed them to leave.

The expedition was supposed to last two years. But suspicion, danger, and animosity would cut it short. Holland wanted no part in a second world war, but after Germany invaded the Netherlands in May of 1940, Dutch soldiers feared the Germans would invade the East Indies next, so they began rounding up any Germans on the islands. They minded little about collateral damage, about apprehending a group of touring Americans hunting for, of all things, plants. As a courtesy, the *Chêng Ho* was ordered to leave the region, to return to the Philippines, and then America. Don't stop, Dutch authorities warned, and don't look back.

David Fairchild defied the order. The boat stopped at seventeen more islands, and on each one he shuffled slowly onto shore to snatch seeds of palms, fruits, and flowers. He moved as fast as his aging body would allow to evade arrest, yet was content to be moved by the currents. He instructed the captain of the *Chêng Ho* that they would take their time.

Epilogue

One day a few autumns ago, after several months of research, I decided it was time to meet David Fairchild. He'd been dead for sixty years, so I was really going to see the remnants of his work. Fairchild took his last breath under a Javanese ficus tree in his Florida garden one day in August of 1954, which seemed fitting for a man who had fallen so deeply in love with the tropics.

The better part of a century later, there's a small army of people near Miami committed to keeping Fairchild's legacy alive. Gardeners, archivists, geneticists, all of whom draw a paycheck from a nonprofit or government agency that wouldn't exist had Fairchild not lived.

I spent days in a small room with taupe tile and a buzzing wall-unit air conditioner where boxes of Fairchild's old letters were stacked to the ceiling. I visited the Kampong, the house that he and Marian had lived in, and stood in their bedroom—hoping to discover what? I didn't know. I imagined Fairchild walking down the stairs and across a small breezeway to the kitchen, still with its original tile, and then I strolled out in his lush green backyard, now a venue for Miami weddings, and stopped to look at the view of Biscayne Bay that Fairchild enjoyed in the phase of his life when he simply sat and watched the lapping waves.

Somehow, though, I didn't feel as if I had truly met Fairchild until I met Mike Winterstein. He asked me to meet him a few miles from the Kampong near an area blocked by a gate. About five and a half feet tall, Winterstein was the kind of USDA employee I had never seen in Washington—his bronze skin and calloused hands made me think he probably hadn't put on a suit since sometime in the seventies. He talked fast and breathless, and when he heard I was poking around, he invited me to see the restricted USDA land where some of Fairchild's old plants still grow.

"I'll take you for a drive around the property," he said. "You can see what it looked like when the man was here."

We whirled around the orchard, taking such fast and sharp turns that it felt as if two wheels of our golf cart came off the ground. Twice I reminded Mike I wasn't in a rush. Twice he assured me that he wasn't, either. He pointed to trees planted in the middle of tall, thick grass. Most of them were mangoes. Each started as a sapling that Fairchild picked up in some corner of the world. Now some were more than fifty feet tall.

I couldn't resist asking Winterstein what was the purpose of keeping alive such old trees when more contemporary mango trees now exist, the fruit's production long ago outsourced abroad. Mangoes that once grew abundantly in Florida are now produced commercially in Mexico, Brazil, and India. And the avocados that helped build Southern California are now imported mostly from Mexico.

"These are the originals," Winterstein said—or in other words, the primary colors. By now, Fairchild's dates from Baghdad in 1903 have been mixed, crossbred, and hybridized millions of times, resulting in the dates in any American supermarket. Winterstein told me how chemists and fruit researchers still use the remnants of Fairchild's old work with mangoes—and in a nice twist of diplomatic karma, it's often foreign researchers who find the most value in the mangoes Fairchild brought to America from other countries. Winterstein explained, "If Israel, for example, is dealing with a pathogen in their commercial mango groves, we can send them *clean* material to use for evaluation plantings." All of which makes Fairchild something of an originator. He could take credit for today's dates and avocados the same way Alexander Graham Bell could claim credit for the iPhone, or Henry Ford for a Ferrari. One person makes a breakthrough, and then innovators make improvements.

Once I had this in mind, I started seeing Fairchild everywhere. On a trip to New York I saw an ad on the subway for a drink called Peachy Keen Nectarine ("with real fruit flavor!"). A high-end restaurant on Washington, D.C.'s Fourteenth Street featured a Meyer lemon salad. In the mornings, I often run around the tidal basin near the Washington Monument. It's silent most days, except during a two-week period each spring when crowds fill the area, kites fill the sky, and a man with a cart sells cherry blossom ice cream.

Fairchild's legacy seemed to have tentacles everywhere, and after a while, my friends grew to expect it. When I'd stab some food item on my plate—a cashew, some kale, a nectarine—and say, "Guess who helped bring this to America," they were at first impressed, but over time, they began to roll their eyes.

But Fairchild's successes are only part of his legacy. He often explained to people that food introduction had two phases: bringing a food across an ocean, and then getting consumers to like it. The second phase was where thousands of crops fell apart. Things like the vegetable pear, also known as the chayote, just petered out, uninteresting to farmers and eaters. Same story with dasheens, uncharismatic root vegetables that couldn't edge out potatoes, carrots, or even jicama for meaningful market share.

I spent months trying to find a mangosteen, the fruit of Southeast Asia that Fairchild considered his favorite. He was perplexed by why people didn't see the magic he did, and disappointed until the day he died that mangosteens never caught on. Then one summer day my neighbor Wendy returned from New York with a grin.

"I found some" was all she said.

There in her kitchen, I tried for the first time the round, purple fruit. After one bite I understood why the mangosteen fizzled. It was delicious—sweet and creamy—but not cut out for long-distance travel. Its rind was too thick, its flesh too mealy, and it bruised too easily. When compared to today's powerhouse crops like bananas, apples, and oranges, mangosteens have a weak résumé.

Too bad, really. Selecting which fruits live and die based on their market appeal seems to be a form of bioeconomic Darwinism. But that's how agriculture works. And it has continued long after Fairchild's era. A hundred years ago, American farmers grew 408 types of commercial tomatoes. Now the number has winnowed to 79. And 207 varieties of corn have become 12. Growing single crops at industrial scale ensures reliable food, but it also brings a greater chance of plant disease. And, if we're being sentimental about it, just a loss of richness about the world.

Which returns me to the question I posed earlier, about whether there's room in today's world for another Fairchild. In all reality, the answer is probably no. The possibility of another food explorer leading an illustrious life seems to have been wiped away by the conveniences of globalization. Farmers now share crops, seeds, and tips at international conferences. I can take a webinar on how to grow the world's best rice, and then buy seeds online. Keeping agricultural secrets is hard. A humble man stumbling on a new food that could reinvigorate America is nearly impossible in a world of multinational food companies whose jurisdiction is the entire planet. As with kale or quinoa, modern culinary spikes are usually the work of marketers, not explorers.

But it'd be hard to argue that the way we do food now isn't overall a good thing. And on this point, I began to think that Fairchild would agree. I ended my search for Fairchild's legacy on Okinawa, the small Japanese island near where Fairchild first saw the cherry blossom trees he'd bring to Washington, D.C. On my daily walks around my neighborhood, I passed a house that had a tree with perfectly pink cherry blossoms that, thanks to the temperate island weather, slowly opened over the course of my stay.

I figured it'd be nice to have those back home, or at least to give to some friends. So I decided I'd engage in the same sort of botanical espionage that Fairchild pioneered. I probably could have just asked the owner of the tree if I could take a small cutting, and she probably, out of sheer bewilderment, would have said yes. But I decided to do the most un-Japanese thing imaginable and steal them instead, if only to feel the adrenaline one time that Fairchild must have felt hundreds.

I procrastinated as long as possible, until the morning of my flight back to Washington. When I walked down the road with a pair of scissors, the woman who owned the tree was pruning her garden.

I hadn't accounted for this, so I made two laps of the neighborhood while I considered my strategy. I lurked around a corner until I saw her disappear from view to the other side of the yard; then I walked briskly toward the tree. I slowed only slightly, and in one smooth arm motion, I cut three bud sticks from her cherry blossom tree, stuffed them in my pocket, and kept walking.

They made their way back to Washington in my suitcase, sealed in a plastic bag with wet paper towels—the closest I could come to Fairchild's method of using damp moss. Forty hours later—lightning fast by any nineteenth-century standard—I had them in my kitchen. I dipped each cutting in a rooting hormone I keep on hand for botanical emergencies, and then stuffed each cutting in a raw potato. I felt satisfied that I had done everything right, and had benefited from modern travel and climate control. Fairchild would be impressed.

And yet, two weeks later, right as the buds might have grown new roots, when I might feel the triumph of successfully moving plant material from one continent to another, the cuttings began to dry out. The blossoms began to flake, and eventually, the flakes fell off.

I'm no botanist, so perhaps my failure can be excused. But the whole exercise seemed to accentuate the accomplishments of a man who did this work a century prior, without the conveniences of modern life.

There's now about as much life in the cuttings as there is on the moon, but I can't muster the courage to throw them away. I don't like looking at dead sticks any more than I like ending this book talking about them. But each morning when I eat breakfast next to them, I sense something poetic that Fairchild might have felt. Botany is sometimes the disappointment of dead sticks. And sometimes, if you're lucky, it's the art of life, growth, and transformation.

California, 1919. Barbour Lathrop and David Fairchild.

ACKNOWLEDGMENTS

My first and most meaningful thanks is to those who farm. To grow food is to power humanity, and I salute those who do.

The day I met David Fairchild was like walking up to a fertile field of dirt at the beginning of spring. My visionary agent, Lauren Sharp, encouraged me to dig, and my sharp and thoughtful editor, Brent Howard, took a chance on the seeds I planted. The soil was rich because Fairchild had the foresight to write things down. I have many times wondered what I'd say to the man. I'd start by thanking him for the trail of bread crumbs.

This project wouldn't have grown legs without Fairchild's living grandchildren—Helene Pancoast, Hugh Muller, David Muller, Marian Weissman, Sally Shankman, Barbara Bates, David Fairchild, and Alice Bell Fairchild—and his great-nephew Gil Grosvenor, and his granddaughters-in-law Jeanne Muller and Katharine Muller, who all offered their time, kindness, and hospitality. Nancy Korber was the modern guardian of Fairchild's legacy as archivist at the Fairchild Tropical Botanic Garden before she passed the baton to Arielle Simon. Marianne Swan and Mary Jo Robertson are the unsung heroes who archived Fairchild's thirteen-thousand-and-counting photographs and guided me through them. My friend and talented photo editor Jessie Wender helped curate the best ones. David Lee gave context to Fairchild's agricultural exploits. And I'd have found much less about Fairchild's home, the Kampong, without Craig Morell, Arlene Lang, Jon Lehman, and David Jones. If this book moves you to care about plants, you might visit (or donate to) the Fairchild Tropical Botanic Garden in Coral Gables, Florida, the National Tropical Botanical Garden in Kalaheo, Kauai, or your local botanical garden or gardening club.

I picked up bushels of agriculture lore thanks to Sara Lee, Susan Fugate, Rachel Donahue, Diane Wunsch, and the long line of librarians before them at the National Agricultural Library, as well as Melanie Harrison with the Agricultural Research Service. There's no bigger public treasure than the Library of Congress, where David Mao, Liz Morrison, and Stephanie Marcus showed extraordinary capability and kindness. Connie Carter, unofficial queen of America's public archives, did all that and baked cookies for my research sessions.

Mike Litterst at the National Park Service offered a tour through cherry blossom history, Kirk Huffman walked me delicately through Fijian cannibalism, and Sarah Seekatz nerded out with me about dates. Mike Winterstein at the USDA plied me with more mango lore (and mangoes) than I could digest, Peter Raven at the Missouri Botanical Garden offered a precise and concise botanical history of Earth, Tom Gradziel at UC Davis helped navigate thorny questions of botanical nomenclature, and Kazuo Ariyoshi of the Yokohama Nursery Company patiently answered, in English, my endless questions about Japanese sakura trees. I must say so bluntly: I consulted many sources, but I offer a special salute to prior scholars of plant hunting, among them Amanda Harris, Philip Pauly, and Marjory Stoneman Douglas.

The National Geographic Society gave Fairchild half a century of adventure and enrichment. I've also benefited from the Geographic's long line of thoughtful editors, writers, and artists, the ones I've worked with and the earlier ones who made our work possible. My gratitude to Renee Braden, keeper of the society's illustrious history, along with the inspired and admired Chris Johns. I'll go broke the day my friends from *Newsweek*—Jeff Bartholet, Karen Breslau, Claudia Kalb, Patti Wingert, Evan Thomas, and Eleanor Clift—send me an invoice.

I wrote the final chapters of this book in Japan, thanks to the hospitality and hijinks of Dan Berg and Vanessa Gomez, who indulged me with *mikans* when my writing got stiff. Andrea Henkel jumped fences with me to investigate Fairchild's wedding. Ryan Prete risked his bachelor's degree to smuggle me a rare book. And the esteemed Will Halicks was my partner in indignation every time the Library of Congress kicked us out at four thirty ("But you close at five!"). This book would be twice as long if I listed all the friends who fueled it with their enthusiasm. You know who you are, and thank you.

A sequoia-sized thanks to the team at Dutton—especially Jamie Knapp, Kayleigh George, Cassidy Sachs, and Caroline Payne—for giving this book life, color, and eyeballs. Liz Flock and Lance Richardson, the other two of my three-pronged writers group, buoyed me through every crisis large and small. My perennial neighbor Wendy Stuart had a way of showing up with rare fruits when I needed them. Bill Press, Sarah Kliff, Sandra Beasley, Spencer Millsap, Lamar Heystek, Fritz Schneider, Jackie Clark, Adam Gerber, Andy Carmona, Catherine Zuckerman, Jeremy Berlin, and Eve Conant critiqued drafts, offered advice, and just generally shoveled coal into the locomotive that pulled this train forward.

To my parents, Arlene and Ron, and my sister, Karen, for inspiring my life's adventures. And to Alanna, my beginning and end, the sun and the moon, who keeps our plants growing.

BIBLIOGRAPHY

An American Lady. *The American Home Cook Book: With Several Hundred Excellent Recipes: Selected and Tried with Great Care, and with a View to Be Used by Those Who Regard Economy, and Containing Important Information on the Arrangement and Well Ordering of the Kitchen: The Whole Based on Many Years of Experience.* New York: Dick & Fitzgerald, 1854.

Annals of the Bohemian Club, Vol. 1. TS, Barbour Lathrop Collection, Fairchild Tropical Botanic Garden. Coral Gables, FL. Date unknown.

Bailey, Beth L. *From Front Porch to Back Seat: Courtship in Twentieth-Century America.* Baltimore: Johns Hopkins University Press, 1989.

Bemmelen, J. F. van, G. B. Hooijer, and Jan Frederik Niermeyer. *Guide Through Netherlands India, Comp. by Order of the Koninklijke Paketvaart Maatschappij (Royal Packet Company).* London: T. Cook & Son, 1906.

Berenson, Edward. *The Statue of Liberty: A Transatlantic Story.* New Haven: Yale University Press, 2012.

Berkeley, M. J. *Journal of the Royal Horticultural Society of London.* London: Ranken & Co., 1877.

Beveridge, Albert J., George Frisbie Hoar, William Jennings Bryan, and William Bourke Cockran. *Great Political Issues and Leaders of the Campaign of 1900.* Chicago: W. B. Conkey, 1900.

Brady, Dorothy S. *Output, Employment, and Productivity in the United States After 1800: Studies in Income and Wealth No. 30.* New York: National Bureau of Economic Research, Distributed by Columbia University Press, 1966.

———. *Output, Employment, and Productivity in the United States after 1800: Studies in Income and Wealth No. 31.* New York: National Bureau of Economic Research, Distributed by Columbia University Press, 1966.

Brands, H. W. *The Reckless Decade: America in the 1890s.* Chicago: University of Chicago Press, 2002.

Bryson, Bill. *One Summer: America, 1927.* New York: Doubleday, 2013.

Buck, Albert H., and Thomas Lathrop Stedman. *A Reference Handbook of the Medical Sciences: Embracing the Entire Range of Scientific and Practical Medicine and Allied Science.* New York: William Wood, 1900.

Buckland, Gail. *The White House in Miniature*. New York: W. W. Norton & Company, 1994.

Burleigh, Nina. *The Stranger and the Statesman: James Smithson, John Quincy Adams, and the Making of America's Greatest Museum: the Smithsonian*. New York: William Morrow, 2003.

Bush, Joseph. *Before Marriage, and After*. London: Charles H. Kelly, 1901.

Chadwick, Mrs. J. *Home Cookery: A Collection of Tried Receipts, Both Foreign and Domestic*. Boston: Crosby, Nicholas, and Company, 1853.

Chauncey, George. *Gay New York: Gender, Urban Culture, and the Making of the Gay Male World, 1890–1940*. New York: BasicBooks, 1994.

Condit, Ira J. *History of the Avocado and Its Varieties in California*. Irvine: California Avocado Association, 1916.

Connelley, William E. *A Standard History of Kansas and Kansans* Vol. 2. Chicago: Lewis Publishing Company, 1918.

Considine, Douglas M., and Glenn D. Considine, eds. *Foods and Food Production Encyclopedia*. New York: Van Nostrand Reinhold, 1982.

Cook, O. F. *Inventory of Foreign Seeds and Plants* Vol. 1. United States Department of Agriculture, Section of Seed and Plant Introduction. Washington, D.C.: Government Printing Office, 1899.

Cook, O. F., Argyle McLachlan, and Rowland Montgomery Meade. *A Study of Diversity in Egyptian Cotton*. Washington, D.C.: Government Printing Office, 1909.

Crago, Jody A., Mari Dresner, and Nate Meyers. *Chandler*. Charleston, SC: Arcadia Publishing, 2012.

Crosby, Alfred W. Jr. *The Columbian Exchange: Biological and Cultural Consequences of 1492*. Westport, CT: Greenwood Press, 1972.

Cunningham, Isabel Shipley. *Frank N. Meyer: Plant Hunter in Asia*. Ames: Iowa State University Press, 1984.

Damerow, Peter. "Sumerian Beer: The Origins of Brewing Technology in Ancient Mesopotamia." *Cuneiform Digital Library Journal*, 2012.

De Blij, H. J. "The Little Ice Age: How Climate Made History." *Annals of the Association of American Geographers* 92, no. 2 (2002): 377–79.

Department of Agriculture inventory reports. National Agricultural Library. Beltsville, MD. 1905–1908.

Diamond, Jared M. *Guns, Germs, and Steel: The Fates of Human Societies*. New York: W. W. Norton & Company, 1998.

Dorsett, P. H., A. D. Shamel, and Wilson Popenoe. *Bulletin No. 445: The Navel Orange of Bahia; With Notes on Some Little-known Brazilian Fruits*. Washington, D.C.: United States Department of Agriculture, Bureau of Plant Industry, 1917.

Douglas, Marjory Stoneman. *Adventures in a Green World: The Story of David Fairchild and Barbour Lathrop*. Coconut Grove, FL: Field Research Projects, 1973.

Dunning, Nelson A. *The Farmers' Alliance History and Agricultural Digest.* Washington, D.C.: Alliance Pub., 1891.

Edge, Laura Bufano. *Andrew Carnegie: Industrial Philanthropist.* Minneapolis: Lerner Publications, 2004.

Epstein, Beryl Williams, and Sam Epstein. *Plant Explorer, David Fairchild.* New York: J. Messner, 1961.

Fairchild, David. *The World as Garden: The Life and Writings of David Fairchild.* Edited by David W. Lee. West Charleston, SC: Createspace, 2013.

———. "Exploring the Klondike of China's Plant Gold." TS, Meyer Collection, Fairchild Tropical Botanic Garden. Date unknown.

———. "Our Flowering Cherry Trees." MS, Fairchild Tropical Botanic Garden. Date unknown.

———. *Garden Islands of the Great East: Collecting Seeds from the Philippines and Netherlands India in the Junk "Chêng Ho."* New York: Charles Scribner's Sons, 1943.

———. *Japanese Bamboos and Their Introduction into America.* Washington, D.C.: Government Printing Office, 1903.

———. *The World Grows Round My Door: The Story of The Kampong, a Home on the Edge of the Tropics.* New York: Charles Scribner's Sons, 1947.

———. *The World Was My Garden.* TS, Family Life, Fairchild Tropical Botanic Garden. Unpublished rough draft.

———. *Three New Plant Introductions from Japan.* Washington, D.C.: Government Printing Office, 1903.

Fairchild, David, Elizabeth Kay, and Alfred Kay. *The World Was My Garden: Travels of a Plant Explorer.* New York: Charles Scribner's Sons, 1938.

Fairchild, George T. *Rural Wealth and Welfare: Economic Principles, Illustrated and Applied in Farm Life.* New York: Macmillan, 1900.

Francatelli, Charles Elmé. *The Modern Cook.* London: W. Clowes and Sons, 1846–1848.

Funigiello, Philip J. *Florence Lathrop Page: A Biography.* Charlottesville: University of Virginia Press, 1994.

Galloway, B. Memorandum (on the History of the Department of Agriculture). 1914. TS, USDA Collection, National Agricultural Library.

Galloway, B. T. *Seeds and Plants Imported During the Period September, 1900, to December, 1903.* Bulletin no. 66. 5501–9896. United States Department of Agriculture, Bureau of Plant Industry. Washington, D.C.: Government Printing Office, 1905.

Gitlin, Marty, and Topher Ellis. *The Great American Cereal Book: How Breakfast Got Its Crunch.* New York: Abrams, 2011.

Glazer, Nathan, and Cynthia R. Field, eds. *The National Mall: Rethinking Washington's Monumental Core.* Baltimore: Johns Hopkins University Press, 2008.

Godey's Lady's Book, 1850. Philadelphia, 1850.

Godoy, Ricardo. "The Evolution of Common-Field Agriculture in the Andes: A Hypothesis." *Comparative Studies in Society and History* 33, no. 2 (April 1991): 395–414.

Goldman, Emma. *Emma Goldman: A Documentary History of the American Years, Vol. 1: Made for America, 1890–1901.* Edited by Candace Falk. Urbana: University of Illinois Press, 2008.

Gollner, Adam Leith. *The Fruit Hunters: A Story of Nature, Adventure, Commerce, and Obsession.* New York: Scribner, 2008.

Goodwyn, Lawrence. *The Populist Moment: A Short History of the Agrarian Revolt in America.* Oxford: Oxford University Press, 1978.

Gray, Charlotte. *Reluctant Genius: Alexander Graham Bell and the Passion for Invention.* New York: Arcade Publishing, 2006.

Green, Tamara M. *The Greek and Latin Roots of English.* Lanham, MD: Rowman & Littlefield, 2003.

Gruen, J. Philip. *Manifest Destinations: Cities and Tourists in the Nineteenth-Century American West.* Norman: University of Oklahoma Press, 2014.

Haber, Barbara. *From Hardtack to Home Fries: An Uncommon History of American Cooks and Meals.* New York: Free Press, 2002.

Harlan, H. V., and M. L. Martini. "Problems and Results in Barley Breeding." In *Yearbook of Agriculture.* Washington, D.C.: Government Printing Office, 1936.

Harris, Amanda. *Fruits of Eden: David Fairchild and America's Plant Hunters.* Gainesville: University Press of Florida, 2015.

Harris, Thaddeus Mason. *Biographical Memorials of James Oglethorpe, Founder of the Colony of Georgia.* Boston: Printed for the Author, 1841.

Hecke, G. H. *Monthly Bulletin of the Department of Agriculture* 1, no. 11. Sacramento: Government of the State of California, 1922.

Helstosky, Carol. *Pizza: A Global History.* London: Reaktion, 2008.

Herschell, George. *Indigestion: The Diagnosis and Treatment of the Functional Derangements of the Stomach, with an Appendix on the Preparation of Food by Cooking with Especial Reference to Its Use in the Treatment of Affections of the Stomach.* Chicago: W. T. Keener, 1905.

Hicks, John D. *The Populist Revolt: A History of the Farmers' Alliance and the People's Party.* Minneapolis: University of Minnesota Press, 1931.

Higginbotham, Don. *George Washington Reconsidered.* Charlottesville: University of Virginia Press, 2001.

Hill, George William. *Yearbook of Agriculture 1897.* Washington, D.C.: United States Department of Agriculture, Government Printing Office, 1898.

Hine, Darlene Clark, William C. Hine, and Stanley Harrold. *The African-American Odyssey: Combined Volume.* New York: Bedford/St. Martin's, 2002.

Hobbs, Frank, and Nicole Stoops. US Census Bureau. *Demographic Trends in the 20th Century.* Washington, D.C.: U.S. Government Printing Office, 2002.

Jacobsen, Hans-Adolf, and Arthur L. Smith Jr. *The Nazi Party and the German Foreign Office*. New York: Routledge, 2007.

James A. "Tama" Wilson Papers, RS 9/1/11, Special Collections Department, Iowa State University Library.

Jansen, A. A. J., Susan Parkinson, and A. F. S. Robertson, eds. *Food and Nutrition in Fiji: A Historical Review*. Suva, Fiji: Department of Nutrition and Dietetics, Fiji School of Medicine, 1990.

Jefferson, Roland, and Alan Fusonie. *The Japanese Flowering Cherry Trees of Washington, D.C.* National Arboretum Contribution No. 4. Washington, D.C.: United States Department of Agriculture, Agricultural Research Service, 1977.

Jeffrey, J. W. *Quarantine Laws and Orders*. Sacramento: California State Commission of Horticulture, 1911.

Jobb, Dean. *Empire of Deception: The Incredible Story of a Master Swindler Who Seduced a City and Captivated the Nation*. New York: Algonquin Books, 2015.

Kamiya, Gary. *Cool Gray City of Love: 49 Views of San Francisco*. New York: Bloomsbury, 2013.

Kazin, Michael. *A Godly Hero: The Life of William Jennings Bryan*. New York: Anchor, 2007.

Keating, John McLeod. *A History of the Yellow Fever: The Yellow Fever Epidemic of 1878, in Memphis, Tenn.* Memphis: Howard Association, 1879.

King, F. H. *Farmers of Forty Centuries: Organic Farming in China, Korea, and Japan*. Mineola, NY: Dover Publications, 2004.

Kirwan, Albert Dennis. *Revolt of the Rednecks: Mississippi Politics 1876–1925*. Lexington: University of Kentucky Press, 1951.

Kjeldsen-Kragh, Søren. *The Role of Agriculture in Economic Development: The Lessons of History*. Copenhagen: Copenhagen Business School Press, 2007.

Koeppel, Dan. *Banana: The Fate of the Fruit That Changed the World*. New York: Hudson Street Press, 2008.

Kohlstedt, Sally Gregory, and David Kaiser. *Science and the American Century: Readings from Isis*. Chicago: University of Chicago Press, 1996.

Kumar, Martha Joynt. *The White House Beat at the Century Mark: Reporters Establish Position to Cover the "Elective Kingship."* College Park: University of Maryland Center for Political Leadership and Participation, 1996.

Lacey, Nick. *Introduction to Film*. New York: Palgrave Macmillan, 2005.

Larson, Erik. *The Devil in the White City: Murder, Magic, and Madness at the Fair That Changed America*. New York: Crown, 2003.

Laszlo, Pierre. *Citrus: A History*. Chicago: University of Chicago Press, 2007.

Lengel, Edward G., ed. *A Companion to George Washington*. Malden, MA: Wiley-Blackwell, 2012.

Lewis, W. Arthur. *Growth and Fluctuations: 1870–1913*. New York: Routledge, 2009.

Liliuokalani. *Hawaii's Story by Hawaii's Queen*. Rutland, VT: Tuttle, 1964.

Mann, Charles C. *1491: New Revelations of the Americas Before Columbus*. New York: Knopf, 2005.

Manufacturers, National Association of. *Transactions of the National Association of Cotton Manufacturers* Vol. 69. Place of publication not identified: E. L. Barry, 1900.

Marlatt, C. L. *An Entomologist's Quest: The Story of the San Jose Scale; The Diary of a Trip around the World, 1901–1902*. Washington, D.C.: Monumental Printing Co., 1953.

———. *How to Control the San Jose Scale*. Washington, D.C.: United States Department of Agriculture, Division of Entomology, 1900.

———. *The Periodical Cicada: An Account of Cicada Septendecim, Its Natural Enemies and the Means of Preventing Its Injury*. Washington, D.C.: U.S. Dept. of Agriculture, Division of Entomology, 1898.

McCarty, Kenneth G. "Farmers, the Populist Party, and Mississippi (1870-1900)." *Mississippi History Now*, July 2003.

McCormick, Leander James. *Family Record and Biography*. Chicago, 1896.

McCullough, David G. *The Wright Brothers*. New York: Simon & Schuster, 2015.

McKinley, William. *The Last Speech of William McKinley, President of the United States, Delivered at the Pan-American Exposition, Buffalo, New York, on the Fifth of September, 1901*. Canton, PA: Kirgate Press of Lewis Buddy, 3rd, 1901.

McMurry, Linda O. *George Washington Carver, Scientist and Symbol*. New York: Oxford University Press, 1981.

Meyer, Frank Nicholas. *Agricultural Explorations in the Fruit and Nut Orchards of China*. Washington, D.C.: Government Printing Office, 1911.

Millard, Candice. *River of Doubt: Theodore Roosevelt's Darkest Journey*. New York: Doubleday, 2005.

Morton, Julia Frances. *Fruits of Warm Climates*. Miami: J. F. Morton, 1987.

Myntti, Cynthia. *Paris Along the Nile: Architecture in Cairo from the Belle Epoque*. Cairo: American University in Cairo Press, 1999.

Napheys, George H. *The Physical Life of Woman: Advice to the Maiden, Wife and Mother*. London: C. Miller, 1893.

Nelson; Ida, Hial, Elmer, Arthur, and Walter. "Sketches of Our Home Life." TS, Amherst College. 1897.

Pauly, Philip J. *Biologists and the Promise of American Life: From Meriwether Lewis to Alfred Kinsey*. Princeton, NJ: Princeton University Press, 2000.

———. *Fruits and Plains: The Horticultural Transformation of America*. Cambridge, MA: Harvard University Press, 2007.

Perrine, Henry. *Tropical Plants: Report [of] the Committee on Agriculture to Which Was Referred the Memorial of Henry Perrine, Asking & Grant of Land in the Southern Extremity of East Florida, Etc.* Washington, D.C.: United States Congress House Committee on Agriculture, 1838.

Peterson, Merrill D. *The President and His Biographer: Woodrow Wilson and Ray Stannard Baker.* Charlottesville: University of Virginia Press, 2007.

———. *Thomas Jefferson and the New Nation: A Biography.* New York: Oxford University Press, 1970.

Pieters, A. J. "Seed Distribution by the United States Department of Agriculture." *The Plant World* 13, no. 12 (1910). Ecological Society of America.

Pillsbury, Richard. *No Foreign Food: The American Diet in Time and Place.* Boulder, CO: Westview Press, 1998.

Poore, Benjamin Perley. "Agriculture of Massachusetts." Lecture, Essex Agricultural Society, October 1, 1856.

Popenoe, Wilson. *Manual of Tropical and Subtropical Fruits: Excluding the Banana, Coconut, Pineapple, Citrus Fruits, Olive, and Fig.* New York: Macmillan, 1920.

Postel, Sandra. *Pillar of Sand: Can the Irrigation Miracle Last?* New York: W. W. Norton & Company, 1999.

Prinz, Jesse J. *Beyond Human Nature: How Culture and Experience Shape the Human Mind.* New York: W. W. Norton & Company, 2012.

Randall, Willard Sterne. *George Washington: A Life.* New York: Henry Holt & Company, 1997.

Rasmussen, Wayne D. "The People's Department: Myth or Reality?" *Agricultural History* 64, no. 2 (spring 1990): 291–299.

Rasmussen, Wayne D., and Douglas E. Bowers. *A History of Agricultural Policy: Chronological Outline.* Washington, D.C.: United States Department of Agriculture, Economic Research Service, 1992.

Ratican, Diane. *Why LA? Pourquoi Paris?: An Artistic Pairing of Two Iconic Cities.* Mansfield, MA: Benna Books, 2014.

Rees, Albert, and Donald P. Jacobs. *Real Wages in Manufacturing, 1890–1914.* United States National Bureau of Economic Research. Princeton, NJ: Princeton University Press, 1961.

Reuther, Walter, Herbert John Webber, and Leon Dexter Batchelor, eds. *The Citrus Industry, Volume I: History, World Distribution, Botany, and Varieties.* Oakland: University of California Press, 1967.

Ricker, John F. *Yuraq Janka: Cordilleras Blanca and Rosko; Guide to the Peruvian Andes.* Banff: Alpine Club of Canada, 1981.

Rorer, S. T. *Good Cooking.* Philadelphia: Curtis Publishing Company, 1898.

Rosengarten, Frederic Jr. *Wilson Popenoe: Agricultural Explorer, Educator, and Friend of Latin America.* Lawai, Hawaii: National Tropical Botanical Garden, 1991.

Ross, Alice. "Health and Diet in 19th-Century America: A Food Historian's Point of View." *Historical Archaeology* 27, no. 2 (June 1993): 42–56.

Rothbard, Murray N. *Conceived in Liberty.* New Rochelle, NY: Arlington House, 1979.

Rowthorn, Chris, and Greg Bloom. *Philippines.* Oakland: Lonely Planet, 2006.

Rutkow, Eric. *American Canopy: Trees, Forests, and the Making of a Nation*. New York: Scribner, 2012.

Samuels, Gayle Brandow. *Enduring Roots: Encounters with Trees, History, and the American Landscape*. New Brunswick, NJ: Rutgers University Press, 1999.

Sanday, Peggy Reeves. *Divine Hunger: Cannibalism as a Cultural System*. Cambridge: Cambridge University Press, 1986.

Schwartz, B. W. "A History of Hops in America." In *Steiner's Guide to American Hops*. New York: Hopsteiner, 1973.

Seaburg, Carl, and Stanley Paterson. *The Ice King: Frederic Tudor and His Circle*. Boston: Massachusetts Historical Society, 2003.

Shambaugh, Benjamin Franklin. *Biographies and Portraits of the Progressive Men of Iowa: Leaders in Business, Politics and the Professions; Together with an Original and Authentic History of the State, by Ex-Lieutenant-Governor B. F. Gue*. Des Moines: Conaway & Shaw, 1899.

Shurtleff, William, H. T. Huang, and Akiko Aoyagi. *History of Soybeans and Soyfoods in China and Taiwan*. Lafayette, CA: Soyinfo Center, 2014.

Siddiq, Muhammad. *Tropical and Subtropical Fruits: Postharvest Physiology, Processing and Packaging*. Ames, IA: Wiley-Blackwell, 2012.

Smith, Andrew F. *Fast Food and Junk Food: An Encyclopedia of What We Love to Eat*. Santa Barbara, CA: Greenwood, 2012.

Smith, Jane S. *The Garden of Invention: Luther Burbank and the Business of Breeding Plants*. New York: Penguin Press, 2009.

Spillane, Joseph F. *Cocaine: From Medical Marvel to Modern Menace in the United States, 1884–1920*. Baltimore: Johns Hopkins University Press, 2002.

St. Johnston, Alfred. *Camping Among Cannibals*. London: Macmillan and Co., 1889.

Stebbing, Edward Percy. *Departmental Notes on Insects That Affect Forestry*. Calcutta: Office of the Superintendent of Government Printing, 1902.

Stoner, Allan, and Kim Hummer. *19th and 20th Century Plant Hunters*. Washington, D.C.: USDA Agricultural Research Service, National Germplasm Resources Laboratory, 2007. 198. Excerpted in *Horticultural Science*.

Talapatra, Sunil Kumar, and Bani Talapatra. *Chemistry of Plant Natural Products: Stereochemistry, Conformation, Synthesis, Biology, and Medicine*. Heidelberg: Springer, 2015.

Tatum, Charles M., ed. *Encyclopedia of Latino Culture: From Calaveras to Quinceañeras*. Santa Barbara, CA: Greenwood, 2014.

Taylor, William A. *Inventory of Seeds and Plants Imported by the Office of Foreign Seed and Plant Introduction During the Period from April 1 to June 30, 1912*. Washington, D.C.: Government Printing Office, 1914.

Thornton, Ian. *Krakatau: The Destruction and Reassembly of an Island Ecosystem*. Cambridge, MA: Harvard University Press, 1996.

Thrum, Thomas G. *Hawaiian Almanac and Annual*. Honolulu: Thos. G. Thrum Publisher, 1912.

Traister, Rebecca. *All the Single Ladies: Unmarried Women and the Rise of an Independent Nation*. New York: Simon & Schuster, 2016.

Tyrrell, Ian R. *Crisis of the Wasteful Nation: Empire and Conservation in Theodore Roosevelt's America*. Chicago: University of Chicago Press, 2015.

United States. Chief of Engineers U.S. Army. War Department. *Report of the Chief of Engineers* Vol. 3. Washington, D.C.: Government Printing Office, 1910.

United States. House of Representatives. United States Indian Affairs Committee. *Hearings by a Subcommittee of the Committee on Indian Affairs* Vol. 3. Washington, D.C.: Government Printing Office, 1920.

United States. Massachusetts Board of Agriculture. Office of the Secretary. *Fourth Annual Report of the Secretary of the Massachusetts Board of Agriculture*. Boston: William White, 1857.

United States. U.S. Department of Agriculture. *Annual Report of the Commissioner of Agriculture for the Year 1880*. Washington, D.C.: Government Printing Office, 1881.

United States. U.S. Department of Agriculture. Secretary of Agriculture. *Annual Reports of the Department of Agriculture for the Fiscal Year Ended June 30, 1900*. Washington, D.C.: Government Printing Office, 1900.

Valeš, Vladimir. *From Wild Hops to Osvald's Hop Clones*. Issue brief. Hop museum in Žatec. Translated by Naďa Žurková and Steve Yates. Prepared for the author, 2015.

Vella, Christina. *George Washington Carver: A Life*. Baton Rouge: Louisiana State University Press, 2015.

Ward, Erica M. *Coachella*. Mount Pleasant, SC: Arcadia Publishing, 2015.

Whitlock, Barbara. Swingle Plant Anatomy Reference Collection. "Walter Tennyson Swingle." August 20, 2009.

Wild, Antony. *Coffee: A Dark History*. New York: W. W. Norton & Company, 2005.

Williams, Thomas, and James Calvert. *Fiji and the Fijians*. New York: D. Appleton and Company, 1859.

Wilson, Stephen. *Feuding, Conflict, and Banditry in Nineteenth-Century Corsica*. Cambridge: Cambridge University Press, 1988.

Zhao, Xiaojian, and Edward J. W. Park. *Asian Americans: An Encyclopedia of Social, Cultural, Economic, and Political History*. Santa Barbara, CA: Greenwood, 2013.

NOTES

Historical nonfiction is the work of hard facts, even if one must admit that some facts are harder than others. Long-ago events that I've recounted rely on the written recollections of those who took part in them, almost all of whom, in this story, have died. In the case of a conflict, I chose the account written closest to the time the event occurred. I made logical assumptions about people and places only when independent sources corroborated a particular claim. Anything within quotes I took from an interview or historical document.

The black-and-white images in this book were almost all acquired from the Fairchild Tropical Botanic Garden in Coral Gables, Florida. The watercolor paintings are courtesy of the U.S. Department of Agriculture Pomological Watercolor Collection, Rare and Special Collections, National Agricultural Library in Beltsville, Maryland. The image of the Yokohama Nursery Company botanical catalogue was granted by the Arnold Arboretum Horticultural Library of Harvard University.

CHAPTER ONE: Chance Encounters

3   **"I had been accustomed":** Fairchild, David. *The World Was My Garden*. TS, Family Life, Fairchild Tropical Botanic Garden. Unpublished draft.

3   **ailing in his stomach:** Fairchild, David, Elizabeth Kay, and Alfred Kay. *The World Was My Garden: Travels of a Plant Explorer*. New York: Charles Scribner's Sons, 1938, p. 47.

4   **who refused to cable money:** Pocket notebook, winter 1894. Fairchild Tropical Botanic Garden. Coral Gables, FL.

4   **as he was at ballroom dancing:** David Fairchild to Marian Bell, 1904. Family Collection, Baddeck, Nova Scotia.

4   **"There I was, with an adventure":** Fairchild. *The World Was My Garden*, p. 47.

4 **Corsicans could be wary of outsiders:** Wilson, Stephen. *Feuding, Conflict, and Banditry in Nineteenth-Century Corsica.* Cambridge: Cambridge University Press, 1988.

5 **"a bandit of a fellow":** Pocket notebook, winter 1894. Fairchild Tropical Botanic Garden. Coral Gables, FL.

5 **folded like an accordion:** Photograph notes, date unknown. Photo file. Fairchild Tropical Botanic Garden. Coral Gables, FL.

7 **"On an errand that was not likely":** Fairchild, David. "Our Plant Immigrants." *National Geographic*, April 1906.

8 **"Americano!":** Fairchild. *The World Was My Garden*, p. 49.

9 **cuttings could later be grown:** Pocket notebook, winter 1894. Fairchild Tropical Botanic Garden. Coral Gables, FL.

9 **Only the southern states could farm:** Dunning, Nelson A. *The Farmers' Alliance History and Agricultural Digest.* Washington, D.C.: Alliance Pub., 1891, p. 454.

10 **"The fare of the Puritan farmers":** Poore, Benjamin Perley. "Agriculture of Massachusetts." Lecture, Essex Agricultural Society, October 1, 1856.

10 **"Porridge for breakfast; bread, cheese, and beer":** Massachusetts State Board of Agriculture. *Fourth Annual Report of the Secretary of the Massachusetts Board of Agriculture.* Boston: William White, 1857.

10 **Slaves tended to get leftovers:** Hedbor, Lars D. H. "Feeding the Slaves." *Journal of the American Revolution*, July 19, 2013. https://allthingsliberty .com/2013/07/feeding-the-slaves/.

10 **"Woody tissue" was harder:** Letheby, Henry. "On Food." *Journal of the Society of Arts*, Vol. 16, 1868, pp. 651–57.

10 **The nineteenth century's avant-garde:** Prinz, Jesse J. *Beyond Human Nature: How Culture and Experience Shape the Human Mind.* New York: W. W. Norton & Company, 2012.

10 **"excess in the quantity and variety":** Francatelli, Charles Elmé. *The Modern Cook.* London: W. Clowes and Sons, 1846, p. viii.

11 **wasn't properly "brought up":** Napheys, George H. *The Physical Life of Woman: Advice to the Maiden, Wife and Mother.* London: C. Miller, 1893, p. 174.

11 **"Eat only the proper amount":** Rorer, S. T. *Good Cooking.* Philadelphia: Curtis Publishing Company, 1898, pp. 145–60.

11 **Some blamed it on eating hot foods:** Ross, Alice. 1993. "Health and Diet in 19th-Century America: A Food Historian's Point of View." *Historical Archaeology* 27 (2). Society for Historical Archaeology: 42–56.

11 **The implied warning:** Herschell, George. *Indigestion: The Diagnosis and Treatment of the Functional Derangements of the Stomach, with an Appendix on the Preparation of Food by Cooking with Especial Reference to Its Use in the Treatment of Affections of the Stomach.* Chicago: W. T. Keener, 1905.

12 **cooking eels with a little parsley:** An American Lady. *The American Home Cook Book: With Several Hundred Excellent Recipes: Selected and Tried with Great Care, and with a View to Be Used by Those Who Regard Economy, and Containing Important Information on the Arrangement and Well Ordering of the Kitchen: The Whole Based on Many Years of Experience.* New York: Dick & Fitzgerald, 1854.

12 **terrapin turtles boiled with salt:** Haber, Barbara. *From Hardtack to Home Fries: An Uncommon History of American Cooks and Meals.* New York: Free Press, 2002.

12 **The foot of a calf:** Chadwick, J. *Home Cookery: A Collection of Tried Receipts, Both Foreign and Domestic.* Boston: Crosby, Nicholas, and Company, 1853.

12 **more than half were farmers:** National Bureau of Economic Research. *Output, Employment, and Productivity in the United States After 1800: Studies in Income and Wealth No. 30.* By Dorothy S. Brady. New York: National Bureau of Economic Research, Dist. by Columbia University Press, 1966.

12 **comfort food:** Romm, Cari. "Why Comfort Food Comforts." *The Atlantic*, April 3, 2015.

12 **just over five feet:** "Charlotte Pearl (Halsted) Fairchild." Kansas State University. Accessed May 1, 2015. https://krex.k-state.edu/dspace/handle/2097/21953.

12 **She had been the first:** Fairchild, David. "A Genetic Portrait Chart." *Journal of Heredity* 12, no. 5 (1921): 213–19.

12 **"Spread with a nice sauce":** *Godey's Lady's Book, 1850.* Philadelphia: Louis A. Godey, 1850.

13 **clumping together oats:** Gitlin, Marty, and Topher Ellis. *The Great American Cereal Book: How Breakfast Got Its Crunch.* New York: Abrams, 2012.

13 **"butterine":** Snodgrass, Katharine. *Margarine as a Butter Substitute.* Stanford, CA: Stanford University Food Research Institute, 1930.

13 **the crowd's Victorian sensibilities:** Koeppel, Dan. *Banana: The Fate of the Fruit That Changed the World.* New York: Hudson Street Press, 2007. pp. 51–52.

14 **Nine million people:** National Bureau of Economic Research. *Output, Employment, and Productivity in the United States After 1800: Studies in Income and Wealth No. 30.* By Dorothy S. Brady. New York: National Bureau of Economic Research, Dist. by Columbia University Press, 1966.

14 **a slender blue-eyed boy:** Fairchild, David. "A Genetic Portrait Chart." *The Journal of Heredity* 12, no. 5 (1921): 213–19.

14 **He wandered through the neighbors' rows:** Epstein, Beryl Williams, and Sam Epstein. *Plant Explorer, David Fairchild.* New York: J. Messner, 1961, p. 41.

14 **"When Wallace came he stayed at our house":** Fairchild. *The World Was My Garden*, p. 14.

15 **thus solidifying his perch:** "Natural Selection: Charles Darwin & Alfred Russel Wallace." University of California Museum of Paleontology. Accessed April 19, 2015. http://evolution.berkeley.edu/evolibrary/article/history_14.

15 **Wallace told Fairchild that:** Fairchild. *The World Was My Garden*, p. 14.

15 **"When the formative years of one's life":** Fairchild. *The World Was My Garden*, p. 6.

15 **Any Kansas boy could find:** Nelson; Ida, Hial, Elmer, Arthur, and Walter. "Sketches of Our Home Life." 1897. TS, Amherst College.

16 **How could you inoculate:** Epstein, Beryl Williams, and Sam Epstein. *Plant Explorer, David Fairchild*. New York: J. Messner, 1961, p. 24.

17 **coincidentally named Isaac Newton:** Rasmussen, Wayne D. 1990. "The People's Department: Myth or Reality?" *Agricultural History* 64 (2). Agricultural History Society: 291–99.

17 **peach yellows that made fruit ripen:** Galloway, B. Memorandum (on the History of the Department of Agriculture). 1914. TS, USDA Collection, National Agricultural Library.

19 **to rival Gustave Eiffel's:** Larson, Erik. *The Devil in the White City: Murder, Magic, and Madness at the Fair That Changed America*. New York: Crown, 2003.

19 **"knowledge people can use!":** Letter from Beverly Galloway to David Fairchild, 1893.

19 **If he timed it right:** Fairchild. *The World Was My Garden*, p. 29.

21 **seven-thousand-ton ocean liner:** Detroit Publishing Co., Publisher, photograph by Johnston, John S. "SS *Fulda*." 1882. Image retrieved from the Library of Congress.

21 **The man was tall and handsome:** Fairchild. *The World Was My Garden*, pp. 30–31.

21 **the number changed each time:** Douglas, Marjory Stoneman. *Adventures in a Green World: The Story of David Fairchild and Barbour Lathrop*. Coconut Grove, FL: Field Research Projects, 1973.

22 **"why don't you collect plant specimens":** "Hunting for New Crops." *The Inter Ocean* (Chicago, Illinois), September 4, 1906.

23 **Fairchild saw him one more time:** Fairchild, David. *The World Was My Garden*. TS, Family Life, Fairchild Tropical Botanic Garden, unpublished draft.

23 **mountain tribespeople in northern Morocco:** Fairchild. *The World Was My Garden*, p. 32.

23 **drawn to the dramatics and prestige:** Douglas, Marjory Stoneman. *Adventures in a Green World: The Story of David Fairchild and Barbour Lathrop*. Coconut Grove, FL: Field Research Projects, 1973.

CHAPTER TWO: One Thousand Dollars

24 **A hundred million years after that:** Raven, Peter. President Emeritus of Missouri Botanical Library. Interview by author. December 16, 2016.

25 **Nine thousand years passed:** Tatum, Charles M., ed. *Encyclopedia of Latino Culture: From Calaveras to Quinceañeras.* Santa Barbara, CA: Greenwood, 2014, p. 473.

25 **"wheat, corn, rice, barley, sorghum, and soy":** Gollner, Adam. *The Fruit Hunters: A Story of Nature, Adventure, Commerce, and Obsession.* New York: Scribner, 2008, p. 22.

26 **the last ice age, eighteen thousand years ago:** De Blij, H. J. *"The Little Ice Age: How Climate Made History, 1300–1850 by Brian Fagan"* [Review]. *Annals of the Association of American Geographers* 92, no. 2 (2002): 377–79.

26 **the process of domestication:** Diamond, Jared. "Evolution, Consequences and Future of Plant and Animal Domestication." *Nature* 418, no. 6898 (2002): 700–07.

26 **Domestication let people:** Raven, Peter. President Emeritus of Missouri Botanical Library. Interview by author. December 16, 2016.

26 **The earliest North Americans:** Diamond, Jared. "Evolution, Consequences and Future of Plant and Animal Domestication." *Nature* 418, no. 6898 (2002): 700–07.

26 **Mexico and South America:** Raven, Peter. President Emeritus of Missouri Botanical Library. Interview by author. December 16, 2016.

27 **early civilizations in Asia and Africa:** Akhunov, Eduard. "Crop Origins for *National Geographic* Magazine." Interview by author. September 22, 2014.

27 **Edible plants tend to reproduce sexually:** "How Do Plants Reproduce Sexually?" Biosciences for Farming in Africa. Accessed March 16, 2016.

27 **produce plants *vegetatively*:** Bradford, Kent. "Plant Reproduction." Interview by author. April 3, 2016.

27 **the first roots of agriculture:** "The Development of Agriculture." Genographic Project, *National Geographic.* Accessed May 21, 2015.

28 **the Columbian Exchange:** Crosby, Alfred W. Jr. *The Columbian Exchange: Biological and Cultural Consequences of 1492.* Westport, CT: Greenwood Press, 1972.

28 **Columbus never set foot:** Strauss, Valerie. "Christopher Columbus: 3 Things You Think He Did That He Didn't." *Washington Post*, October 14, 2013.

28 **Smallpox alone is thought to have diminished:** Mann, Charles C. *1491: New Revelations of the Americas Before Columbus.* New York: Knopf, 2005.

28 **a heavily wooded continent:** Pillsbury, Richard. *No Foreign Food: The American Diet in Time and Place.* Boulder, CO: Westview Press, 1998.

28 **barley, wheat, and peaches:** Mann, Charles C. "How the Potato Changed the World." *Smithsonian Magazine*, November 2011.

28 **a sustainable system for growing food:** Diamond, Jared. *Guns, Germs, and Steel: The Fates of Human Societies.* New York: W. W. Norton & Company, 1998.

28 **James Oglethorpe, the British general:** Harris, Thaddeus Mason. *Biographical Memorials of James Oglethorpe, Founder of the Colony of Georgia.* Boston: Printed for the Author, 1841, p. 128.

28 **support silk, hemp, and flax:** Rothbard, Murray N. *Conceived in Liberty.* New Rochelle, NY: Arlington House, 1979, pp. 609–10.

28 **Before he was president:** Higginbotham, Don. *George Washington Reconsidered.* Charlottesville: University of Virginia Press, 2001, p. 75.

29 **investigating the optimal fertilizer:** Randall, Willard Sterne. *George Washington: A Life.* New York: Henry Holt & Company, 1997, pp. 209–10.

29 **his revelation that cows, rather than horses:** Lengel, Edward G., ed. *A Companion to George Washington.* Malden, MA: Wiley-Blackwell, 2012.

29 **"The greatest service which can be rendered":** Peterson, Merrill D. *Thomas Jefferson and the New Nation: A Biography.* New York: Oxford University Press, 1970. p. 537.

29 **Farmers accounted for 90 percent:** U.S. Department of Agriculture, Economic Research Service. *A History of Agricultural Policy: Chronological Outline.* By Wayne D. Rasmussen and Douglas E. Bowers. 1992.

29 **just over half:** *Output, Employment and Productivity in the United States after 1800: Studies in Income and Wealth* No. 30. By Dorothy S. Brady. New York: National Bureau of Economic Research, Dist. by Columbia University Press, 1966. Table 2.

29 **courses on horticulture:** Rasmussen, Wayne, D. "Lincoln's Agricultural Legacy." National Agricultural Library. Accessed May 21, 2015. https://www.nal.usda.gov/Lincolns-agricultural-policy.

30 **"It is now generally conceded":** U.S. Department of Agriculture. *Annual Report of the Commissioner of Agriculture for the Year 1880.* Washington, D.C.: Government Printing Office, 1881, pp. 19–20.

30 **"The high-pitched, screaming voices":** Fairchild. *The World Was My Garden,* p. 32.

30 **"Sitting on the sea-wall [in Naples]":** "Scenes in Charming Old Naples." *Chicago Sunday Tribune,* November 18, 1894.

31 **An Italian painter:** Fairchild. *The World Was My Garden,* p. 32.

31 **a view of Mount Vesuvius:** Jepson, Tim. *National Geographic Traveler: Naples and Southern Italy.* Washington, D.C.: National Geographic, 2007, p. 65.

31 **"pestiferous ragamuffins":** Fairchild, David. Pocket notebook. Undated. Fairchild Tropical Botanic Garden. Coral Gables, FL.

31 **"thirteen characters who were all killed":** Fairchild. *The World Was My Garden,* p. 33.

32 **Paul Mayer, a marine biologist:** Fairchild, David. Pocket notebook. Undated. Fairchild Tropical Botanic Garden. Coral Gables, FL.

32 **"As a boy I watched termites":** Fairchild. *The World Was My Garden,* unpublished draft. Fairchild Tropical Botanic Garden. Coral Gables, FL.

32 **where pizza was invented:** Helstosky, Carol. *Pizza: A Global History.* London: Reaktion, 2008.

34 **"The professor and I":** Fairchild. *The World Was My Garden*, p. 35.

35 **the era's average salary:** Rees, Albert, and Donald P. Jacobs. National Bureau of Economic Research. *Real Wages in Manufacturing, 1890–1914*. Princeton, NJ: Princeton University Press, 1961, pp. 120–27.

35 **Lathrop seemed a peculiar man:** Douglas, Marjory Stoneman. *Adventures in a Green World: The Story of David Fairchild and Barbour Lathrop*. Coconut Grove, FL: Field Research Projects, 1973, p. 9.

36 **"Well, don't you think you'd better":** Fairchild. *The World Was My Garden*, p. 37.

36 *Bank of Scotland, 19 Bishopsgate Street Within:* Fairchild, David. Pocket notebook. Undated. Fairchild Tropical Botanic Garden. Coral Gables, FL.

CHAPTER THREE: East of Suez

37 **"How foolish I would be":** Fairchild. *The World Was My Garden*, unpublished draft. Fairchild Tropical Botanic Garden. Coral Gables, FL.

38 **W. A. Taylor, assistant pomologist:** *Proceedings of the Twenty-Fourth Session of the American Pomological Society: Held in Sacramento, Cal., January 16–18, 1895*. Topeka: American Pomological Society, 1895, pp. 175–76.

38 **The fruit itself was larger:** Reuther, W., et al., eds. *The Citrus Industry, Volume I: History, World Distribution, Botany, and Varieties*. Oakland: University of California, 1967.

38 **four major original citrus:** Karp, David. "Mandarin Oranges, Rising Stars of the Fruit Bowl." *New York Times*, February 1, 2016.

38 **fruits' hardy Asian ancestors:** Karp, David. "Citrus Phylogeny (for *National Geographic*)." Interview by author. April 2016.

38 **Americans in the 1890s:** Pabor, W. E. "Our Plant Immigrants." The *Sun* (Jacksonville, FL), July 7, 1906.

39 **"real value" to American citrus growers:** Fairchild. *The World Was My Garden*, p. 50.

39 **The saplings would bolster:** Geisseler, Daniel, and William R. Horwath. "Citrus Production in California." University of California, Davis, June 2016, pp. 1–4. https://apps1.cdfa.ca.gov/FertilizerResearch/docs/Citrus-Production_CA.pdf.

39 **Ted Nichols, was studying:** "Dartmouth Physics: Ernest Fox Nichols." *Dartmouth Undergraduate Journal of Science*. October 9, 2012. http://dujs.dartmouth.edu/2012/10/ernest-fox-nichols-2/#.V0IYoa6rS1t.

39 **"Incredible as it may seem":** Fairchild. *The World Was My Garden*, unpublished draft. Fairchild Tropical Botanic Garden. Coral Gables, FL.

41 **the French sculptor Frédéric-Auguste Bartholdi:** Berenson, Edward. *The Statue of Liberty: A Transatlantic Story*. New Haven: Yale University Press, 2012, pp. 22–29.

41 **"You approach Java with a feeling":** Fairchild, David. "Sumatra's West Coast." *National Geographic*, November 1898: 449–64.

43   **a jungle of rattan palms:** Fairchild, David. *Garden Islands of the Great East: Collecting Seeds from the Philippines and Netherlands India in the Junk "Chêng Ho."* New York: C. Scribner's Sons, 1943, p. 8.

43   **"as hot as liquid fire":** Fairchild. *The World Was My Garden*, p. 71.

45   **one made of rolled oats:** Markham, Charles Edwin. "California at the World's Fair." *The Californian Magazine*, November 1893: 762–71.

45   **Termites struck Fairchild as ironic:** Fairchild. *The World Was My Garden*, p. 66.

45   **a calculation he completed twice:** Fairchild, David. Pocket notebook. Undated. Fairchild Tropical Botanic Garden. Coral Gables, FL.

46   **Lathrop said he was "shocked":** Fairchild. *The World Was My Garden*, p. 80.

47   **several wise investments:** Funigiello, Philip J. *Florence Lathrop Page: A Biography*. Charlottesville: University of Virginia Press, 1994, p. 25.

47   **"a lawyer cannot tell the truth":** Douglas, Marjory Stoneman. *Adventures in a Green World: The Story of David Fairchild and Barbour Lathrop*. Coconut Grove, FL: Field Research Projects, 1973, p. 5.

47   **"The entire city buzzed":** Kamiya, Gary. *Cool Gray City of Love*. New York: Bloomsbury, 2013, p. 209.

47   **"a newspaperman":** Annals of the Bohemian Club, Vol. 1. TS, Barbour Lathrop Collection, Fairchild Tropical Botanic Garden. Coral Gables, FL. Date unknown.

47   **a front-row seat to important events:** Fairchild, David. "Uncle Barbour." 1934. TS, Barbour Lathrop Collection, Fairchild Tropical Botanic Garden. Coral Gables, FL.

48   **He quit his job:** Douglas, Marjory Stoneman. *Adventures in a Green World: The Story of David Fairchild and Barbour Lathrop*. Coconut Grove, FL: Field Research Projects, 1973, pp. 8–9.

48   **"sire of high jinks":** Douglas, Marjory Stoneman. *Adventures in a Green World: The Story of David Fairchild and Barbour Lathrop*. Coconut Grove, FL: Field Research Projects, 1973, p. 7.

48   **Bryan's wife annoyed everyone:** Fairchild, David. "Uncle Barbour." 1934. TS, Barbour Lathrop Collection, Fairchild Tropical Botanic Garden. Coral Gables, FL.

48   **the great Chicago dynasty of Robert McCormick:** McCormick, Leander James. *Family Record and Biography*. Chicago, 1896. p. 309.

49   **A sight that delighted Fairchild:** Fairchild. *The World Was My Garden*, p. 81.

49   **Lathrop banished him from the hotel:** Fairchild, David. "Uncle Barbour." 1934. TS, Barbour Lathrop Collection, Fairchild Tropical Botanic Garden. Coral Gables, FL.

49   **"I'm not accustomed to it":** Fairchild. *The World Was My Garden*, p. 81.

50   **officials in New York and Connecticut deployed fire engines:** Thornton, Ian. *Krakatau: The Destruction and Reassembly of an Island Ecosystem*. Cambridge, MA: Harvard University Press, 1996, p. 24.

50 **a chain of protruding volcanoes:** Fairchild, David. "Sumatra's West Coast." *National Geographic*, November 1898: 449–64.

50 **He assured her that:** Fairchild. *The World Was My Garden*, p. 83.

CHAPTER FOUR: Guest and Protégé

51 **Only after she delivered her first child:** Fairchild, David. "Sumatra's West Coast." *National Geographic*, November 1898: 455–56.

51 **Fairchild shook it to test its strength:** "Bamboo in the South." *Goldsboro Daily Argus* (Goldsboro, NC), July 21, 1903.

51 **"the most beautiful and useful of plants":** Fairchild, David. *Japanese Bamboos and Their Introduction into America*. Washington, D.C.: Government Printing Office, 1903.

52 **"He didn't propose to spend the rest of his life":** Fairchild, David. "Uncle Barbour." 1934. TS, Barbour Lathrop Collection, Fairchild Tropical Botanic Garden. Coral Gables, FL.

52 **He made all the major decisions:** Douglas, Marjory Stoneman. *Adventures in a Green World: The Story of David Fairchild and Barbour Lathrop*. Coconut Grove, FL: Field Research Projects, 1973.

52 **"the public morality":** "Discovering the Decades: 1850s." City of Alexandria, VA. Accessed October 28, 2015. https://www.alexandriava.gov /historic/info/default.aspx?id=28408.

54 **Lathrop stared at the lens:** Fairchild. *The World Was My Garden*, p. 84A.

54 **Lathrop stood up and threw his napkin:** Fairchild. *The World Was My Garden*, p. 92.

54 **"I was the guest and protégé":** Fairchild, David. "Uncle Barbour." 1934. TS, Barbour Lathrop Collection, Fairchild Tropical Botanic Garden. Coral Gables, FL.

54 **Two others had come prior:** Pauly, Philip J. *Fruits and Plains: The Horticultural Transformation of America*. Cambridge, MA: Harvard University Press, 2007, p. 126.

54 **Lathrop identified himself as "bohemian":** "The Literature of Bohemia." *The Westminster Review* 79 (spring 1863): 32.

54 **The fashion of the so-called Gay Nineties:** Chauncey, George. *Gay New York: Gender, Urban Culture, and the Making of the Gay Male World, 1890–1940*. New York: BasicBooks, 1994.

55 **"It's a collection expedition":** Fairchild, David. "Uncle Barbour." 1934. TS, Barbour Lathrop Collection, Fairchild Tropical Botanic Garden. Coral Gables, FL.

56 **a system of cogs with teeth:** Coulter, John Merle. *Botanical Gazette Volume 30*. Chicago: University of Chicago Press, 1900, pp. 127–28.

56 **Swampy jungle lined both sides:** Fairchild, David. "Uncle Barbour." 1934. TS, Barbour Lathrop Collection, Fairchild Tropical Botanic Garden. Coral Gables, FL.

57 **Without one specimen collected:** Fairchild, David. "Uncle Barbour." 1934. TS, Barbour Lathrop Collection, Fairchild Tropical Botanic Garden. Coral Gables, FL.

57 **"You're a worker, Fairchild":** Douglas, Marjory Stoneman. *Adventures in a Green World: The Story of David Fairchild and Barbour Lathrop.* Coconut Grove, FL: Field Research Projects, 1973, p. 17.

57 **Collecting useful things couldn't be done:** Fairchild, David. "Uncle Barbour." 1934. TS, Barbour Lathrop Collection, Fairchild Tropical Botanic Garden. Coral Gables, FL.

57 **"If you're going to travel with me":** Fairchild. *The World Was My Garden,* p. 83.

59 **"what do you think we should collect?":** Handwritten notes for "Uncle Barbour." 1934. Barbour Lathrop Collection, Fairchild Tropical Botanic Garden. Coral Gables, FL.

59 **a Catholic priest appeared:** Fairchild. *The World Was My Garden,* p. 84.

60 **his first taste of a banana:** Handwritten notes for "Uncle Barbour." 1934. Barbour Lathrop Collection, Fairchild Tropical Botanic Garden. Coral Gables, FL.

60 **"If I was a botanist":** Fairchild, David. "Uncle Barbour." 1934. TS, Barbour Lathrop Collection, Fairchild Tropical Botanic Garden. Coral Gables, FL.

61 **Just over seven thousand Spanish people:** Hine, Darlene Clark, William C. Hine, and Stanley Harrold. *The African-American Odyssey: Combined Volume.* Upper Saddle River, NJ: Prentice Hall, 2002, p. 376.

61 **nine days before the agreement was signed:** "The California Gold Rush." PBS. September 13, 2006. http://www.pbs.org/wgbh/amex/goldrush/peopleevents/e_goldrush.html.

61 **to defend it from Indians:** House of Representatives, United States Indian Affairs Committee. *Hearings by a Subcommittee of the Committee on Indian Affairs,* Vol. 3. Washington, D.C.: Government Printing Office, 1920, pp. 704–706.

61 **The only other catch:** Sonneborn, Liz. *Chronology of American Indian History: The Trail of the Wind.* New York: Facts on File, 2001.

62 **its first agricultural depression:** Pauly, Philip J. *Fruits and Plains: The Horticultural Transformation of America.* Cambridge, MA: Harvard University Press, 2007.

62 **"the highest authority on horticultural subjects":** Shambaugh, Benjamin Franklin. *Biographies and Portraits of the Progressive Men of Iowa: Leaders in Business, Politics and the Professions; Together with an Original and Authentic History of the State, by Ex-Lieutenant-Governor B. F. Gue.* Des Moines: Conaway & Shaw, 1899, pp. 135–37.

63 **a set of chimes at midnight:** "A New Year Ushered In." *New York Times,* January 1, 1897.

63 **Fairchild and Lathrop were floating in the dark:** Douglas, Marjory Stoneman. *Adventures in a Green World: The Story of David Fairchild and Barbour Lathrop.* Coconut Grove, FL: Field Research Projects, 1973, p. 18.

CHAPTER FIVE: The Listless Pacific

65 **delighting the hotel's owner so much:** Fairchild. *The World Was My Garden,* pp. 85–86.

65 **It dawned on Fairchild first:** Fairchild, David. Pocket notebook. Undated. Fairchild Tropical Botanic Garden. Coral Gables, FL.

66 **Native Hawaiians:** Thrum, Thomas G. *Hawaiian Almanac and Annual.* Honolulu: Thos. Thrum Publisher, 1912, p. 20.

66 **In December of 1893:** Cox, Francis M. *Message from the President of the United States to the Two Houses of Congress at the Beginning of the Second Session of the Fifty-third Congress with the Reports of the Heads of Departments and Selections from Accompanying Documents.* Washington, D.C.: Government Printing Office, 1894, pp. 35–48.

67 **"Uncle Barbour was a great raconteur":** Fairchild, David. "Uncle Barbour." 1934. TS, Barbour Lathrop Collection, Fairchild Tropical Botanic Garden. Coral Gables, FL.

67 **"What's the finest fruit":** Fairchild, David. "Uncle Barbour." 1934. TS, Barbour Lathrop Collection, Fairchild Tropical Botanic Garden. Coral Gables, FL.

67 **"It's the wampi":** Fairchild. *The World Was My Garden,* p. 87.

67 **rough, pale skin that would pass for a yellow grape:** Lower, Elsie E. *Clausena lansium.* 1911. USDA Pomological Watercolors, National Agricultural Library, Beltsville, MD.

67 **the wampi would one day:** Morton, Julia F. *Fruits of Warm Climates.* Miami, FL: J. F. Morton, 1987, pp. 197–98.

68 **"incomprehensible":** Fairchild. *The World Was My Garden,* p. 89.

68 **He witnessed a man fall:** Fairchild. *The World Was My Garden,* p. 89.

68 **North German Lloyd:** "Prominent People on Board." Hapag-Lloyd Insight. Accessed February 25, 2016. https://www.hapag-lloyd.com/en/news-insights/insights/2015/08/prominent-people-on-board_42541.html.

68 **"the delightfulest":** Jobb, Dean. *Empire of Deception: The Incredible Story of a Master Swindler Who Seduced a City and Captivated the Nation.* New York: Algonquin Books, 2015.

68 **"Pshaw, I don't believe it":** Fairchild, David. "Uncle Barbour." 1934. TS, Barbour Lathrop Collection, Fairchild Tropical Botanic Garden. Coral Gables, FL.

68 **they stared straight and walked away:** Nicholson, Evelyn Louise. *Diary of a Trip to Australia 1897.* University of Sydney Library, 1999. Accessed online: http://adc.library.usyd.edu.au/data-2/p00067.pdf.

69   **a small lyrebird:** Fairchild. *The World Was My Garden*, p. 91.

69   **there were more than five hundred:** "Genus: *Eucalyptus* L'Her." U.S. National Plant Germplasm System. January 27, 2009. https://npgsweb.ars-grin.gov/gringlobal/taxonomygenus.aspx?id=4477.

69   **he had been lured down under:** Blanchard, Frieda Cobb. "Nathan A. Cobb: Botanist and Zoologist, a Pioneer Scientist in Australia." *Asa Gray Bulletin* 3, no. 2 (1957).

69   **Developing governments:** Huettel, R. N., and A. N. Golden. "Nathan Augustus Cobb, the Father of Nematology in the United States." United States Department of Agriculture, Agricultural Research Service. Accessed April 25, 2016. http://www.ars.usda.gov/News/docs.htm?docid=9626.

69   **He presented a small wheel:** Fairchild. *The World Was My Garden*, p. 91.

70   **On special occasions:** Wells, Kathryn. "Australian Food and Drink." Australia.gov.au. April 7, 2015. http://www.australia.gov.au/about-australia/australian-story/austn-food-and-drink.

70   **Fairchild directed the conversation:** Fairchild, David. Pocket notebook. Undated. Fairchild Tropical Botanic Garden. Coral Gables, FL.

70   **a Boston man named Tudor:** Seaburg, Carl, and Stanley Paterson. *The Ice King: Frederic Tudor and His Circle.* Boston: Massachusetts Historical Society, 2003.

70   **He passed the shrinking cube:** Fairchild. *The World Was My Garden*, p. 97.

70   **eating human flesh out of necessity:** Sanday, Peggy Reeves. *Divine Hunger: Cannibalism as a Cultural System.* Cambridge: Cambridge University Press, 1986, pp. 151–53.

71   **The wealthy partook most often:** Jansen, A. A. J., Susan Parkinson, and A. F. S. Robertson, eds. *Food and Nutrition in Fiji: A Historical Review.* Suva, Fiji: Department of Nutrition and Dietetics, Fiji School of Medicine, 1990.

71   **so sought-after:** Williams, Thomas, and James Calvert. *Fiji and the Fijians.* New York: D. Appleton, 1859, pp. 179–80.

71   **"It is as good as *bakolo*":** St. Johnston, Alfred. *Camping Among Cannibals.* London: Macmillan, 1889, p. 229.

72   **a regular display of slaughter:** St. Johnston, Alfred. *Camping among Cannibals.* London: Macmillan, 1889, p. 229.

72   **the king was led to believe:** Fairchild. *The World Was My Garden*, p. 96.

73   **Later he learned that Lathrop:** Fairchild, David. "Uncle Barbour." 1934. TS, Barbour Lathrop Collection, Fairchild Tropical Botanic Garden Coral Gables, FL.

73   **For Fairchild, it was the farthest:** Fairchild, David. "Travel Journal." Fairchild Collection. Fairchild Tropical Botanic Garden. Coral Gables, FL.

73   **The first to discover Hawaii:** Zhao, Xiaojian, and Edward J. W. Park. *Asian Americans: An Encyclopedia of Social, Cultural, Economic, and Political History.* Santa Barbara, CA: Greenwood, 2013, p. 239.

73   **She tried, with her limited military:** Liliuokalani. *Hawaii's Story by Hawaii's Queen.* Rutland, VT: Tuttle, 1964.

74 **someone else from the Department:** Fairchild, David. Pocket notebook. Undated. Fairchild Tropical Botanic Garden. Coral Gables, FL.

75 **crawled off dizzy and sick:** Fairchild. *The World Was My Garden*, p. 100.

75 **He talked with a man:** Fairchild, David. "Travel Journal." Fairchild Collection. Fairchild Tropical Botanic Garden. Coral Gables, FL.

76 **it struck him that, in comparison, Vesuvius:** Fairchild, David. "Travel Journal." Fairchild Collection. Fairchild Tropical Botanic Garden. Coral Gables, FL.

76 **the musicians played the soft, slow notes:** Fairchild, David. Pocket notebook. Undated. Fairchild Tropical Botanic Garden. Coral Gables, FL.

76 **keen to return to the Bohemian Club:** Fairchild, David. "Uncle Barbour." 1934. TS, Barbour Lathrop Collection, Fairchild Tropical Botanic Garden. Coral Gables, FL.

77 **"I had never beheld so many":** Fairchild. *The World Was My Garden*, p. 104.

77 **George Fairchild greeted:** Fairchild, David. Pocket notebook. Undated. Fairchild Tropical Botanic Garden. Coral Gables, FL.

77 **Fairchild recalled stories:** "Kansas Items of Interest." *Hutchinson Gazette*, July 29, 1897.

CHAPTER SIX: One Cause, One Country

81 **Harvey's Ladies and Gentlemen's Oyster Saloon:** Boese, Kent. "Lost Washington: Harvey's Restaurant." Greater Greater Washington, June 3, 2009. Accessed April 28, 2015.

81 **Every president:** Sheir, Rebecca. "The Tasty History of D.C.'s Restaurant Scene." WAMU 88.5, January 17, 2014. Accessed October 28, 2015.

81 **soft-spoken and reserved:** Grubin, David, and Judy Crichton. "Spirit of the Age." Transcript. In *America 1900*. PBS. November 3, 1998.

82 **recommended Swingle for the job:** Whitlock, Barbara. Swingle Plant Anotomy Reference Collection. "Walter Tennyson Swingle." August 20, 2009.

84 **an old man who let only to young men:** Fairchild. *The World Was My Garden*, unpublished draft. Fairchild Tropical Botanic Garden. Coral Gables, FL.

84 **They discussed their travels and their futures:** Swingle, Walter. Letter to David Fairchild. December 20, 1898.

84 **a roomful of Florida citrusmen:** Whitlock. "Walter Tennyson Swingle." 2009.

85 **"My god":** Fairchild, David. "Early Days of SPI." Speech, Washington, D.C., October 9, 1922.

85 **Newsboys yelled, "Extra *Star*!":** Fairchild, David. "Early Days of SPI." Speech, Washington, D.C., October 9, 1922.

86 **"I hereby place my services":** Kazin, Michael. *A Godly Hero: The Life of William Jennings Bryan*. New York: Anchor, 2007, p. 86.

86 **the ship exploded:** The Learning Network, *New York Times* index.html. "Feb. 15, 1898 | U.S. Battleship Maine Explodes in Havana Harbor." February 15, 2012.

87 **311 to 6:** "The War of 1898: The Spanish-American War." Hispanic Division, Library of Congress. https://www.loc.gov/rr/hispanic/1898/index .html.

88 **They gloated:** Cosmas, Graham A. "Securing the Fruits of Victory: The U.S. Army Occupies Cuba, 1898–1899." *Military Affairs* 38, no. 3 (1974): 85–91.

88 **Congress investigated why so many soldiers:** Alger, R. A. "The Food of the Army During the Spanish War." *North American Review* 172, no. 530 (1901): 39–58.

88 **Soldiers marveled at:** *The Cuba Review and Bulletin,* Vol. 10. New York: Munson Steamship Line, 1911–1912, p. 15.

89 **one of the strangest résumés in American history:** *United States Congressional Serial Set.* 1888–1889. Washington, D.C.: Government Printing Office, 1889, p. 401.

89 **In Wilson's wood-paneled office:** Pieters, A. J. "Seed Distribution by the United States Department of Agriculture." *The Plant World* 13, no. 12 (1910): 292–96.

89 **It wasn't uncommon for packets:** Fairchild, David. "Early Days of the Seed Distribution Program." Unpublished essay. Date unknown.

89 **stories of farmers in the Upper Mississippi Valley:** "Rise of Industrial America, 1876–1900: Rural Life in the Late 19th Century." Library of Congress. Accessed April 27, 2015.

91 **He had scrawled:** Fairchild, David. Personal notes on page margins, 1898. Fairchild Tropical Botanic Garden. Coral Gables, FL.

91 **While Fairchild spoke:** Fairchild. *The World Was My Garden*, p. 106.

91 **whose populist campaign had riled farmers:** Blaine, Mary Kate. "Rise of the Populists and William Jennings Bryan." The Gilder Lehrman Institute of American History.

93 **"Don't let them crowd you out":** Fairchild. *The World Was My Garden.* unpublished draft. Fairchild Tropical Botanic Garden. Coral Gables, FL.

93 **In 1898, there were just 1,600 people:** George, Paul S. "Miami: One Hundred Years of History." *South Florida History* 24, no. 2 (1996). www.historymiami. org/Fastspot/research-miami/topics/history-of-miami/index.html.

93 **In 1829, Henry Perrine:** Perrine, Henry. *Tropical Plants: Report [of] the Committee on Agriculture to Which Was Referred the Memorial of Henry Perrine, Asking & Grant of Land in the Southern Extremity of East Florida, Etc.* Washington, D.C.: United States Congress House Committee on Agriculture, 1838, p. 14.

94 **Eventually, his limp body:** McIver, Stuart. "Massacre the Day an Island Died Indian Key Was Once the Capital of Dade County." *Sun Sentinel* (Florida). August 11, 1985.

94   **The Royal Palm, a five-story temple:** Piket, Casey. "Miami's First Luxury Hotel." Miami History. January 15, 2012.

95   **"I was thrilled to find tropical territory":** Fairchild. *The World Was My Garden*, p. 113.

95   **Fairchild returned to Washington:** Fairchild. *The World Was My Garden*, p. 113.

95   **a new appropriation of twenty thousand dollars:** Allen, E. W. 1901. "Appropriations for the U.S. Department of Agriculture." *Science* 13 (328). American Association for the Advancement of Science: 572–74.

96   **A nervous collapse:** Fairchild. "The Early Days of SPI." Unpublished essay. Fairchild Tropical Botanic Garden. Coral Gables, FL.

96   **"David," he said, "you're no more fit":** Fairchild. "The Early Days of SPI." Unpublished essay. Fairchild Tropical Botanic Garden. Coral Gables, FL.

97   **"I do not approve of it at all":** Fairchild. "The Early Days of SPI." Unpublished essay. Fairchild Tropical Botanic Garden. Coral Gables, FL.

97   **a gold USDA seal:** Letter with golden seal found by the author. *National Geographic* archives. March 2016.

98   **Wilson suggested that Fairchild look:** Fairchild. *The World Was My Garden*, p. 117.

CHAPTER SEVEN: Crossing Countries

99   **"California," he reported, "is to us":** Nordhoff, Charles. "California: How to Go There and What to See by the Way." *Harper's New Monthly Magazine* 44, no. 264 (1873).

99   **Now those heading west:** Gruen, J. Philip. *Manifest Destinations: Cities and Tourists in the Nineteenth-century American West*. Norman, OK: University of Oklahoma Press, 2014, p. 31.

100 **The summer had brought:** "Heavy Rains Affect American Crops." *Chicago Daily Tribune*, June 17, 1898.

100 **Each success brought bursts:** Brands, H. W. *The Reckless Decade: America in the 1890s*. Chicago: University of Chicago Press, 2002, p. 23.

100 **The Transcontinental Railroad connected:** "Railroad Maps, 1828–1900." Collection Connections. U.S. Library of Congress. Accessed April 29, 2016.

101 **Delicacies like mutton chops:** Butler, Stephanie. "Dining Across America in Rail's Golden Age." History. December 13, 2012. http://www.history.com/news/hungry-history/dining-across-america-in-rails-golden-age.

101 **a long-nosed plant enthusiast:** Chamberlin, Susan. "The Life of Dr. Francesco Franceschi and His Park (Part II)." Pacific Horticulture Society, 2002. Accessed April 29, 2016.

101 **The squash had originated:** Reader, Laurel. "Zucchini: A Treat in the Heat." *Master Gardener Journal*, 2013. http://cals.arizona.edu/maricopa/garden/html/pubs/0403/zucchini.html.

102 **Each morning a passenger on board:** Fairchild. *The World Was My Garden*, p. 120.

102 **expensive paintings and first-class libraries:** "Comfort, Courtesy, Safety, Speed." Ocean Crossings, 1870–1969, On the Water, Smithsonian National Museum of American History. Accessed April 29, 2016. americanhistroy.si.edu/onthewater/exhibition/5_3.html.

102 **Lathrop was always granted the best cabin:** Douglas. *Adventures in a Green World*, p. 13.

103 ***"Kingston, Jamaica, was the first foreign port":*** Fairchild. *The World Was My Garden*, p. 121.

103 ***"Eaten after peeling off the thick rind":*** Fairchild, David. Pocket notebook, 1898. Fairchild archive. National Tropical Botanic Garden.

103 **a lumpy reddish fruit called an akee:** Newton, Amanda Almira. *Blighia sapida (fruit)*. 1924. USDA Pomological Watercolors, National Agricultural Library, Beltsville, MD.

103 **"Mr. Lathrop had an extraordinary palate":** Fairchild. *The World Was My Garden*, p. 122.

104 **He rarely missed the opportunity:** Fairchild. *The World Was My Garden*, p. 123.

104 **The vegetable pear would later:** Passmore, Deborah Griscom. *Sechium edule*. 1910. USDA Pomological Watercolors, National Agricultural Library, Beltsville, MD.

104 **"Mr. Lathrop was enthusiastic":** Fairchild. "Plant Exploration." Unpublished draft of autobiography. Fairchild Tropical Botanic Garden. Date unknown.

104 **alternating between potatoes and wet moss:** Husby, Chad. "Botanical Travel." Telephone interview by author. April 18, 2016.

104 **wet cigarette paper, banana leaves, and sorghum moss:** Harris, Amanda. "Packing Methods." Telephone interview by author. March 7, 2016.

105 **a "Dago dazzler":** Fairchild. *The World Was My Garden*, p. 119.

105 **His associates at the USDA:** Fairchild, David. "Uncle Barbour." 1934. TS, Barbour Lathrop Collection, Fairchild Tropical Botanic Garden. Coral Gables, FL.

106 **Wilson's agricultural report for 1897:** James A. "Tama" Wilson Papers, RS 9/1/11, Special Collections Department, Iowa State University Library.

106 **"The Old World contains many things":** United States. Department of Agriculture. *Yearbook of Agriculture 1897*. By Geo. Wm. Hill. Washington, D.C.: Government Printing Office, 1898, p. 11.

106 **Yet America's farmers were finding:** Hicks, John D. *The Populist Revolt: A History of the Farmers' Alliance and the People's Party*. Minneapolis: University of Minnesota Press, 1931, p. 54.

106 **the newest railroad, the newest oil discovery:** Kirwan, Albert D., *Revolt of the Rednecks: Mississippi Politics 1876–1925*. Lexington: University of Kentucky Press, 1951.

106 **"There is a screw loose":** Polk, Leonidas L. *Progressive Farmer*, April 28, 1887. Accessed April 30, 2016.

107 **America's doctrine of expansion:** Goodwyn, Lawrence. *The Populist Moment: A Short History of the Agrarian Revolt in America*. Oxford: Oxford University Press, 1978.

107 **The nation was buried beneath:** McCarty, Kenneth G. "Farmers, the Populist Party, and Mississippi (1870–1900)." Mississippi History Now. July 2003.

107 **Kansas farmers began to burn their crop:** Brands, H. W. *The Reckless Decade: America in the 1890s*. Chicago: University of Chicago Press, 1995, pp. 177–81.

107 **being stuck in a business:** Goodwyn, *The Populist Moment: A Short History of the Agrarian Revolt in America*.

107 **People in China had farmed for thousands of years:** King, F. H. *Farmers of Forty Centuries: Organic Farming in China, Korea, and Japan*. Mineola, NY: Dover Publications, 2004.

108 **"What farmers need to do is raise less corn":** Connelley, William E. *A Standard History of Kansas and Kansans*, Vol. 2. Chicago: Lewis Publishing Company, 1918, p. 1150.

108 **the wicked conditions nearly drove him to suicide:** Millard, Candice. *River of Doubt: Theodore Roosevelt's Darkest Journey*. New York: Doubleday, 2005.

108 **Another tuber, which appeared similar to a potato:** Fairchild. *The World Was My Garden*, p. 124.

109 **transferred the virus that caused Caracas fever:** Fairchild, David. "Uncle Barbour." 1934. TS, Barbour Lathrop Collection, Fairchild Tropical Botanic Garden. Coral Gables, FL.

109 **"I was badly frightened":** Fairchild. *The World Was My Garden*, p. 124.

109 **fracture, gangrene, funeral:** Fairchild. *The World Was My Garden*, p. 9.

CHAPTER EIGHT: Alligator Pears

111 **Agriculturally, the Andes stood alone:** Ricker, John F. *Yuraq Janka: Cordilleras Blanca and Rosko; Guide to the Peruvian Andes*. Banff: Alpine Club of Canada 1981, p. 41.

111 **living with the planet's most fickle climate:** Godoy, Ricardo. 1991. "The Evolution of Common-Field Agriculture in the Andes: A Hypothesis." *Comparative Studies in Society and History 33*, no. 2 (1991): 395–414. http://www.jstor.org/stable/178907.

111 **"A pinch of seed may come half around the world":** Fairchild. *The World Was My Garden*, p. 205.

112 **hamburger in the 1870s:** Smith, Andrew F. *Fast Food and Junk Food: An Encyclopedia of What We Love to Eat*. Santa Barbara, CA: Greenwood, 2012, p. 322.

112 **delicacy of broiled eels:** An American Lady. *The American Home Cook Book, with Several Hundred Excellent Recipes. Selected and Tried with Great Care, and with a View to Be Used by Those Who Regard Economy, and*

Containing Important Information on the Arrangement and Well Ordering of the Kitchen. The Whole Based on Many Years of Experience. New York: Dick & Fitzgerald, 1864, p. 51.

112 **The Incas built their entire diet:** "Origin and History." International Year of Quinoa 2013. http://www.fao.org/quinoa-2013/what-is-quinoa/origin-and-history/en/. Further proof that quinoa peaked late: The UN's Food and Agriculture Organization dubbed 2013 the International Year of Quinoa.

112 **"A Scotchman told me":** Fairchild. *The World Was My Garden*, p. 128.

112 **surprise Peruvian and Bolivian farmers:** DePillis, Lydia. "Quinoa Should Be Taking Over the World. This Is Why It Isn't." *Washington Post*, July 11, 2013. https://www.washingtonpost.com/news/wonk/wp/2013/07/11/quinoa-should-be-taking-over-the-world-this-is-why-it-isnt/.

113 **"as a medicine . . . to remedy catarrh":** U.S. Department of Agriculture, Section of Seed and Plant Introduction. *Inventory of Foreign Seeds and Plants.* By O. F. Cook. Vol. 1. Washington, D.C.: Government Printing Office, 1899, p. 46.

113 **Peru's global claim had been over potatoes:** "Preserving Potato Diversity in Peru." American Museum of Natural History. April 26, 2013. http://www.amnh.org/explore/news-blogs/news-posts/preserving-potato-diversity-in-peru.

113 **Farmers had bred types:** Godoy, Ricardo. 1991. "The Evolution of Common-Field Agriculture in the Andes: A Hypothesis." *Comparative Studies in Society and History 33*, no. 2 (1991): 395–414.

113 **in the satchel of the English circumnavigator Francis Drake:** Mann, Charles C. "How the Potato Changed the World." *Smithsonian*, November 2011.

113 **Thomas Jefferson had served at the White House:** Rupp, Rebecca. "Are French Fries Truly French?" *National Geographic*, The Plate. January 8, 2015. http://theplate.nationalgeographic.com/2015/01/08/are-french-fries-truly-french/.

114 **a plant called coca:** Fairchild, David. "Uncle Barbour." 1934. TS, Barbour Lathrop Collection, Fairchild Tropical Botanic Garden. Coral Gables, FL.

115 **Lathrop never heard back:** Douglas, Marjory Stoneman. *Adventures in a Green World: The Story of David Fairchild and Barbour Lathrop.* Coconut Grove, FL: Field Research Projects, 1973, p. 11.

115 **"a flow of saliva and leaves a peculiar numbness":** Talapatra, Sunil Kumar, and Bani Talapatra. *Chemistry of Plant Natural Products: Stereochemistry, Conformation, Synthesis, Biology, and Medicine.* Heidelberg: Springer, 2015, p. 777.

115 **The suffix "caine":** "Cocaine." Online Etymology Dictionary. Accessed April 30, 2015.

115 **The large pharmaceutical company Parke-Davis:** Spillane, Joseph F. *Cocaine: From Medical Marvel to Modern Menace in the United States, 1884–1920.* Baltimore: Johns Hopkins University Press, 2002, pp. 67–75.

116 **His favorite was an ornamental tree:** Fairchild, David. "Uncle Barbour." 1934. TS, Barbour Lathrop Collection, Fairchild Tropical Botanic Garden. Coral Gables, FL.

116 **there simply wasn't capacity:** U.S. Department of Agriculture. Section of Seed and Plant Introduction. *Inventory of Foreign Seeds and Plants.* By O. F. Cook. Vol. 1. Washington, D.C.: Government Printing Office, 1899.

116 **mentioned in his obituary:** "David Grandison Fairchild." Everglades Digital Library. Accessed July 6, 2015. http://everglades.fiu.edu/reclaim/bios/fairchild.htm.

116 **their word for testicle:** Green, Tamara M. *The Greek and Latin Roots of English.* Lanham, MD: Rowman & Littlefield, 2008, p. 5.

117 **the fruit could withstand a mild frost:** U.S. Department of Agriculture, Section of Seed and Plant Introduction. *Inventory of Foreign Seeds and Plants.* By O. F. Cook. Vol. 1. Washington, D.C.: Government Printing Office, 1899.

117 **"A valuable find for California":** Fairchild. *The World Was My Garden,* p. 130.

117 **He agreed that a fruit so hardy:** Fairchild, David. "Uncle Barbour." 1934. TS, Barbour Lathrop Collection, Fairchild Tropical Botanic Garden. Coral Gables, FL.

117 **nearly a thousand avocados were packed:** Fairchild, David. "Uncle Barbour." 1934. TS, Barbour Lathrop Collection, Fairchild Tropical Botanic Garden. Coral Gables, FL.

118 **written instructions that only mature trees would fruit:** U.S. Department of Agriculture, Section of Seed and Plant Introduction. *Inventory of Foreign Seeds and Plants.* By O. F. Cook. Vol. 1. Washington, D.C.: Government Printing Office, 1899.

118 **Hollywood in 1886 or near Miami in 1894:** Condit, Ira J. *History of the Avocado and Its Varieties in California* 2. California Avocado Association, 1916: 105–44.

119 **a twentieth-century variety called *Fuerte*:** Condit, Ira J. *History of the Avocado and Its Varieties in California* 2. California Avocado Association, 1916: 105–44.

119 **a mail carrier in Fallbrook, California:** Gollner, Adam Leith. *The Fruit Hunters: A Story of Nature, Adventure, Commerce, and Obsession.* New York: Scribner, 2008, p. 10.

119 **an artist to sketch his avocado:** Hass, Rudolph G. R. G. HASS Plant Pat. 139. US Patent Office, filed April 17, 1935, and issued April 27, 1935.

121 **neighborhood of La Habra Heights:** *Year Book of the California Avocado Association.* Los Angeles: California Avocado Society, 1971, p. 16.

121 **name it after himself, Rudolph Hass:** *Year Book of the California Avocado Association.* Los Angeles: California Avocado Society, 1934, p. 24.

121 **His posture and attire and the coif of his mustache:** Douglas, Marjory Stoneman. *Adventures in a Green World: The Story of David Fairchild and Barbour Lathrop.* Coconut Grove, FL: Field Research Projects, 1973, p. 24.

121 **His mule slipped:** Fairchild. *The World Was My Garden*, p. 131.

122 **and soft-wooded evergreen tree named *bella sombra*:** Fairchild, David. "Uncle Barbour." 1934. TS, Barbour Lathrop Collection, Fairchild Tropical Botanic Garden. Coral Gables, FL.

123 **the United States' diplomatic residence in Petrópolis:** Fairchild. *The World Was My Garden*, p. 132.

123 **a distinctive dwarf mango called *Itamaraca*:** Fairchild, David. "Reminiscences of Early Plant Introduction in South Florida." *Proceedings of the Florida State Horticultural Society* 51 (1938): 11–13.

123 **"flattened like a tomato":** Fairchild. Pocket Notebook. Fairchild Tropical Botanic Garden. Coral Gables, FL.

124 **originated in the East African tropics of Ethiopia:** Wild, Antony. *Coffee: A Dark History*. New York: W. W. Norton & Company, 2005, p. 25.

124 **red dust from coffee fields:** Fairchild. *The World Was My Garden*, p. 134.

CHAPTER NINE: Grapes of a Venetian Monk

125 **to drink alkaline water:** Buck, Albert H., and Thomas Lathrop Stedman. *A Reference Handbook of the Medical Sciences: Embracing the Entire Range of Scientific and Practical Medicine and Allied Science*. New York: William Wood, 1900.

125 **"crusty person":** Fairchild. *The World Was My Garden*, p. 162.

125 **repeated enemas of tea:** Keating, John McLeod. *A History of the Yellow Fever. The Yellow Fever Epidemic of 1878, in Memphis, Tenn.* Memphis: Howard Association, 1879, p. 69.

125 **Windsor broad beans, also known as fava beans:** Berkeley, M. J. *The Journal of the Royal Horticultural Society of London*. London: Ranken & Co., 1877, p. 172.

126 **A woman had offered him:** Fairchild, David. "Uncle Barbour." 1934. TS, Barbour Lathrop Collection, Fairchild Tropical Botanic Garden. Coral Gables, FL.

126 **the city's zoo had a single horse:** Fairchild. *The World Was My Garden*, p. 137.

128 ***"more extensive trial":*** U.S. Department of Agriculture, Section of Seed and Plant Introduction. *Inventory of Foreign Seeds and Plants*. By O. F. Cook. Vol. 1. Washington, D.C.: Government Printing Office, 1899, p. 28.

128 **To bemuse each other:** "Postcard." Walter Swingle to David Fairchild. 1899. Fairchild Tropical Botanic Garden. Coral Gables, FL.

129 **$338.50 after twelve months in transit:** Harris, Amanda. *Fruits of Eden: David Fairchild and America's Plant Hunters*. Gainesville: University Press of Florida, 2015, p. 52.

129 **"It has puzzled me":** Ibid.

129 **450 new plants sent by Fairchild:** U.S. Department of Agriculture. *Secretary of Agriculture. Annual Reports of the Department of Agriculture for*

the Fiscal Year Ended June 30, 1900. Washington, D.C.: Government Printing Office, 1901, p. 5.

129 **"Through the generosity of Hon. Barbour Lathrop":** Ibid.

130 **he credited not just himself:** "Field Reports." United States. U.S. Department of Agriculture, Section of Seed and Plant Introduction. *Inventory of Foreign Seeds and Plants.* By O. F. Cook. Vol. 1. Washington, D.C.: Government Printing Office, 1899.

130 **slow-moving swirls of straw, eggshells:** "Venice As It Is To-Day." *New York Times,* February 21, 1896.

130 **The monk escorted him:** Fairchild, David. "Uncle Barbour." 1934. TS, Barbour Lathrop Collection, Fairchild Tropical Botanic Garden. Coral Gables, FL.

130 **Fairchild took his portrait:** Fairchild. *The World Was My Garden,* p. 138.

130 **The seedless grape variety:** Bradford, Dr. Kent. UC Davis Department of Plant Sciences. "Plant Reproduction and Cloning." Interview by author. April 3, 2016.

130 **A California horticulturist:** Fairchild. *The World Was My Garden,* pp. 263–82.

131 **potential of tweaking genes:** Smith, Jane S. *The Garden of Invention: Luther Burbank and the Business of Breeding Plants.* New York: Penguin Press, 2009.

131 **He imagined that a plum with no pit:** Fairchild. *The World Was My Garden,* p. 139.

131 **Hotel Bauer-Grünwald:** Fairchild, David. "Uncle Barbour." 1934. TS, Barbour Lathrop Collection, Fairchild Tropical Botanic Garden. Coral Gables, FL.

131 **"To my delight, the gondola turned":** Fairchild. *The World Was My Garden,* p. 139.

131 **The man promised:** Fairchild. *The World Was My Garden.* Unpublished draft. Fairchild Tropical Botanic Garden. Coral Gables, FL.

132 **Adding to the pleasantly sweet taste:** Fairchild, David. "Uncle Barbour." 1934. TS, Barbour Lathrop Collection, Fairchild Tropical Botanic Garden. Coral Gables, FL.

132 **"This grape should be given the most serious attention":** U.S. Department of Agriculture, Section of Seed and Plant Introduction. *Inventory of Foreign Seeds and Plants.* By O. F. Cook. Vol. 1. Washington, D.C.: Government Printing Office, 1899.

133 **the most popular grape in America:** "Thompson Seedless." UC Integrated Viticulture. Accessed September 8, 2015. http://iv.ucdavis.edu/Viticultural_Information/?uid=132.

133 **The crème-colored building:** "Shepheard's Hotel: British Base in Cairo." *Life Magazine,* December 14, 1942, 119–23.

134 **the greatest outpost in the world:** Fairchild, David. "Uncle Barbour." 1934. TS, Barbour Lathrop Collection, Fairchild Tropical Botanic Garden, p. 84.

134 **Turkish soldiers passed by:** Peters, Elizabeth. *Crocodile on the Sandbank.* New York: Dodd, Mead, 1975. (Fictionalized description of Shepheard's Hotel based on personal visits in 1900.)

134 **Their expertise in farming:** Postel, Sandra. *Pillar of Sand: Can the Irrigation Miracle Last?* New York: W. W. Norton & Company, 1999, p. 3.

134 **"The seed is used as a medicine":** U.S. Department of Agriculture, Section of Seed and Plant Introduction. *Inventory of Foreign Seeds and Plants.* By O. F. Cook. Vol. 1. Washington, D.C.: Government Printing Office, 1899, p. 26.

134 **the Egyptian pea:** Fairchild, David. "Uncle Barbour." 1934. TS, Barbour Lathrop Collection, Fairchild Tropical Botanic Garden, p. 89.

135 **It had originated sometime around 3000 BC in Pakistan:** Cotton's true origin remains largely a mystery, as it is believed to have been domesticated independently on both sides of the world. Evidence of cotton has been found in caves in Mexico as well as in Egypt's Nile Valley, both dating back more than five thousand years, before the Vikings or Columbus arrived in the Western Hemisphere. Such a coincidence would be a little like the ancient Greeks and the ancient Moche culture of South America each inventing algebra on their own, without ever knowing the other existed.

135 **Upland cotton, the yellow-flowered relative:** Pauly, Philip J. *Fruits and Plains: The Horticultural Transformation of America.* Cambridge, MA: Harvard University Press, 2007, p. 101.

135 **Muhammad Ali, had been given cotton:** Rivlin, Helen Anne B. "Muḥammad Ali." *Encyclopedia Britannica.*

136 **"Paris on the Nile":** Myntti, Cynthia. *Paris Along the Nile: Architecture in Cairo from the Belle Epoque.* Cairo: American University in Cairo Press, 1999.

136 **"a variety with a long":** Fairchild, David. "Our Plant Immigrants." *National Geographic,* January 1906, p. 190.

136 **The long fibers were:** Cook, O. F., Argyle McLachlan, and Rowland Montgomery Meade. *A Study of Diversity in Egyptian Cotton.* Washington, D.C.: Government Printing Office, 1909, pp. 18–22.

136 **became known as "Egyptian cotton":** Manufacturers, National Association Of. *Transactions of the National Association of Cotton Manufacturers.* Vol. 69. Place of Publication Not Identified: E. L. Barry, 1900, p. 168.

136 **"If you think it is such a good thing":** Fairchild. *The World Was My Garden,* p. 141.

137 ***"superior, both in amount of flesh":*** U.S. Department of Agriculture, Section of Seed and Plant Introduction. *Inventory of Foreign Seeds and Plants.* By O. F. Cook. Vol. 1. Washington, D.C.: Government Printing Office, 1899, p. 65.

137 ***"ripened for the table twenty days earlier":*** U.S. Department of Agriculture, Section of Seed and Plant Introduction. *Inventory of Foreign Seeds and Plants.* By O. F. Cook. Vol. 1. Washington, D.C.: Government Printing Office, 1899, p. 66.

137 *"recommended for irrigated Western lands"*: U.S. Department of Agriculture, Section of Seed and Plant Introduction. *Inventory of Foreign Seeds and Plants.* By O. F. Cook. Vol. 1. Washington, D.C.: Government Printing Office, 1899, p. 68.

137 *"grows in regions which are dry"*: U.S. Department of Agriculture, Section of Seed and Plant Introduction. *Inventory of Foreign Seeds and Plants.* By O. F. Cook. Vol. 1. Washington, D.C.: Government Printing Office, 1899, p. 791.

137 *"gives a brilliant color"*: U.S. Department of Agriculture, Section of Seed and Plant Introduction. *Inventory of Foreign Seeds and Plants.* By O. F. Cook. Vol. 1. Washington, D.C.: Government Printing Office, 1899, p. 66.

138 **A. J. Chandler was at the time:** "David Fairchild and the Introduction of Egyptian Cotton." Chandlerpedia, Chandler Museum Arizona. Accessed August 1, 2015. http://archive.chandlermuseum.org/Exhibits/Cotton_and_Goodyear /01._David_Fairchild_and_the_Introduction_of_Egyptian_Cotton.

138 **A new, long-staple variety raised:** Crago, Jody A., Mari Dresner, and Nate Meyers. *Chandler.* Charleston, SC: Arcadia Publishing, 2012, p. 73.

CHAPTER TEN: *Citrus Maxima*

141 **The Netherlands India Steam Navigation Company:** Bemmelen, J. F. van, G. B. Hooijer, and Jan Frederik Niermeyer. *Guide Through Netherlands India, Comp. by Order of the Koninklijke Paketvaart Maatschappij (Royal Packet Company).* London: T. Cook & Son, 1906.

141 **Even Lathrop, one of the nineteenth century's:** Fairchild, David. "Uncle Barbour." 1934. TS, Barbour Lathrop Collection, Fairchild Tropical Botanic Garden. Coral Gables, FL.

141 **He and Lathrop were technically researchers:** Fairchild, David. "Uncle Barbour." 1934. TS, Barbour Lathrop Collection, Fairchild Tropical Botanic Garden. Coral Gables, FL.

142 **"The native market yielded little":** Fairchild, David. "Uncle Barbour." 1934. TS, Barbour Lathrop Collection, Fairchild Tropical Botanic Garden. Coral Gables, FL.

143 **"At each place we met":** Fairchild, David. "Uncle Barbour." 1934. TS, Barbour Lathrop Collection, Fairchild Tropical Botanic Garden. Coral Gables, FL.

144 **A dog with no hair:** Fairchild, David. "Uncle Barbour." 1934. TS, Barbour Lathrop Collection, Fairchild Tropical Botanic Garden. Coral Gables, FL.

145 **"the feuds of poor whites":** Fairchild. *The World Was My Garden.* Unpublished draft. Fairchild Tropical Botanic Garden. Coral Gables, FL.

145 **The artillery didn't work:** Fairchild, David. "Uncle Barbour." 1934. TS, Barbour Lathrop Collection, Fairchild Tropical Botanic Garden. Coral Gables, FL.

145 **The captain sent a second officer:** Fairchild. *The World Was My Garden*, p. 150.

145 **"Joke and do comic ridiculous things":** Fairchild, David. "Uncle Barbour." 1934. TS, Barbour Lathrop Collection, Fairchild Tropical Botanic Garden. Coral Gables, FL.

146 **a citrus fruit shaped curiously like a pear:** Krieger, Louis Charles Christopher. *Citrus grandis.* USDA Pomological Watercolors, National Agricultural Library, Beltsville, MD.

147 **"Seeds of a large and very sour variety":** U.S. Department of Agriculture, Bureau of Plant Industry. *Seeds and Plants Imported During the Period September, 1900, to December, 1903.* By B. T. Galloway. Bulletin No. 66, 5501–9896. Washington, D.C.: Government Printing Office, 1905, p. 15.

147 **The spoils of the war:** "The World of 1898: The Spanish-American War." Hispanic Division, Library of Congress. http://loc.gov/rr/hispanic/1898/intro.html.

147 **five hundred million Chinese:** Grubin, David, and Judy Crichton. "Spirit of the Age." Transcript, quote by Walter Lafeber. In *America 1900*. PBS. November 3, 1998.

147 **giving a razor to a babe:** Halsall, Paul. "Albert Beveridge: The March of the Flag." Modern History Sourcebook, Fordham University August 1997. http://legacy.fordham.edu/halsall/mod/1898beveridge.asp.

148 **After an American soldier:** Grubin, David, and Judy Crichton. "Spirit of the Age." Transcript, quote by Walter Lafeber. In *America 1900*. PBS. November 3, 1998.

148 **Andrew Carnegie, who offered:** Edge, Laura Bufano. *Andrew Carnegie: Industrial Philanthropist.* Minneapolis: Lerner Publications, 2004, p. 95.

148 **"An American military presence":** Wilson, James. Letter to David Fairchild. Fairchild Tropical Botanic Garden. 1900.

149 **"The time is not yet ripe":** Fairchild, David. Letter to James Wilson. Fairchild Tropical Botanic Garden. March 5–14, 1900.

149 **McKinley sent a portly federal judge:** White, William Allen. "Taft, a Hewer of Wood." *American Magazine*, May 1908, p. 19–32.

150 **For forty centuries, China:** King, F. H. *Farmers of Forty Centuries: Organic Farming in China, Korea, and Japan.* Mineola, NY: Dover, 2004.

150 **its population, which seemed to rise:** Banister, Judith. "A Brief History of China's Population." In Poston, Dudley L. Jr., and David Yaukey, *The Population of Modern China.* Boston: Springer, 1992, pp. 51–57.

150 **Chickens hung, often alive:** King, F. H. *Farmers of Forty Centuries: Organic Farming in China, Korea, and Japan.* Mineola, NY: Dover, 2004.

150 **"an overpowering stench":** Fairchild. *The World Was My Garden*, p. 144.

152 *Worthy of consideration:* U.S. Department of Agriculture, Bureau of Plant Industry. *Seeds and Plants Imported During the Period September, 1900, to December, 1903.* By B. T. Galloway. Bulletin No. 66, 5501–9896. Washington, D.C.: Government Printing Office, 1905, p. 194.

153 **"Surely only a nightmare could fill my brain":** Fairchild. *The World Was My Garden*, pp. 157–58.

154 **"which so well illustrates Mr. Lathrop's warm heart":** Fairchild. *The World Was My Garden*, p. 159.

157 **"He will not be moved":** Fairchild. *The World Was My Garden*. Unpublished draft. Fairchild Tropical Botanic Garden. Coral Gables, FL.

157 *Prinz Heinrich* **that had two smokestacks:** Fairchild. *The World Was My Garden*, p. 161.

CHAPTER ELEVEN: Lemons, Leaves, and the
Dawn of New Light

161 **one thousand plants, including foods, shrubs, and trees:** Fairchild. *The World Was My Garden*. Unpublished draft. Fairchild Tropical Botanic Garden. Coral Gables, FL.

161 **But the Department's chief:** Fairchild. *The World Was My Garden*, p. 166.

162 **Fairchild cautioned that denying Lathrop:** Harris, Amanda. *Fruits of Eden: David Fairchild and America's Plant Hunters*. Gainesville: University Press of Florida, 2015, p. 57.

163 **Beer had been around:** Damerow, Peter. "Sumerian Beer: The Origins of Brewing Technology in Ancient Mesopotamia." *Cuneiform Digital Library Journal*, 2012. cdli.ucla.edu/pubs/cdlj/2012/cdlj2012_002.html.

163 **Over centuries, Bavarian and nearby Bohemian breweries:** Harlan, H. V., and M. L. Martini, "Problems and Results in Barley Breeding." In *Yearbook of Agriculture: 1936*. Washington, D.C.: Government Printing Office, 1936.

163 **American beer, by contrast, was full of harsh bitterness:** Geiling, Natasha. "In Search of the Great American Beer." Smithsonian.com, July 30, 2014.

163 **in the Pacific Northwest:** Schwartz, B. W. "A History of Hops in America." In *Steiner's Guide to American Hops*. New York: Hopsteiner, 1973.

163 **"American hops may be dismissed":** Geiling, Natasha. "In Search of the Great American Beer." Smithsonian.com, July 30, 2014.

164 **The nearby growers had formed a cartel:** Fairchild. *The World Was My Garden*, p. 168.

164 **the Semš hop was new:** Valeš, Vladimir. *From Wild Hops to Osvald's Hop Clones*. Issue brief. 2015. Hop museum in Žatec. Translated by Naďa Žurková and Steve Yates. Prepared for the author.

164 **In 1853 Semš saw sprouting in his yard:** U.S. Department of Agriculture, Bureau of Plant Industry. *Seeds and Plants Imported During the Period September, 1900, to December, 1903*. By B. T. Galloway. Bulletin No. 66, 5501–9896. Washington, D.C.: Government Printing Office, 1905, p. 29.

164 **"How could I hope to convert them":** Fairchild. *The World Was My Garden*, p. 168.

166 **"I suggested that a tablet":** Fairchild. *The World Was My Garden*, p. 169.

167 **The Woman's Christian Temperance Union:** "Early History." Woman's Christian Temperance Union. Accessed February 3, 2016. http://www.wctu
.org/history.html.

168 **The United States entered the new century:** Cooper, John Milton. "Enhanced Transcript." Transcript. In *America 1900*. PBS. November 3, 1998.

168 **the magic of telephones:** John, Richard R. "Telephony." Electronic Encyclopedia of Chicago 2005. http://www.encyclopedia.chicagohistory.org/pages/1236.html.

168 **moviemakers began to populate:** Lacey, Nick. *Introduction to Film*. Houndmills, U.K., and New York: Palgrave Macmillan, 2005, p. 92.

168 **the Washington Monument:** United States. Corps of Engineers, U.S. Army. War Department. *Report of the Chief of Engineers* U.S. Army. Vol. 3. Washington, D.C.: Government Printing Office, 1910, pp. 2673–74.

168 **The presidential election of 1900:** Miller Center, University of Virginia. "William McKinley: Campaigns and Elections." Accessed October 9, 2016. https://millercenter.org/president/mckinley/campaigns-and-elections.

169 **"Bigger intellectually, bigger hopefully":** Beveridge, Albert J., George Frisbie Hoar, William Jennings Bryan, and William Bourke Cockran. *Great Political Issues and Leaders of the Campaign of 1900*. Chicago: W. B. Conkey, 1900, p. 600.

169 **an enormous elephant:** Beveridge, Albert J., George Frisbie Hoar, William Jennings Bryan, and William Bourke Cockran. *Great Political Issues and Leaders of the Campaign of 1900*. Chicago: W. B. Conkey, 1900, p. 596.

169 **"The Department of Agriculture has been extending":** McKinley, William. Speech, State of the Union Address, Washington D.C., December 3, 1900.

169 **He had acquired some disease:** "Obituary: George Fairchild." Unknown newspaper. Fairchild Tropical Botanic Garden. Coral Gables, FL.

170 **his life's work published:** Fairchild, George T. *Rural Wealth and Welfare: Economic Principles, Illustrated and Applied in Farm Life*. New York: Macmillan, 1900.

170 **"grief and loneliness":** Fairchild. *The World Was My Garden*, p. 180.

170 **"pushing on.":** Pancoast, Helene. "Fairchild's character." Interview by author. July 2015.

170 **a two-thousand-year-old grandparent:** Texas AgriLife Extension Service. "Greeks and Romans Grew Kale and Collards." Aggie Horticulture Aggie Horticulture. Accessed October 2, 2016. http://aggie-horticulture.tamu.edu/archives/parsons/publications/vegetabletravelers/kale.html.

171 **"The ease with which it is grown":** U.S. Department of Agriculture, Bureau of Plant Industry. *Seeds and Plants Imported During the Period September, 1900, to December, 1903*. By B. T. Galloway. Bulletin No. 66, 5501–9896. Washington, D.C.: Government Printing Office, 1905, pp. 45–46.

171 **it drew salt into its body:** "Kale." American Heritage Vegetables. Accessed October 2, 2016. http://lichen.csd.sc.edu/vegetable/vegetable.php?vegName=Kale.

171 **its biggest consumers restaurants:** Greenfield, Rebecca. "How McDonald's Could Conquer Kale." May 12, 2015. http://www.bloomberg.com/news/articles/2015-05-12/how-mcdonald-s-could-conquer-kale.

171 **chemists discovered it had more iron:** Oaklander, Mandy. "Here's Why Kale Is So Good for You." *Time Magazine.* January 2, 2015.

171 **"I could not understand why":** Fairchild. *The World Was My Garden*, p. 170.

172 **the prospect of dried table grapes:** U.S. Department of Agriculture, Bureau of Plant Industry. *Seeds and Plants Imported During the Period September, 1900, to December, 1903.* By B. T. Galloway, Bulletin No. 66, 5501–9896, Washington, D.C.: Government Printing Office, 1905, p. 79.

172 **tiny green beans known as lentils:** U.S. Department of Agriculture, Bureau of Plant Industry. *Seeds and Plants Imported During the Period September, 1900, to December, 1903.* By B. T. Galloway. Bulletin No. 66, 5501–9896, Washington, D.C.: Government Printing Office, 1905, p. 85.

173 **the first budded pistachio trees:** Fairchild. *The World Was My Garden*, p. 177.

173 **"I would find seedless lemons":** Fairchild. *The World Was My Garden*, p. 177.

174 **all for a small nut:** Schutt, Ellen Isham. *Anacardium occidentale.* 1909. USDA Pomological Watercolors, National Agricultural Library, Beltsville, MD.

175 **to import cashews from places like India:** Perez, Agnes. "USDA ERS—Fruit and Tree Nuts: Trade." Fruit and Tree Nuts: Trade. Updated August 25, 2016. http://www.ers.usda.gov/topics/crops/fruit-tree-nuts/trade.aspx.

175 **Buffalo, New York, wasn't anyone's first choice:** University at Buffalo Libraries. "Pan-American Exposition of 1901." Accessed October 16, 2015. http://library.buffalo.edu/pan-am/.

175 **two large pavilions:** "Map of Pan-American Exposition Held in Buffalo in 1901." In University of Maryland Libraries. 1901.

175 **the seventy-five-thousand-square-foot palace of agriculture:** "Colors of Nature in Agriculture Building." *Buffalo Evening News*, January 30, 1901.

175 **watermelons, cauliflowers, and new varieties of tomatoes:** *Vegetable Exhibit, North Section.* Photograph. University of Buffalo, Buffalo, NY.

175 **the biggest agricultural trade show:** *Report of the Board of General Managers of the Exhibit of the State of New York at the Pan-American Exposition; Transmitted to the Legislature, March 27, 1902.* Albany: J. B. Lyon, 1902, pp. 61–62.

176 **Farmers took turns wandering:** Durkee, J. H. "Report of the Agricultural Exhibit." Pan-American Exposition of 1901, University at Buffalo Libraries. Accessed February 2, 2016.

176 **"serves to deepen your faith":** Hartt, Mary Bronson. "How to See the Pan-American Exposition." *Everybody's Magazine,* July 1901, pp. 488–91.

176 **the other side of the Atlantic:** Lewis, W. Arthur. *Growth and Fluctuations, 1870–1913.* New York: Routledge, 2009, pp. 136–45.

176 **Europe's patchwork of small countries:** Kjeldsen-Kragh, Søren. *The Role of Agriculture in Economic Development: The Lessons of History.* Copenhagen: Copenhagen Business School Press, 2007, pp. 174–75.

177 **last speech McKinley would ever give:** McKinley, William. *The Last Speech of William McKinley, President of the United States, Delivered at the Pan-American Exposition, Buffalo, New York, on the Fifth of September, 1901.* Canton, PA: Printed by the Kirgate Press of Lewis Buddy, 3rd, 1901.

177 **"a disturbed anarchist":** Goldman, Emma. *Emma Goldman: A Documentary History of the American Years, Vol. 1: Made for America, 1890–1901.* Edited by Candace Falk. Urbana: University of Illinois Press, 2008, p. 79.

CHAPTER TWELVE: On the Banks of the Tigris

178 **a hundred-thousand-dollar "cottage":** Funigiello, Philip J. *Florence Lathrop Page: A Biography.* Charlottesville: University of Virginia Press, 1994, p. 108.

178 **One evening:** Fairchild. *The World Was My Garden,* unpublished draft. Fairchild Tropical Botanic Garden. Coral Gables, FL.

179 **In Washington, groups of farmers:** Moore, Sam. "Ten Agricultural Inventions That Changed the Face of Farming in America." *Farm Collector,* August 2008.

179 **a city of dairy and citrusmen:** *California Cultivator* 16, no. 1 (January 4, 1901).

179 **Before movie stars:** Ratican, Diane. *Why LA? Pourquoi Paris?: An Artistic Pairing of Two Iconic Cities.* Mansfield, MA: Benna Books, 2014, p. 56.

180 **"They were soon at my heels":** Fairchild. *The World Was My Garden,* p. 209.

180 **When the Nile floods:** Nixon, Scott W. "Replacing the Nile: Are Anthropogenic Nutrients Providing the Fertility Once Brought to the Mediterranean by a Great River?" *Ambio* 32, no. 1 (2003): 30–39.

180 **two petitions—one for men and the other for women:** *The 1897 Petition Against the Annexation of Hawaii.* 1897. National Archives and Records Administration. https://www.archives.gov/education/lessons/hawaii-petition.

180 **A Nevada congressman:** House Joint Resolution 259, 55th Congress. "The Newlands Resolution" (July 7, 1898). U.S. National Archives.

181 **"I cannot but be sad":** Fairchild. *The World Was My Garden,* p. 103.

181 **tropical products Americans were increasingly using:** "May Grow Our Own." *El Dorado Daily Republican* (El Dorado, KS), October 11, 1900.

181 **A Chinese minister's wife:** Fairchild. *The World Was My Garden,* unpublished draft. Fairchild Tropical Botanic Garden. Coral Gables, FL.

181 **he sent unripe specimens to Washington:** Fairchild. *The World Was My Garden*, p. 220.

182 **"Look where one will":** Mitra, Rajendralala. "The Parsis of Bombay." Lecture, Bethune Society, Calcutta, 1880.

182 **women in long yellow and red robes:** "Women and Children of the East." *National Geographic*, April 1907.

182 **"an insanitary labyrinth":** Lees, Andrew. *The City: A World History*. New York: Oxford University Press, 2015, p. 86.

182 **"The best Indian mangoes":** Fairchild. *The World Was My Garden*, p. 223.

182 **introduced by the Portuguese:** Joglekar, Rahul. "King of Mangoes Comes to See the Queen." India Ink, *New York Times*, May 10, 2013.

183 **The Douglas Bennett Alphonso:** Popenoe, Wilson. *Manual of Tropical and Subtropical Fruits: Excluding the Banana, Coconut, Pineapple, Citrus Fruits, Olive, and Fig*. New York: Macmillan, 1920. p. 18.

183 **Fairchild hired a group of children:** Douglas. *Adventures in a Green World*, p. 35.

184 **Straining to be polite:** Fairchild. *The World Was My Garden*, p. 228.

184 **"It certainly is a good way":** Fairchild. *The World Was My Garden*, p. 232.

185 **The close, fuzz-less relative:** Considine, Douglas M., and Glenn D. Considine, eds. *Foods and Food Production Encyclopedia*. New York: Van Nostrand Reinhold, 1982, p. 1331.

185 **Farmers in Iowa, Texas, and California:** *Proceedings of the Thirty-Eighth Convention of the American Pomological Society*. Columbus, OH: F. J. Heer Printing Company, 1922, p. 204.

185 **genealogy has secured the Quetta's presence:** "Nectarine Historic Cultivars." UC Davis Fruit & Nut Research and Information Center. December 12, 2013. http://fruitandnuteducation.ucdavis.edu/fruitnutproduction/PeachNectarine/Peach_Nect_FlFr/Nect_cv/.

186 **the biggest intersection of the world:** "Bagdad as a Railroad Centre." *New York Times*, January 25, 1903.

186 **a lush era of Islam:** "Bagdad." *New York Times*, June 17, 1900. Adapted from *Leslie's Popular Monthly*.

186 **Iron from England:** "Bagdad." *New York Times*, June 17, 1900. Adapted from *Leslie's Popular Monthly*.

186 **"Baghdad buttons":** "Bagdad." *New York Times*, June 17, 1900. Adapted from *Leslie's Popular Monthly*.

186 **"Women in black gowns and masks":** Fairchild. *The World Was My Garden*, p. 238.

186 **new strains of wheat, millet, barley:** Fairchild. *The World Was My Garden*, p. 240.

188 **the suckers made the ocean voyage:** Fairchild. *The World Was My Garden*, p. 241.

188 **Coachella Valley High School named its mascot:** Ward, Erica M. *Coachella*. Mount Pleasant, SC: Arcadia Publishing, 2015, pp. 60–61.

190 **"The food was bad on the boat":** Fairchild. *The World Was My Garden*, unpublished draft. Fairchild Tropical Botanic Garden. Coral Gables, FL.

190 **"the queen of tropical fruits":** "Hunting for New Crops." *The Inter Ocean* (Chicago, Illinois), September 4, 1906.

190 **"It has a beautiful white fruit pulp":** Fairchild, David. "Our Plant Immigrants." *National Geographic*, April 1906, p. 194.

191 **"I had a hell of a time":** Fairchild, *The World Was My Garden*, unpublished draft. Fairchild Tropical Botanic Garden. Coral Gables, FL.

192 **In Lathrop's later retelling:** Fairchild, David. "Uncle Barbour." 1934. TS, Barbour Lathrop Collection, Fairchild Tropical Botanic Garden. Coral Gables, FL.

192 **"What kept you so long?":** Fairchild. *The World Was My Garden*, p. 249.

193 **to eat with two narrow sticks:** Fairchild. *The World Was My Garden*, p. 258.

193 **a yellow plum known as a loquat:** Fairchild, David. *Three New Plant Introductions from Japan*. Washington, D.C.: Government Printing Office, 1903.

193 **"puckerless persimmon":** Wilson, Robert. "The Puckerless Persimmon—Fit Food for the Gods." *Pittsburgh Press*, January 22, 1911.

193 **zoysia grass, a rich green lawn specimen:** Forrester, Gary. "Zoysiagrass." Home & Garden Information Center, Clemson University. January 2016. http://www.clemson.edu/extension/hgic/plants/landscape/lawns/hgic 1212.html.

CHAPTER THIRTEEN: Bell's Grand Plan

194 **The invitation came from Gilbert Grosvenor:** Fairchild. *The World Was My Garden*, p. 194.

194 **or at the very least, to keep it alive:** Grosvenor, Gil. "National Geographic History." Interview by author. February 2015.

195 **"one of the most extensively traveled men":** "Cotton Views." *Houston Post*, September 17, 1904.

195 **"the closest thing to a social headquarters":** Tyrrell, Ian R. *Crisis of the Wasteful Nation: Empire and Conservation in Theodore Roosevelt's America*. Chicago: University of Chicago Press, 2015, p. 29.

195 **He built a briefing room:** Kumar, Martha Joynt. *The White House Beat at the Century Mark*. University of Maryland, College Park: Center for Political Leadership and Participation. p. 7. marthakumar.com/communications/white_house_beat.pdf.

195 **the "White House":** Office of the Curator, the White House. "Inside the White House: History." The White House. Accessed May 5, 2015. https://www.whitehouse.gov/about/inside-white-house.

195 **Victorian décor:** Buckland, Gail. *The White House in Miniature*. New York: W. W. Norton & Company, 1994, p. 76.

195 **Then he started to invite:** "Theodore Roosevelt Renovation: 1902." White House Museum. Accessed May 5, 2016. http://www.whitehouse museum.org/special/renovation-1902.htm.

195 **audiences applaud and cheer:** Burleigh, Nina. *The Stranger and the Statesman: James Smithson, John Quincy Adams, and the Making of America's Greatest Museum: the Smithsonian.* New York: Morrow, 2003, p. 3.

195 **"The government enterprise":** Fairchild, David. "Plant Immigrants." Lecture, Address to the National Geographic Society, Washington D.C., 1903.

196 **Bell had invited Fairchild:** Fairchild. *The World Was My Garden*, unpublished draft. Fairchild Tropical Botanic Garden. Coral Gables, FL.

197 **Wilson assigned Fairchild:** U.S. Department of Agriculture, Bureau of Plant Industry. *Seeds and Plants Imported During the Period September, 1900, to December, 1903.* By B. T. Galloway. Bulletin No. 66, 5501–9896, Washington, D.C.: Government Printing Office, 1905, Introduction by D. Fairchild, p. 7.

197 **"This branch of our government":** Fairchild. *The World Was My Garden*, p. 286.

197 **the largest office building:** Glazer, Nathan, and Cynthia R. Field, eds. *The National Mall: Rethinking Washington's Monumental Core.* Baltimore: Johns Hopkins University Press, 2008, p. 183.

198 **"Of the nearly 4,400 new introductions":** U.S. Department of Agriculture, Bureau of Plant Industry. *Seeds and Plants Imported During the Period September, 1900, to December, 1903.* By B. T. Galloway. Bulletin No. 66, 550–9896, Washington, D.C.: Government Printing Office, 1905, Introduction by D. Fairchild, p. 8.

199 **"circumnavigate Africa":** Fairchild. *The World Was My Garden*, p. 363.

199 **"This obviously entails a great risk":** "Curious African Tribes." *New York Times*, September 30, 1900.

199 **"I was much disappointed":** Fairchild. *The World Was My Garden*, p. 273.

199 **The bickering over land:** Iweriebor, Ehiedu E. G. "The Colonization of Africa." Africana Age, Schomberg Center for Research in Black Culture, New York Public Library. Accessed April 5, 2016. http://exhibitions.nypl .org/africanaage/essay-colonization-of-africa.html.

199 **landing required an unreliable method:** Fairchild, *The World Was My Garden*, p. 273.

201 **It was a Kaffir orange:** Fairchild, David. "The Kafir Orange: An Edible Member of the Strychnine-Producing Genus Which Succeeds in the United States." *The Journal of Heredity* 4, no. 3 (1913): 148–53.

201 **the carissa plum:** "Carissa, Natal Plum." Growables: Grow Florida Edibles. Accessed January 3, 2015. http://www.growables.org/information/ TropicalFruit/carissa.htm.

201 **"We tore the pineapples to pieces":** Fairchild. *The World Was My Garden*. Unpublished draft. Fairchild Tropical Botanic Garden. Coral Gables, FL.

201 **a bespoke three-story redbrick mansion:** "Building Permits." *Sunday Herald* (Washington, D.C.), June 14, 1891.

202 **Money flowed freely:** Gray, Charlotte. *Reluctant Genius: Alexander Graham Bell and the Passion for Invention*. New York: Arcade, 2006, p. 416.

202 **on whose rosters, one after another:** *Directory of the Washington Academy of Sciences*. Washington, D.C.: Judd & Detweiler Printers, 1893.

202 **Each Wednesday evening:** Fairchild. *The World Was My Garden*, p. 290.

202 **"exploration" or "curiosity":** Grosvenor, Gil. "National Geographic History." Interview by author. February 2015.

203 **Only after Bell patented:** Lorna MacDonald librettist. *The Bells of Baddeck*. Baddeck, Nova Scotia, July 2015.

203 **Fairchild reminded Bell:** Grosvenor, Gil. "National Geographic History." Interview by author. February 2015.

203 **Mr. Bell was at his charming best:** Fairchild. *The World Was My Garden*, p. 290.

204 **"The president joked, they laughed":** "The 'Kitchen Cabinet' of the President." *New York Times*, August 8, 1909.

204 **"the strenuousest of the strenuous":** "The 'Kitchen Cabinet' of the President." *New York Times*, August 8, 1909.

204 **an offhanded suggestion:** Fairchild. *The World Was My Garden*, unpublished draft. Fairchild Tropical Botanic Garden. Coral Gables, FL.

204 **It was Bell's idea:** Muller, Hugh. Interview by the author. July 2015.

205 **for two hours, Fairchild listened:** Fairchild. *The World Was My Garden*, unpublished draft. Fairchild Tropical Botanic Garden. Coral Gables, FL.

205 **a cursory engagement:** "Feminine Chat." *Harrisburg Star-Independent*, December 10, 1902. And Harris, Amanda. *Fruits of Eden: David Fairchild and America's Plant Hunters*. Gainesville: University Press of Florida, 2015, pp. 107–108.

205 **"Concentration proved difficult":** Fairchild. *The World Was My Garden*, p. 311.

CHAPTER FOURTEEN: A Brain Awhirl

206 **"his intellect":** Marian Bell to David Fairchild. January 4, 1905. Washington, D.C. Letter found by the author.

207 **courting begun to change:** Bailey, Beth L. *From Front Porch to Back Seat: Courtship in Twentieth-Century America*. Baltimore: Johns Hopkins University Press, 1989, p. 3.

207 **a new term: "dating":** Wilson, Brenda. "Sex Without Intimacy: No Dating, No Relationships." NPR. June 8, 2009. http://www.npr.org/templates/story/story.php?storyId=105008712. This act of dating was true for another couple. The same three months Fairchild pursued Marian, Teddy Roosevelt's niece Eleanor was getting to know her

future husband, Franklin, who happened to be her fifth cousin once removed.

207 **her parents might have matched her:** Traister, Rebecca. *All the Single Ladies: Unmarried Women and the Rise of an Independent Nation.* New York: Simon & Schuster, 2016.

208 **half the population . . . under twenty-three:** Hobbs, Frank, and Nicole Stoops, U.S. Census Bureau. *Demographic Trends in the 20th Century.* CENSR-4. Washington, D.C.: U.S. Government Printing Office, 2002, p. 1.

208 **"If, in marrying, you get nothing":** Bush, Joseph. *Before Marriage, and After.* London: Charles H. Kelly, 1901, p. 24.

208 **Gertrude Mercer Hubbard:** Fairchild. *The World Was My Garden,* p. 311.

208 **the high-altitude attic:** Fairchild. Pocket notebook. November 1904 to January 1905.

208 **a woody climbing vine:** "Camoensia Maxima." JStor Global Plants. Accessed May 6, 2016. https://plants.jstor.org/compilation/camoensia.maxima.

208 **a candidate for a new American garden shrub:** Fairchild. Pocket notebook. November 1904 to January 1905.

208 **Washington Charity Ball:** *Washington Charity Ball.* New Willard Hotel, Washington D.C., January 1904. Dance card and program found by the author.

209 **He wrote "supper":** *Washington Charity Ball.* New Willard Hotel, Washington D.C., January 1904. Dance card and program found by the author.

209 **Marian made regular trips:** Harris, Amanda. *Fruits of Eden: David Fairchild and America's Plant Hunters.* Gainesville: University Press of Florida, 2015, pp. 104–105.

209 **Marian had been drawn:** Fairchild, David. TS "Marian," Fairchild Papers, Fairchild Tropical Botanic Garden. Coral Gables, FL.

209 **a collection of finely sculpted angels:** "The Shattered Angels." *New York Times,* October 15, 1905.

210 **"a self-reliant and beautiful woman":** Harris, Amanda. *Fruits of Eden: David Fairchild and America's Plant Hunters.* Gainesville: University Press of Florida, 2015, pp. 104–05.

210 **Clara Barton . . . invited eighteen-year-old Marian:** Johnson, Ryan. "Angel of the Battlefield." American Red Cross. Accessed March 26, 2014. http://www.redcross.org/news/article/Angel-of-the-Battlefield.

210 **"accomplish no good":** Harris, Amanda. *Fruits of Eden: David Fairchild and America's Plant Hunters.* Gainesville: University Press of Florida, 2015, p. 103.

210 **her parents worried about:** Muller, Hugh. "Daisy Bell." Interview by author. July 2015.

211 **Fairchild took her hand:** Fairchild. Pocket notebook. November 1904 to January 1905.

211 **"That music was so deep":** Letter from David Fairchild to Marian Bell. January 13, 1905.

212 **He knocked over a candle:** Fairchild. *The World Was My Garden*, p. 311.

212 **Charles Lang Freer wanted to donate:** Harris, Amanda. *Fruits of Eden: David Fairchild and America's Plant Hunters.* Gainesville: University Press of Florida, 2015, p. 103.

212 **"Did you ever look at a friend's photograph":** David Fairchild to Marian Bell. January 31, 1905. Washington, D.C. Letter found by the author.

213 **"There is no use in my trying":** David Fairchild to Marian Bell. February 13, 1905. Wilmington, NC. Letter found by the author.

213 **"My friend—you know who":** David Fairchild to Marian Bell. February 13, 1905. Washington, D.C. Letter found by the author.

214 **"Uncle Barbour, this is Marian":** Fairchild. *The World Was My Garden*, p. 457.

215 **an engagement necklace:** "Current Comment." The Wilmington *Morning Star*, May 16, 1905.

217 **"My dear Daddysan":** Fairchild, David. *The World as Garden: The Life and Writings of David Fairchild.* Edited by David W. Lee. West Charleston, SC: Createspace, 2013, p. 109.

217 **Marian's dowry could be:** Harris, Amanda. *Fruits of Eden: David Fairchild and America's Plant Hunters.* Gainesville: University Press of Florida, 2015, p. 110.

218 **two tickets to Roosevelt's inaugural ball:** *Inaugural Ball.* Pension Building, Washington D.C., March 4, 1905. Ticket and dance card found by the author.

218 **creamed oysters, French peas:** *Program for the Inaugural Ball.* Washington, D.C., 1905.

218 **The blooms were Marian's:** Epstein, Beryl Williams, and Sam Epstein. *Plant Explorer, David Fairchild.* New York: J. Messner, 1961, p. 124.

218 **"My Marian, my own darling":** David Fairchild to Marian Bell. April 24, 1905. Washington, D.C. Letter found by the author.

219 **who traded seasons:** Muller, Hugh. "Daisy Bell." Interview by author. July 2015.

219 **white accordion chiffon dress:** "Diplomats Join in Merry Dance." *Washington Times*, May 11, 1905.

CHAPTER FIFTEEN: Cherry Trees with No Cherries

220 **In the 1880s, he watched:** "San Jose Scale." California State Integrated Pest Management Program. March 15, 2016.

220 **an expedition to Asia:** U.S. Department of Agriculture, Division of Entomology. *How to Control the San Jose Scale.* By Charles L. Marlatt. Washington, D.C. 1900.

221 **"Mr. and Mrs. Ladybug":** "Ladybugs Are Shielded." *The Nebraska Advertiser* (Nemaha, NE), June 13, 1902.

221 **In the 1870s, it had been Marlatt:** Pauly, Philip J. *Biologists and the Promise of American Life: From Meriwether Lewis to Alfred Kinsey.* Princeton, NJ: Princeton University Press, 2000.

221 **his scale-hunting trip:** Marlatt, C. L. *An Entomologist's Quest: The Story of the San Jose Scale; The Diary of a Trip Around the World, 1901–1902.* Washington, D.C.: Monumental Printing Co., 1953.

222 **infestations of periodical cicadas:** Marlatt, C. L. *The Periodical Cicada: An Account of Cicada Septendecim, Its Natural Enemies and the Means of Preventing Its Injury.* Washington, D.C.: U.S. Dept. of Agriculture, Division of Entomology, 1898.

222 **They wanted space:** Fairchild. *The World Was My Garden*, p. 313.

223 **Bells gifted them an automobile:** Fairchild. *The World Was My Garden*, p. 313.

223 **a wartime ambulance driver:** Pancoast, Helene. "Daisy Bell." Interview by author. July 2015. Coconut Grove, Florida.

223 **"Like children, we waded":** Fairchild. *The World Was My Garden*, p. 316.

223 **chickpea muffins:** Fairchild, David. "Uncle Barbour." 1934. TS, Barbour Lathrop Collection, Fairchild Tropical Botanic Garden. Coral Gables, FL.

223 **Fairchild ordered 125 of them:** Yokohama Nursery Company. *Botanical Catalog.* 1901. The Arnold Arboretum at Harvard University.

223 **Uhei Suzuki, was so pleased:** Ariyoshi, Kazuo. "Sakura trees." Interview by author. February 2016. Yokohama, Japan.

223 **just ten cents apiece:** Fairchild. *The World Was My Garden*, unpublished draft. Fairchild Tropical Botanic Garden. Coral Gables, FL.

225 **He carried his camera:** Fairchild. *The World Was My Garden*, p. 415.

225 **"We are much given to claiming":** "Gives Washington Pride a Setback." *Washington Herald*, May 5, 1910.

225 **beaches, polo fields, baseball diamonds:** "Washington's Parks." *Washington Post*, November 8, 1914.

226 **a consular officer in Japan:** Parsell, Diana. "Eliza Scidmore." Interview by author. March 2016. Washington, D.C.

226 **"Why bother with cherry trees":** Fairchild, David. "Our Flowering Cherry Trees." MS, Fairchild Tropical Botanic Garden. Date Unknown.

226 **Every tree Fairchild imported brought demand:** "Garden Sites in Streets." *Washington Post*, May 7, 1910.

226 **one boy from each school:** Fairchild. *The World Was My Garden*, p. 412.

226 **"the most noted writer on Japan.":** Fairchild, David. "Our Flowering Cherry Trees." MS, Fairchild Tropical Botanic Garden. Date Unknown.

227 **"Washington would one day":** Rutkow, Eric. *American Canopy: Trees, Forests, and the Making of a Nation.* New York: Scribner, 2012, p. 205. And in "Arbor Day." *Washington Star*, May 1908.

227 **Japanese and Korean people . . . into segregated schools:** Pauly, Philip J. *Fruits and Plains: The Horticultural Transformation of America.* Cambridge, MA: Harvard University Press, 2007, p. 148.

228 **a fireworks display in his honor:** Samuels, Gayle Brandow. *Enduring Roots: Encounters with Trees, History, and the American Landscape.* New Brunswick, NJ: Rutgers University Press, 1999, p. 78.

228 **"There is nothing in the American life":** "Cherry Trees of Japan." *New York Times*, August 31, 1909.

228 **three hundred finest cherry blossom trees:** Fairchild, David. "Our Flowering Cherry Trees." MS, Fairchild Tropical Botanic Garden. Date Unknown.

229 **three hundred trees turned into two thousand:** U.S. Department of Agriculture. *The Japanese Flowering Cherry Trees of Washington, D.C.* By Roland Jefferson and Alan Fusonie. National Arboretum Contribution No. 4. Washington, D.C.: Agricultural Research Service, 1977, p. 9.

229 **they rose to the highest levels of government:** U.S. Department of Agriculture. *The Japanese Flowering Cherry Trees of Washington, D.C.* By Roland Jefferson and Alan Fusonie. National Arboretum Contribution No. 4. Washington, D.C.: Agricultural Research Service, 1977, p. 4.

229 **thirteen-day trip to Washington:** U.S. Department of Agriculture. *The Japanese Flowering Cherry Trees of Washington, D.C.* By Roland Jefferson and Alan Fusonie. National Arboretum Contribution No. 4. Washington, D.C.: Agricultural Research Service, 1977, p. 10.

230 **trouble making up his mind:** Miller Center, University of Virginia. "William Taft: Impact and Legacy." Accessed May 7, 2016. http://miller-center.org/president/taft/impact-and-legacy.

230 **[Taft description]:** "American Experience: TV's Most-watched History Series." PBS. Accessed October 7, 2015. http://www.pbs.org/wgbh/americanexperience/features/biography/presidents-taft/.

231 **a stodgy introvert:** Miller Center, University of Virginia. "William Taft: Life Before the Presidency." Accessed February 8, 2016. http://miller-center.org/president/biography/taft-life-before-the-presidency.

231 **the prospect of catastrophe:** U.S. Department of Agriculture. *The Japanese Flowering Cherry Trees of Washington, D.C.* By Roland Jefferson and Alan Fusonie. National Arboretum Contribution No. 4. Washington, D.C.: Agricultural Research Service, 1977, p. 10.

231 **vulnerable to corrosion:** Fairchild, David. "Our Flowering Cherry Trees." MS, Fairchild Tropical Botanic Garden. Date unknown.

231 **"Young stock would undoubtedly":** Letter from Charles Marlatt to James Wilson. January 19, 1910. Bureau of Entomology, USDA, Washington, D.C.

231 **"serious infestations":** Letter from Charles Marlatt to James Wilson. January 19, 1910. Bureau of Entomology, USDA, Washington, D.C.

232 **Chinese *Diaspis*:** U.S. Department of Agriculture. *The Japanese Flowering Cherry Trees of Washington, D.C.* By Roland Jefferson and Alan Fusonie.

National Arboretum Contribution No. 4. Washington, D.C.: Agricultural Research Service, 1977, p. 10.

232 **wood-boring** *lepidopterus* **larvae:** Stebbing, Edward Percy. *Departmental Notes on Insects That Affect Forestry.* Calcutta: Office of the Superintendent of Government Printing, 1902, p. 44.

232 **"Every sort of pest imaginable":** Fairchild. *The World Was My Garden*, p. 413.

232 **a surge of support for people like Marlatt:** Samuels, Gayle Brandow. *Enduring Roots: Encounters with Trees, History, and the American Landscape.* New Brunswick, NJ: Rutgers University Press, 1999, p. 68.

233 **the president ordered the trees burned:** U.S. Department of Agriculture. *The Japanese Flowering Cherry Trees of Washington, D.C.* By Roland Jefferson and Alan Fusonie. National Arboretum Contribution No. 4. Washington, D.C.: Agricultural Research Service, 1977, p. 15.

233 **A news item:** "Destroy Tokio Gift Trees." *New York Times*, January 29, 1910.

234 **"To destroy the cherry trees":** "Topics of the Times." *New York Times*, January 31, 1910.

234 **Ozaki received David Fairchild:** Fairchild, David. "Our Flowering Cherry Trees." MS, Fairchild Tropical Botanic Garden. Date unknown.

235 **"We are more satisfied":** McClellan, Ann. *The Cherry Blossom Festival: Sakura Celebration.* Piermont, NH: Bunker Hill, 2005, p. 34.

235 **"memorial of national friendship":** U.S. Department of Agriculture. *The Japanese Flowering Cherry Trees of Washington, D.C.* By Roland Jefferson and Alan Fusonie. National Arboretum Contribution No. 4. Washington, D.C.: Agricultural Research Service, 1977, p. 19.

235 **Three thousand and twenty trees:** National Park Service. "Cherry Blossom Festival." U.S. Department of the Interior, National Park Service. Accessed May 10, 2016. https://www.nps.gov/subjects/cherryblossom/index.htm.

235 **trees were fumigated twice:** Letter from Yoshinao Kozai to L. O. Howard. January 29, 1912.

236 **"minute and careful examination":** Letter from Spencer Cosby to Yukio Ozaki. April 4, 1912.

236 **The wife of the Japanese ambassador:** U.S. Department of Agriculture. *The Japanese Flowering Cherry Trees of Washington, D.C.* By Roland Jefferson and Alan Fusonie. National Arboretum Contribution No. 4. Washington, D.C.: Agricultural Research Service, 1977, p. 37.

236 **Gardeners planted extras:** U.S. Department of Agriculture. *The Japanese Flowering Cherry Trees of Washington, D.C.* By Roland Jefferson and Alan Fusonie. National Arboretum Contribution No. 4. Washington, D.C.: Agricultural Research Service, 1977, p. 20.

236 **a shipment of flowering dogwoods:** U.S. Department of Agriculture. *The Japanese Flowering Cherry Trees of Washington, D.C.* By Roland Jefferson and Alan Fusonie. National Arboretum Contribution No. 4. Washington, D.C.: Agricultural Research Service, 1977, p. 44.

236 **bright white blooms:** U.S. Department of Agriculture. Natural Resources Conservation Service. "Flowering Dogwood" Plant Guide. By Sarah Wennerberg. USDA NRCS National Plant Data Center.

236 **a cottage industry around them:** Litterst, Mike. "Cherry Tree Maintenance." Interview by author. March 3, 2016.

CHAPTER SIXTEEN: The Urge to Walk

241 **the only reason she married him:** Fairchild, David. "Early Days of SPI." Speech, Washington, D.C., October 9, 1922.

243 **"no more tramps together":** Douglas. *Adventures in a Green World*, p. 41.

244 **"envoys of agriculture":** Farlow, Laura. "Envoys of Agriculture." *The Strand*, May 1908, pp. 385–91.

244 **"Don't waste time and postage":** Fairchild. *The World Was My Garden*, p. 157.

245 **Missouri Botanical Garden:** Shurtleff, William, H. T. Huang, and Akiko Aoyagi. *History of Soybeans and Soyfoods in China and Taiwan*. Lafayette, CA: Soyinfo Center, 2014, p. 2601.

245 **something practical, like making musical instruments:** Cunningham, Isabel Shipley. *Frank N. Meyer: Plant Hunter in Asia*. Ames: Iowa State University Press, 1984.

245 **"It was a characteristic sight":** Fairchild, David. "Exploring the Klondike of China's Plant Gold." Date unknown. TS, Meyer Collection, Fairchild Tropical Botanic Garden. Coral Gables, FL.

245 **sweating so profusely:** Photograph of Frank N. Meyer Collection, National Agricultural Library, Beltsville, MD.

245 **"His eager face was sparkling":** Fairchild. *The World Was My Garden*, p. 315.

245 **"What don't we know of the world":** Fairchild, David. "Exploring the Klondike of China's Plant Gold." Date unknown. TS, Meyer Collection, Fairchild Tropical Botanic Garden. Coral Gables, FL.

247 **"Better small and fine":** Fairchild, David. "Exploring the Klondike of China's Plant Gold." Date unknown. TS, Meyer Collection, Fairchild Tropical Botanic Garden. Coral Gables, FL.

247 **Alexander Graham Bell could tell:** Fairchild. *The World Was My Garden*, p. 316.

248 **"makes its appearance on the Peking market":** Fairchild, David. *Early Days of the Seed Distribution Program*. Unpublished essay. Date unknown.

248 **Chinese outlaws, murderous thieves:** "Capital's Columbus Starts This Week On a World-Wide Two-Year Search." *Washington Post*, August 15, 1909.

249 **"I am pessimistic by nature":** Cunningham, Isabel Shipley. *Frank N. Meyer: Plant Hunter in Asia*. Ames: Iowa State University Press, 1984.

249 **"a beautiful job":** Harris, Amanda. *Fruits of Eden: David Fairchild and America's Plant Hunters*. Gainesville: University Press of Florida, 2015, p. 126.

249 **"to enrich the United States of America":** Frank Meyer to David Fairchild. October 11, 1907. Peking. National Agricultural Library.

250 **Drummond:** Douglas. *Adventures in a Green World*, p. 40.

250 **"I . . . never dreamed":** Letter from Barbour Lathrop to David Fairchild. February 5, 1904. Fairchild Tropical Botanic Garden. Coral Gables, FL.

250 **"The work of plant introduction":** Douglas. *Adventures in a Green World*, p. 45.

251 **to protect their design:** McCullough, David G. *The Wright Brothers*. New York: Simon & Schuster, 2015.

252 **"I don't trust him an inch":** McCullough. *The Wright Brothers*, p. 190.

252 **large board of tetrahedral cells:** Author visit to the Alexander Graham Bell National Historic Site. Baddeck, Nova Scotia. July 2015.

253 **an equal hunger for detail:** Muller, Hugh. "Alexander Graham Bell." Interview by author. July 2015.

253 **large discoveries were the sum of small ones:** Burleigh, Nina. *The Stranger and the Statesman: James Smithson, John Quincy Adams, and the Making of America's Greatest Museum: the Smithsonian*. New York: Morrow, 2003, p. 3.

253 **"I sensed vaguely in 1907":** Fairchild. *The World Was My Garden*, p. 333.

253 **the *June Bug*:** "Record Flight of Aeroplane." *Morning Tribune* (Altoona, PA), June 23, 1908.

253 **"frail but trim, with its struts":** Fairchild. *The World Was My Garden*, pp. 341–42.

254 **the feat had been accomplished:** "Wins Aeroplane Trophy." *Washington Post*, July 5, 1908.

255 **"the sky would be full of aeroplanes":** Fairchild. *The World Was My Garden*, p. 344.

255 **Frank Meyer returned from China:** Shurtleff, William, H. T. Huang, and Akiko Aoyagi. *History of Soybeans and Soyfoods in China and Taiwan*. Lafayette, CA: Soyinfo Center, 2014, p. 550.

255 **his fingernails so long:** Fairchild, David. "Exploring the Klondike of China's Plant Gold." Date unknown. TS, Meyer Collection, Fairchild Tropical Botanic Garden. Coral Gables, FL.

255 **they curled upward:** Harris. *Fruits of Eden*, p. 134.

255 **a thin-skinned watermelon:** "Kansas Man's Discovery." *Leavenworth Times*, July 8, 1909.

255 **feed for livestock, food for humans:** Department of Agriculture inventory reports. National Agricultural Library. Beltsville, MD. 1905–1908.

257 **He arrived with twenty tons:** Cunningham, Isabel. *Frank Meyer, Agricultural Explorer*. Arnoldia 44, no. 3 (1984): 25.

257 **two rare white-cheeked gibbons:** Cunningham. *Frank Meyer, Agricultural Explorer*, p. 10.

257 **"western devil":** Harris. *Fruits of Eden*, p. 126.

257 **heavy boots and a round wool hat:** Fairchild, David. "Exploring the Klondike of China's Plant Gold." Date unknown. TS, Meyer Collection, Fairchild Tropical Botanic Garden. Coral Gables, FL.

257 **hungry bears, tigers, and wolves:** "Capital's Columbus Starts This Week on a World-Wide Two-Year Search." *Washington Post*, August 15, 1909.

258 **He imitated the bandits:** Constance Carter. "Plant Hunters." Journeys and Crossings, Library of Congress. Accessed May 12, 2016. https://www.loc.gov/rr/program/journey/planthunter-tran script.html.

258 **"Hotel of 1000 bedbugs":** Cunningham, Isabel Shipley. *Frank N. Meyer: Plant Hunter in Asia.* Ames: Iowa State University Press, 1984, pp. 34–35.

259 **twenty cents per fruit:** Meyer, Frank Nicholas. *Agricultural Explorations in the Fruit and Nut Orchards of China.* Washington, D.C.: Government Printing Office, 1911, p. 204.

259 **salary to 1,400 dollars:** "The People Who Stand for Plus." *The Outing Magazine*, October 1908, pp. 69–76.

259 **"Frank Meyer is back":** David Fairchild to Gilbert Grosvenor. 1908. National Geographic Library. Washington, D.C.

260 **Meyer grudgingly accepted the invitation:** Fairchild. *The World Was My Garden*, p. 347.

260 **"I will be famous":** Harris. *Fruits of Eden*, p. 134.

CHAPTER SEVENTEEN: Outlaws, Brigands, and Murderers

261 *Dynaspidiotus meyeri:* "Aspidiotus Meyeri Marlatt, 1908." Global Biodiversity Information Facility. Accessed January 12, 2016. http://www.gbif.org/species/110093968.

261 **weaving classes:** Armstrong, Selene. "Dugmore to Give Benefit Lecture." *Washington Times*, March 15, 1910.

261 **"The greatest danger":** Marlatt, Charles. "Plant Quarantine #37." Lecture, Society of American Florists, August 21, 1919.

262 **"It would be eminently unfair":** Fairchild, David. "The Independence of American Nurseries." Lecture, American Forestry Association, January 1917.

262 **typhus, yellow fever, and malaria:** Hawkins, Stephanie L. *American Iconographic: National Geographic, Global Culture, and the Visual Imagination.* Charlottesville: University of Virginia Press, 2010, pp. 88–89.

262 **"dirty," "destroy," "dangerous":** Marlatt, Charles. "Pests and Parasites: Why We Need a National Law to Prevent the Importation of Insect-Infested and Diseased Plants." *National Geographic*, April 1911.

263 **"Now that you have had your fingers burned":** Marlatt, Charles Lester. *An Entomologist's Quest: The Story of the San Jose Scale: Diary of a Trip around the World 1901–1902.* Washington, D.C.: Monumental Printing Co., 1953, p. 330.

263 **"Chinese Wall":** Harris. *Fruits of Eden*, p. 176.

263 **called his bluffs distortions:** U.S. Congress. House Committee on Agriculture. April 28, 1910 sess. H. Doc. Hearing Transcript. 1910. Acquired from the Center for Legislative Archives, National Archives and Records Administration, pp. 542–43.

264 **Ladies' Garden Clubs:** Marlatt, Charles Lester. *An Entomologist's Quest: The Story of the San Jose Scale: Diary of a Trip around the World 1901–1902.* Washington, D.C.: Monumental Printing Co., 1953, p. 329.

264 **After the islands' 1898 annexation:** Hawaii wouldn't become an actual state until 1959, but its domestic status for the purpose of commerce began almost as soon as the Kingdom of Hawaii's flag came down.

264 **steamships from Hawaii:** Jeffrey, J. W. *Quarantine Laws and Orders.* Sacramento: California State Commission of Horticulture, 1911. p. 12.

264 **prohibit the shipment of all fruits:** Cook, A. J. "An Alarming Fruit Pest." *The California Outlook*, January 13, 1912, p. 11.

264 **travelers were glad to oblige:** Hecke, G. H. *Monthly Bulletin of the Department of Agriculture.* Vol. 11. Sacramento: Government of the State of California, 1922, pp. 567–76.

265 **He marched to Marlatt's office:** Fairchild. Pocket notebook. *"Disagreement with C. Marlatt."* Date unknown. Fairchild Tropical Botanic Garden. Coral Gables, FL.

265 **seized, fumigated, and burned:** Jeffrey, J. W. *Quarantine Laws and Orders.* Sacramento: California State Commission of Horticulture, 1911, pp. 12–13.

267 **the *Youth's Companion*:** "In The Youth's Companion." *Roxboro Courier* (Roxboro, NC), May 8, 1912.

267 **kids could convince their parents:** "A Famous Feast of Frogs." *Donaldsonville Chief* (Donaldsonville, LA), April 12, 1913.

267 ***Technical World* magazine:** Clark, Edward B. "Plant Hunter in the Wilds." *Technical World Magazine*, July 1911, pp. 519–24.

267 **"coolies and carts":** "The People Who Stand for Plus." *The Outing Magazine*, October 1908, pp. 69–76.

269 **Pests and Parasites:** Marlatt, Charles. "Pests and Parasites: Why We Need a National Law to Prevent the Importation of Insect-Infested and Diseased Plants." *National Geographic*, April 1911.

269 **regularly published photographs:** "First Photo Published in National Geographic." National Geographic. Accessed February 15, 2016. http://photography.nationalgeographic.com/photography/photographers/first-photo-article.html.

269 **alfalfa-leaf weevil [and National Geographic story]:** Marlatt, Charles. "Pests and Parasites: Why We Need a National Law to Prevent the Importation of Insect-Infested and Diseased Plants." *National Geographic*, April 1911.

270 **"The whole trend of the world":** Fairchild, David. "The Independence of American Nurseries." *American Forestry*, April 1917, pp. 213–16.

271 **the October issue's leading story:** Fairchild, David. "New Plant Immigrants." *National Geographic*, October 1911, pp. 879–907.

272 **longest tenure for any cabinet secretary:** Manweller, Mathew, ed. *Chronology of the U.S. Presidency*. Santa Barbara: ABC-CLIO, 2012, p. 748.

272 **had mellowed, even humbled:** Wilson, James. Notes. Date unknown. Department of Agriculture, National Agricultural Library.

272 **President Wilson's victory:** Miller Center, University of Virginia. "Woodrow Wilson: Campaigns and Elections." Accessed October 13, 2015. http://millercenter.org/president/biography/wilson-campaigns-and-elections.

273 **"efficiency":** Wilson, Woodrow. First Inaugural Address, Washington, D.C., March 4, 1913.

273 **Plant Quarantine Act:** The Plant Quarantine Act, U.S. Dept. of Agriculture, Office of the Secretary (August 20, 1912) (enacted).

273 **which, conveniently, Marlatt controlled:** Marlatt, C. L. "Recent Work of the Federal Horticultural Board." *Journal of Economic Entomology* 17, no. 4 (1924): 437.

274 **Meyer's work was the most meaningful:** Fairchild. *The World Was My Garden*, p. 406.

275 **Plant exploration offered not only problems but solutions:** "Frank Nicholas Meyer (1875–1918)." Arnold Arboretum of Harvard University. Accessed May 16, 2016.

275 **a young man in Altadena, California:** Harris. *Fruits of Eden*, p. 137.

275 **an upgrade in budget, adventure, and . . . glory:** Rosengarten, Frederic Jr. *Wilson Popenoe: Agricultural Explorer, Educator, and Friend of Latin America*. Lawai, Hawaii: National Tropical Botanic Garden, 1991.

CHAPTER EIGHTEEN: Fly the Coop

277 **He visited his family:** Cunningham, Isabel Shipley. *Frank N. Meyer: Plant Hunter in Asia*. Ames: Iowa State University Press, 1984.

278 **bread and sausage, and drank only tea:** Harris, Amanda. *Fruits of Eden: David Fairchild and America's Plant Hunters*. Gainesville: University Press of Florida, 2015, p. 201.

278 **Meyer held a ticket:** Frank N. Meyer papers. Archives of the Arnold Arboretum of Harvard University.

280 **"I wish I had seven bodies.":** Cunningham. *Frank N. Meyer*, p. 226.

282 **salary that Fairchild granted him:** Rosengarten, Frederic Jr. *Wilson Popenoe: Agricultural Explorer, Educator, and Friend of Latin America*. Lawai, Hawaii: National Tropical Botanic Garden, 1991, p. 19.

282 **"The chief tried always to help me":** "David Fairchild, Plantsman." Fairchild Tropical Botanic Garden Bulletin 18, no 3 (July 1963).

283 **[Navel orange introduction story]:** U.S. Department of Agriculture, Bureau of Plant Industry. *Bulletin No. 445: The Navel Orange of Bahia; With*

Notes on Some Little-Known Brazilian Fruits. By P. H. Dorsett, A. D. Shamel, and Wilson Popenoe. February 10, 1917.

284 **two trees to his former neighbor:** "Who Put the Navel in Navel Oranges?" NPR. April 18, 2009. http://www.npr.org/templates/story/story.php?storyId=103250589.

284 **"in her doorway":** Laszlo, Pierre. *Citrus: A History.* Chicago: University of Chicago Press, 2007, p. 37.

284 **state horticultural contest:** Boulé, David. "Navel Orange Produced a Big Bang in the Golden State." *Sacramento Bee.* January 2, 2016. http://www.sacbee.com/opinion/california-forum/article52340530.html.

285 **"a dignified look":** Harris. *Fruits of Eden,* p. 146.

285 **His office had become a bottleneck:** Fairchild. *The World Was My Garden,* p. 425.

285 **"Carrying on profound research":** Fairchild. *The World Was My Garden,* p. 423.

286 **the law would deter young people:** Fairchild. *The World Was My Garden,* pp. 425–26.

287 **fruits and vegetables could be dehydrated:** Greensmith, Maurice. *Practical Dehydration.* London: Food Trade Press, 1971.

287 **Carver visited Fairchild:** McMurry, Linda O. *George Washington Carver, Scientist and Symbol.* New York: Oxford University Press, 1981, p. 169.

287 **empowered farmers to diversify:** Vella, Christina. *George Washington Carver: A Life.* Baton Rouge: Louisiana State University Press, 2015.

287 **"We must do something now":** McMurry, Linda O. *George Washington Carver, Scientist and Symbol.* New York: Oxford University Press, 1981, p. 170.

288 **Horst brought twenty-six types of vegetables:** Fairchild, *The World Was My Garden,* p. 460.

CHAPTER NINETEEN: Sad and Mad and So Utterly Unnecessary

289 **"thrilling":** Fairchild. *The World Was My Garden,* p. 422.

289 **Brazilian cherries, cashew wine, guava jelly:** Morton, Julia Frances. *Fruits of Warm Climates.* Miami: J. F. Morton, 1987, pp. 371–74.

289 **only a fraction passed inspection:** Taylor, William A. *Inventory of Seeds and Plants Imported by the Office of Foreign Seed and Plant Introduction During the Period from April 1 to June 30, 1912.* Washington, D.C.: Government Printing Office, 1914, p. 29.

290 **The country lacked a strong military:** Beauchamp, Zack, Timothy B. Lee, and Matthew Yglesias. "40 Maps That Explain World War I." Vox.com. August 4, 2014. http://www.vox.com/a/world-war-i-maps. Map #33.

290 **"Every reform we have won":** Peterson, Merrill D. *The President and His Biographer: Woodrow Wilson and Ray Stannard Baker.* Charlottesville: University of Virginia Press, 2007, p. 59.

291 **Popenoe family business:** Harris. *Fruits of Eden,* p. 165.

291 **"It will be a race"**: Cunningham, Isabel Shipley. *Frank N. Meyer, Plant Hunter in Asia.* Ames: Iowa State University Press, 1984, p. 220.

292 **hit by a hurricane:** Harris. *Fruits of Eden*, p. 207.

292 **more arduous every day:** Bell, C. Ritchie. "Frank N. Meyer: Plant Hunter in Asia by Isabel Shipley Cunningham." *Isis* 76, no. 4 (1985): 618–19.

292 **"Heimweh":** Shurtleff, William, H. T. Huang, and Akiko Aoyagi. *History of Soybeans and Soyfoods in China and Taiwan.* Soyinfo Center, 2014, p. 764.

292 **"The specter of a lonely old age":** Cunningham. *Frank N. Meyer, Plant Hunter in Asia*, p. 209.

292 **"At eighteen":** Cunningham. *Frank N. Meyer, Plant Hunter in Asia*, p. 220.

293 **wild pear forests in the region of Jehol:** Fairchild, David. "An Agricultural Explorer in China." *Asia: The American Magazine on the Orient* 21, no. 1 (January 1921): 7–13.

293 **"put a little less officialness":** Cunningham. *Frank N. Meyer, Plant Hunter in Asia*, p. 38.

293 **"We have only one life to live":** Letter from David Fairchild to Frank Meyer. March 25, 1917. National Agricultural Library, Beltsville, MD.

294 **"The loneliness and the hardships":** Letter from Frank Meyer to David Fairchild. February 10, 1917. National Agricultural Library, Beltsville, MD.

294 **"nervous sleeplessness":** Cunningham. *Frank N. Meyer, Plant Hunter in Asia*, p. 217.

294 **"the paralyzing effect":** Cunningham. *Frank N. Meyer, Plant Hunter in Asia*, p. 220.

294 **"It is difficult to imagine":** Letter from David Fairchild to Frank Meyer. May 2, 1917. National Agricultural Library, Beltsville, MD.

295 **"I tried to write for a few nights":** Letter from Frank Meyer to David Fairchild. May 22, 1917. National Agricultural Library, Beltsville, MD.

295 **"The change from 'roughing it'":** Letter from Frank Meyer to David Fairchild. May 22, 1917. National Agricultural Library, Beltsville, MD.

296 **"Proposed Resignation":** Cunningham. *Frank N. Meyer, Plant Hunter in Asia*, p. 225.

296 **"Is it strange that a man":** Letter from Frank Meyer to David Fairchild. May 22, 1917. National Agricultural Library, Beltsville, MD.

296 **kill all unnecessary animals:** Letter from Frank Meyer to David Fairchild. June 5, 1917. National Agricultural Library, Beltsville, MD.

297 **"We are all much grieved":** Letter from David Fairchild to Frank Meyer. June 29, 1917. National Agricultural Library, Beltsville, MD.

298 **"a bad piece of business":** Letter from Frank Meyer to David Fairchild. October 24, 1917. National Agricultural Library, Beltsville, MD.

298 **"the serious questions of plant introduction work":** Letter from David Fairchild to Frank Meyer. July 27, 1917. National Agricultural Library, Beltsville, MD.

299 **"Food . . . Don't Waste It":** *Food: Don't Waste It.* Philadelphia: Committee on Public Safety, Department of Food Supply, 1914. https://archive.org/details/CAT31157947.

299 **"No one can adequately describe":** Fairchild. *The World Was My Garden,* p. 458.

300 **"I thought for a moment":** Fairchild. *The World Was My Garden,* p. 464.

300 **"You speak in one of your recent letters":** Letter from David Fairchild to Frank Meyer. July 27, 1917. National Agricultural Library, Beltsville, MD.

301 **"What would become of our social structure":** Letter from Frank Meyer to David Fairchild. August 1, 1917. National Agricultural Library, Beltsville, MD.

301 **"I have become so calloused":** Letter from Frank Meyer to David Fairchild. September 8, 1917. National Agricultural Library, Beltsville, MD.

301 **"As I am writing we hear":** Letter from Frank Meyer to David Fairchild. February 1, 1918. National Agricultural Library, Beltsville, MD.

302 **"Do not become despondent":** Letter from David Fairchild to Frank Meyer. March 6, 1918. National Agricultural Library, Beltsville, MD.

303 **He had lost weight:** Sokobin, Samuel. "U.S. Consulate Report on the Death of Frank Meyer." June 12, 1917. National Agricultural Library, Beltsville, MD.

304 **"In the glorious luxuriance":** USDA Agricultural Research Service, National Germplasm Resources Laboratory. *19th and 20th Century Plant Hunters.* By Allan Stoner and Kim Hummer. 2007. Excerpted in *Horticultural Science* 42, no. 2 (2007): 197–99.

304 **"Times certainly are sad and mad":** Letter from Frank Meyer to David Fairchild. May 18, 1918. National Agricultural Library, Beltsville, MD.

305 **he considered Meyer's death a mystery:** Fairchild. *The World Was My Garden,* p. 455.

305 **"they will all be his":** Fairchild. *The World Was My Garden,* p. 455.

305 **Meyer left one thousand dollars:** "Last Will and Testament of Frank N. Meyer." National Agricultural Library. Beltsville, MD.

305 **The Meyer Medal:** Harrison, Melanie. "The Meyer Medal." E-mail interview by author. February 23, 2016. U.S. Department of Agriculture, Agricultural Research Service, Plant Genetic Resources Conservation Unit.

CHAPTER TWENTY: *Wij Zijn Amerikanen*

306 **Fairchild watched the animal struggle:** Fairchild, David. *Garden Islands of the Great East: Collecting Seeds from the Philippines and Netherlands India in the Junk "Chêng Ho."* New York: C. Scribner's Sons, 1943, pp. 83–84.

306 **Fairchild mostly gave up:** Pauly, Philip J. *Biologists and the Promise of American Life: From Meriwether Lewis to Alfred Kinsey.* Princeton: Princeton University Press, 2000, p. 88.

306 **Quarantine #37:** Kohlstedt, Sally Gregory, and David Kaiser, eds. *Science and the American Century: Readings from Isis.* Chicago: University of Chicago Press, 2013, p. 52.

306 **ominous disease:** Marlatt, C. L., et al. *Plant Regulatory Announcements.* January–June 1922. Washington, D.C.: U.S. Government Printing Office, 1922, p. 81.

307 **"If the average American knew":** Marlatt, Charles Lester. "Protecting the United States from Plant Pests." *National Geographic,* August 1921, 205–18.

307 **"the most tremendous of all experiences":** Fairchild, David. "The Jungles of Panama." *National Geographic,* February 1922, 131–46.

307 **new explorers spent lavishly:** Harris, Amanda. *Fruits of Eden: David Fairchild and America's Plant Hunters.* Gainesville: University Press of Florida, 2015, pp. 214–232.

307 **He met a smart and pretty bamboo researcher:** Rosengarten, Frederic J. *Wilson Popenoe: Agricultural Explorer, Educator, and Friend of Latin America.* Lawai, Hawaii: National Tropical Botanic Garden, 1991, pp. 89–98.

308 **He told his staff:** Fairchild. *The World Was My Garden,* p. 473.

308 **Florida . . . an attractive place to vacation:** Florida Center for Instructional Technology. "Florida's Land Boom." University of South Florida, 2002. http://fcit.usf.edu/florida/lessons/ld_boom/ld_boom1.htm.

308 **people even bought land underwater:** Bryson, Bill. *One Summer: America, 1927.* New York: Doubleday, 2013, chapter 19.

308 **Florida became a new frontier:** Boulton, Alexander O. "The Tropical Twenties." *American Heritage* 41, no. 4 (May/June 1990): 88–95.

308 **"the Kampong":** Fairchild, David. *The World Grows Round My Door: The Story of the Kampong, a Home on the Edge of the Tropics.* New York: C. Scribner's Sons, 1947.

308 **The steamships of earlier days:** Douglas, Marjory Stoneman. *Adventures in a Green World: The Story of David Fairchild and Barbour Lathrop.* Coconut Grove, FL: Field Research Projects, 1973, p. 53.

310 **Fairchild often hosted Lathrop . . . along with the Bells:** Fairchild. *The World Was My Garden,* p. 420.

310 **"the major romance in the story of my life":** Fairchild. *The World Was My Garden,* p. 81.

310 **One obituary would say thirteen:** "Barbour Lathrop: Botanist Who Spent Fifty Years in Quest of Rare Plants Dies at 80." *New York Times,* May 18, 1927.

310 **"His blue eyes sparkle":** Fairchild. *The World Was My Garden,* p. v.

311 **"What's the most interesting thing":** Pancoast, Helene. "DF as Granddad." Interview by author. Fall 2014. Coconut Grove, FL.

313 **"in our philosophy dangers to health lurk":** Fairchild, David. *Garden Islands of the Great East: Collecting Seeds from the Philippines and Netherlands India in the Junk "Chêng Ho."* New York: C. Scribner's Sons, 1943, p. 15.

315 **faraway people ate papaya leaves:** Siddiq, Muhammad, ed. *Tropical and Subtropical Fruits: Postharvest Physiology, Processing and Packaging.* Ames, IA: Wiley-Blackwell, 2012.

315 **balance blood sugar, boost immunity:** Myszko, Amy. "Papaya Leaf Tea Benefits." SFGATE, *San Francisco Chronicle.* Accessed February 2, 2016. http://healthyeating.sfgate.com/papaya-leaf-tea-benefits-10422.html.

315 **"I know there are many people":** Fairchild, David. *Garden Islands of the Great East: Collecting Seeds from the Philippines and Netherlands India in the Junk "Chêng Ho."* New York: Charles Scribner's Sons, 1943, p. 99.

316 **they began rounding up any Germans:** Jacobsen, Hans-Adolf, and Arthur L. Smith Jr. *The Nazi Party and the German Foreign Office.* New York: Routledge, 2007, p. 143.

316 **The boat stopped at seventeen more islands:** Zuckerman, Bert. "The Voyage of the Cheng Ho." *Garden News,* 1993, 14–15.

INDEX

NOTE: Page references in *italics* refer to figures and photos.

Hubbard, Gertrude Mercer, 208, 219, 266
hybridization, 286

I
Ichang lemon, 302
India, Fairchild's plans and travels,
　　181–183. 140–141
indigestion (dyspepsia), in nineteenth
　　century, 11
insects. *See also* quarantine of plants
　boll weevil, 262
　Dynaspiridiotus meyeri name, 261
　Fairchild's study of termites, 45–50, 57
　infestation of cherry trees, 231–237
　Marlatt's work as entomologist,
　　220–222
　Mediterranean fruit fly, 264
　USDA Division of Entomology, 221, 248
inspection of plants. *See also* quarantine
　　of plants
　of cherry trees, 230–232, 263–264
　at seaports and airports, 314
　states' responsibility for, 222, 264
"In the Woods" (Fairchilds' home),
　　222–223, 226, 251, 299–300
irrigation, in Egypt, 134
Italy, Fairchild in, 20–23, 130–133, 170–172
Itamaraca mango, 123–124

J
Jamaica, Fairchild and Lathrop in, 102–104
Jannovitch (Egyptian) cotton, 135–139
Japan. *See also* cherry trees
　Fairchild and Lathrop in, 190–193
　U.S.-Japan relations, 227–237
　war with China (1937), 313
Java. *See also* Malay Islands
　Fairchild and Lathrop in, 140–142
　Marian Fairchild's interest in, 241
Jefferson, Thomas, 29, 113
Johnson, Hiram, 264
June Bug (biplane), 253

K
kale, 170–171
"Kampong" (Fairchilds' Florida home),
　　308–310, 317–318

Kansas State University (Kansas State
　　Agricultural College), 14, 77
karyokinesis, 32, 34
kava ceremony, 73
Kellogg, John Harvey, 13
knapsack sprayer, *18*
Knox, Philander, 230, 231

L
Ladies' Garden Clubs of America, 264
ladybugs, 220–221
Lathrop, Barbour. *See also* food
　　exploration destinations
　biographical information, 47–48, 52
　Bohemian Club home of, 48, 54–55, 76,
　　122, 157, 250
　characterization of, 51–55, 66–67, 82,
　　157, 162
　collection expedition plans of, 55–64,
　　74–76, 90
　death of, 310
　decline of, 249–251
　Fairchild's first meeting with, 20–23
　Fairchild's Java sponsorship by, 33–36,
　　37–38, 46–50
　on Fairchild's marriage, 241–243
　first meeting with Marian, 214–215
　friendship with Fairchild, 156, 178,
　　213–214, 310
　Java sponsorship offered to Fairchild
　　by, 33–38, 40–41, 46–50
　late life of, 308–310
　Meyer Medal awarded to, 305
　photos of, *216, 309, 323*
　sexual orientation of, 48, 54–55
　tension between Wilson and, 96–98,
　　100–102, 128–130, 198
　as USDA "special agent," 283
　yellow fever of, 109–110, 125–126
Lathrop, Bryan (brother), 46–49
Lathrop, Florence (sister), 178, 225
Lathrop, Jedediah Hyde (father),
　　47–48
Lease, Mary Elizabeth, 108
LeDuc, William G., 30
lemons
　Ichang lemon, 302
　Meyer lemon, 259
　seedless, 173–174